The single European market and beyond

In recent years we have become obsessed with being 'ready for 1992'. Yet despite the hype how many people understand what '1992 and all that' will actually entail?

The Single European Market and Beyond offers a detailed account of both the practicalities involved and the principles behind them. It falls into four parts. Part I serves as an introduction to the subject and provides an overview. It examines the Single European Act (1986) – which set the 31 December deadline – in some detail. Dennis Swann argues that the 1986 Act is best understood in terms of three key ideas – completing, deepening and widening the Community. Part II examines the completion of the market in terms of the 1986 Act. Part III is concerned with the deepening and widening of particular aspects of the Act. It focuses on issues such as European Monetary Union, the Social Charter, environmental policy and political union, and takes account of the countries now considering or actively seeking full membership – including the East European countries. Part IV comprises a discussion of the three issues most likely to shape Europe's future: the Single Market, EMU and political union and rounds off with an account of the new Treaty on European Union.

The single European market and beyond

A study of the wider implications of the Single European Act

Edited by
Dennis Swann

London and New York

First published 1992
by Routledge
11 New Fetter Lane, London EC4P 4EE

Simultaneously published in the USA and Canada
by Routledge
a division of Routledge, Chapman and Hall, Inc.
29 West 35th Street, New York, NY 10001

Typeset in Garamond by Selectmove Ltd.
Printed and bound in Great Britain by
Mackays of Chatham PLC, Chatham, Kent

British Library Cataloguing in Publication Data
A catalogue record for this title is available from the British Library.

Library of Congress Cataloguing in Publication Data
Swann, Dennis
The Single European market and beyond: a study of the wider implications of
   the Single European Act/edited by Dennis Swann.
      p. cm.
   Includes bibliographical references and index.
   ISBN 0–415–06160–1. — ISBN 0–415–06161–X (pbk)
   1. European Monetary Union. 2. Monetary policy–European Economic
   Community countries. 3. European Economic Community countries–
   Economic conditions. 4. Europe 1992. I. Swann, Dennis.
   HG930.5.S56 1992
   341.24'2—dc20   91-33934 CIP

Contents

Figures and Tables

Contributors

David Allen is a Senior Lecturer in Politics in the Department of European Studies at Loughborough University of Technology.

Kenneth Button is Professor of Applied Economics and Transport and Director of the Applied Microeconomics Research Group in the Department of Economics at Loughborough University of Technology.

David Llewellyn is Professor of Money and Banking and Head of the Department of Economics at Loughborough University of Technology and Chairman of the Loughborough University Banking Centre.

Christopher Milner is Professor of Economics in the Department of Economics at Loughborough University of Technology.

Dennis Swann is Professor of Economics in the Department of Economics at Loughborough University of Technology.

Brian Tew is External Professor in the Department of Economics at Loughborough University of Technology and a member of the Loughborough University Banking Centre.

Tony Westaway is a Senior Lecturer in Economics in the Department of Economics at Loughborough University of Technology.

Preface

Recently the year 1992 has been a major focus of public attention. Politicians, government departments, leaders of industry and commerce and members of the European Communities Commission have been exhorting the public to become aware of it. Up and down the land conferences have been held to explain what it is all about and answer the question of whether we are ready for it. However, focusing on 1992 is somewhat misleading as it suggests that the completion of the single market in that year is all that is at stake. In fact, as this book endeavours to show, though the single market is a key element, 1992 has other implications. The Single European Act of 1986, which has been the mainspring of European activity, has, directly or indirectly, implications that are monetary, social, environmental, regional, technological and, last but by no means least, political and international. We ignore these at our peril. This book is designed to explore not only the single market concept but also these wider aspects.

As the editor of this book I am grateful to my colleagues, in European studies as well as economics, who have generously collaborated to produce this volume. Thanks are also due to Brenda Moore, Su Spencer, Lorraine Whittington and Joyce Tuson who have borne the main burden of getting the manuscript into its final form.

Dennis Swann
Loughborough
December 1991

Abbreviations

ACP	African, Caribbean and Pacific Ocean Countries
ASEAN	Association of South East Asian Nations
ATM	Automated Teller Machine
CAP	Common Agricultural Policy
CCP	Common Commercial Policy
CEN	Capital Export Neutral
CEP	Common Energy Policy
CET	Common External Tariff
CIN	Capital Import Neutral
CMLR	Common Market Law Reports
COMECON	Council for Mutual Economic Assistance
CRS	Computer Reservation System
CSCE	Conference on Security and Cooperation in Europe
CTP	Common Transport Policy
DDR	German Democratic Republic
EAGGF	European Agricultural Guidance and Guarantee Fund
EBRD	European Bank for Reconstruction and Development
EC	European Community (ies)
ECB	European Central Bank
ECSC	European Coal and Steel Community
ECU	European Currency Unit
ecu (hard)	Rival European Currency Unit proposed by UK
ecu	Unit of European Community Currency in eventual state of EMU
EEA	European Economic Area
EEC	European Economic Community
EFTA	European Free Trade Association
EIB	European Investment Bank
EMCF	European Monetary Cooperation Fund
EMF	European Monetary Fund
EMU	Economic and Monetary Union
EPC	European Political Cooperation

ERDF	European Regional Development Fund
ERM	Exchange Rate Mechanism
ESCB	European System of Central Banks
ESF	European Social Fund
ESPRIT	European Strategic Programme for Research and Development in Information Technology
EURATOM	European Atomic Energy Community
EUT	European Union Treaty
G7	The seven leading industrial nations
G24	The group of twenty four western developed economies
GATT	General Agreement on Tariffs and Trade
GDP	Gross Domestic Product
GNP	Gross National Product
GSP	General System of Preferences
IGC	Inter-Governmental Conference
IMF	International Monetary Fund
MEP	Member of the European Parliament
MFA	Multi-Fibre Arrangement
MFN	Most Favoured Nation
NATO	North Atlantic Treaty Organisation
NTB	Non-Tariff Barrier
RACE	Research and Development in Advanced Communications Technologies for Europe
R&TD	Research and Technological Development
SAD	Single Administrative Document
SEA	Single European Act
SEM	Single European Market
UTA	Union de Transports Aeriens
VAT	Value Added Tax
VER	Voluntary Export Restraint
WEU	Western European Union
2+4	East and West Germany plus four other European countries

Part I

Setting the scene

Chapter 1

The single market and beyond – an overview

Dennis Swann

The Precipitating Act

A key event in the quest for European union, from which so much subsequently flowed, was the signing in 1986 by the twelve member states of the European Communities of the Single European Act (SEA). Their signature, and subsequent ratification of the Act broadly achieved two things. First, the Act modified the founding treaties which gave rise to the three European Communities,[1] – amending the Paris treaty of 1951 which created the European Coal and Steel Community (ECSC), the Rome Treaty of 1957 which brought into being the European Atomic Energy Community (EURATOM) and the other Rome Treaty of 1957, which called into existence the European Economic Community (EEC). It was this latter treaty that was the main focus of attention in the SEA and the contents of this book reflect its importance.

Second, it brought certain major cooperative arrangements more firmly within the framework of what may be termed the Community process. Here we are thinking primarily of foreign policy coordination under European Political Cooperation (EPC) and, to a lesser extent, the European Monetary System (EMS), both intergovernmental arrangements and not formal products of the founding European Community treaties.

More specifically the achievements of the SEA were as follows:

(a) It granted new decision-making powers to the Council of Ministers and European Parliament, designed to facilitate the implementation of the aims of all the founding treaties, but particularly those of the EEC treaty.
(b) It sought to speed up the process of completing the Single European Market (SEM) as originally envisaged in the EEC treaty (see this chapter) and set the target date for completion at 31 December 1992.
(c) It placed certain areas of economic and social policy more firmly within the ambit of Community competence and reinforced others, focusing not only on monetary cooperation but also on social, regional, science, technology and environmental policies.
(d) The above relate to the economic and social aspects of the founding

treaties but, in addition, the SEA formally recognized the key role of EPC. We could summarize the post-SEA situation by saying that the sought-after European union was to be built on the twin pillars of the three European Communities on the one hand and EPC on the other.

The signing and ratification of the SEA was in due course followed by further significant decisions. Two are worth highlighting at this point. First, the heightened role for monetary cooperation envisaged in the SEA, was complemented by a proposal that the Community should seek progressively to achieve economic and monetary union (EMU). This development was foreshadowed in the preamble to the SEA which referred to the continuing validity of the Community's commitment to EMU, dating from 1972. Second, the modification of the Community's decision-making powers and the confirmation of EPC's key role were followed by a proposal that the Community should seek to develop political union, though views of course differed as to what such union implied.

The plan of the book

This first chapter aims to provide an overview of the process of European union from the founding treaties to the present. Subsequent chapters develop specialist themes. In chapter 2 David Allen explains how the SEA came about and discusses in detail the institutional and decision-making changes contained in it. The rest of the book covers topics which come under the headings either of the completing, deepening or widening of the European Community. Part II is devoted to completion – i.e. carrying to completion the original aims set out in the founding treaties. In chapter 3 Dennis Swann deals with the problem of the residual Non-Tariff Barriers (NTBs) which had to be swept away if the completion of the SEM envisaged in the SEA was to be achieved. In chapter 4 Tony Westaway discusses the fiscal dimension of the single market – an area of Community endeavour where only limited progress had been made prior to the SEA. Fiscal progress was essential not only for the free movement of goods and services but also for the free movement of production factors. Also fiscal reform was essential for business integration across frontiers. This free movement of services forms the core of chapters 5 and 6. In chapter 5 David Llewellyn focuses on the creation of a European financial common market whilst in chapter 6, Kenneth Button analyses the process of and problems arising from the liberalization of transport services (surface, maritime and particularly air). The completion of the single market was bound to have implications for the rest of the world. The question of access – whether the Community was going to establish a relatively open trading relationship with the rest of the world or create 'fortress Europe' – is one of several issues discussed by Christopher Milner and David Allen in chapter 7.

In Part III the emphasis shifts to deepening and widening the Community. Deepening mainly concerns the introduction of new policy commitments – not only economic and social but also political. As we noted earlier, the preamble to the SEA recollects the earlier commitment to EMU. The possibility of pressing forward from the existing EMS was therefore a property of the SEA. The SEA did in fact modify the monetary provisions of the Rome (EEC) Treaty but, as we noted earlier, the twelve subsequently agreed to reactivate EMU. The history of the Community in the monetary sphere and the problems raised by the new EMU proposal are discussed in detail by Brian Tew in chapter 8. The SEA also paved the way for a more vigorous approach in the sphere of social policy, giving rise to the Social Charter; regional policy, hence the economic and social cohesion provisions; and research, technology and environmental policy. These deepening issues are discussed by Dennis Swann in chapter 9.

Chapter 10 is also concerned with deepening in the sense that, as we noted earlier, the SEA formally recognized the role of EPC in the search for European union. But in addition there has for a long time been a recognition that the decision-making machinery of the EEC particularly was in need of further development. The commitment to achieving greater economic integration within an expanded Community of twelve gave even greater urgency to this issue. This urgency was not dictated purely by a desire for greater speed and efficiency: it was also increasingly linked with the democratic implications of the Community system. Subsequently these issues were thrown into the melting pot by the proposal to proceed to political union. The issues raised by all these developments are discussed by David Allen in chapter 10.

The period since the signing and ratification of the SEA has also been one in which the possibility of further widening Community membership has also been on the agenda. Widening has had a twofold dimension. First, the prospect of the completion of the internal market alarmed members of the European Free Trade Area (EFTA) who feared that they might be excluded from its benefits. The idea of a closer relationship between the EFTA and the twelve in the form of a European Economic Area Treaty, and the possibility of full Community membership for some, has been under discussion.[2] Second, the revolutionary changes in eastern Europe, together with a shift towards free enterprise economic systems there, have raised the possibility of closer relations between eastern and western Europe. The shape of the future relationship, is also discussed by David Allen in chapter 10. In chapter 11 three of the authors add some final thoughts. Details of the new Treaty on European Union appear in chapter 12.

European integration: the original blueprint

The first significant essay in European post-war economic integration occurred in 1951 when six European states – France, Italy, West Germany, Belgium, the Netherlands and Luxembourg – brought into existence the ECSC to which we referred earlier. This was a limited arrangement as the integration exercise applied only to coal and steel. The years immediately following were disappointing to those who desired greater European unity. The grand proposals for a European defence community and a European political community both failed. However, in 1955 the integration process got underway again and in 1957 the six signed the EEC and EURATOM treaties. The former was to prove by far the most significant, though at the time great hopes were held out for EURATOM. In what follows we will concentrate solely on the EEC.[3]

The EEC, which came into existence on 1 January 1958, was based on what is technically called a common market. Internally this had eight main implications.

Member states were to remove the customs duty (or tariff) protection which they applied to goods sold to each other. They also had to remove any charges equivalent in effect to customs duties. For example, the Italian government imposed what it called a statistical levy on imports and exports. This had to be discontinued, as in the view of the Commission and Court of Justice it was equivalent in effect to a customs duty.

Member states also had to dismantle quantitative restrictions (or quotas) on goods sold to each other. They had to discontinue the imposition of measures equivalent to quantitative restrictions. One of the celebrated examples of this was provided by the *Cassis de Dijon* case[4] where West Germany had introduced a law which banned the sale of liqueurs of low alcohol content. French Cassis de Dijon, manufactured from blackcurrants, failed to meet the standard and imports into Germany were banned. The effect of this rule was equivalent to the imposition of a zero import quota.

These measures, designed to create internal free trade in goods, were complemented by a requirement to progressively abolish restrictions on the freedom to supply services across frontiers such as banking, insurance and general professional services.

It was recognized that though tariffs and quotas, and charges equivalent to tariffs and measures equivalent to quotas, might be removed; and that though restrictions on the freedom to supply services might be lifted, nevertheless free and undistorted trade in goods and services would not arise inevitably. In other words, various NTBs could exist which would frustrate the integration process: the Rome Treaty therefore provided the Community institutions with powers to control the NTBs, including powers to:

(a) control and ban cartel practices and abuses by dominant firms which restricted competition in inter-state trade, divided markets, etc;

(b) regulate and ban state aids which gave home producers unfair competitive advantages;

(c) harmonize product standards, as otherwise goods and services produced in one state might not be saleable in another because of the differences in national standards;

(d) ban discrimination in public purchasing which gave artificial advantages to home produced goods;

(e) control practices of state trading monopolies (not to be confused with nationalized industries) which prohibited or discriminated against competing imports;[5]

(f) harmonize the structure, base and rates of indirect taxes (including turnover taxes and excise duties) in order to prevent competitive distortions and assist in the removal of frontier controls.

In order to complete the common market, the freedom to supply goods and services was to be accompanied by the free and undistorted movement of factors of production. Labour, capital and enterprise (freedom of enterprise being termed the right of establishment) should be able to locate anywhere within the common market. Finally, the Rome Treaty placed an absolute ban on discrimination based on nationality.

It cannot be emphasized too much that the Rome Treaty foreshadowed an integration process based on free competition – the unification or integration of previously separate markets was to be accomplished through the medium of competitive trade interpenetration and not by interventionist methods.

All this was to be achieved within a twelve-year transition period to end on 31 December 1969. The reader will appreciate that the SEA commitment to create a SEM was not new. Moreover, the fact that the SEA assigned 31 December 1992 as the date for the accomplishment of the SEM served to underline the extent to which the Community had fallen behind schedule. It is true that tariffs and quotas were abolished within the original transition period,[6] but it is also true that measures equivalent to quotas, factors inhibiting the freedom to supply services, many NTBs and factors which inhibited and distorted the flow of factors, continued to fragment what was supposed to be a single European market. We shall return to this when discussing the subject of Eurosclerosis.

The internal measures designed to create free movement were complemented by the external, protective provisions of the Common Commercial Policy (CCP), central to which was a requirement to establish within the transition period a Common External Tariff (CET). Each member state agreed to impose the same level of customs duty protection on goods imported from outside the Community. The implication of the CCP was that member states ceased to be sovereign in respect of import protection and negotiations concerning the level of the CET became Community matters. The same was true in respect of import quotas and other protective devices such as anti-dumping duties.

Not all economic activity fell within the ambit of these common market provisions. Agriculture was subject to a separate Common Agricultural Policy (CAP) which typically consisted of arrangements at the Community frontier to raise the import price of foodstuffs, stimulating competing internal supplies, and to combine this with support buying and export subsidies in cases where supply inside the Community exceeded demand. In the main the SEA did not affect the basic CAP arrangements, but the 1992 SEM programme did indicate that further measures would have to be introduced in respect of veterinary and phytosanitary controls.

Transport was also subject to a special regime – indeed, as with agriculture, the Rome Treaty called for a separate Common Transport Policy (CTP). The treaty did not spell out its nature in great detail, but the features which were revealed were essentially liberalizing in character. In 1961 and 1962 the EC Commission unveiled plans which envisaged a more competitive approach to a sector which had been characterized by a high degree of regulation. Quota and licensing restrictions were to be relaxed, greater pricing freedom was to be enjoyed and factors which distorted competition between countries and different transport modes were to be harmonized. All this applied to surface transport (road, rail and inland waterway), but in practice only limited progress was made – so little that in 1983 the European Parliament decided, successfully as things turned out, to take the Council of Ministers to the Court of Justice because of the Council's failure to act. The CTP only applied to road, rail and inland waterway, and so the position of air and maritime transport was surrounded by uncertainty and for a considerable period they therefore escaped attention. We shall return to all these issues, as the need for progress was highlighted in the 1992 SEM programme.

In passing we should note that while none of the founding treaties referred to the need for a Common Energy Policy (CEP), nevertheless the Community has endeavoured to develop one. With rather limited success, the Community's approach has been a fourfold one consisting of the adoption of Community energy targets and balance sheets; the implementation of policies which give rise to the rational use of energy; the elaboration of emergency procedures; and lastly, the use of all the Community's financial instruments to provide grants and loans to the energy sector with the aim of reducing import dependency. In practice, the CEP played no really significant role in the emergence of the SEA. Subsequently however, the Commission recognized that a single market for energy could help to realize the 1992 goal, and in 1988 it addressed a communication to the Council of Ministers surveying the areas for action.[7]

The EEC treaty did contain specific provisions relating to social policy but they had a relatively limited impact. In the original conception, social policy had a threefold aspect. First, the French were concerned about the competitive disadvantage they might suffer as a result of their commitment to the 'equal-pay-for-equal-work' principle. The treaty therefore required this principle to be adopted by all the Community member states. Second, the signatories to the treaty agreed on the need to promote better living and working conditions and agreed that progressive harmonization and improvement was desirable. No obligations were placed on the member states to achieve this. Instead it was assumed that the effect of the common market together with the existence of harmonizing provisions within the treaty would favour such developments. Third, the treaty expressly created a European Social Fund (ESF), channelling monies to social ends such as the retraining and resettlement of workers. We shall return to the social issue as the SEA contained provisions directly relevant to the development of Community social policy and the preamble foreshadowed what came to be known as the Social Charter.

The EEC treaty did not provide for the Community to develop a conventional active regional policy. It is true that the preamble did refer to the desirability of reducing differences between various regions and reducing the backwardness of the less favoured regions, but this was in the nature of a grand aspiration. In practice, the task of regional grant giving was a national responsibility, though the European Investment Bank (EIB), through its loan operations, did direct the bulk of its resources towards infrastructure improvements in poorer regions. The Community did exercise a control over regional aid-giving, but this was motivated by a desire to prevent unfair competition and was concerned with its NTB implications. We return to the subject of active regional policy later since the SEA emphasizes its importance under the heading of economic and social cohesion.

The Rome Treaty contained no specific provisions concerning the active steering of industrial development. Here there was a clear contrast with the Paris Treaty which gave the old High Authority (and now the EC Commission) significant general powers of intervention and influence in respect of outputs, prices and investment in the steel and coal sectors.[8] By the time the Rome Treaty came to be negotiated, the buoyancy of the western European economy, together with the West German attachment to free market principles, disposed the contracting parties to produce a treaty in which free competition formed the dominating ethos. We shall return to the subject of industrial policy later, as a limited form of industrial policy did emerge in due course, notably collaboration in research and technology and cross-frontier business integration, matters which were further emphasized in the SEA.

In this review of Rome Treaty economic policy it is essential that something be said about macro-economic policy. The key point is that the Rome Treaty sought to develop a Community based on a common market but not on EMU. The treaty did contain provisions relating to the conduct of monetary policy, but even a cursory glance at these leads to the conclusion that the treaty did not envisage centralized control over macro-economic management. In broad terms, the conduct of monetary policy was left in the hands of member states, who were also free to alter exchange rates, and even apply protection, although this could be revoked by Council. However, it was clearly recognized that economic integration gave rise to increased economic interdependence, and to that end the treaty emphasized the need for consultation and coordination. We shall return to this subject also, for though the treaty contained no specific provision relating to monetary union, full EMU was subsequently placed on the agenda.

In order to implement all these aims the Rome Treaty created a series of interacting institutions.[9] These included the European Commission, (now responsible for all three Communities), whose role is to initiate policy proposals and help to administer agreed policies – and here the Commission is responsible for administering competition rules as they apply to cartels and dominant firms, state aids, public purchasing and so on. Of central importance is the Council of Ministers which is in effect the Community's law-maker since it alone can place the official stamp on draft regulations and draft directives emanating from the Commission. In addition the Community machinery included a Parliamentary Assembly and an Economic and Social Committee. Originally the Parliament was indirectly elected and delegates were nominated by the national parliaments. Both these bodies were essentially consultative as the treaty indicated that on a range of issues the Council of Ministers would not be acting lawfully if it did not first consult them. But the Parliamentary Assembly had certain teeth – it could for example dismiss the whole Commission. Finally, the Rome Treaty provided for a Court of Justice whose tasks were to decide whether member states had failed to fulfil treaty obligations; to review the legality of Council or Commission acts; to review any failure to act by the Council of Ministers or Commission where the treaty so obliged them; and to give preliminary rulings on points of Community law at the request of national courts of member states. A fairly simple budgetary system was also established.

Anticipating somewhat the shape of the present-day Community, we should note that the original six members in due course increased to nine when Denmark, the Irish Republic and the United Kingdom joined in 1973. In 1981 the number rose to ten with the accession of Greece and in 1986 the membership increased to twelve with the adherence of Spain and Portugal.

Post-transition optimism

The picture we have just painted is of an EEC as it was envisaged in the transition period up to 1969. When this period came to an end, the six could have decided that their task was at an end, and concluded that no further institutional and policy developments were called for beyond those already spelled out in the Rome Treaty. In practice, the integration process did not end there: thanks to a series of summit meetings of heads-of-state and government, further institutional developments were taken on board and new policy areas were opened up including three major institutional changes.

First, the Community budget, whose task was to raise finance in order to fund the various Community policies and activities, was significantly developed. Looking beyond the simple system of direct contributions from member states, the 1969 Hague summit envisaged a system in which the Community was endowed with its own resources to be introduced progressively alongside an enhanced budgetary role for the Parliament. These resources were increased at the Fontainebleau summit of 1984 and Brussels summit of 1988, and principles of budgetary control and management were progressively put in place. Agreements concerning the way in which budget monies should be spent, particularly as they affected poorer members of the Community, were an important part of the package deal which led to the adoption of the SEM proposal and we shall return later to the Community budget. Another significant step forward was the decision, flowing from summit meetings in Paris in 1974 and Rome in 1975, that the European Parliament should be directly elected by the people. As we shall see, the emergence of the first directly elected European Parliament in 1979 was an important milestone in the build-up to the SEA. It was partly because of the enhanced authority which the Parliament enjoyed that it felt sufficiently confident to launch the idea of a European Union Treaty. Third, the importance of summit meetings of heads-of-state and government in the onward movement of European unity is all too obvious. In 1974 it was decided that these meetings should henceforth be dignified with the title of the European Council. As already noted, in the post-SEA system, the position of the European Council as the supreme body presiding over the twin pillars – economic and political – of European unity was formally confirmed and institutionalized.

The post-1969 period also saw a number of policy developments within the ambit of the Community decision-making system. Four were of particular relevance in the light of the SEA. In 1972 it was agreed that a European Regional Development Fund (ERDF) should be established, enabling the Community henceforth to be involved in regional grant-giving. The ERDF came into existence in 1975. Its relevance will be more apparent when we discuss the economic and social cohesion provisions of the SEA and the way in which poorer countries were intended to benefit from expenditures deriving from the Community budget.

Earlier we noted that the original Rome Treaty did not provide for an active industrial policy – that is to say, the business of steering the industrial development of the Community was basically left to competitive and market forces. Nevertheless, in 1970 the EEC Commission did put forward proposals for a Community industrial policy,[10] though it cannot be said that they resulted in conspicuous success. The main ingredients included the need to create a European industrial base – in effect a SEM and thus hardly a new idea – and the desirability of fostering cross-frontier business organization, notably by developments in company law and company taxation fields. When we discuss the 1992 SEM programme, it will be apparent that relatively little had been achieved in either of these two areas.

In 1971 the Commission tabled proposals concerning collaboration in research and technological development.[11] These met with a favourable response at the 1972 Paris summit and significant amounts of Community budget resources were subsequently channelled in this direction. This theme will be covered later, as under the SEA technology collaboration has been singled out as a key area of future Community cooperative effort.

The Community also opened up a policy on the environment. The Rome Treaty did not address this issue but, at the path-breaking Paris summit of 1972, heads-of-state and government called for an environmental action programme. Again, this is a topic to which we shall return as environmental policy was specifically built into the Rome Treaty by the SEA.

As we have noted, social policy did feature in the treaty, in contrast to environmental issues. But it was of limited significance and it was therefore significant that at the 1972 Paris summit the development of a more vigorous approach to social issues was emphasized. Here again the SEA built on these earlier developments notably by developing the idea of a Social Charter.

Several important new policy initiatives were taken in what can best be described as an intergovernmental, rather than a Community, framework. The first was a decision in 1970 to establish a foreign policy cooperation system known as the EPC mechanism, a possibility opened up by a decision taken at the Hague summit in 1969.[12] The second intergovernmental initiative was the establishment in 1979 of the EMS, which was a limited step towards monetary union.[13] An attempt to develop an EMU by 1980 had been foreshadowed by the Hague summit of 1969, but arrangements launched in the early 1970s subsequently ran aground; the EMU commitment was not formally abandoned, but it was for a period put in abeyance following discussions at the Paris summit of 1974. The SEA of course highlighted both EPC and the role of monetary cooperation, including EMU, and we shall return to these later in this chapter.

The onset of Eurosclerosis

One thing is clear: the Community of the early 1970's was extremely dynamic – a sign of this was the decision by the ebullient Paris summit of 1972 to establish a European union by the end of the decade. However, by the time Leo Tindemans, Prime Minister of Belgium, delivered his report on the subject in 1975, some of the steam had gone out of the system. The EMU proposal had run into the ground and Tindemans was talking about a two-tier Community in which those who had the will and ability to forge ahead with EMU could do so while the rest could lag behind, though they would not be released from the need to fall into line ultimately.

Indeed the later 1970s and notably the early 1980s were increasingly characterized by lack of progress, a state which came to be termed 'Eurosclerosis'. The reasons for this were various. One was that the recessions which followed in the wake of the oil price increases of 1973 and 1979 led to the emergence of protective responses which inhibited the drive to open up national markets. By 1981, when the EC Commission addressed a communication to the Council of Ministers on the state of the internal market, what it had to say was far from flattering:

> The customs union, the implementation of which is intended to ensure the internal market, is proving to be increasingly inadequate for the achievement of this aim. The substance of what has been achieved is instead being jeopardized and undermined by the fact that old barriers have survived for too long and new barriers have been created.[14]

But recession was not the only cause of Eurosclerosis. Other factors included the successive enlargement of the Community which not only diverted energies but also created a growing diversity of national interests. In addition, the completion of the original liberalizing blueprint took place in competition with new policies being developed, some of which we have indicated. A major distracting factor was the continuing conflict over the CAP and the Community budget, and at the centre of both these wrangles was the UK. From the outset the British government had indicated that it wished to secure major reforms in the CAP and from 1980 onwards was deeply dissatisfied with the UK's treatment in the European budget. Wrangling over both of these issues continued until 1984 and persisted to a lesser extent until 1988. But in both these years, the European Council agreed to major reforms of the CAP and made significant adjustments to the Community budget; the Fontainebleau agreement of 1984 was particularly important in releasing Community energies from internal bickering – indeed after the summit, President Mitterand observed 'There is not a single dispute left to settle'.[15] This was a little optimistic but it contained more than a grain of truth.

Another factor which slowed progress was procedural weakness within Community decision-making machinery. This had long been recognized – witness the European Council decision in 1978 to set up a committee of three wise men to address the issue. A good instance of the length of time it could take the Community to get things done is provided by the case of merger regulation. The need, recognized by the Commission as early as 1965, was explicitly to have a merger-controlling power, to complement provisions which already existed in respect of cartels and dominant positions. Such a proposal was tabled as a draft regulation end in 1973. It finally became law in modified form at the end of 1989, thanks partly to the impetus provided by the SEA's commitment to a SEM.

The turn of the tide

Eventually the log-jam was broken. Details of the emergence of the SEA, its institutional content and implications will be dealt with in detail by David Allen in the next chapter. We shall therefore content ourselves with a brief account appropriate for an overview.

Undoubtedly, a key ingredient of the SEA was the self-confidence of the directly elected European Parliament which set in motion discussions culminating in 1984 in a proposal for a European Union Treaty (EUT). This EUT, if agreed, would have radically altered the Community's decision-making structure, a change the Parliament felt essential, since the Community was failing to make essential decisions and particularly failing to respond imaginatively to problems such as the recession and competition from countries like Japan and the US. This failure was at least in part due to the institutional blockages referred to earlier. An EUT would have brought both economic and foreign policy matters within the ambit of the union decision-making machinery, strengthened the position of the Commission, progressively phased out national vetoes, and finally, given the European Parliament an enhanced legislative (as opposed to its largely consultative) role, similar to that of national political systems. Parliament was destined to be disappointed but nevertheless, as David Allen shows, some progress could be claimed. Indeed, it seems evident from the history of the European Community that although proposals tend to move in big leaps, actual results are characterized by small but remorselessly steady accretions.

The initiative did not only lie with the European Parliament. In October 1981 the French government submitted to its partners a memorandum on the revitalization of the Community.[16] Its emphasis was wholly on the need to reinvigorate the Community's efforts in the fields of economic, social and cultural policy and it contained no proposals for institutional innovation. It was followed by the German-Italian initiative of November 1981,[17] which proposed the adoption of a European Act; drafts of this, together with a declaration on European integration were addressed to the European Council and Parliament. The draft act was centrally concerned with institutional matters and looked to the creation of a European union. The European Council submitted this to the foreign ministers for study and the results of these studies were picked up at the European Council in Stuttgart in 1983; upon that occasion the heads-of-state and government signed the Solemn Declaration on European Union.[18]

This latter sounded very promising but closer inspection revealed that the main body of the declaration consisted largely of a somewhat cautious reaffirmation of the need to make progress on European union. The final provision, where concrete action might have been expected, was characterized by hesitancy: it declared that European union was already being achieved by deepening and broadening the scope of existing European activities. The European Council would subject the declaration to a review when progress towards European union justified it, and such a review would take place not later than five years from the signature of the declaration. In the light of such a review, a decision would be made as to whether the progress achieved should be incorporated in a treaty on European union: in short, member states could sign the declaration without committing themselves to any immediate radical change.

The next crucial step occurred in 1984 at the Fontainebleau summit. It was a significant milestone for two reasons. First, it made a major contribution to solving the bitter disputes which had plagued the Community for several years. In particular, real progress was made towards reforming the agricultural surplus problem and therefore curbing excessive budget spending, and this was to be achieved by instituting milk quotas. The UK also secured a more durable settlement of its own budget dispute. These bold decisions paved the way for an increase in the own-resource base of the Community budget. Second, with the atmosphere significantly improved, member states were willing to contemplate further progress to European union. A committee was set up to study the creation of a people's Europe (the Adonnino Committee); and an Ad Hoc Committee on Institutional Affairs (the Dooge Committee) was also established. The Dooge discussions were the more important, but the Adonnino Committee did make important recommendations on the need for the free movement of people – a subject to which we return later.

Both committees reported to the European Council in Brussels in March 1985.[19] The Dooge Committee suggested the establishment of an intergovernmental conference (IGC) to negotiate a European union treaty, and the IGC was agreed at the Milan summit in July 1985.

The negotiations which followed involved not just the ten member states but also the Commission and the Parliament together with Spain and Portugal which were just about to become full members. The Commission made a number of important proposals to the IGC many of which found their way into the subsequent Act. A key Commission proposal, the Cockfield Report,[20] emphasized the need to complete the internal market. This was not new – as we have seen, the Commission had been harrying the Council of Ministers on the subject for several years. A French memorandum of 1980 had emphasized its importance, the Copenhagen summit had assigned it a high priority and it had been underlined in the Solemn Declaration. The novelty of the Cockfield Report lay in its detailing of the specific measures which still remained to be adopted before the single market could be said to have been achieved – some 300 measures were suggested. The report was particularly attractive to the UK which favoured a practical approach emphasizing the need to finish properly the building of a common market, rather than rushing off to initiate further grandiose and unrealistic proposals.

The results of the IGC negotiations were reported at the Luxembourg summit in December 1985 and the resulting SEA was duly signed in February 1986.[21] Ratification followed, in some cases after procedural complications which are discussed in detail by David Allen. The SEA entered into force on 1 July 1987.

The Single European Act

The Single European Act formally placed the three European Communities and EPC at the centre of the search for European union. The European Council was clearly recognized as the supreme over-arching body. The role and institutional arrangements concerning EPC were spelled out in detail and are discussed by David Allen in the next chapter.

The SEA also reformed the decision-making processes of the three founding treaties. The main changes related to the Rome (EEC) Treaty. They were three in number and are all discussed in detail by David Allen in the next chapter:

(a) The voting arrangements in the Council of Ministers, both in respect of the provisions relating to the completion of the single market and in respect of other policies, such as economic and social cohesion and research and technology, were recast.
(b) The legislative relationship between the Council of Ministers and the European Parliament was also reformed.
(c) An additional court was to be grafted onto the Court of Justice.

The Act declared that the Community should aim to complete the internal market by the 31 December 1992. It also specified that the EEC internal market should comprise an area without internal frontiers.

The Act inserted into the Rome (EEC) Treaty new provisions on macro-economic policy implying that the need to ensure convergence of economic and monetary policy was a key aim. In this member states would take account of experience both in the EMS and with the development of the European Currency Unit (ECU), which had not featured previously in the treaty. Perhaps more significant was the fact that the preamble to the Act recollected that the 1972 Paris summit had committed itself to the goal of EMU. While not committing members to full membership of the EMS as an instrument deriving its authority from the Rome Treaty, these provisions did help to move matters in that direction.

The SEA also modified the Rome Treaty's provisions concerning social policy. Member states were encouraged to pay particular attention to instituting improvements in the working environment. The key point was that though the original Rome Treaty placed no compulsion on member states, the new Act subjected these social-improvement proposals to a majority voting procedure. The SEA also required the Commission to seek a dialogue between labour and management at the European level. The Social Charter itself owed its existence to an aspiration in the SEA preamble which had been endorsed by the signatories. The SEA also gave rise to innovations in what is called economic and social cohesion. Most interestingly the aspiration of the Community to reduce disparities between the various regions and reduce backwardness in least favoured regions, which had only been in the preamble to the old treaty, was shifted into the main body of the amended treaty. The SEA also required that expenditure under the Community budget be directed to these ends. This was realized in 1988 when the Community budget was reformed and increased provision was made for so-called structural funds.

New provisions were also added to the Rome Treaty which declared that the Community's aim should be to strengthen the scientific and technological basis of European industry to encourage it to become more competitive at an international level. A clutch of new articles designed to facilitate this were also provided. This development had been foreshadowed in the Commission's memorandum, 'Towards A European Technology Community',[22] which it contributed to the IGC discussions of 1985. Finally the SEA added to the treaty powers which quite explicitly provided for a Community competence in matters concerning the environment. All four of these policy developments are discussed by Dennis Swann in chapter 9.

The dimensions of the single market

Although many individual aspects of the single market are dealt with in detail in later chapters, not all are covered and so in this overview the treatment is deliberately uneven – those which come later will be economically outlined but those which are not dealt with subsequently will be treated in greater depth.

Before turning to our overview, it is important to stress that the detailed list of measures specified in the Cockfield Report did not exhaust all the actions needed to complete the single market – some measures were not specified. For example, the need for a merger-controlling power, to which we referred earlier, was not included in the Cockfield Report list (see chapter 3). Nevertheless when the merger regulation finally appeared it did specifically cite the single market as a reason for its introduction. Another example is provided by corporation taxation. It has long been held by the Commission that corporation tax rates and the system of corporation taxation itself needed to be harmonized if distortions in the flow of capital between different states were to be prevented. Yet no measure to this end was included in the Cockfield Report, though proposals were made in 1988 (see chapter 4). Then again, some areas of activity called for no additional enabling measures; rather the requirement was for the enforcement of existing powers, the policing of state aids being an obvious example (see chapter 3) among several others.

What did completing the single market entail? The Cockfield Report emphasized the need to do away with internal frontier controls in their entirety.[23] The SEA reiterated this – 'the internal market shall comprise an area without internal frontiers'. Moreover this area without frontier controls was to apply across the board, to goods, services, persons and capital. The Commission was of the view that in the short term, checks and controls were to be relaxed and rationalized, though in the long term they were destined to go.

An obvious short-term measure was cutting down the documentation involved in the movement of goods. A move to this end was achieved (ahead of the SEA) in December 1984 when the Council of Ministers agreed to a Single Administrative Document (SAD). The SAD came into operation at the beginning of 1988: however it was proposed that from the beginning of 1993 the SAD will be eliminated.

The total elimination of border controls in respect of goods could not however be accomplished by such a development alone. Customs duties and quotas may have gone, but other grounds for control still existed. The most obvious of them was a product of the system of indirect taxation, notably the arrangements concerning VAT. The Community long ago agreed to harmonize indirect taxes around the VAT principle, but widely differing national rates still continued to exist. Competitive distortions have been prevented by using the destination system whereby goods destined for export have had VAT remitted (known as zero-rating), the appropriate rate of VAT being imposed in the country of destination, thereby preventing competitive unfairness. However in order to stop fraud – zero rated goods being sold at home rather than abroad – and to stop citizens popping over the border to buy goods in lower VAT-rate countries, border controls have been essential. Only when VAT rate harmonization or approximation has been achieved and the special VAT treatment of exports has ceased would such controls appear to be redundant (see chapter 4).

The SEA also calls for the complete free movement of persons – a matter about which there has been, and no doubt will continue to be, considerable controversy. Mrs Thatcher has been forthright on this subject. In her famous, to some infamous, speech at Bruges in 1988 she declared 'it is a matter of plain common sense that we cannot totally abolish frontier controls if we are also to protect our citizens from crime and stop the movement of drugs, or terrorists, and of illegal immigrants'.[24] The UK argued that though the SEA envisaged easier passage for nationals of member states, it did not intend this to apply to nationals of third countries; therefore it could maintain border controls if only to control third country nationals. This may be a convenient piece of logic chopping, but nevertheless there is no doubt that the SEA did provide support for UK resistance since one of the declarations at the end of the act guarantees that nothing in it shall prevent states taking such measures as they consider necessary to control third country immigration, terrorism, crime, drug-trafficking and illicit trade in art and antiques.

There is a serious problem here since, before removing border controls, member states do need to be assured that adequate alternative safeguards exist. These require developments such as adequate policing at the common external frontier by all the other member states and arrangements which guarantee that the ability to apprehend criminals, terrorists and drug traffickers is not undermined.

Two approaches have been followed here. First, some countries – notably France, Germany, Belgium, Netherlands and Luxembourg – have sought to develop a comprehensive treaty abolishing all frontier controls on the movement of people between them. The now famous Schengen Treaty, signed in June 1990, began life in 1984 as a Franco-German endeavour, which the Benelux countries joined in in 1985. The Schengen Treaty will not be operative until all the states have ratified the arrangement – this is currently expected by the end of 1991. Second, and in the light of the Adonnino Committee's aspirations, ministers of justice and international affairs have sought agreement on a piecemeal basis on subjects such as the right of asylum. An important agreement on this latter subject (though without the adherence of Denmark) was reached in Dublin in June 1990, with the result that asylum-seekers are now guaranteed that at least one state will process applications, and situations where individuals are shuffled from state to state will not arise. Individual developments such as this, though less spectacular than the Schengen Treaty, should as they accumulate, help to ease the frontier control problem progressively.

Under the Schengen agreement the five parties agreed to shift controls away from their internal borders to their external frontier. To this end they agreed on a common list of countries whose citizens require visas to enter the zone; a common right of asylum policy; and to pool their crime data in a giant computer; to let their police forces pursue criminals on each others' territories; and have undertaken to narrow national differences in narcotics policies. There would be no border controls for people travelling between the five states and passport controls on flights between the Schengen Treaty partners would be scrapped.

While topics such as the SAD, tax frontiers, and emotive subjects such as the free movement of people have tended to catch the limelight, a glance at the Cockfield Report clearly indicates that a good deal of the required legislative activity would be dominated by the need to deal with more down-to-earth veterinary and phytosanitary controls referred to earlier. In other words, member states were going to want to continue to institute border checks and controls until they could be assured that animal diseases had been eliminated, pesticide residues had been reduced to acceptable limits, and so on. Over sixty of the 300 SEA measures were related to such mundane but vital issues.

A crucial requirement of the single market is to harmonize technical standards, food products and pharmaceuticals being high on the list. While considerable progress towards this goal was made in the period leading up to the SEA, much still remained to be done. The original harmonization process was extremely time-consuming and was further complicated by the fact that many of these standards soon became obsolescent. A key feature of the Cockfield approach to the standards problem was streamlining so that harmonization would henceforth be confined to essentials and the rest left to mutual recognition. Cases such as *Cassis de Dijon* cited earlier had helped to clarify the issue – this is all discussed in greater detail in chapter 3.

As indicated earlier, state aids though not requiring any specific enactment were recognized as a problem; indeed, the more barriers were removed and competitive forces brought to bear, the more states might seek to protect their industries by other means such as subsidies. The Cockfield Report therefore required the Commission to produce an inventory of aids and a report on state aid policy, and the first such report emerged in 1989.[25] Public procurement had been subjected to specific Community directives since as early as 1971; the Cockfield Report indicated that the directives needed to be tightened up and hitherto exempt areas brought under control. Basic anti-trust policy concerning cartels and dominant positions was not in need of further legislative attention but a power to control mergers was needed – though not specifically referred to. A need for a directive on take-over bids was however specifically identified, and while this was linked with anti-trust policy it was also seen as part of a batch of proposals designed to encourage cross-frontier business integration. This general topic is discussed later in this chapter; state aids, public procurement and mergers are all discussed in more detail in chapter 3.

The fiscal policy content of the Cockfield Report was substantial – in excess of thirty measures were proposed. It has never been suggested that income taxes should be the objects of harmonization although the Cockfield Report did call upon the Community to address income tax problems arising in connection with workers crossing frontiers daily. In the original draft directive of 1979 it was suggested that such workers should be taxed in their country of residence and that husbands and wives should be taxed separately. We have already discussed the subject of corporation tax harmonization. The bulk of the Cockfield Report's fiscal measures were in fact concerned with two other issues. One was the need to achieve fiscal neutrality in cross-frontier business situations, i.e. the problems arising in connection with subsidiary-to-parent dividend payments, capital gains taxes arising in connection with acquisitions and the double taxation burden imposed when transfer payments disputes arose. Cross-frontier business integration is further discussed below. The other was the need to deal with a whole range of matters concerning VAT and harmonizing rates; in the case of excises there was a need to determine the fiscal structure in respect of a number of products such as wine, cigarettes, mineral oils as well as to prescribe rates. Successfully tackling the indirect tax problem of course carried with it the possibility of helping to get rid of frontier controls. It is also worth mentioning that just as the Commission envisaged a new approach to technical standards, it also adopted a new one in respect of tax rates; that is to say approximation rather than absolute harmonization would suffice. Fiscal issues are discussed in detail in chapter 4.

The Cockfield Report also sought to complete the internal market in respect of services, the prime focus being financial services, notably insurance and banking, and transport. Key features of this area of policy are the concepts of freedom to supply services and right of establishment. The latter would be the case if a UK insurance company set up a subsidiary in Germany and the subsidiary insured risks in Germany. Freedom to supply services would be exemplified by the UK parent itself insuring the German risk, i.e. a cross-frontier transaction. It is true that according to the *Reyners*[26] and *Van Binsbergen*[27] cases, in the post-transition period the right of establishment and freedom to supply services could be invoked in the courts and all discrimination on grounds of nationality was automatically prohibited. However this did not dispose of all the problems since member states regulated these activities with consumer and depositor protection very much in mind and the regulatory standards adopted in one jurisdiction might not satisfy those demanded in another. Harmonization was therefore called for. Some progress was made, as for example in the case of the right of establishment in non-life insurance but freedom to supply services in such business continued to elude agreement. In short both these principles needed to be applied to the various kinds of insurance business and also to banking and other financial activities. The Cockfield Report contained a raft of proposals to this end. These and related matters are discussed in detail in chapter 5. Again a new approach was adopted: harmonization would only apply to the key regulatory issues, the rest would be left to mutual recognition.

In transport the Cockfield Report recognized that there was a major need for progress in air and maritime transport both of which, as we explained earlier, had for a long period remained in limbo. The prime need in the case of air transport was to apply the cartel rules to air passenger transport, to provide specifically for fare flexibility and to open up the bilateral (country to country) restrictions on access to routes – in other words to allow freedom to supply air services.[28] The other areas of action specified by the Cockfield Report related to access to the inland waterway freight market, liberalization of coach services and the need in the case of international road haulage to make progress in respect of two issues which had been specified in the Rome Treaty way back in 1957. These required the member states to increase the quota of international licences and to allow such hauliers to carry out domestic hauls in another member state as an incidental aspect of an international haul. This is referred to as cabotage. These measures and the problems surrounding them are discussed in detail in chapter 6.

The Cockfield Report also called for further measures to facilitate the free movement of labour and to encourage greater international mobility in the professions by coordinating training and recognizing qualifications. The original approach had been a sectoral one and could be time-consuming – it took seventeen years to achieve agreement on the architectural profession! However in 1988 the Council of Ministers took a step forward by adopting a directive which embodied a more general approach. It applied to all those professions where access was limited by the state and required at least three years' university training or its equivalent. Broadly it enabled a qualified professional in one member state to become a member of the equivalent profession in another member state without having to requalify. The free movement of capital was also on the agenda, though the measures listed were specified in terms of particular kinds of transaction. The main text of the Cockfield Report did refer to the need to monitor the existing system of exchange controls. In the event, as revealed in chapter 5, the Community took the bull by the horns and decided that exchange controls should be abolished.

The fact that the Cockfield Report contains important proposals for action in respect of cross-frontier business organization is already apparent from what has gone before. Those mentioned above do not however exhaust the stock of Cockfield proposals. The idea that efforts should be made to facilitate various forms of cross-frontier business organization has been a long-standing feature of the collection of measures constituting the Community's industrial policy. Apart from proposals to harmonize various aspects of national company law (e.g. the fifth company law directive which is aimed at giving workers a role in the running of public limited companies), the Commission had over the years striven unsuccessfully to introduce three specific collaborative measures. The first was a directive designed to harmonize national company laws so as to enable cross-frontier mergers to occur. The second was a regulation which would establish, side by side with national laws, a system of Community company law which would enable a European company or *Societas Europea* to be formed. The third was a regulation which would create a European economic interest grouping. The latter would be available to persons as well as companies, would have a cross-frontier character and be particularly helpful to small- and medium-size undertakings. Happily this proposal was adopted by the Council of Ministers in 1985.

The Cockfield Report also addressed the subject of intellectual and industrial property. Notable was a proposed regulation for a Community trade mark. The ability to obtain, by means of a single application, a trade mark covering all the member states was thought to be a useful device for enabling firms to adapt their businesses to the enlarged European market.

The benefits of completion

The Cockfield Report did not estimate the benefits of completing the single market. Rather the Community acted first and calculated afterwards. One of the most publicized studies was known as the Cecchini Report, whose detailed evidence ran to sixteen volumes,[29] though some more digestible summaries were produced.[30]

The Cecchini Report approached the problem from both a micro and macro angle. The micro-economic analysis focused, sector by sector, on the benefits derived from the removal of trade barriers (customs formalities and related delays); the removal of barriers to production (barriers to the play of competition such as those connected with public procurement and technical standards); and the greater enjoyment of economies of scale and the reduction of costs caused by increased competitive pressures which economists describe as the reduction of X-inefficiency. On various assumptions these benefits ranged from 4.3 – 6.4 per cent of the Community total Gross Domestic Product (GDP). It should be emphasized that these were once-and-for-all gains. Looking at it from a macro-economic angle, allowing for the full range of interactive effects, the estimated gain amounted to 4.5 per cent of Community GDP. However it was argued that these beneficial effects helped to reduce constraint on macro-economic management. A variety of more favourable scenarios were therefore envisaged, the most plausible of which was a declared increase in the medium term in Community GDP of 7 per cent and the creation of 5 million new jobs.

Though this was not an enormous prize, it has to be said that it was well above the levels usually associated with trade liberalization exercises which have tended to be extremely low – often in the order of 1 per cent of GDP or less. While not doubting the probability of some gain, there are those who have criticized these estimates. One such is Merton Peck who suggested that the report overestimated the gains by a factor of two or three.[31] Peck also made the important point that the Cecchini gains depended on adherence to rules of the game – that is to say member states would have to implement directives, and would have to accept the unpleasant consequences of intensified competition without resorting to subsidies and covert discrimination. Firms would have to compete and not collude or merge their way out of trouble, the Commission would have to enforce the competition rules remorselessly and Court of Justice rulings would have to be obeyed. This latter however, was not inevitable; it was reported in 1990 that at the beginning of the year there were fifty-three outstanding cases where governments had ignored court rulings on non-implementation of directives or abuse of single market rules.[32] Companies and individuals could be fined but not governments, although that could be changed if the Community's constitution were to be rewritten.

Monetary union and a new constitution?

Until 1988 the shape of European unity was that specified by the SEA. The SEA was not really revolutionary in its impact, but was rather an act of consolidation and completion which also embodied useful policy and institutional accretions. What is remarkable is that within the space of two years all this was to be transformed. At the Hanover summit in June 1988 the European Coouncil, recalling the 1972 commitment to EMU contained in the preamble to the SEA, asked the President of the Commission, Jacques Delors, together with the central bank governors, another member of the Commission and three others, to examine the progressive realization of EMU. They were to report back to the Madrid summit in June 1989, where the now famous Delors Report[33] was considered. It recommended a three-stage approach to EMU culminating in a single currency. The summit agreed to proceed to stage one of EMU and agreed that preparatory work should begin on organizing another IGC to determine the subsequent stages. Stage one required members to participate in the Exchange Rate Mechanism (ERM) of the EMS. Notably the UK had not done this, as it was far from happy about the prospect of EMU, though it had agreed to meet the ERM requirement when certain conditions were satisfied. These included a reduction of the UK inflation rate, the abolition of exchange controls by other member states and the completion of the internal market. In fact, the UK jumped the gun and joined the ERM in October 1990 while the real rate of inflation was still high. The subject of EMU is discussed in detail in chapter 8, where various alternative UK schemes, including the idea of competing currencies and the hard-ecu, will also be discussed. It should be added that German experience with monetary union in the lead-up to the political union of East and West Germany was likely to influence thinking about the feasibility of the Delors plan.

A series of factors were propelling the Community still further forward. First, there was concern about a 'democratic deficit' in the Community. At one point Jacques Delors let slip the speculation that by the mid-1990s perhaps 80 per cent of economic legislation would derive from Brussels. Even if only half true, the statement pointed to the emergence of a democratic gap. Since Community law is supreme, national parliaments would necessarily be consigned to rubber stamping the actions of the Council of Ministers. The European Parliament on the other hand is largely consultative. It does not provide a substitute for national parliaments in that the Council of Ministers does not legislate through it and is not accountable to it in the way typical of representative democracies. Some change, possibly a redefined role for the Parliament in relation to the Council of Ministers, would be needed. Not surprisingly all kinds of ideas began to be canvassed.

Second, the debates about EMU also provoked thoughts about a European constitution. EMU would shift control over monetary affairs to the centre, to a European central bank to be known as 'Eurofed'. How would those concerned with monetary, and indeed budgetary policy be made accountable?

The third and major factor was external. The changes in eastern Europe and in the general international atmosphere had several implications. The changes were of such a magnitude that it was increasingly felt that the EPC mechanism was inadequate to bear the weight of the new challenge. The changes also implied the possibility of new members, but a larger Community would slow down decision-making in the absence of institutional reform. The increasing prospect of German reunification was another powerful influence. The rest of the Community felt that German unity would be a safer and more acceptable prospect if it was to take place within a Europe which was more united. The Germans too were increasingly warm to European unity, and where previously there was always the fear that Community membership would debar them from following the path to German reunification, after 1990 this was no longer a concern.

At the Strasbourg summit in December 1990 the need for more rapid progress led the European Council to conclude that the IGC on EMU should start in December 1990. Eleven states also adopted the Social Charter, under its official title of Community Charter of the Fundamental Rights of Workers. The UK withheld its assent – Margaret Thatcher and Jacques Delors were not on the same wavelength on this aspect of the SEA.

Early in 1990 Jacques Delors aired some ideas on constitutional reform in which he maintained that the subject justified its own IGC. This won the support both of the French President and German Chancellor, and in April 1990 they issued a joint appeal for European Union. The two Dublin summits which followed decided that a parallel IGC should be convened in December 1990, to be devoted to political union. There were however different views as to what this meant and the UK reception was cool. In her Bruges speech in 1988, Margaret Thatcher declared that her first guiding principle was that 'willing and active cooperation between independent sovereign states'[34] was the best way to build a European Community. Federalism was not mentioned in her critique of Europe's future, but she made her feelings plain when she expressed her opposition to the suppression of nationhood and to fitting British customs and traditions into an 'identikit European personality'.[35] The two IGCs were anyway convened in December 1990 and discussions continued into 1991. The prospects for the IGC on political union were not improved by a marked lack of unity on the Gulf Crisis. These two ICGs are discussed further in chapters 8, 10, 11 and 12.

Chapter 2

European union, the Single European Act and the 1992 programme

David Allen

Introduction

In the mid-1980s, as Dennis Swann noted in the previous chapter, the European Community began to emerge from the doldrums. In 1984 the European Council, meeting at Fontainebleau, reached an agreement that was to mark the beginning of the end of the budget wrangle that had bedevilled the EC for some ten years.[1] The British government had made the achievement of equitable budgetary arrangements an absolute condition to be fulfilled before any further development of the EC could be permitted. The decision to complete the internal market by the end of 1992 was taken in principle at the Brussels European Council meeting of March 1985. The Cockfield Report, which detailed some 300 measures necessary to achieve this objective, was accepted at the next European Council meeting held in Milan in June 1985. At this meeting the European Council also decided, despite the objections of Britain, Denmark and Greece, to hold an IGC under the forthcoming Luxembourg presidency to consider the revising the Rome Treaty and drafting a treaty on political cooperation and European security.[2] The IGC resulted in agreement on the SEA[3] which was eventually ratified in July 1987, following referenda in Denmark (1986)[4] and Ireland (1987). In February 1988 Jacques Delors as President of the European Commission was able to say that the 'third stage of the rocket'[5] was in place when the European Council accepted his financial package, after further refining of its budgetary and CAP reforms. This package provided for substantial increases in EC structural funds which were to be increased from ECU 7 billion in 1987 to ECU 14 billion in 1993. The idea was to provide elements of compensation to those member states that were likely to initially lose out as a result of the completion of the internal market.

The combination of the SEA with its decision-making reforms along with the compensatory financial package ensured that the single market programme rapidly gathered momentum in the second half of the 1980s – to such an extent that it was soon accepted, both inside and outside the EC, that the 1992 deadline would be met. For the first time the remaining wealthy members of EFTA began to contemplate seriously the dangers of being left outside the EC after 1992; and both the United States and Japan showed concern about the likely future impact of a post-1992 EC on the international economy. As the achievement of the single market programme became accepted advocates of further integration began to seek further ways of deepening the EC. Even before the dramatic changes in the Soviet Union and eastern Europe, which culminated in the unification of Germany within the EC in 1990, there were calls for more progress towards an ultimate, albeit ill-defined, goal of European union. More specifically notions of EMU and of political union were placed on the agenda. This internal dynamic of integration was boosted considerably by the events of 1989 and 1990 in eastern Europe. Most EC States, in particular France and Germany, believed that the EC could best cope with German unity and the collapse of the cold war structures in Europe by speeding up the process of consolidating or deepening the European Community. The result, again with Britain's reluctant support, was the decision of the European Council, meeting in Rome in December 1990, to convene two new IGCs on EMU and political union respectively.

To an extent these developments have tended to overshadow the single market programme. The SEA was increasingly seen as an initial first amendment to a Rome Treaty that would require more dramatic changes if it was to meet the challenges of the new Europe in the 1990s. Even the EC's new enlarged structural funds seemed to pale into insignificance when compared with estimates of the sums that would be required to assist the Soviet Union and the newly liberated states of eastern Europe in their transition to market economies. The EC is now increasingly faced not only with the question of deepening but also with the possibility of further enlarging, as both the EFTA, eastern European states, not to mention Turkey, Cyprus, Malta and Morocco, all manoeuvre for position.

However the 1992 programme and the SEA both represent actual achievements rather than aspirations, and any understanding of the way that the EC is likely to evolve in the future requires an understanding of its recent and current experiences. Similarly recent developments can only be properly understood in the context of what went before them. The EC has always developed incrementally via a series of intergovernmental deals, some of which have led to the transfer of powers and competences from the member states to Community institutions, but all of which have sought to build upon, rather than replace, that which has gone before. The progress has not always been either steady or smooth, rather it has been ratchet-like with many examples of advance and eventual spillover from one economic area to another including from economics to politics – but with few examples of regression or spillback. The 1992 programme and the SEA represent key developments in the evolution of the European Community and it is the aim of this chapter to examine their political origins, substance and significance and so place them in the context of that evolution. In chapter 10 some of the themes and experiences considered below will be projected forward in an attempt to shed some light on the likely future evolution of the EC in the new Europe of the 1990s.

The evolution of EC decision-making

The EC has to date gone through three stages of institutional development[6] and may well be on the verge of a fourth. From 1957 until 1965 the EC institutions set about the tasks given them in the original treaty using the procedures laid down in that treaty. Thus internal trade restrictions were abolished and common policies established by the European Commission, exercising its sole right of initiative, making legislative proposals (regulations, directives and decisions) to the Council of Ministers which in turn, under the organization of the rotating presidency, took decisions. These decisions were arrived at, depending on the rules laid down in the treaty either by unanimous, simple or weighted majority voting – though in practice before 1966, few votes were taken by simple majority. In some cases, notably with regard to restrictive practices and the running of the CAP, the Council exercised its right to authorize the Commission to take legislative action on its own accord. In these cases a system of management committees were established so that the Council could both supervise and, to a degree, control subsequent Commission action.

The Common Assembly, as the European Parliament was then called, consisted of unelected delegates from the national parliaments of the member states. It had no legislative or budgetary powers but it could, by an absolute majority, pass a motion of censure on the Commission. This was not considered to be a very effective power as the Council of Ministers had the sole right to nominate or renominate members of the Commission. The Council was obliged to receive the Assembly's opinion on any Commission legislative proposal but it was not obliged to take any notice of that opinion. The Community budget was financed by national contributions although Article 201 of the treaty provided for the eventual introduction of an own-resources system of funding. The Court of Justice was accepted by all member states as the ultimate arbiter of legality in a Community legal system which recognized the superiority of EC law over national legislation. Given the vagueness and ambiguity of much of the treaty and given the broad political as well as economic objectives alluded to in its preamble, the Court's role as the ultimate interpreter of that treaty was inevitably political. It is generally accepted that the Court has sought wherever possible to use its role to advance the cause of European unity and as such was probably in a position to be more effective in this direction than the Common Assembly during this first period.

This period came to an end in 1965 when a French boycott of Community decision-making institutions was eventually resolved in what became known as the Luxembourg Compromise.[7] In essence this represented an agreement to disagree between France and the other five EC member states over how far the Council should go towards seeking unanimous agreement (even where the treaty provided for majority voting) on issues that individual states regarded as vital to their national interests. Although the Compromise was just that and had no legal standing in the EC system, it had an important impact on decision-making in the Council: it has been interpreted as meaning that any member state could in fact exercise a veto on any issue that it determines will affect its vital national interests. In consequence decision-making in the Council slowed down dramatically; for though the veto has only rarely been formally used, its existence ensured that decisions were endlessly postponed until unanimous agreement could be reached.[8] For our purposes the significance of the Luxembourg Compromise was that it created a decision-making deadlock in the Council which had to be rectified in the SEA in order that the 1992 programme might be achieved.

In relation to events in the mid 1980s one other aspect of the EC's 1965 constitutional crisis is instructive. The problem initially arose because France under De Gaulle (not unlike Britain under Thatcher) became concerned about the advance of supra-nationality in the EC which was linked with a perceived loss of French national sovereignty. The Commission had attempted to advance the EC by putting forward a package deal which linked something that France wanted – the completion of the CAP – with a switch of EC financing from national contributions to an own-resources system. The Commission further argued that if the new system of EC financing was accepted then the European Parliament would need some powers of control over the budget. The French took exception to this attempted supra-national advance and were successful in the short term in preventing it. Much the same situation arose in 1985 when this time the Commission led by Jacques Delors was successful in linking something that Britain wanted – the completion of the single market – with a reform of the EC institutions involving an extension of the power of the Parliament and an increase in the policy areas covered by Community competence.

At the Hague summit of 1969 a number of decisions were taken that involved both the prospective widening and deepening of the EC. It has long been a contention of some British politicians that these are two incompatible notions. Thus in the 1970s the British government supported the applications for membership of Greece, Spain and Portugal partly because it believed that these would hold up or even render impossible further extensions of supra-nationality and the power of Community institutions. As we shall see in chapter 10 much the same argument was deployed at the end of the 1980s when the British government saw a further enlargement of the EC to include EFTA and some eastern European countries as a way of preventing both EMU and political union. However the experience of 1969–73 should have taught the British government a lesson for during this period the EC not only completed the process of enlargement to include Britain, Ireland and Denmark but also set itself the ambitious target of both EMU and progress towards political cooperation, particularly in the area of foreign policy. In 1970 the system of EPC[9] was established whereby EC member states, operating on the basis of consensus without a treaty, but underpinned by the Luxembourg (1970) and Copenhagen (1973) Reports, sought to harmonize and coordinate their foreign policy positions and, where possible, undertake common action together. In the early days the attraction of EPC for many member states lay in the fact that it was intergovernmental, it operated outside the framework of the Rome Treaty and it was managed exclusively by the state holding the EC Council presidency. Therefore all Community institutions and in particular the Commission could be excluded. All these aspects of the EPC system, which developed extensively between 1970 and 1985,[10] were to be altered by the inclusion of a separate Title III in the SEA dealing with 'Provisions on European cooperation in the sphere of foreign policy'.

Although the possibility of taking significant majority votes in the Council ended in 1966 the EC, spurred on by the Hague summit managed to maintain its momentum up to around 1973. Apart from enlargement and the establishment of new policies and objectives, progress was also made on EC financing, with the gradual introduction of a system of own-resources after 1970 – albeit one that was to prove contentious until reformed in 1984 and again in 1988. Furthermore the introduction of this new financing system, which became fully effective by 1975, was accompanied by granting minimal budgetary powers to the European Parliament.[11] These powers were added to in 1975 when the Financial Provisions Treaty gave the Parliament the final say on the adoption of the Budget as a whole. This power was to be exploited by the Parliament after it was first directly elected in 1979. Poor publicity was attracted by the Parliament in the early 1980s as it attempted to use rejection of the budget to extend its overall influence. This played a part in persuading those who, like Spinelli, wished to see the Parliament develop further, to direct their attention towards increasing the Parliament's legislative as opposed to budgetary powers. As we shall see, this view was reflected in the European Parliament's own draft treaty on European union in 1984 and appeared, much weakened, in the cooperation procedure outlined in the SEA.

However despite the optimism apparent at the Paris summit of 1972, which marked the accession of the three new members, the decade that was to follow is generally regarded as a time of relative retrenchment for the Community. This second period in the institutional life of the Community from 1973 to 1984 was described in the previous chapter as one of Eurosclerosis. In substantive terms it was marked by a long and occasionally bitter struggle between Britain and the Commission and the other member states over the reform of both the budget and the CAP which had begun to generate unwanted and costly surpluses. Though a regional fund was established and although the EMS was developed towards the end of the 1970s little else was achieved and in a number of areas, worsening international circumstances forced the member states to consider national rather than Community solutions to their problems. Where the Community was used it tended to be defensively and negatively *vis-à-vis* the outside world as in the Multi-Fibre Agreement or the various steel and shipbuilding crisis measures that were introduced to try and protect the European market from outside competition.

In institutional terms the EC got itself bogged down because of the threat of the veto in the Council and because the Commission itself became markedly more timid in the exercise of its sole right of initiative. Many felt that the Commission was behaving more like a bureaucracy than an executive[12] and that with enlargement there were just too many Commissioners chasing too few substantive portfolios: Britain, France, Germany and Italy all claimed two Commission posts, the other members one each. Within the Commission the principle of 'juste retour' extended remorselessly down through the bureaucracy so that permanent officials could only rise so far on merit before they came up against the member states insisting that certain senior posts be determined by nationality rather than ability. Even where posts were available they were often snapped up by members of the Commissioners' personal 'cabinets' who exploited their privileged positions to seek more permanent employment in the Commission. Above all the Commission suffered from a crisis of leadership. Neither Presidents Ortoli, Jenkins nor Thorn were able to raise the morale and profile of the Commission sufficiently above the collective gloom hanging over the Community to seize the initiative in the way that Jacques Delors was able to do from 1984 onwards.

Though, as we have seen, the European Parliament managed to secure some budgetary powers, it continued to play little part in the legislative process. Great store was set by the decision in principle, taken at the Paris summit of 1974, to allow direct elections to the Parliament. But these did not in fact first take place until 1979 and then not under a common electoral system but utilizing the many different national electoral systems. Only in the external sphere, where the EC was seen more and more to be an actor of some significance in the international system, was any real progress made towards further integration. This was partly because of the development of EPC, though this was often criticized for being more about procedure than policy; and it was partly because of the growing importance of economic and trade matters – the business of the EC – in international politics. One consequence of this growing external role was a realization that the economic and political aspects of external policy could no longer be separated as rigidly as the EC and EPC structures suggested. Furthermore it would not be long before the Community's external agenda might have to be expanded into the security sphere, for so long under the exclusive authority of NATO. The London Report of 1980[13] raised this possibility for the first time as well as introducing into EPC a series of measures designed to aid the member states in their collective approach to international crises – the EC states had been severely embarrassed by the fact that their response to the Soviet invasion of Afghanistan had taken six weeks to formulate.

During the period of Eurosclerosis there was no shortage of proposals, reviews and reports designed to get the Community moving again. These tended to centre on the theme of European union which was understood in most of western Europe to be more of a process than a fixed end-state. The exception of course was Britain where the notion of federalism was frequently confused with centralization and where the goal of European union was assumed to involve the transfer of all authority or sovereignty to a central European state. In Britain, both Labour and Conservative governments generally sought to limit the federalist damage done by these numerous attempts to revitalize the EC whilst at the same time trying to ensure that practical or pragmatic reforms to make the EC as it stood work better were adopted. Thus when it came to the consideration of majority voting in the SEA Britain was anxious to have it applied to internal market issues but was equally anxious to prevent its extension to new areas of Community competence. Similarly the UK has taken the lead in advocating pragmatic reforms of EPC such as the establishment of a small secretariat or the consideration of security issues, but has resisted attempts to make a common foreign or defence policy a formal EC treaty objective subject to treaty procedures such as majority voting.

The term European union first emerged in Paris in 1972 when the EC heads of government agreed to 'transform before the end of the decade, the whole complex of the relations of Member States into a European Union'.[14] This was reaffirmed at the 1974 Paris summit at which the Belgian Prime Minister, Leo Tindemans, was given the task of consulting his fellow EC leaders and drawing up a Report on European Union. By the time that the report[15] was produced the EC was already consumed with its own crisis and no member was prepared to seriously consider its findings. However in placing great emphasis on the EC's external role and on the internal reform of its institutions, Tindemans was to point the way to future, more productive attempts to advance the EC – in particular the SEA. In 1979 the Spierenburg Report looked at various ways in which the Commission might function more effectively within the EC system as it stood, while the report of the Committee of Three sought a more radical shake-up of the whole institutional structure. It was not however until the start of the 1980s that things began to move. As Britain mounted its campaign for the reform of the budget, others began to look beyond the immediate quarrels and ask where the Community was headed.

Relaunching the Community

The incentives to try and get the EC going were numerous. We have already mentioned the fact that there was continuous pressure from the early 1970s, amongst some member state governments and a number of prominent individuals, to develop European union. This had not relented; in fact it was given a boost by the direct election of the European Parliament and the presence within that Parliament of a number of fervent advocates of European union – in particular Altiero Spinelli.

Another incentive came from the fact that national attempts to solve the economic problems of the 1970s had all by and large failed and a number of governments, encouraged by their business élites, were turning once again to consider Community solutions. The failure of western European national economic strategies was best illustrated by the growing unease that was exhibited by a number of states about Japan's rapid rise to economic power. Just as the 'defi americaine' had produced an incentive to establish the common market in the 1960s, so the Japanese threat inspired many to advocate the advantages of completing the internal market in the 1990s. Support for the notion of getting the EC moving again via the instrument of the single market was also encouraged by the general decline of the left in western Europe at the start of the 1980s. The notion of a deregulated, free market Europe appealed to the new governments of the right in Britain and West Germany while the failure of the French national socialist experiment removed any opposition that might have been expected from President Mitterrand. Indeed by the time in early 1984 that France took up the presidency of the EC, Mitterrand was anxious to distract attention from recent national economic traumas by launching and leading a great European initiative. The fact that Jacques Delors, a close friend of Mitterrand as well as being his potential successor, had just become President of the Commission also made a considerable difference, for he was to play an important leadership role in getting both the 1992 programme and the SEA off the ground.

If the rise of Japan provided one incentive for renewed activity at EC level so too did changes in the relationship between the United States and western Europe. These were partly the consequence of relative American decline and partly the result of changes in the relationship between the United States and the Soviet Union. Economically western Europeans worried about the growing US budget and trade deficits. They also worried about the possibility of the US completing deals with the Japanese over, for instance, market sharing or high technology research and development, which might in turn adversely affect European interests. Politically and militarily, the west Europeans began to worry about the nature of the American security guarantee. Whether they sought to bolster NATO or to prepare for its replacement, all the EC members, with the exception of Ireland, began in the

1980s to consider either developing a security role for the EC as an extension of EPC, or building up Western European Union (WEU) as a bridge between the EC and NATO. The onset of the new cold war, marked by the Soviet invasion of Afghanistan and the anti-Soviet hostility of the new Reagan administration, made a number of EC member states, in particular West Germany, very uncomfortable because they had a considerable stake in better relations with the East that had been a feature of the 1970s. On this issue, as well as over the Middle East and Central America, the Europeans, operating within EPC, found themselves not directly opposed to the United States, but exhibiting clear differences of interpretation. What was emerging was some sort of European identity which might provide the basis for extending the objectives of EPC towards the establishment of a common foreign policy.[16] Superpower hostility was to provide an incentive for renewed European cooperation in the early 1980s. But the sudden transformation in US–Soviet relations bought about by the arrival of Mr Gorbachev and his new thinking was to maintain this cooperation in the second half of the decade. A number of EC states received a very real fright when the Americans and the Soviets came close to agreement at Reykjavik in October 1986 for it seemed as if European interests could be easily ignored or bargained away.[17] Proposals to eliminate nuclear weapons in Europe and to cut strategic arsenals threatened to destroy the strategic links between Europe and the United States, to place great pressure on the British and French nuclear forces and to leave western Europe at the mercy of superior Soviet conventional forces. No wonder then that even before the dramatic events in eastern Europe that marked the end of the cold war, the EC member states were prepared in 1985 and 1986 to consider the development of EPC as part of their proposed revival of the EC.

Finally all the Community institutions, with the possible exception of the Council of Ministers, were anxious to both add new competences to the Community agenda and to reform the Community's decision-making process and thus to enhance and extend their own authority. Whilst the Commission, Parliament and Court all had communautaire reasons for advocating deepening and reform they were joined in 1984 not only by those member states, like Italy, France, West Germany and the Benelux countries who also wanted to make progress towards European union but also by those like Britain and Denmark who had a specific interest in the 1992 programme and thus in any reforms necessary to make that programme work. As we shall see it was the particular skill of France and Germany working together and in cooperation with Delors that ensured that the new EC menu contained not just the 1992 programme but a number of other Community delicacies (some not so palatable to the British and Danes!) as well.

The first sign of movement came from the new directly elected European Parliament. In July 1981 this adopted a resolution submitted by the 'Crocodile Club', a group of pro-federalist MEPs led by Altiero Spinelli, that was designed to give a fresh impetus to the process of European union. An Ad Hoc Committee on Institutional Affairs was set up and given the task of drawing up a draft treaty on European union.[18] This draft treaty was duly completed and on 14 February 1984 the European Parliament approved it by a large majority. It is worth spending a moment on some of the detail of the draft treaty, as most observers[19] would agree with Jacques Delors' implicit answer to his own question, from his speech in Bruges on 17 October 1989, 'do you think that it would have been possible to convene the IGC that produced the SEA had Parliament not thrown its weight behind the idea on the basis of the draft European union treaty which it had adopted at the initiative of that great European, Altiero Spinelli?' Although the SEA disappointed many of those who supported the proposals in the draft treaty it is also significant that many of them are once again on the agenda of the IGC on political union.

First of all Spinelli was anxious to increase the level of democratic participation in the European union that he sought in the draft treaty. There were not however to be any new institutions for the Parliament had insisted on reform rather than revolution. Under the draft treaty the Commission and the Parliament would have much larger roles. The Commission was destined to become the sole executive body of the union – drawing up and implementing the budget, initiating and implementing union action and representing the union in external relations (all tasks which were at present shared with the Council of Ministers). The Parliament would have been given joint or colegislative power with the Council and both institutions would also be given the right of initiative (at present the Commission has the sole right of initiative). It was anticipated that the Parliament and the Council would work much like the two houses of the US Congress (with the European Parliament approximating to the House of Representatives and the Council to the Senate). They were to be given the joint power to raise revenue independent of national parliaments and to adopt the union budget. They would also jointly share in the investiture of the Commission. The Council, which would take all decisions by qualified majority voting would thus share the legislative, budgetary and treaty ratifying powers that it previously held exclusively. The European Council would become a union institution and its main function would be to appoint the President of the Commission and to decide, using the ill-defined principle of subsidiarity, which areas of cooperation would be assigned to the union. The inclusion of the principle of subsidiarity is an indication of the cautious nature of the draft treaty for it was designed to prevent the member states being frightened off. The understanding of the principle enshrined in the draft treaty (which is also being applied to the political union deliberations) is that the member states will retain general competence or responsibility for all areas except those entrusted to the union by the treaty. Thus the union, under these proposals, would only be given those tasks which the member states cannot execute independently or which they cannot execute as effectively. In other words the union remains subsidiary to the member states.

The inclusion of the principle of subsidiarity and the interpretation of it given above is obviously designed to cope with the fears that states like Britain and France have about the potential loss of national sovereignty under a European union. Subsidiarity, interpreted in this way has thus been enthusiastically adopted by the British government as a principle that can be usefully applied to all discussions about European union – the SEA and more recently political union. However it has been pointed out by several observers that subsidiarity can be interpreted in a number of ways.[20] It is true that in the draft treaty subsidiarity has been seen as the 'protector of the freedom of smaller units (the member states) from the unwelcome attentions of larger ones (Community institutions)'.[21] Adonis and Tyre,[22] in a letter to the Financial Times, argue that the term is a mere platitude in that it can mean 'as much decentralization as possible or as much centralization as necessary'. They cite eight contradictory definitions some of which support the British government's understanding of the term (that things should not be done at Community level unless they cannot be done at national level). Other definitions give powers to the higher authorities on grounds that Commission officials would find most agreeable. Even if the British understanding of subsidiarity is accepted, it remains an open-ended one and still begs the question as to who should decide – the European Council or the Court of Justice – whether a task can be executed independently or effectively at the national level. Another participant in the Financial Times debate[23] pointed out that in recent years there have been any number of proposals for action now at national level to be taken at Community level; but very few suggesting anything that could be done at a national level that is now done at Community level (though, it must be admitted, some of the more extreme suggestions concerning the renationalization of the CAP would fit into this category!). This particular correspondent ended up by arguing that 'subsidiarity is nothing more than a somewhat threadbare rhetorical device employed by those who wish to disguise, for various reasons, the ever increasing powers and authority of EC institutions'.[24]

The draft treaty was all very well but it was the response of national governments that really mattered given the fact that the European Parliament had no real power other than to place the issue of European union firmly on the agenda. It has to be said that, despite Spinelli's aspirations, the evolution of the 1992 Programme, the SEA and the subsequent IGCs owed little to the demands from or the involvement of the mass public. Spinelli had hoped that the draft treaty would capture the imagination of mass movements in Europe so that governments would be forced to respond to a popular demand for European union. In fact there was no such development, it is hard even to argue that the second (1984) or third (1989) round of direct elections to the European Parliament had much influence on the issues under consideration.

Direct elections in most EC member states were fundamentally determined by local and national issues with little real discussion of Community matters. What occurred was essentially the product of intergovernmental bargaining between the member states, with the Commission playing a very important role and with a number of transnational business groups (such as the Round-table of European Industrialists, organized under the chairmanship of Pehr Gyllenhammer of Volvo) exerting a growing pressure for the single market at both the national and Community levels.[25]

As we have seen, by the start of the 1980s European policy makers were beginning to lose faith in national solutions to their various economic problems and were once again beginning to show an interest in European solutions. Thus in the early 1980s Etienne Davignon on behalf of the Commission was able to set up, with the twelve major electronics companies in the EC, the European Strategic Programme for Research and Development in Information Technology (ESPRIT) which they were then able to jointly sell to their national governments. The Research for Advanced Communications Technologies (RACE) programme emerged in much the same way with the Commission, national governments and private business élites all working together. Politically too, things began to stir in the early 1980s with the launching of a German-Italian initiative for a European act designed mainly to link EPC with the EC. The idea was that the act would be reviewed after five years and transformed into a treaty of European union. This proposal was consistently diluted until it was published as the Solemn Declaration on European Union at the Stuttgart European Council meeting in 1983 and in the words of Britain's permanent representative at the time was 'sunk without trace'.[26] The failure of the Solemn Declaration to deal with the question of bringing security cooperation into EPC or to provide stronger links between EPC and the EC meant that both these issues remained to be faced when drafting the SEA.

The idea of completing the single market as a response to the failure of national policies and to the threat from Japan and the United States had, as we have seen, developed steadily during the early 1980s with considerable encouragement from influential transnational business élites. The European Council meeting in Copenhagen in 1982 had instructed the Council 'to decide, before the end of March 1983, on the priority measures proposed by the Commission to reinforce the internal market' but it took the appointment of Jacques Delors as president of the Commission to get the process under way. Delors was looking for an idea that would re-ignite the European idea and the beginning of 1985 was a particularly good time to launch the 1992 programme because of developments during the French presidency in the first half of 1984. President Mitterrand was determined first of all to resolve the British problems with the Community budget that had proved so divisive over the years (one incentive for the French was that they too were likely to soon become net contributers to the European budget!). He saw an opportunity to build on the renewed expressions of enthusiasm for European union such as were demonstrated by the European Parliament's draft treaty and in this way put pressure on the British to accept a compromise on the budget. French strategy was based on the assumption that the British government, now firmly committed to membership of the EC, would be very sensitive to any attempt by the core member states to move to a higher level of integration, possibly without Britain. Paul Taylor's argument that British diplomacy 'therefore had to balance two objectives: satisfying specific interests and staying in the game'[27] and that 'a measure of compromise in the former had become necessary to achieve the latter'[28] is thus particularly perceptive and holds good for most of the period that we are discussing. Once Britain had decided that its future lay within the EC then the threat of exclusion became a real one and required the British to go along however reluctantly with both the SEA and the IGCs on EMU and political union. From this point onwards Britain has always had an interest in processes, like the SEA or the IGCs, which revolve around amending the Rome Treaty (a treaty amendment requires the unanimous agreement and ratification by all member states) rather than the creation of a new treaty or treaties which could be achieved by those states who so wished, if necessary without British or Danish participation.

At the first European Council meeting of the French presidency, which was held in Brussels in March of 1984 a deal was almost struck to resolve the budget dispute. This failed mainly, as the French and Germans saw it, because of Mrs Thatcher's intransigence. At one point at this meeting, Chancellor Kohl rose threatening to leave, and in so doing managed to convey both to the British and to his other colleagues a significant warning, namely that as far as he was concerned the British could either 'take it or leave it'.[29] President Mitterrand too sought to exploit the difficulty of the British position by speaking positively to the European Parliament about its draft treaty and by calling for a conference of those within the EC who were prepared to stand up and be counted on both the issue of the budget and the further deepening of the Community. He actually called for a new treaty which could of course be agreed by an inner core of EC states free from the dangers of the British veto. Mitterrand, encouraged by Kohl took this notion further when the European Council next met at Fontainebleau in June by holding up the business for several hours whilst he waxed lyrical about his dreams of Europe. The result of this pressure on Britain was that agreement on the European budget was reached at Fontainebleau and the European Council was able to move the Community agenda on with little real obstruction from the British who were obliged to make some concessions to European union in order to stay in the game. Mrs Thatcher even turned up at Fontainebleau with her own set of proposals contained in a document called 'Europe – the future'. The main emphasis of this document was on the need to complete the internal market, to improve the EC's external relations capability and to achieve both these objectives within the institutional system as it stood rather than via significant reforms or new common policies. However at Fontainebleau it was in fact agreed that two committees would be set up, one to investigate ways of giving substance to the notion of a 'citizen's Europe' (the Adonnino Committee) and one to look into the possibility of institutional reform and related matters (the Dooge Committee).

The Dooge Committee reinforced the linkages that had begun to be made between various items on the integration menu – in particular, the completion of the internal market, the strengthening of EPC and institutional reform were all firmly linked together to the dismay of the British representative on the Committee who was Malcolm Rifkind. Dooge reported to the Brussels European Council in 1985 and much of the Committee's report bore the echoes of the Parliament's draft treaty. Thus in policy terms Dooge called for the establishment of a genuine internal market, increased economic convergence, the creation of a technological community, the strengthening of the EMS, the mobilization of the necessary resources, the promotion of the common values of civilization and the search for an external identity that would include external policy, security and defence matters. Institutionally, however, the Dooge Committee did not stick so closely to the draft treaty proposals. Instead of calling for colegislative powers for the Parliament and the Council, the elimination of the veto and a strengthened Commission, Dooge argued for changes in practice, less bureacracy and a restricted resort to majority voting. The British insisted that none of this could affect the Luxembourg Compromise and also entered a number of other reservations against any strengthening of the European Parliament and against suggestions that the Commission President might nominate his own team.

While the Dooge Committee was drawing up its report Delors was settling into the Commission Presidency and getting down to the business of raising the profile of the single market programme. In a speech to the European Parliament on 14 January 1985 he mentioned the idea of a 1992 deadline for the first time and this notion was approved by the same European Council meeting in Brussels that received the Dooge Report. In Brussels the European Council laid particular emphasis on 'action to achieve a single large market by 1992 thereby creating a more favourable environment for stimulating enterprise, competition and trade'. It also called upon the Commission 'to draw up a detailed programme with a specific timetable before its next meeting'. This was the mandate for the Commission to draw up the White Paper on Completing the Internal Market, which became known as the Cockfield Report. This was presented to and accepted by the European Council meeting in Milan in June 1985.

The major impact of adding the deadline of 1992 for the completion of the internal market was to put pressure on the member states to agree the other aspects of what had become accepted as a package – in particular there was a need to reach a fairly swift agreement on the necessary institutional changes. At Brussels, the Dooge Committee did not go along with the European Parliament's preferred option of calling for a new treaty. Instead it proposed that the Article 236 procedure for the amendment of the existing treaty be used. The Committee therefore proposed the calling of an IGC to negotiate a draft treaty based on the 'aquis communautaire' (the Rome Treaty and all subsequent EC legislation), the Dooge report itself and the Solemn Declaration on European Union (which had not quite sunk without trace). It was also suggested that the IGC should be guided by the spirit of the Parliament's own draft treaty.

At the Milan summit the French proposal that an IGC be convened, with the amendment of EC decision-making amongst other things on its agenda, carried the day, mainly because of the support it attracted from Germany and Italy. The British, the Greeks and the Danes voted against an IGC at the European Council but subsequently accepted one at a meeting of EC foreign ministers held in July 1985. The Luxembourg presidency was charged with convening the IGC during the latter part of 1985 with a view to reporting to the European Council in Luxembourg in December. The IGC was to consider the revision of the Treaty of Rome and the drafting of a treaty on political cooperation and European security. The British had failed in their attempt to prevent any linkage between the internal market programme and institutional reform but they had at least succeeded in ensuring that there would not be a new treaty and that any treaty amendments proposed by the IGC would be subjected to unanimous acceptance and ratification by the member states.

The Milan summit predetermined a great deal of the IGCs work as a number of relevant agreements were concluded there. First and most important was the accord on the single market but there was also agreement on technological cooperation, on the idea of a people's Europe (which was to influence the social policy provisions) and on the future of the EMS and the role of the ECU. Despite receiving detailed proposals from Britain and a Franco-German text the heads of government were not able to agree on guidelines for the EPC treaty but they were clear that this would be linked with any proposed amendments to the Rome Treaty and not dealt with as a separate issue, as some states, notably Britain would have preferred. The details of the SEA were therefore sorted out in the IGC during the autumn of 1985, at the European Council meeting in Luxembourg in December 1985 and at a subsequent EC foreign ministers meeting held later on in December. The text of the SEA was formally adopted on 17 February 1986 in Luxembourg and on 28 February in the Hague. Article 236 states however that treaty amendments (such as the SEA) only come into force 'after having been ratified by all the existing member states in accordance with their respective constitutional requirements'. It was for this reason that the SEA did not formally amend the treaty until July 1987 although in practice many of its provisions (for instance on majority voting) had already begun to influence the work of the Community's institutions.

The Single European Act

The SEA consists of a preamble and four titles dealing with common provisions, provisions amending the treaties that established the European Communities, treaty provisions on European cooperation in the sphere of foreign policy and general and final provisions.[30] The preamble restates the objective of creating a European union based on the EC treaties and on the treaty on foreign policy cooperation. It reaffirms member states' commitment to the preservation of human rights and democracy and specifically refers to the indispensability of the European Parliament in this context. The preamble also relates the extension of common policies and the establishment of new objectives, as well as the proposed reform of the institutions, to a determination to improve the economic and social situation. Finally the preamble records the objective of 'the progressive realization of economic and monetary union' and 'notes' both the introduction of the EMS and the fact that the Community and the Central Banks of the member states have taken a number of measures intended to implement monetary cooperation.

In Article 2 of the SEA the existence and composition of the European Council is recorded for the first time but there is no mention of what it is supposed to do within the EC system. In particular the relationship between the European Council and the ordinary Council of Ministers remains unclear. At present any decisions taken by the European Council which relate to EC legislation have to be formally noted by the Council of Ministers before they can become Community law. Some observers have argued that the separate reference to the European Council in the SEA effectively precludes its members (the EC heads-of-state or government and the President of the European Commission) from ever acting as the Council of Ministers.

The most important institutional changes to be found within the SEA relate to the provisions for an increased use of qualified (or weighted) majority voting in the Council and the introduction of a new cooperation procedure between the Council and the Parliament in some areas of Community activity. The provisions for qualified majority voting are mainly to be found in the section of the SEA dealing with the internal market. Articles 8A, 8B, 8C, 28, 57(2), 59, 70(1) and 83 of the EC Treaty are all amended to replace unanimity with qualified majority voting and Article 100A is added to Article 100. Under Article 100, which covers the key area of the approximation or harmonization of laws, the Council had to act unanimously and was only allowed to issue directives. The new Article 100A in the SEA allows the Council, for the purposes of achieving the single market by the end of 1992, to act by qualified majority and to adopt measures and not be restricted to directives. The UK was instrumental in ensuring that Article 100A(2) was also inserted into the SEA retaining unanimity for fiscal provisions, the free movement of persons, and the rights and interests of employees. Britain remains adamant that border controls (which some EC states have already removed under the Schengen Agreement – see Chapter 1) must be kept in place in order to control terrorism and the spread of diseases like rabies.

Although the SEA extends qualified majority voting into a number of areas it still disappointed those states like France, Germany, Italy and the Benelux countries which along with the Commission said they would like to have seen the principle more broadly extended. The SEA represents a sort of triumph for the minimalist British position in that it makes concessions to the need to reform the decision-making process but then goes on to severely restrict those concessions. As well as the exceptions provided in Article 100A(2), Article 99 is altered to allow for the European Parliament to be consulted but unanimity is to be preserved for the harmonization of VAT rates, excise duties and other forms of indirect taxation – all matters of political sensitivity to Britain. More generally the SEA provides for further derogations whereby under certain circumstances a member state will be able to implement national measures on the grounds of 'major needs' (under Article 18 of the SEA, adding Article 100A(4) to the Rome Treaty) or to protect the working and natural environments. There are a number of other clauses that have the potential to be abused by the member states but it has to be said that to date there have been few examples of this sort of activity. It is the failure of some states to implement internal market directives agreed to in the Council that has provided a much more serious challenge to the achievement of the 1992 objective, than their ability to claim derogations under the SEA.

Despite the limitations discussed above, the effective reintroduction of qualified majority voting[31] has had the desired effect of enabling the Council to take decisions. First of all in December 1986 the Council changed its rules of procedure to allow any member state or the Commission itself to call for a formal vote. In the past only the state holding the presidency could do this and so it could if it wished prevent a decision going against it by refusing to call for a vote. Even before the SEA came into force the Council began to alter its voting habits, suggesting that unanimity was more a matter of political will than legal obligation. Thus before 1986 majority votes in the Council rarely reached double figures for a full year whilst in 1986, forty-three items of legislation were adopted on a majority basis during the Dutch presidency and fifty-five during the British presidency. Since then most presidencies have been able to report significant progress of internal market measures through the Council; and in the current debate about political union there is considerable pressure to extend this voting system to many other areas of the treaty and EPC. As we saw earlier, the original treaty had provided for both majority and qualified majority voting, but this had effectively been halted by the Luxembourg Compromise. The present status of the Luxembourg

Compromise remains unclear. There was an attempt in the IGC to clarify it which not surprisingly failed and Mrs Thatcher continued to insist, when pressed, that it remained unaffected by the SEA. However in practice it seems unlikely that the Luxembourg Compromise will play much of a part in the future evolution of the EC.

The reason why the theoretically continuing existence of the Luxembourg Compromise is important to Britain and to one or two other EC states with relatively strong national parliaments relates to the question of national democratic control and scrutiny of EC business. At the IGC on the SEA and in the current IGCs, Britain has taken the lead in arguing that rather than increase the powers of the European Parliament the member states should expand and enhance national systems of scrutiny. However an expansion of qualified majority voting in the Council makes it much harder for national parliaments to hold ministers accountable for decisions taken in the Council for they can always argue that they were outvoted. The fact that the Council holds both its meetings and votes in secrecy just serves to make the task that more difficult.

When it came to considering how democracy could be best enhanced in the new system of decision-making the participants in the IGC came up with the cooperation procedure which gives the European Parliament more say in EC legislation on the internal market than Britain would have liked but considerably less than it would have got under its own draft treaty or if the Italian proposal had been accepted. Like the restricted use of majority voting the emergence of the cooperation procedure, which was essentially based on the proposals of the Commission and West Germany in the IGC, has to be seen as a successful piece of damage limitation by Britain for the maximalist proposal was rejected which would have introduced codecision-making for the EP with the Council, effectively giving each institution a veto. The cooperation procedure which is applied in ten areas where the treaty was amended to provide for majority voting is very complex but does not significantly increase the legislative power of the European Parliament. It does however represent a foot in the legislative door for the Parliament which will be anxious to build upon this in the political union IGC.

The cooperation procedure[32] effectively added a second reading to the original legislative system under which the Council was required to consult the Parliament on any proposed legislation. The cooperation system starts in the same way as before with the Commission sending a proposal for legislation to the Council and the Parliament. The Parliament then issues an opinion and the Commission decides whether or not to alter its proposal in the light of that opinion. Under the original system the Commission proposal, whether amended or not would then go to the Council for decision. Under the cooperation procedure the Council can no longer take a final decision but is required to adopt a common position on the Commission proposal by a qualified majority. Once this common position has been adopted the Parliament has another go at it and can do one of four things. It can accept the Council's position or it can do nothing in which case after three months the Council can adopt its position unaltered. However if the Parliament can muster an absolute majority of its members (260 votes) then it can either reject or amend the Council's common position. If the Parliament rejects the common position outright then the Council can only adopt it by a unanimous vote. On the question of amendment the Parliament quickly decided to adopt its own rules of procedure so that when it came to this second reading it would limit itself to considering only amendments that would return the proposal to the form suggested by the Parliament's original opinion. In other words, there was a decision that at the second-reading stage the Parliament would not attempt to introduce new proposals but would content itself with defending its first-reading conclusions.

Any amendments that the Parliament comes up with under this formula are then transmitted back to the Commission which has one month to decide whether it will revise its proposal to accommodate the Parliament. The proposal then goes back to the Council which can do one of four things within a period of three months. It can adopt the Commission's proposal by a qualified majority; it can by unanimous vote alter the Commission proposal to take account of the Parliament's proposed amendments (which have not been taken up by the Commission); it can by unanimous vote just alter the Commission's proposal to suit its own taste; or it can simply fail to act, in which case the Commission proposal lapses – though the Parliament can authorize a one-month extension to this last procedure if it wants to.

Although extremely complex, the cooperation procedure has in fact worked quite well in practice without necessarily enhancing the Parliament's powers. Since the SEA came into force, and up to the end of 1990[33] 162 proposals were adopted under the cooperation procedure. Of the amendments requested by Parliament on the first reading, 58 per cent were accepted by the Commission and 46 per cent by the Council. On the second reading, seventy common positions of the Council were approved by the Parliament and ninety-two amended; of these 50 per cent were accepted by the Commission and 26 per cent by the Council. In the words of the Commission's twenty-fourth general report 'the inclusion of Parliament in the decision-making process appears to have improved the texts and not disturbed the procedure'.[34] Reading that, MEPs, anxious to assert democratic control over Community procedures and keen to extend the authority of their Parliament, might feel that they had been damned with faint praise. One interesting side effect of the cooperation procedure on the organization of the European Parliament may be to bring about closer working relations between some of the many party groupings. For Parliament to exert authority under the cooperation procedure it will have to put a majority together – something it has only had to do in the past in order to elect its own president – and this may encourage the development of two broader left- and right-of-centre coalitions gathered round the present Socialist and Christian Democrat groups.

The SEA also gave the European Parliament new powers over both the admission of new members to the EC and the conclusion of agreements between the EC and other states or international organizations. The SEA amended both Articles 237 and 238 so that the assent of the Parliament (via an absolute majority of its members) was now required in both cases. This gave the Parliament powers over international agreements similar to those exercised by the US Senate and enabled the Parliament to exercise a degree of political conditionality over concessions offered by the EC. The Parliament has already delayed approval of certain arrangements with Israel in protest against Israeli conduct in the occupied territories. More significantly the Parliament would have to approve any decisions to allow either EFTA or eastern European states into the EC in the future.

The SEA affects the powers and role of the Commission in several ways. First of all the cooperation procedure does nothing to reduce the Commission's exclusive right to initiate legislative proposals or indeed to withdraw them at any time if it feels that either the Parliament or the Council have distorted them. Second Article 10 of the SEA supplements Article 145 of the EC Treaty to provide a framework within which the Council can delegate powers to the Commission. This is not new of course because the Council has been delegating powers for some time while usually requiring the Commission to consult with a committee representing the interests of the member states – the various CAP management committees are good examples of this. As a result a large number of committees with differing regulatory powers have grown up and the purpose of SEA Article 10 is to provide an overall framework for the delegation of powers.

The Commission naturally hoped that this would lead to it being given more rather than less discretion but this is not how it has worked out. The Comitology Decision adopted by the Council in June 1987 prescribed three basic types of Committee, composed of representatives of the member states and the Commission. These were: advisory committees which could offer opinions on Commission measures but not refer them to the Council; management committees which could refer Commission measures to the Council if a qualified majority disagree with them; and regulatory committees which could refer Commission measures to the Council if there were not a qualified majority in favour of them. The Parliament was greatly opposed to the idea of Regulatory Committees for it was felt that their existence would undermine the Parliament's own control of the Commission. The Comitology Decision set up a tussle between the Commission and the Council over the delegation of implementing powers. In general the Council has been reluctant to grant those powers generously to the Commission. Although the IGC suggested that the Council give priority to the advisory committee (as opposed to the more restrictive management and regulatory committees), up to the end of 1990 in all internal market proposals the Council has only opted for the advisory system of regulating Commission implementation twelve times out of the thirty-eight proposed by the Commission.

Finally it should be noted that the SEA provided for the introduction of a new Court of First Instance to try and speed up the judicial process by hearing, in the first instance, certain classes of action such as staff cases and cases involving individuals (such as complex competition cases). The new court would not be allowed to hear cases brought by member states or Community institutions but should leave the Court of Justice with more time to consider them, provided of course that not too many of the first instance cases end up in the Court of Justice on appeal.

Taken together the institutional and decision-making changes effected by the SEA add up to a lot less than was anticipated in the Parliament's draft treaty but they do nevertheless represent progress of a sort. They have ensured the success to date of the single market programme and they provide a point of departure for all the EC institutions to build upon in the new round of negotiations centred on the political union IGC (see chapter 10).

Although the internal market measures form the bulk of Title II of the SEA five other subsections add new competences, and deepen the treaty. These cover monetary capacity, social policy, economic and social cohesion, research and technological development and the environment. On the question of monetary capacity a new section has been added to the Rome Treaty thus further consolidating the EC process as previously the EMS mechanisms were not formally part of them. Most important from the British perspective, the new EC Article 102A explicitly stated that any further development of EMU that required institutional changes would be subject to the Article 236 process – an IGC and a treaty amendment. The inclusion of the monetary arrangements was opposed by Britain who believed that Germany would support this position. In fact Kohl reneged on his deal with Thatcher and it was the German compromise text that was in the end adopted. But the UK, once again, ensured that it would have a say over any future EMU arrangements and effectively prevented the further consolidation of European monetary arrangements without the UK. However these decisions were only postponed and the UK now finds itself, five years on, participating in an IGC to develop EMU.

The social policy provisions were very general because there was little agreement in the IGC but they were used as a base to push the Social Charter through the 1989 Strasbourg European Council. Similarly the mechanism established in the subsection on economic and social cohesion allowed the funding of the structural funds to be doubled by 1993 – an essential element of Delors' European union package. The environmental subsection gives a solid treaty base to an important new area, but having made the gesture the member states nevertheless ensured that any environmental decisions in the

Council would be subject, in the first instance, to unanimity. Similarly, having agreed to an effort to strengthen the scientific and technological base in the EC by creating a Community competence in the SEA, the UK and Germany still insisted on the preservation of unanimity. Though the UK has gone along with a significant extension of Community competence in the SEA it has retained the ability to frustrate the full exercise of that competence; thus Britain has been able to keep funding of the European space programme at minimal levels. In so doing of course the UK has given the Community institutions and its fellow member states sound reasons for wanting to move beyond the SEA in the new IGC on political union.

European political cooperation

Title III of the SEA provided a Treaty for European Political Cooperation (EPC) which, though it established a number of links with the EC, nevertheless still preserved the distinction between EPC and the formal EC Treaty process. Thus in the parts of the SEA dealing with amendments to the Rome Treaty the member states are referred to as such; but in the parts dealing with EPC they are referred to as the high contracting parties. This failure to fully integrate EPC and the EC under one common treaty (as opposed to within a 'Single' European act) has been viewed as one of the major failures of the IGC-SEA exercise and as a result is a major agenda item for the current political union IGC (see chapter 10). Nevetherless, as we have argued above, the fact that the Rome Treaty amendments and the EPC Treaty were published in a single act (which the French wanted to call the Act of European Union) is still of some significance.

The EPC Treaty which emerged from the IGC deliberations was prepared at official level not by the Dondelinger Group (which worked on the EC Treaty aspects of the SEA) but by the EPC Political Committee (which brought together the political directors of member states' foreign offices. The text did not prove difficult to resolve and essentially represents a consensus between the texts submitted by Britain on the one hand and France and Germany on the other, at the Milan Summit.

The treaty itself consists of a single article, Article 30 divided into twelve points, most of which serve to codify the practices of EPC that have evolved over the years within the framework of the Luxembourg Report (1970), the Copenhagen Report (1973) and the London Report (1981) and the Solemn Declaration of European Union (1983). Article 30(1) describes the objective of EPC as being 'to endeavour jointly to formulate and implement a European foreign policy'. This is the first mention of a European foreign policy and it is perhaps significant that the word endeavour is used; it is, after all, possible to 'endeavour for ever' without actually being seen to fail and it is hard to imagine how a commitment to endeavour, as opposed to succeed, could ever be enforced.

Moreover the member states have been fairly cautious about the means they are committed to employing in pursuit of this vague objective. EPC was always intended to complement and coordinate national foreign policies rather than replace them. Article 30(2) talks of the need for the states to inform and consult one another on foreign policy matters to ensure that their combined influence was exercized as effectively as possible through the coordination, convergence and implementation of common actions. The EPC states are committed to consult one another before taking up national positions and to not taking up national positions or undertaking national actions that might 'impair their effectiveness as a cohesive force in international relations'. There have of course been any number of occasions when the spirit of these provisions has been breached by unilateral actions but EPC has proved to be very resilient over the years. It would be much harder to either turn a blind eye or just accept maverick behaviour if EPC was fully integrated into the EC treaty system and thus subjected to the possibility of actions concerning breaches of the Rome Treaty being brought before the Court of Justice.

The SEA dealt with the machinery of EPC in Articles 30(3) and 30(10) and this amounted mainly to a codification of the practices that have developed since 1970. The role of the Commission, so long disputed in the early days of EPC, was confirmed as was the habit of discussing EPC business in the EC Council of Ministers, as well as in the special EPC foreign ministers meetings. The leadership, management and representative role of the Presidency was confirmed, as was the position of the political committee and the European correspondents group. The one EPC institutional innovation dealt with in Title III was to be found in Article 30(10g) which provided for the establishment of a Brussels-based Secretariat for EPC, to assist the presidency. The member states had resisted the creation of any central institutions for some time because they wished to preserve at all costs the intergovernmental nature of EPC. The fact that it was separate from the goldfish bowl that is Brussels was seen as a positive asset for some time. However the problems of distinguishing between the economic and political aspects of many contemporary international issues combined with the immense burden of work that EPC imposed on the presidency country caused the member states to relent and agree, on pragmatic rather than 'communautaire' grounds, to the establishment of the EPC Secretariat.

The Secretariat has now been set up and operates from the Council building in Brussels. It is headed up by an Ambassador appointed for five years who works with five representatives from the national foreign offices. These five officials provide a degree of continuity across five successive Presidencies; each one is appointed one year before his (or her) country assumes the Presidency, manages the Presidency within the Secretariat and remains for one year after. It has become the established practice that all working group and some political committee meetings are now held in

Brussels at the Secretariat rather than, as before, in the capital of the individual country's presidency. Elsewhere in the EPC treaty, emphasis is placed on the need to maintain consistency between the external policies of the EC and policies agreed in EPC – Article 30(5). It has also become clear, as EPC has developed, that whatever decisions are taken within the EPC framework, many of the tools of foreign policy at the European level such as economic sanctions or development aid are to be found within the EC framework. Logic would therefore suggest that increasingly more and more EPC business will be transacted in Brussels and in all probability the role of the Secretariat will grow. At present however the larger member states are doing their utmost to restrict the level of EPC activity in Brussels and thus preserve the intergovernmental nature of the process.

We have already seen that in the 1980s a number of attempts were made to add security issues to the EPC agenda. Article 30(6) dealt with security; even its relatively mild wording proved extremely contentious and led to Ireland holding a referendum to ascertain whether ratification of the SEA (with its EPC treaty) was compatible with Irish neutrality. The commitment that eventually emerged was to 'coordinate positions more closely on the political and economic aspects of security' – in other words not on the defence aspects of security. To ensure that this wording was not interpreted as a challenge to established security arrangements, Article 30(6c) made clear that these provisions should not 'impede closer cooperation in the field of security' between some member states within the framework of WEU or NATO. At the time the main problem with the security dimension lay in the fact that not all members of the EC were members of NATO, and of those who were, not all were members of WEU. We have also argued above that there were differences of emphasis between those who saw the addition of security issues to the EPC agenda as an act designed to make the Europeans more effective members of NATO and those who saw it as a potential alternative to NATO. When the SEA was drawn up Europe was still divided by the cold war; by the time that these issues were next considered – in the IGC on political union – the end of the cold war meant that the search had begun for a new European 'security architecture' and the EC was being seriously mooted as an alternative defence structure to NATO. Finally in the security area Article 30(6b) refers to 'maintaining the technological and industrial conditions necessary for security'. This represented a first very cautious attempt, enthusiastically supported by Delors, to involve EC institutions in security matters, initially via the creation of a European procurement base.

The remaining articles effectively further codified EPC practice as it had developed. Article 30(7) dealt with attempts to cooperate and develop common positions in international organizations like the United Nations where the EC countries have more and more come to be seen as a significant bloc – to such an extent that Britain and France have come under some pressure to reconsider their possession of two seperate permanent seats in the Security Council. The EC countries regularly vote together and they are also able to muster collective support for individual members, as when Britain sought assistance in obtaining a Security Council resolution to back its actions in the Falklands.[35] Article 30(8) dealt with relations with third countries and, more importantly, regional groupings. The EC has become progressively more involved in a series of regional dialogues which have both an economic and a political dimension. Therefore EC and EPC competences had to be coordinated in the European-Arab dialogue or in dealings with organizations like the Association of South-East Asian Nations (ASEAN) or the Gulf Cooperation Council. Most of the EC's dealings with third countries now have some sort of political dimension to them – recent dealings with east European countries would be a good example – and so the need to closely coordinate EPC and EC activity is becoming greater.

Although the twelve increasingly act together in international politics we have seen that they nevertheless maintain national foreign policies and national foreign services. Within EPC there is a great deal of cooperation between embassies abroad and this was covered by Article 30(9). However this cooperation has definite limits attached to it mainly because the EC member states remain direct economic competitors in third country markets and trade promotion represents a growing aspect of overseas diplomatic work. It does not therefore seem very likely that cooperation between national foreign services will be soon replaced by the development of a European diplomatic service. The odd attempts at creating joint embassies in obscure countries have not been very successful. Finally, Article 30(12) provided for the revision of Title III after five years and this process has now been subsumed into the work of the IGC on political union.

The SEA represents the first major revision of the Rome Treaty and without it it is clear that the 1992 programme could not have been as successfully implemented as it has been. Others might argue that without the inspiration of the single market the sort of reforms that are to be found in the SEA would not have been possible; whatever view one takes it is clear that the 1992 programme and the SEA are inseparable from one another and that together they represent a major advance within and towards European union. In 1985 the EC put an end to the period of Eurosclerosis, set itself ambitious new targets, began the reform of its institutions and reinvigorated an integrative dynamic. This meant that by the start of the 1990s the EC was contemplating not just consolidation and completion of the single market but greater deepening, in the form of EMU and political union, and widening, with the prospect of both EFTA and eastern European countries seeking membership. It must also be said that without the stimulus of the 1992 programme and the SEA the EC would have been in poor shape to face the challenges that have arisen because of the dramatic changes in East–West relations.

Part II

Completing the 1992 single market

Chapter 3

Standards, procurement, mergers and state aids

Dennis Swann

We indicated in chapter 1 that a key feature of the SEA was the commitment to complete the internal market by 31 December 1992. Some 300 individual measures were identified in the Cockfield Report (later reduced to 279) as being necessary before a truly single market could be said to exist. In other words, though tariffs and quotas had long been removed by the nine[1], many NTBs to free and undistorted movement of goods and services still remained in existence. In this chapter we discuss four particular NTBs.

Standards

The original philosophy

The original Rome Treaty was an imaginative document. Those who drafted it anticipated most if not all of the problems which could arise in the process of creating a common market[2] including that of standards. The drafters recognized that governments and national industrial bodies (such as the British Standards Institute, AFNOR in France and DIN in Germany) intervened in the market on a considerable scale: governments produced standards in the form of regulations which were legally binding, but national industrial bodies on the other hand devised standards which were essentially in the nature of voluntary specifications. A third type of problem emerged in connection with testing and certification procedures designed to ensure conformity to existing regulations and standards. A barrier arose when an importing country demanded an additional certification procedure to that required in the country of origin.[3] This has been the case in pharmaceuticals as we shall see later.

These legal and voluntary standards were devised for a variety of purposes. Products might be literally standardized in order to facilitate compatibility and interconnection and to provide for the scale economies deriving from long runs of production. Often they were laid down in order to protect users against physical injury and deception, and as an example of the former we could cite the case of drugs and proprietary medicines. The need for government surveillance and control here is all too obvious – experience with products such as thalidomide leaves no room for doubts on that score. In the case of foods, standards must be established in respect of flavourings, colourings, preservatives, emulsifiers and other additives – the British ban on the use of the sweetening agent cyclamate is a case in point. There are many areas where danger and discomfort call for controls – noise and pollutants emitted by road vehicles are such instances.

When the consumer is not likely to be harmed he may nevertheless be deceived. It may therefore be decided that products should be labelled so as to indicate what they contain, but standards sometimes proceed beyond this to the use of compositional rules. Thus in the case of foodstuffs a particular designation may be reserved for products which meet the compositional requirements prescribed by the national regulation. Manufacturers may be free to bring to market products which do not satisfy the compositional rules but will be debarred from using the reserved designation.[4] Thus, for example, the German food purity laws laid down stringent rules regarding the permitted ingredients for beer and prohibited the use of all additives. The word 'beer' was reserved for products which satisfied these conditions. Imported beers which used other ingredients, but no additives, could be sold but could not use the description 'beer'.[5]

Standards of the kind we have discussed were generally viewed as serving the public interest, but this was not invariably the case, as some were designed to protect special interests. The famous Italian pasta law whereby products described as pasta could only be made from durum wheat was introduced to assist a small but powerful group of farmers in the south of Italy. Prior to that pasta made from a mixture of soft wheat and durum wheat had accounted for 50 per cent of Italian pasta consumption but after the law was promulgated the proportion fell close to zero.[6] Whatever the original motivation one thing is clear – to the extent that standards differed significantly between states they undoubtedly constituted a form of NTB. Broadly speaking either differing standards meant that goods of a particular designation could not be exported, with a consequent loss of competition across frontiers; or, if they were to be exported, they had to be adapted to the rules of each national export market. Either way the economies of large-scale production, in the form of long runs of a standardized product, were to some degree sacrificed. One solution was to harmonize standards. The Commission saw other virtues in such a process. For example, it could raise the quality of life in matters such as safety and the environment since a Community standard could be based on the best national practice available. Moreover consumer choice would be increased. The idea that harmonization would lead to less variety was held to be erroneous. Although products were subject to harmonization in certain essential aspects they still exhibited wide variations in styling and performance. The motor car was said to be a case in point.

Articles 100–2 of the Rome Treaty provided the necessary harmonizing powers. Article 100 enabled the Council of Ministers, on a proposal from the Commission, to issue unifying directives when the laws, regulations or administrative actions of the member states directly affected the setting up or operation of the common market. A directive was not directly binding on individuals or businesses. Rather it was addressed to member states and required them to modify their national laws and regulations so as to bring their provisions into line with those specified in the directive.

Three features of this system are worthy of particular note. First, Articles 100–2 did not require absolute harmonization, but indicated the less demanding requirement of approximation of laws. It is nevertheless acceptable to use the more widely-used term harmonization. Second, this harmonization could only be decided by Council on the basis of unanimity. Third, harmonization measures fell either into the total or the optional category. Total harmonization required that all products covered by a directive had to conform to the standards set out in the directive. In such a case national standards had to be abolished and the Community standard substituted. Total harmonization was usually adopted when consumer safety was involved (as with cosmetics), though this approach was also adopted in the case of textile labelling, which was purely informational. Optional harmonization permitted the parallel existence of both Community and national rules. Manufacturers who produced in accordance with the Community standards acquired access to all national markets, while those who continued to apply only national standards had access to only their home market.

It should be emphasized that the decision to approach the standards problem via the process of harmonization was itself a reflection of the view which was taken of the right of member states to indulge in protective action. In chapter 1 we described the Rome Treaty as a document which obliged member states to dismantle all forms of internal protection. This picture is not wholly correct. Thus while Article 30 and those following required members to remove all quantitative restrictions, and all measures of equivalent effect, Article 36 provided an escape clause. It recognized that quantitative restrictions could be justified on grounds of public morality, public order, public safety; the protection of the health and life of humans, animals and plants; the protection of national treasures; and the protection of industrial and commercial property. It was this second category which was particularly relevant in the context of standards.

Quite clearly many national standards were devised to protect humans, animals and plants from injury and therefore a refusal by a state to import goods which did not satisfy its standards of protection was entirely legitimate. Not surprisingly it was therefore concluded that the only way round the problem was to harmonize standards – only then would states be divested of their need and treaty-based right to oppose imports.

The Commission accordingly launched a programme of standards harmonization which it proposed to work through, product by product. This led to some progress – by 1985 182 directives concerned with industrial products had been adopted and a significant number had also been agreed in the area of foodstuffs. The industrial products covered included motor vehicles, metrology (measuring) instruments, solvents and other dangerous substances and electrical equipment. In the case of foodstuffs directives had been adopted governing labelling, additives, materials coming into contact with food (a framework directive and several specific directives) as well as compositional matters (jams, jellies and marmalades).[7] Despite all this there was still a long way to go; in truth the system was unable to keep up with the problem – harmonization was a tedious process in which the Commission and Council of Ministers allowed themselves to be caught up in the detail of harmonizing particular products. Given the need to achieve unanimity progress was bound to be slow and more members threatened even slower progress. Not only that but directives were quickly out of date due to technical progress.[8]

Two measures of the inadequacy of the system are provided by the following facts. Pelkmans points out that the Community in the seventies and early eighties produced on average little over ten technical directives a year,[9] whereas the West German DIN Institute had produced a total of 23,000.[10] In the case of foodstuffs the harmonization programme drawn up in 1969 and updated in 1973 was still by 1985 only two-fifths of the way to completion.

The new approach

By 1985 the Commission was aware that a new streamlined method was needed. In this it was, as so often is the case, aided by the Court of Justice whose observations in the *Cassis de Dijon*[11] and other rulings pointed the way to a new approach. The reader will be aware that in the Cassis case the relevant West German authority had refused the import of the French blackcurrant liqueur because its alcohol content fell below the prescribed minimum German standard. The latter was 32 per cent although this was reduced to 25 per cent for drinks of the Cassis type. Since Cassis contained only 15 – 20 per cent it failed to qualify. In its ruling the Court made two remarks which, while relating to the specific case, had fundamental implications for all other products.

First, there was no valid reason why a product which had been lawfully produced and marketed in one member state should not be introduced in another member state. Second, while member states had the power via Article 36 to block imports, this was only effective to the extent that such actions were necessary to satisfy mandatory requirements relating in particular to the effectiveness of fiscal supervision, the protection of public health, the fairness of commercial transactions and the defence of the consumer.

By interpretation this meant that free circulation was the rule. Where there were no threats to health, safety, and so on, free imports should be allowed. Only where such threats existed was harmonization needed. In other words just because one country had a different view about how, for example, chocolate should be made using innocuous ingredients, this was not a ground for refusing to import chocolate made in a different way but also using innocuous ingredients, since no threat to health existed which mandated anything so extreme as an import ban. The new case law emphasized the concept of proportionality. According to the Commission 'the touchstone is the "principle of proportionality" which means that legal measures must not go further than is genuinely necessary to achieve the desired objective'.[12] If, as the West German authorities argued, regulation was necessary to prevent the consumer from being deceptively sold weak liqueur then this could be achieved by contents-labelling. It followed from all this that much of the harmonization was not really necessary and should be confined to cases where there was a genuine threat and where no valid alternative existed.

Therefore in 1985, as part of the discussions leading up to the SEM programme, the Commission announced that it had devised a new approach to harmonization; this was put to the Council of Ministers and adopted. The general principles, as supplemented by the procedural changes sanctioned in the SEA, are as follows, though it should be emphasized that this is a complex matter and we shall seek merely to provide a summary of the main points.

Following the Cassis and other cases, free importation of goods legally marketed in another member state was the overriding principle and with it went the implication of mutual recognition of other country standards. Only when health, safety, and so on were threatened and a refusal to import becomes valid would harmonization be implemented. When a technical harmonization directive[13] was called for the Commission and Council of Ministers would not be involved in the actual detail, but rather would concentrate on identifying the objectives to be attained, such as essential safety requirements for products to qualify for free movement. The SEA simplified this process by allowing such harmonizing decisions to be based on majority voting. The actual task of devising the details of the standards was off-loaded onto European standards bodies, such as the European Committee for Standardization (CEN) and the European Committee for Electrotechnical Standardization (CENELEC) which both include non-EC states.[14] These non-EC states have also modified their decision-making arrangements and current rules allow for majority votes with countries having different voting strengths according to size. Governments are obliged to presume that if a product is manufactured according to these standards then it complies with the fundamental requirements stipulated in the directive and must be granted free access. In the absence of European standards, conformity to national standards temporarily carries the same benefit. If however a product is not manufactured in accordance with the European standard then the onus is on the producer to prove that fundamental safety and health requirements are met.[15] In order to prevent new obstacles to trade a standstill arrangement was agreed in 1983. It came fully into force at the beginning of 1985. Member states were obliged to notify proposals for new technical standards in advance. A standstill then had to be instituted while the Commission and other member states considered whether it was likely to create a barrier which might therefore necessitate remedial action, either by banning or by harmonization. The Cockfield Report noted that its limited coverage needed to be extended to cover a wider range of industrial products as well as food and pharmaceuticals.

Two others points need to be stressed. The SEA stipulated that under the modified harmonization procedure, proposals concerning health, safety, environmental protection and consumer protection 'will take as a base a high level of protection'. This was part of what is now referred to as the Article 100A procedure. The SEA also gave rise to Article 100B which provided that in 1992 the Commission would ascertain what laws, regulations, and directives had not been harmonized, and in respect of them the Council might decide that member states should be obliged to recognize other states' laws and regulations.

The Community has made effective use of this new approach to technical harmonization, typical examples being the directive concerned with simple pressure vessels,[16] and that concerned with toys.[17]

In the case of food special arrangements have applied. It would have been possible to devise recipe laws involving detailed regulations on the composition and manufacturing characteristics of each foodstuff. The alternative approach was that, provided consumers were given adequate information on the nature and composition of foodstuffs, it was not necessary to define these elements in law and in the event the Community chose the latter. The Commission declared that it was not desirable to confine the culinary riches of the twelve to a legislative strait-jacket. This would stifle innovation and commercial flexibility. The tastes and preferences of consumers should not be a matter for regulation.[18]

This meant that mutual recognition was the key principle. However there were certain issues which could not be allowed to escape the regulatory process. These included public health standards; additives (allowable substances and allowable concentrations); materials and articles coming into contact with foodstuffs (such as permitted packaging materials); labelling (protection of consumers against misleading descriptions and manufacturers against unfair competitive practices); official inspections designed to ensure that manufacturers comply with rules relating to health and safety protection. This is important because under conditions of free importation other states will have to rely on the vigilance of their partners, i.e. on the efficacy of the inspection system in the country of manufacture. In all these cases (except public health) there was a need for general harmonizing directives though in practice this was mainly a matter of amending existing directives, the exception being food inspection which called for a new directive.

The Commission made substantial progress on foodstuffs. Amended directives on additives[19] and materials in contact with foodstuffs[20] emerged in 1988 and in 1989 their labelling[21] and inspection[22] were also covered. In 1987 a Commission communication was issued on the situation in respect of the public health monitoring of foodstuffs together with an action programme for cooperation at Community level.[23] Various amendments to directives on fruit jams[24], and so on, were also issued.

The Commission indicated in the Cockfield Report that apart from foodstuffs particular effort was needed in the information and telecommunications sector and in construction, where there was a major need to facilitate interconnection and compatibility. Pharmaceuticals is another area where progress has been slow and was first addressed by the Commission in 1962,[25] since when two particular problems have obtruded. First, while there has been a degree of harmonization of pre-market testing by national registration authorities, products can only be released if they are licensed in the state in which they are to be sold. The situation where a product if licensed by one state is automatically accepted by all the others still eludes the Community; national vetoes still obtain despite the introduction of various regulating mechanisms. The Commission was required by 1990 to come up with proposals for removing the remaining barriers to the free movement of pharmaceuticals, and three possibilities were canvassed: a system of mutual recognition; a single Community authorization system; or some intermediate arrangement. It seems doubtful whether the Community will meet the 1992 deadline in this sector. Pharmaceutical products are also subject to various forms of government price control since to a large extent they are not purchased privately, and national governments have tended to set higher prices for the products of their own industries. The Cockfield Report proposed that there should be greater pricing transparency. Whilst the 1988 directive[26] may not have totally eradicated the problem of price discrimination, it is recognized that it should help to remove some discrepancies.

Procurement

The Cockfield Report explicitly singled out public procurement as a field for further legislative action. As in the case of standards, the Community had made progress prior to the SEA but there were gaps and weaknesses in the policy which needed remedying. Before discussing the treaty powers, the original policy and the programme of action in connection with the SEM, we need to consider the size and nature of the public purchasing problem.

Table 3.1 Macro-economic importance of public sector purchasing (billion units of national currency and ECUs, 1989)

	Belgium BF	France FF	Germany DM	Italy Lira	UK £	Total ECU
GDP	4,402	4,282	1,754	720,682	319	2,566
Total government expenditure	2,599	2,048	788	336,515	137	1,183
Total government expenditure/GDP	59.4%	47.8%	45.4%	46.6%	42.9%	46.1%
Public purchasing:						
Government	288	369	131	60,215	38	227
Public enterprises	480	235	77	34,226	32	157
Total	768	604	208	94,441	70	384
Total public purchasing/						
Total government expenditure	29.5%	29.4%	26.3%	28.6%	51.0%	32.4%
Total public purchasing/GDP	17.5%	14.1%	11.8%	13.1%	21.8%	15.0%

Source: European Communities Commission, *Research on the 'Cost of Non-Europe', Basic Findings*, vol.5, part A, Luxembourg, OOPEC, 1988, p.26.

The significance of public procurement

The public sector – that is to say central and local government together with public enterprises – is a major spender in the economic systems of western economies. The macro-economic importance of public sector purchasing in a selection of Community countries is indicated in Table 3.1. On average total government expenditure in the five states in 1984 was 46.1 per cent of national GDP. However government expenditure includes such items as wages and salaries, and transfer payments, whereas we are only interested in the purchases by the state of goods and services. Public purchasing as a percentage of total government spending was on average 32.4 per cent, and as a percentage of national GDP was 15 per cent. It was also apparent that in respect of this large block of spending, import penetration was much lower than for the economy as a whole. This is shown in the 1985 data contained in Table 3.2.

Table 3.2 Public sector import penetration from EC and non-EC sources (%)

	Belgium	France	Germany	Italy	UK
National import penetration*	43	20	22	19	22
Apparent public sector import penetration+	21	16	12	1	4

Source: European Communities Commission, *Research on the 'Cost of Non-Europe'. Basic Findings*, vol. 5, part A, Luxembourg, OOPEC, 1988, p. 12.
Notes: *Imports/(national production + imports).
         +Purchases reported to be of foreign origin/total purchases (total purchases include those of unreported origin).

It is a generally accepted fact that public spending does not always take place in a non-discriminatory way; rather than accepting the cheapest or best offers, institutions in the public sector have often adopted 'buy-national' attitudes. The motives for this are various and the Cecchini study suggested several.[27] One is strategic: there is a desire in all countries to maintain a national capability to supply notably in respect of defence systems, power generation (especially nuclear) and telecommunications. There is also pressure to support declining sectors where non-national purchasing would lead to unemployment. The report cites coal, railway rolling stock, shipbuilding and heavy fabrication and also observed that environmentally-damaging industries tend to support local (but not national) businesses – coal mining and the nuclear industry were given as examples. The study also revealed the tendency to support emerging high technology sectors, such as new telecommunications systems and lasers. Finally there are general political reasons – some goods are extremely visible such as cars and tableware and public authorities fear criticism if they buy these from foreign sources.

Treaty powers

The Rome Treaty did not contain provisions specifically related to the public purchasing problem. Nevertheless it did provide general powers which could be brought to bear; Article 7 pronounced a general ban on discrimination on grounds of nationality and enabled the Council, on a proposal from the Commission, to enact measures designed to prohibit this. In addition, as we saw earlier, Article 30 et seq prescribed a prohibition on both quantitative restrictions on imports and exports and on measures having equivalent effect. The actual policy of the Community in respect of public purchasing is in fact based on Article 30 and those following. It has to be emphasized that those provisions were largely negative in tone and such interdictions were recognized as being insufficient. Rather, a positive obligation to purchase without discrimination was necessary and the specific measures discussed below represent a response to that need.

The first act by the Community was the adoption by the Council of Ministers in 1970 of a directive which gave effect to the ban on discriminatory practices.[28] The directive prohibited measures, imposed by law, regulation or administrative practice, which prevented the supply of imported goods from other member states, which granted domestic products a preference or which made the supply of imported goods more difficult or costly than domestic products.

The EC Commission recognized that a general directive would not suffice and that there was a need to produce specific directives relating to particular kinds of public purchasing. The initial focus was public works contracting, and in 1971 the Council adopted two directives: the first[29] swept away all obstacles to freedom to supply services and the second drew up common rules for the awarding of contracts;[30] a separate decision[31] established an advisory committee on public works contracting. The second directive related to contracts of one million ECUs and more, but left those relating to energy and water for separate treatment. As a result of this directive, contractors throughout the Community were hopefully guaranteed free and effective competition on all major public works contracts offered by member states. Contractors were informed of pending contracts through the Community's official journal and competent authorities were obliged to accept tenders from all qualified contractors in the Community and were required to award contracts on purely economic, non-discriminatory grounds; all discrimination of a purely technical nature was to be eliminated, and a complaints procedure was established.

The public works directive was accompanied by a proposal for a directive on public procurement, and here the Commission encountered some intransigence on the part of the Council of Ministers. In order to add weight to its argument the Commission commissioned a study aimed at uncovering the reasons why intra-Community public procurement had reached a stagnant level. The resulting report by Charpentier and Clark in 1974 declared 'the common market of public procurement does not exist'.[32] It recommended that purchases of public utilities should be excluded from attempts to liberalize public procurement – the reason given was that the opening up of such spending would damage their research and development activities. This concession seems to have eased the way to an agreement and a public supply contracts directive [33] together with a related decision[34] were duly adopted late in 1976.

Under the directive, central, regional and local authorities seeking to award public contracts in excess of 200,000 ECUs were required to publish a notice in the official journal giving potential tenderers all the information they needed to make an offer. Contracting authorities were required to award contracts on the basis of the best offers, i.e. there should therefore be no discrimination as between home and foreign bids. The directive permitted both open and restricted procedures: under the former a call for tender is published and any supplier is entitled to submit a bid; under the latter, bidders are selected on the basis of their capabilities and are then invited to submit bids as in an open tender. In cases of urgency the time given for bidders to bid could be shortened, this is referred to as the accelerated procedure; public supply contracts awarded by bodies administering transport, water, energy and telecommunications services were however exempted from the new arrangements. The associated decision, referred to above, merely made the advisory committee for public works into an advisory committee for public contracts – in other words it was required to oversee both the 1971 and 1976 arrangements.

These were the specific powers which existed prior to the SEA. Two further points are however necessary to mention. First, external pressures led to some modification of the rules. We are referring here to the impact of activities in the GATT. In the 1970s trade negotiations began to focus on the problem of NTBs and the Tokyo round of 1973–9 led to the adoption of a code of public procurement which came into operation in 1981.[35] The Commission endeavoured to comply by proposing quite generous modifications to the 1976 directive. This met with resistance from the Council of Ministers, but it was eventually induced to accept the minimum changes necessary in order to conform to the 1981 code.[36] The threshold for central, or federal, contracts was reduced to 144,000 ECU and the time limits for receipt of tenders were extended. Second, in 1980 the Commission adopted a directive which increased its powers to investigate the financial relationships between governments and their public undertakings.[37] This was primarily motivated by the need to control covert state aids such as advancing capital at less than commercial rates. However it also enabled the

Commission to root out cases of financial compensation being extended to public enterprises whose purchasing policies were designed to support home industries. The value of the directive was unfortunately reduced by virtue of the fact that enterprises in several sectors were exempted. More will be said about this measure when we come to discuss state aids.

Loopholes

Despite all this activity, experience suggested that the effects of these public purchasing directives were symbolic rather than substantive, and there was ample evidence that Community law continued to be flouted. For example, in 1981 the Commission had to institute cases against France and Ireland;[38] both were accused of encouraging and promoting the purchase of domestic goods in preference to imported ones, a clear breach of Article 30 of the Rome Treaty and of the obligations set out in the 1970 directive. In a communication from the Commission to the Council in 1984 the conclusion reached was exactly the same as that of Charpentier and Clark ten years earlier – it referred to a 'virtually non-existent' or 'Uncommon Market' in respect of public procurement.[39]

The lack of impact was due to two main factors. First, as we have noted earlier, certain sectors were specifically excluded, and in addition certain purchases, such as military equipment, were completely outside the scope of the 1976 directive, as were services except those concerned with public works. Second, the authorities concerned with public procurement either failed to implement the rules or exploited the loopholes. As an example of the former McLachlan reports that Italian governmental bodies felt no compulsion to advertise public works contracts.[40] As an example of the latter we can turn to the Commission's 1984 communication for details: it noted that purchasers indulged in over-zealous division of projects or underestimated contract values in order to avoid coverage by the directives. Purchasing departments systematically resorted to restricted procedures which as the Commission observed ought 'in the spirit of the Community directives . . . to have been used in exceptional circumstances only'.[41] Non-competitive or negotiated tendering (where there are no open bids and perhaps only one tenderer) was still extensively used and it was far from clear that its use was always justified. In a significant number of what they claimed were extremely urgent cases purchasing authorities resorted to accelerated procedures thereby reducing the possibility of foreign participation, since the time limit for the submission of offers was curtailed.

The Cockfield Report and after

The Cockfield Report identified three main areas for future legislative activity. First, the existing directives needed to be tightened up – their provisions needed to be clarified and the loopholes blocked. Second, it was desirable that the purchasing of services should be brought under control – the Commission instanced dataprocessing as an area where a major impact could be made. Third, it was essential that the exempt areas should be brought under public supply contracts rules.

In 1988 a directive was adopted which significantly modified the 1976 public supply arrangements,[42] making the open procedure the rule, and restricted and negotiated procedures the exception. The use of these two methods now required the production of a written justification and such a report could be demanded by the Commission. The time limit for bids in open and restricted procedures has been extended; the directive also explicitly provided for the use of a negotiated procedure in order to restrict the use of the single-tender approach. Time limits for the accelerated procedure in cases of extreme urgency have been extended and the directive also called for a much more searching report on the contract-letting activity of each member state.

In 1989 a directive was approved amending the 1971 public works arrangements.[43] The threshold size was raised to 5 million ECUs, partly to take account of inflation and partly to assist smaller firms. Modifications were introduced which were designed to curb the use of exceptional procedure and time limits for bids were extended and in the same year the Council introduced arrangements for monitoring the operation of both basic directives and the setting-up of appeals procedures.[44]

In respect of the excluded sectors – water, energy, transport and telecommunications – the Commission presented proposals in 1988 which gave rise to considerable debate, touching upon fairly contentious issues. However in February 1990 a political agreement on both public works contracting and public purchasing in these areas was announced. The main features of the common position were as follows. The proposed directive would apply not only to public sector buyers but also to those in the private sector if they carried on the previously excluded activity on the basis of special or exclusive rights granted by the state. Purchases of energy and fuels by entities producing power would not be caught, pending further development of the CEP. Air and sea transport were not included in view of measures taken to introduce more competition in those fields (see chapter 6). The thresholds above which the purchasing rules would apply were to be ECU 5 million in public works, ECU 400,000 in supply contracts in water, energy and transport and ECU 600,000 in supply contracts in telecommunications. The proposed directive would also take account of the non-existence of reciprocity arrangements. Special rules would apply to supply-contracts where more than 50 per cent of goods are of non-Community origin and where the Community has not concluded a public purchasing agreement (on a bilateral or multilateral basis) with the supplier. In such cases if the bid by an EC enterprise is not more than 3 per cent higher than the bid from the third country then the Community bid must be chosen (see also chapter 7 on the external aspect).

The future

Does all this mean that a SEM in public procurement is now in sight? The answer is not necessarily: services have yet to be dealt with; defence is still largely excluded; the 1992 deadline will not be met in all cases – in the hitherto-excluded sectors, Greece and Portugal will have until the end of 1997 to come into line. However the most important point relates to attitudes. The Community can adopt directives 'until the cows come home' but a true SEM depends upon those responsible for public-sector purchasing making value-for-money their sole criterion. The omens are not good. When those conducting the Cecchini study interviewed public purchasers they found considerable evidence of deeply-entrenched discriminatory attitudes. Two quotations indicate the nature of the problem. In the case of France they reported, 'Purchasers in ministries seem under clear instructions to buy French. "Acheter Français" is a slogan. . . .'[45] As for Belgium they observed, 'On the question as to whether there is any "pressure" to buy Belgian, some individuals within the ministries initially denied this quite strongly, but then indicated, by their attitude to the opening of the market, that they are in favour of buying Belgian supplies'.[46]

Mergers

In the case of anti-trust policy, unlike the areas of standards and public procurment, the Cockfield Report did not suggest that there was a need for any new legislative measures relating to the mainstream provisions contained in the Rome Treaty.[47] Nevertheless the need to provide a specific power to control mergers has long been recognized, at least by the Commission, and when it was finally agreed the enabling regulation did emphasize its essential role in the realization of the SEM.

The anti-trust problem

Cartels and business concentrations are an obvious device which can frustrate the process of integration through trade. There is plenty of evidence that prior to tariff and quota disarmament various forms of business arrangement, sometimes international in membership, existed which restricted trade flows and allocated and partitioned markets. It was recognized that where initially such devices did not exist, as the trade barriers went down, businessmen might resort to various practices in order to offset the effects of the removal of protection.

The anti-trust problem can be divided into three main compartments: restrictive arrangements (cartels) between otherwise independent firms; the practices of dominant (or even monopoly) firms; phenomena such as mergers which can create conditions of dominance or monopoly.

Instances of cartels abound in Community case law. For example, there are price agreements whereby firms in one member state, when selling to another, agree on the prices which they will charge for exports. Sometimes indeed, such firms may create a separate company which will conduct the export sales of all the participants – this is known as a common selling syndicate. Such arrangements were common in the fertilizer industry. Parallel price behaviour may indeed be international in character, thus in the *Aniline Dye* case[48] the Commission and Court of Justice had to deal with a situation in which equal and simultaneous price movements were made by ten firms – six were from common market countries but three were Swiss and one was British. As a result of international agreements, each home market may be reserved for home producers, and quota agreements may be entered into whereby home and foreign firms agree not to overstock the home market. Firms supplying a home market may enter into reciprocal exclusive dealing arrangements whereby signatory suppliers will only supply signatory dealers, and signatory dealers will only buy from signatory suppliers. If most of the dealers in a member state are locked into the arrangement, non-signatory suppliers, perhaps located in another member state, may have difficulty in penetrating the market. Firms in a member state may operate an aggregated rebate system in which domestic purchasers enjoy a progressive scale of rebate dependent on the (usually annual) volume of purchases from the signatory firms as a totality. The effect of this is to induce domestic purchasers to buy from the domestic firms rather than to import.

In respect of the dominant firm problem, it is not difficult to see how such a firm would, for example, be in a powerful position to induce domestic dealers to deal exclusively with it, and as a result importation would be reduced or even eliminated.[49] Equally a dominant firm might seek to eliminate inconvenient foreign rivals by predatory price cuts or by cutting off supplies of essential materials or components which it alone possesses. Mergers and takeovers can also have adverse effects on the flow of trade. Thus in the now famous *Continental Can* case the burden of the Commission's case was that Continental Can, already dominant in the German market, had taken over one of its few remaining competitors in the shape of Thomassen & Drijver-Verblifa of the Netherlands.

The Rome Treaty rules

The Rome Treaty anticipated these problems but only partially. The key anti-trust provisions were found in Articles 85 – 90 – the substantive law being contained in Articles 85, 86 and 90. Article 85 addressed the restrictive business practice (cartel) problem; Article 85 (1) prohibited a range of practices (we will call them agreements) which restricted competition in the common market and affected trade between member states; Article 85(2) declared prohibited agreements to be automatically void. However in Article 85(3) we encounter the exemption aspect, which holds out the possibility that the Article 85(1) prohibition may not apply if an agreement 'contributes to improving the production or distribution of goods or to promoting technical progress'. There were, however, a number of caveats including:

(a) Any agreement which contributes to such an improvement must allow consumers a fair share of the resulting benefit.
(b) The agreement in achieving the improvement and the fair sharing must not impose restrictions which are not indispensable to the attainment of those objectives. In other words, if an agreement is to get through it must impose no more restrictions than are absolutely essential.
(c) The agreement must not allow the parties to eliminate competition in respect of a substantial part of the products in question. All these conditions are cumulative.

Article 86 deals with the dominant firm problem. It provides that 'Any abuse by one or more undertakings of a dominant position within the Common Market or a substantial part of it shall be prohibited as being incompatible with the Common Market in so far as it may affect trade between member states'. There are three important elements to this:

(a) There must be a dominant position in the common market or a substantial part of it.
(b) Dominance is not the sin, it is the abuse thereof.
(c) There must be the possibility of an effect on trade between the member states – this is typical of the Rome Treaty approach.

Mention must also be made of Article 90 which relates to public enterprises – public undertakings and undertakings to which the state grants special or exclusive rights. Broadly speaking it applies the competition rules of Articles 85 and 86 to such enterprises,[50] though it includes a caveat to the effect that for certain types of public enterprise the application of these rules should not obstruct the discharge of the tasks assigned to them.

Quite early on the Council of Ministers approved a regulation[51] which granted the Commission the powers necessary to implement Articles 85 and 86, including powers relating to the notification of agreements, the commanding of information from enterprises and the imposition of fines and penalties. Thus armed the Commission mounted an attack on anti-trust abuses, but it is not part of our remit to discuss these in detail. Suffice it to say that broadly speaking price fixing, output restricting and market-sharing cartels which had a significant impact on competition and carried with them no counterbalancing advantages, have invariably been condemned, and in some cases extremely heavy fines have been imposed. The Commission has however recognized that some forms of collabora tion can be beneficial, such as specialization and in such cases has been willing to grant them an exemption. Indeed whole categories of agreement have been subject to block exemption; provided they met certain conditions they were automatically exempt without the need for individual scrutiny. In respect of market-dominating enterprises the Commission has attacked a series of practices including the use of loyalty rebates, predatory price-cutting and the cutting-off of supplies of inputs to a competitor dependent on them.

The quest for a merger regulation

The reader however will be aware that no reference has been made to any power to control mergers; indeed the Rome Treaty made no explicit reference to this problem, in marked contrast to the Paris Treaty which enabled the old High Authority (now the EC Commission) to prohibit mergers in coal and steel, which allowed the firms concerned to determine prices or hinder effective competition.

Quite early on the Commission addressed the issue of controlling mergers, and in 1963 commissioned two reports on aspects of the merger problem, one of which was required to consider the possibility that Articles 86 and 85 might be applicable to mergers. On the basis of these findings the Commission produced a report in 1965 in which it ventured the view that Article 86 was certainly applicable. As one illustration the Commission cited the hypothetical example of a dominant enterprise selling below cost, driving another enterprise towards bankruptcy and forcing it to merge. This was a clear offence under Article 86 and could therefore be attacked under existing powers. Nevertheless Article 86 posed a major problem: it required the existence of a dominant position before any action could be taken. On the vital question of what could be done to prevent a dominant position from coming into existence in the first place the Commission was completely silent. Not surprisingly it began to look covetously at the Paris Treaty whose merger provisions contained no such inhibition.

In 1973 two significant events occurred. First, the Court of Justice handed down its judgement in the now famous *Continental Can* case. It concerned the take-over activities of the American company which had established a holding company Europemballage. Continental had acquired a majority holding in a major West German can producer Schmalbach and this holding was transferred to Europemballage, who made a bid for the Dutch firm Thomassen & Drijver-Verblijfa, also a can producer. The Commission then intervened opposing the latter acquisition, which in turn provoked an appeal to the European Court of Justice. The Court decided that the Commission had failed to prove that Schmalbach had a dominant position in the West German container market[52] (establishing the existence of a dominant position is step number one in applying Article 86). However on the key legal point the Court accepted that Article 86 did indeed apply to mergers. It went on to say:

> There may therefore be abusive behaviour if an undertaking in a dominant position strengthens that dominant position so that the degree of control achieved substantially obstructs competition, i.e. so that the only undertakings left in the market are those which are dependent on the dominant undertaking with regard to their market behaviour.[53]

Despite this, in 1973 the Commission decided to request the introduction of a separate merger-controlling regulation and a draft proposal to this end was submitted to the Council of Ministers. The Commission suggested that mergers should be regarded as incompatible with the common market if they were liable to affect inter-state trade and the merged enterprises acquired or enhanced their ability to hinder effective competition. Smaller mergers judged in terms of combined assets and market share were to be excluded from control; certain large mergers judged in terms of the value of combined assets would have to be pre-notified and there would be a three-month suspension period during which the Commission might start proceedings. If it did, a decision had to be given within nine months. No explicit provision was made whereby increases in efficiency might be traded off against a lessening of competition but exemption from prohibition might be given for mergers which were necessary for the attaining of a priority Community objective. A crucial feature of the Commission's proposal was that it would no longer be necessary to prove the existence of a dominant position before a merger could be attacked.

In the event, the Council of Ministers were not disposed to accept the Commission's proposal.[54] Nor, despite its success in the *Continental Can* case, did the Commission exercise its merger-controlling power in any *formal* decision although it was employed in a number of informal settlements of merger cases. In 1981 the Commission endeavoured to revive the merger control proposal but again without success.

The breakthrough

Ultimately the Commission succeeded in its quest but as the reader will have gathered this was a sensitive issue and considerable concessions had to be made. What factors contributed to the ultimate success of the Commission? First, the commitment to complete the SEM highlighted the need for action and not more procrastination. Second, two highly energetic and forceful commissioners held the competition portfolio successively at a crucial period – namely Peter Sutherland and Sir Leon Brittan. Peter Sutherland relaunched the proposal in 1987 and secured broad approval though despite this some member states notably Britain, France and West Germany harboured deep reservations. Finally, as in *Cassis de Dijon* case, the Court of Justice helped to break the log-jam.

This occurred in the *Philip Morris* judgment[55] handed down in 1987. This case involved an agreement by Philip Morris to acquire a 30 per cent interest in a competing cigarette manufacturer Rothmans from its South African owner Rembrandt. After lengthy negotiations the arrangements were blessed by the Commission but were opposed by two other tobacco companies British American Tobacco and R.J. Reynolds. The matter was then tested before the Court of Justice. In its ruling it indicated that the Article 85 prohibition, to which we referred earlier, could also be applied to situations where by agreement a company acquired a minority holding in another, and the holding enabled the acquiring company to control the commercial conduct of the acquired company. An attractive feature of using the Article 85 prohibition in such circumstances was that it did not require proof of the existence of a dominant position.

This ruling was extremely welcome to the Commission. It indicated to those states who were opposed to the proposed merger regulation that the Commission now had an enhanced capability to control mergers. Moreover Peter Sutherland, on behalf of the Commission, indicated an intention to use it if the Council of Ministers continued to deny them the regulation. In fact the Commission proceeded to carry out its threat. For example, in the take-over of British Caledonian by British Airways, which had been passed by the British Monopolies and Mergers Commission, it forced British Airways to give up some routes to smaller rivals. It also successfully blocked the take-over of Irish Distillers by the GC & C Brands consortium. Increasingly companies contemplating major mergers, which previously would not have dreamed of calling upon Brussels, were disposed to seek the Commission's prior opinion. Equally important was the fact that the *Philip Morris* judgment threw up a host of unresolved procedural issues. It was bound to occur to the resisting member states that a regulation was now positively desirable: without it they could not be certain what would happen; with it they could set limits to the Commission's activities. Intensive negotiations followed in which the Commission had to give ground but they culminated in an agreement in December 1989 granting the Commission a power to control mergers.

The regulation

The regulation[56] actually referred not to the control of mergers but to the control of concentrations between undertakings. The word concentration applies to two situations: where previously independent enterprises merge, and where, by means of the acquisition of securities, assets, and so on, one enterprise obtains control over another. Joint ventures whereby enterprises coordinate their activity but remain independent were not included.

The concentrations to which the regulation applied should have a Community dimension. For this purpose the aggregate world-wide turnover of all undertakings should be more than ECU 5,000 million and the aggregate Community-wide turnover of each (of at least two) undertaking should be more than ECU 250 million. However when each (of at least two) undertaking achieved more than two-thirds of its aggregate Community-wide turnover in one and the same member state, then the concentration fell outside the scope of the regulation. The ECU 250 million figure is designed to exclude relatively insignificant transactions where, metaphorically, whales acquire minnows. The two-thirds figure was devised to exclude acquisitions which were essentially national in their impact. All three criteria were manipulated by member states in a way which restricted the Commission's field of action – they would no doubt argue that this was designed to keep the Commission's workload to manageable proportions while it built up its capacity and experience in dealing with merger cases. The threshold figures were to be reconsidered at the end of four years: to the extent that they are high and remain high, national anti-trust authorities will exercise a significant role in determining the nature of the structural adaptation to the SEM.

Of crucial importance are the criteria for appraising concentrations, which are to be judged according to whether they are compatible with the common market. A concentration which creates or strengthens a dominant position, and as a result impedes effective competition in the common market or a substantial part of it, is incompatible with the common market. This dispenses with the need for a dominant position to exist *ab initio*. On the face of it it sounds as if the impact on competition is the only criterion, but the regulation states that in making the appraisal other factors should be taken into account, including the development of technology and economic progress. This has led some to suspect that considerations other than the preservation of competition might be invoked in defence of mergers.[57] Sir Leon Brittan however is reported as saying that coompetition would be the sole criterion. It should be added that the revised draft regulation of November 1988 went a long way towards incorporating a Williamson-type efficiency trade-off – this obviously did not prove acceptable. Incidentally market shares of 25 per cent or less are deemed not liable to impede effective competition, a qualification which is contained in the preamble to the regulation and not in the main body of the text.

Concentrations with a Community-dimension should be notified to the Commission and must not be put into effect prior to notification, or for at least three weeks after notification. The Commission has a month to decide whether to take proceedings against a concentration and four months to make a decision which is much quicker than the procedures suggested in 1973.

The Commission could forbid an incompatible concentration; it could order a divestiture if an unlawful concentration had already been implemented; enforcement powers and fines were also provided for.

Broadly speaking the Commission has the sole right to adjudicate on concentrations with a Community dimension and the arrangement is therefore referred to as a 'one-stop-shop' system. This seems to avoid conflicts between the national and Community anti-trust enforcement agencies over who should deal with a particular concentration and was a key issue in the negotiations. However, the dividing line was slightly less clear-cut in practice because of two qualifications which might in future give rise to some friction. A member state could claim that a problem of market dominance arises in a distinct market within its national territory. If the Commission was persuaded it could either deal with the case itself or leave it to the member state concerned to apply its national law, which provision was inserted at the insistence of West Germany. Member states could also take appropriate measures to protect legitimate interests, including public security, freedom of the press and the prudential rules of financial institutions; in which case a member state could prevent a merger or attach conditions to it.

As a final point, the preamble to the regulation makes it clear that the new instrument should be the sole mechanism for dealing with concentrations with a Community dimension. This apparently does not mean that Articles 85 and 86 do not apply to mergers: for that to be so the Council of Ministers would have to secure an amendment to the treaty under Article 236, and this they have not done. Rather, the position now is that if a merger fulfills the condition of being a concentration with a European dimension, it would be dealt with on the basis of the new regulation, and previous implementing powers no longer apply.

Turning up the heat

The achievement of the SEM demands not merely legislative activity but also increased vigour in the enforcement of the existing competition rules. This is certainly true in the case of the anti-trust dimension. A glance at the Commission's 1986 report on competition policy[58] indicates that it was well aware of the need to intensify the attack on cartels and other forms of divisive business behaviour. We will cite three instances of its response.

The first is the *Polypropylene* case.[59] In 1986 the Commission imposed under Article 85 a fine of ECU 57.85 million on fifteen major petrochemical producers for collusion in respect of price fixing and market sharing. This was followed in 1989 by the imposition of a record fine of ECU 60.5 million on twenty-three major chemical companies who had carved up the £6 billion European market for PVC and low-density polyethylene. Again, price fixing and the allocation of output quotas were key features of the violations.[60]

The second was the bold decision by the Commission in 1988 to use its power under Article 90 (see page 68) to issue a directive requiring member states to liberalize the operation of public undertakings in the field of telecommunications terminal equipment. As well as ending their monopoly to import, supply, connect up and service they were also required to publish technical specifications so that suppliers in other parts of Community could adapt their equipment to the characteristics of each national network.[61] This was challenged by France.

Finally, there is further evidence of the high profile approach when Commissioner Sutherland stated, in the light of the Commission's enhanced powers to attack mergers, that Article 90 would be employed to attack the take-over activities of public undertakings.[62]

Intensified enforcement would of course require extra manpower; the Commission would need an infusion of extra staff to handle the fifty or so concentration cases it could expect to encounter each year. It has also been pointed out that so far the Commission had only scratched the surface when it came to attacking cartels in services, notably in areas such as insurance.[63]

State aids

State aids provide an excellent illustration of the fact that the SEM was not destined to be achieved merely by filling gaps in the Commission's legislative armoury. Rather it also required the vigilant and intensified application of the existing treaty powers. In 1990 Sir Leon Brittan emphasized the point when he observed:

> the creation of the Single market is opening up a whole new world of opportunity for Europe's industry, which is already bringing a new dynamism into our economies ... but as the barriers come down and the competitive environment becomes tougher, so Member states will be under heavy domestic pressure to put their protective hand over particular companies, industries or economic sectors by maintaining aid which could nullify the whole venture.

He went on to say: 'It is in the interests of all Member states that the Commission keeps a strict eye on their development – something we fully intend to do'.[64] The Cockfield Report anticipated this problem by calling for an inventory of state aids and a report setting out the implications for future state aid policy.

State aid takes many forms including grants, straight tax reductions, more indirect assistance such as equity participations, guarantees and soft loans, together with horizontal aids in connection with such things as R&TD, small- and medium-size enterprises and exports to third countries. The first inventory of state aid covered the period 1981–6.[65] The original calculations somewhat overstated the amount of Italian and Irish aid and

Table 3.3 Aid to manufacturing (excluding steel and shipbuilding) (average for 1981–6)

	Italy	Greece	Ireland	Belgium	Netherlands	France	Luxembourg	UK	Germany	Denmark
(a)	8.2	13.9	7.3	4.5	4.1	3.6	3.5	2.9	2.9	1.7
(b)	3067	n.a.	2216	1373	1419	1223	1079	757	940	609

Source: European Communities Commission, First Survey on State Aids in the European Community, Luxembourg, OOPEC, 1989, p.12; Second Survey on State Aids in the European Community, OOPEC, 1990, Annex 1.

Notes: (a) percentage of value added.
  (b) ECU per employee.

the data in Table 3.3 allow for subsequent corrections. The report indicated that EC state aid in the period 1981–6 averaged ECU 104.3 billion which represented 3 per cent of EC GDP. State aid per employed person was ECU 771. State aid per employee, and as a percentage of value added, in manufacturing in the various member states (excluding steel and shipbuilding) is shown in Table 3.3; Greece and Ireland are well to the top of the list with Denmark at the bottom.

The Rome Treaty stance

State aid was specifically covered by Rome Treaty Articles 92–4 while Article 90 applied the rules on competition, including those relating to aids to public enterprises. Article 92 (1) enunciates the basic principle. Aids which threaten to distort competition are incompatible with the common market in so far as they favour the production of certain goods or certain enterprises and affect trade between member states. (The latter phrase reflects the fact that whilst general, across-the-economy measures can be attacked under Articles 101 and 102, they are not caught by the Article 92 ban; it is assumed that they may be compensated for by other across the board factors such as exchange rates.) The prohibition in Article 92 was qualified in two ways: some aids were definitely excepted, such as aids of a social character, aids in connection with natural disasters and aids to assist areas of West Germany disadvantaged by the geographical division (which latter point is obviously no longer relevant). Some aids might be excepted, such as aids for regional development, aids to particular industries (sectoral aids), aids to promote a project of common European importance and aids to remedy a serious disturbance in the economy of a member state. Other categories could be added, and the Commission had the task of keeping aids under review. Member states should inform the Commission of new aids and of alterations to existing ones, an area on which there has been a good deal of backsliding. The Commission vets aids and a refusal to accept its decision leads to referral to the Court of Justice.[66]

The policy stance prior to the Cockfield Report

Regional aid has been permitted but the aid instruments themselves and the intensity of aid have been subject to control. Broadly speaking this latter feature has consisted of aid ceilings with the height of the ceiling (which is not an automatic entitlement) being graduated according to the severity of local economic conditions.

Sectoral aid has also been allowed; policy has consisted of general rules together with particular codes for certain industries. The general rules have emphasized the importance of selectivity, transparency, temporariness and appropriateness. Selectivity has emphasized the need only to assist firms or industries which have had a reasonable prospect of ultimately standing on their own feet. Transparency, a word much loved by the Commission, has emphasized the need to grant aid in a way which enabled its intensity to be assessed. Any doubts about the legitimacy of the Commission's concern on this score should be set at rest by a contemplation of the British government's behaviour in the *Rover* case! Temporariness has emphasized the idea that assistance merely to prop up ailing enterprises was not acceptable; aid should be coupled to restructuring and an eventual phasing-out of assistance. Appropriateness has drawn attention to the desirability of relating measures to a mature assessment of market fundamentals and of not merely reacting hastily to the needs of the moment. The impact of the aid needs to be properly evaluated. Thus an aid system which consisted of a levy on all the enterprises in a sector including those which were efficient was likely to penalize efficiency. This was the basis upon which the Commission opposed a system of aid to the French textile industry.[67] Special aid rules were devised for industries such as shipbuilding, textiles, steel and coal (the latter two under ECSC rules) which have faced particularly fierce third country competition.

General aid schemes have also been high on the Commission's list of major problems. These tended to increase in the 1970s in the wake of the depressed conditions which flowed from the oil price increases. As their title suggests they had no specifically designated objective and could be applied on an individual, sectoral or regional basis as the national need arose. The Commission's view has been that they should be made more specific; however, given that governments considered it beneficial to have such powers, the Commission tended not to intervene at the time when they passed such laws. Rather, the Commission would wait until the laws were implemented in some particular way and would then consider them under the appropriate rules. A good example is provided by the *Philip Morris* case.[68]

Export aids in connection with sales to other member states have also been consistently opposed.

Aid rules have tended to respond to trends in the nature of government aid-giving. In 1974 guidance was given in response to the disposition of governments to help firms seeking to meet rising standards of environmental protection[69] (see chapter 9). By 1980 the Commission had become concerned about the financial relationship between governments and their public corporations – we mentioned this in connection with the vetting of public procurement. Obviously the concern of the Commission is that capital could be provided at favourable rates and that this would give the corporations an artificial competitive edge when competing with firms in the same industry in other member states who operate on a private basis. In order to regulate more effectively the activities of member states in relation to their public enterprises, the Commission in 1980 took the controversial step of adopting a directive[70] requiring states to provide data on the financial relationships between themselves and their public corporations. This provoked strong opposition from some member-state governments. They challenged the Commission's action in the Court of Justice, but in the event the Court supported the Commission.[71] There was also a growing tendency for sectoral aid to take the form of state participation in the capital of private undertakings. The Commission maintained, and has been supported by the Court of Justice, that this constituted an aid if the capital was injected at less than commercial terms. The Court made this clear in the 1984 *Intermills* case[72] when it said that loans advanced on more favourable terms than are available in the market, and equity capital advanced when private investors would not do so, were just as much aids as a capital grant.

After the Cockfield Report

The intensified attack on state aids emphasized the need for more publicity to be given to the state aid issue so that governments could be made increasingly aware of the demands of the Rome Treaty. Apart from publishing policy guidelines the Commission had accepted the need to supply more detailed information on its decisions on aid cases.

The Commission has also indicated that it intends to gradually move to a position where aids may be declared illegal for purely procedural reasons: in other words aids which might otherwise be acceptable under the treaty rules will be declared illegal if member states do not follow the proper procedure, for example, in respect of notifying the Commission in advance.

The Commission has also followed a policy of requiring the repayment of aid which has been granted illegally. This is not a new departure but it is one which the Commission has followed systematically in recent years. The *Rover* and *Renault* cases were spectacular instances.

Renault was a state-owned company which was also in considerable financial difficulty. However its régie (public enterprise) status meant that it could not go bankrupt. The clash between the Commission and the French government over Renault originally centred on equity injections and loans going back to 1984. The Commission maintained that these capital contributions contained aid elements and decided to proceed against them. The French government for its part did not see these as notifiable aids but as transactions to be reported under the 1980 directive (see page 77) relating to financial relationships between governments and public undertakings. The case came to a head when in 1987 the French government notified the Commission of its intention to pay off Renault's FF12 billion debt to the Credit National. This was to be part of a package whereby Renault would change its status from régie to a legal entity under normal commercial law.

Ultimately what appeared to be a settlement was reached and this was published as a formal Commission decision in 1988.[73] First, certain earlier loans were deemed to be illegal; they had to be repaid or would have to bear a normal commercial rate of interest, and any interest subsidy up to the date of the decision also had to be recouped. Second, a capital contribution of FF8 billion and the FF12 billion debt write-off were declared to be compatible with the common market. Third, and this was a crucial element of the settlement, the debt write-off had to be preceded by a change in the legal status of Renault. Additionally, Renault had to complete a restructuring plan involving significant cuts in car and truck production capacity.

The subsequent controversy arose because the Commission alleged that neither of these latter terms had been met. A change of government had led to a backtracking on the legal status issue. Also Renault had undertaken to cut car production capacity by 15 per cent and truck production capacity by 30 per cent. The Commission however reckoned that the cuts had only amounted to 5 and 9 per cent respectively and therefore decided to demand the repayment of FF8.4 billion by Renault. This the French government opposed; intensive bargaining then occurred. Ultimately in May 1990 the Commission and the French government came to an amicable settlement.[74] In the light of the fact that some capacity cuts had taken place and that Renault was in the process of becoming a public limited company (with an involvement by Volvo) the repayment was scaled down to FF6 billion. FF3.5 billion was to be repaid, the remaining FF2.5 billion was to stand as a long-term debt on Renault's balance sheet.

The Commission's intensified approach to state aids has also manifested itself in the adoption of yet further specific rules in areas where aid giving has been particularly intense. In 1986 it published a framework for state aid for R&TD[75] and in 1989 did the same in respect of assistance to the motor vehicle industry.[76] The R&TD provisions were particularly interesting. The Commission is broadly sympathetic to such aid since it helps to strengthen European competitiveness. The general principle is that aid for basic industrial research should not exceed 50 per cent of the gross cost of a project or programme. As the activity gets nearer to the market place the Commission will look for progressively lower levels of assistance.

In 1988 the Commission also redefined its approach to regional aid.[77] Regional aid could be justified under the exemptions prescribed in either Article 92(3)(a) or 92(3)(c). Article 92(3)(a) related to more serious situations where the standard of living is abnormally low or there is serious under-employment. By contrast Article 92(3)(c) merely referred to aid designed to facilitate the development of certain economic regions. Apparently in approving regional aid in the past, little use has been made of Article 92(3)(a): now however, with the accession of three more Mediterranean countries and the SEA's emphasis on economic and social cohesion, this has had to change. The 1988 regional aid communication identified the areas or regions which could benefit under Article 92(3)(a) and established for them a uniform and relatively high aid ceiling. It also specified generally lower and differential aid ceilings for other regions which could benefit, on the basis of Article

92(3)(c). The height of these aid ceilings depended on the region's relative socio-economic position within its own country, though the better-off a country is relative to the Community average the more serious the region's socio-economic position should be to qualify for any given aid ceiling.

Sir Leon Brittan indicated that a key feature of the Commission's future policy would be to switch the emphasis away from a concentration on new aid proposals to a review of existing aid schemes. Apparently high on the list of phenomena to be looked at are export aids (notably to third countries), general investment aids, aids which arise in connection with state involvement in public enterprises and industrial policy aids designed to maintain national champions.

Chapter 4

The fiscal dimension of 1992

Tony Westaway

In this chapter, the initial focus continues to be on NTBs as obstacles to the creation of a SEM. The discussion opens with a consideration of the problems posed by indirect taxes. In the second part of the chapter, the spotlight shifts to a consideration of the way fiscal factors may also distort the flow, not of goods and services, but of factors of production – specifically capital. The discussion rounds off with a brief account of fiscal measures introduced to facilitate cross-frontier business organizations.

Introduction

The role of fiscal policy

Changes to a government's fiscal policy stance are usually announced by the finance minister or chancellor of the exchequer in an annual budget, or public expenditure statement, followed by a period of parliamentary debate. In these eagerly awaited debates, the finance minister discusses a wide range of issues relating to both public expenditure and taxation. Government expenditure is devoted to the provision of a multitude of goods and services. These range from the provision of law and order, defence and roads to education and health services. The reason for intervention is usually justified by reference to some form of market failure.

The reasons for potential market failure and hence government intervention in the provision of these goods and services are however numerous. First, a government will provide goods and services for the benefit of the community that it feels would not be adequately provided if left to the free market. Clearly this is a contentious area and governments will present differing views on the amount of education or health service that should be provided by the state as opposed to the private sector. Thus the government not only has to decide on the amount of expenditure to devote to each of these areas, but it also has to decide on the most equitable method of raising the revenue to fund this expenditure.

Second, some goods have external or spillover effects. A selfish individual or producer may ignore the wider social benefits or costs incurred in the consumption or production of an item and thus the government may choose to intervene to help achieve a more socially desirable allocation of goods and services. For example, a penal tax may be imposed on goods whose consumption needs to be discouraged because their consumption harms others, such as the consumption of tobacco and alcohol, while subsidies may be given to those areas of consumption that would be under-provided by the free market, such as innoculations against contagious disease or lead-free petrol.

The second broad role of fiscal policy is to redistribute a nation's resources. This may be through a progressive tax system in which the rich contribute a greater percentage of their income in tax than the poor, or it may be in the form of a social security expenditure designed to relieve poverty due to unemployment, old age or illness. Alternatively redistribution may be on a regional basis, with greater subsidies going to the poorer regions of a country and higher taxes being imposed on the richer regions.

Finally, fiscal policy has been used as a major instrument in controlling the macro-economy. Until recently this role would have been governed by Keynesian demand management policies, but now governments are more concerned with the supply side of the economy. Thus changes in fiscal policy are used to remove disincentives to production and employment within the economy.

The issues that arise from this multidimensional policy debate not only involve decisions about the size and distribution of public-sector expenditure but also the relative merits of alternative sources of finance. Throughout the European Community these decisions are made at both the central and local government levels. They reflect concern about issues such as the size and structure of the country's social security spending programme, the level and distribution of public sector expenditure on defence, education, roads and health, the control of pollution, scarce energy resources and smoking amongst many others.

Clearly member states will place differing emphases on both the scope and range of public expenditure in addition to the relative merits of alternative sources of revenue. In addition, public expenditure and taxation may distort the allocation of resources within the Community, intentionally or otherwise, and if one of the prime objectives of a common market is to be achieved these distortions need to be removed or at least minimized.

Market distortion and the objectives of tax harmonization

The process of removing disparities in national tax structures to the point where they no longer affect the operation of free markets and hence the allocation of resources between member states, can be referred to as tax harmonization. As has been seen, a common market is established to allow the free movement between members states not only of goods and services, but also of the factor inputs (such as labour, technology and physical capital) used to create them, together with the financial capital needed to fund economic activity. Fiscal policy should not, therefore, be designed so as distort choice between member states and hence influence this free movement of resources.

Fiscal policy is concerned with both public expenditure and taxation at both the national and local levels. This chapter will confine the discussion, in the main, to that of harmonization of taxation at the central government level and in particular with value added tax (VAT), excise duties and corporation tax. The reason for this restriction is that these are the main areas with which the EC has been concerned, and the implications of this will be discussed later in the chapter.

For the benefit of those readers who are not familiar with public finance literature it is worth clarifying some of the ways in which taxation can distort markets and hence interfere with free trade. Further examples of identified trade distortion within the Community will be discussed later in the text.

It should be said at the outset that, though some of the distortions due to tax differences are intentional, the majority result from historical accident. Simply bringing together twelve economies which have different roles for fiscal policy will inevitably result in unintentional trade distortion unless adjustments are made. Many of these tax differences will be jealously guarded and any attempt to interfere with them may be seen by some as infringements of an individual country's fiscal sovereignty, a point of which the Commission is well aware.

Taxes are usually considered as belonging to one of two categories, direct and indirect. Though it can be argued that this distinction has little meaning for economic analysis it is one that will be followed here if simply to comply with most of the public finance literature. A direct tax can be loosely defined as one which is levied directly upon the person or company on whom it ultimately falls. Examples of this type of tax include income tax, which falls on individual earnings, and corporation tax, which applies to the profits of a company.

An indirect tax, on the other hand, is not necessarily levied on the individual on whom it ultimately falls but is usually a charge incorporated in the price of a product or service. The consumer ultimately pays the tax in the form of a higher price, but the tax is actually levied on the seller of the item. Examples of indirect taxes include VAT and excise duties.

In general terms, direct taxes are usually levied on factors of production while indirect taxes are levied on consumption. Also in broad terms it is easier to alter the location of production in response to differences in tax, than to alter the location of consumption. Thus it has been argued that direct taxes are more likely to distort trade than indirect taxes;[1] there are exceptions to this generalization and that is where we shall begin.

There are examples of cross-border shopping within Europe and this may be seen as a problem in densely populated border areas. For example, lower VAT rates and excise duties in Northern Ireland have benefited shoppers from the south whilst Luxembourg, with its modest tax rates, attracts a considerable number of shoppers from its European neighbours: anyone travelling to Luxembourg may be surprised to find such a large number of petrol stations in a country with such a small population!

If an indirect tax, such as VAT, was applied on an origin basis – applied to a good at the rate applicable in the country of origin of the good – then market distortion is likely to become a more serious problem. The nature of this distortion is best explained by use of a simple, if somewhat contrived, example. Let us assume that the VAT rate on cars in country A is 25 per cent whilst in country B the rate is 10 per cent. Assume that the final manufacturing cost of a car, including an allowance for profit, is the same in both countries, say £10,000. The car from country A will sell for £12,500 (£10,000 + 25%) while that from country B will sell for £11,000 (£10,000 + 10%) in both country A and country B and thus have a clear price advantage over its competitor in both markets. This advantage is due entirely to tax differences and has nothing to do with the basic costs of manufacture, which were the same in both countries.

The European Community, however, currently utilizes a destination system for VAT. In effect this means that goods are exported free of VAT and the local VAT rate is applied to the total price of the good in the country of destination. All goods of similar type will therefore carry the same rate of tax regardless of the country of manufacture – thus both cars will sell for £12,500 in country A and for £11,000 in country B. In order for this system to work, exports are made free of tax with VAT being imposed on imports.

Even under the destination principle, there remain certain taxes which are levied on the intermediate stages of production which are not rebated on export and which will not be levied on imports. These include local business rates and taxes on fuel used to transport goods, both of which raise the costs of production.

Turning to direct taxes, one of the largest sources of tax revenue in most countries is personal income tax. Large differences in income tax rates could interfere with the free working of the labour market within the Community. Arguably if a person considers that their earnings are taxed too heavily in one country they can move to a country where the income tax situation is more favourable. However, in reality the decision to move will be influenced by a wide range of considerations of which the income tax regime is likely to play a small role. For most individuals consideration of family ties, differences in language, differences in the cost of living especially housing, and their children's educational opportunities are likely to be more important than income tax differences. The EC has not proposed harmonization of income tax. Given the lack of international mobility of labour this will therefore leave income tax as a major independent tax policy instrument for national governments.

Corporation tax differences are, however, likely to have a greater impact. Many governments have attempted to attract productive industries to their country by, for example, offering state aid in the form of subsidies or regional incentives (these issues are discussed in chapter 3) or by offering tax incentives such as lower rates of corporation tax. The gains from a very low rate of corporation tax may outweigh losses such as increased transport costs or labour retraining costs incurred by moving production to a new location. The decision of where to locate industry will be determined by differences in tax rates rather than differences in efficiency of production. Firms may therefore locate in high-cost but low-tax areas and in terms of economic criteria this leads to inefficient levels of production within the EEC. In addition it will encourage other countries to retaliate and lower their rates of corporation tax, a battle from which all countries will ultimately suffer.

Jurisdiction

Jurisdiction refers to the thorny question of who is entitled to collect a particular tax. Suppose a French company designs a new product in its research laboratory in Germany, manufactures it in Italy and sells it in Greece: in which country should the corporation tax on the profits of the product be paid? All four member states may claim a share of the tax on the income generated. Clearly if the tax regimes in the four countries differ then multinational companies will have plenty of scope to rearrange their accounts so as to minimize their tax liability.[2]

In theory, certain types of tax make the question of jurisdiction easier to resolve. Property tax, which forms the basis of much local government finance, is paid to the government in whose country the property is located. Indirect taxes on the other hand might be either levied at the country of supply (origin), making them production taxes, or at the country of purchase (destination), making them consumption taxes, if they are consumed in the country they are purchased. In most cases, the two places are the same but some interesting differences do arise.

Consider the case of VAT payments. The destination principle means that exports are purchased without VAT being added and VAT is applied in the country of destination. However, for individual purchases this is different. An international visitor to Scotland may buy a case of Malt Whisky, on which UK VAT and excise duty is paid. This will be refunded when the goods are exported and then local taxes are paid when the goods are imported into the country where the product is consumed, subject to the individual's duty free allowance. The treatment of services is however different. If the visitor had his or her hair cut before returning home then the service would be consumed in his or her country of residence but the VAT was paid in Scotland.

The Commission's approach to removing market distortion[3]

In providing for the establishment of a common market the 1957 Rome Treaty was concerned with removing obstacles to the free movement of goods, services and factors of production within the Community. Articles 95–9 specifically related to the taxation of products whilst Article 100 provided the legal basis for the harmonization of direct taxation. In particular, Articles 95–8 were concerned with preventing the use of taxes to discriminate between similar domestic and imported goods. For example Article 95 (1) prevents higher taxation on imported goods than similar domestic goods while Article 95(2) applies to goods in competition with each other and prohibits taxation of the sort that affords internal protection.

In its initial form Article 99 provided for the harmonization of indirect taxes in the interests of the common market. This was amended by the SEA to ensure that legislation concerning turnover taxes, excise duties and other indirect taxes were harmonized to the extent that they ensured the 'establishment and functioning of the internal market'. In other words this gave the conditions necessary to remove fiscal frontiers, which are particularly prevalent in the case of indirect taxes. Every time a product crosses a border between two countries then tax checks need to be made. Clearly this hinders the envisaged free movement of goods and services.[4]

Despite the fact that VAT had been accepted as the main turnover tax throughout the Community, there was not a common VAT base until the sixth directive on VAT was accepted by the European Council on 17 May 1977, coming into force by 1979. Similar progress on the structure of excise duties and corporation taxes still seems a very long way off.

Initially it was also assumed that rates of duty and tax would eventually be harmonized throughout the community. The Cockfield Report changed the emphasis from harmonization to approximation, recognizing that a degree of difference would not seriously affect the free movement of goods and services. These views were enshrined in the 1987 proposals for VAT reform. As December 1992 approaches the Commission has been taking an increasingly flexible approach; for excise duties it has been currently proposing a minimum rate of duty in the belief that market competition will bring the rates closer together.

The emphasis in 1991 shifted to ensuring that the principle of abolishing fiscal frontiers is not put at risk. The Cecchini Report estimated the cost of frontier formalities – physical, administrative and other barriers – to the free movement of goods across borders. The abolition of fiscal frontiers (though they must be accompanied by the removal of other barriers) is seen as a major ingredient in the completion of the internal market.

The remainder of the chapter is devoted to examining the progress made by the Commission in dealing with the problems of distortion and frontiers arising in connection with VAT, excise duties and corporation tax. But before we proceed with that discussion it is important to point out that while most harmonization activity now takes place on a majority-voting basis, following the SEA fiscal matters still require unanimity. This is bound to slow down the process of achieving agreement.

Valued added tax

Harmonization

VAT was adopted as the EEC turnover tax as long ago as 1967 following the recommendations of the 1963 Neumark committee.[5] Nevertheless, simply adopting a uniform method of taxation did not mean that potential market distortions were removed and many problems still remained. However, before considering these problems, it is necessary to ask why VAT was chosen as the main EEC turnover tax in preference to others.

Prior to the adoption of VAT, four alternative forms of taxation on the purchase of goods were in evidence. West Germany, Luxembourg and the Netherlands used a cumulative multi-stage cascade system, under which tax payments were calculated on the final price of a company's product at each stage of the production process. This price included all taxes paid by companies producing goods as part of the previous stages of the production process. In consequence if several companies are involved in producing an item then the tax payments will increase at a cumulative rate with companies further down the production process paying tax on the tax already paid by companies in the early stages of production.

Table 4.1 illustrates this process by reference to the tax payments of three companies, R, S and F, involved in a multi-stage production process. (Calculations are based on an assumed tax rate of 10 per cent.) The raw materials needed to make one unit of the product are produced by company R for £10 to which is added £1 in tax; it is assumed that company R does not need to buy inputs from any other company. Company S thus buys these raw materials for £11.00 and adds £9.00 in value, turning the product into its semi-finished stage. This gives a price at the end of this second stage of £20 to which is added a further 10 per cent in tax or £2.00. Company F then buys the semi-finished product for £22 and turns it into the final product by adding £8.00 in value. The price at the end of the final product stage is £30.00 to which is added £3.00 in tax to give a final selling price of £33.00 per unit of output. As can be seen from the table, this final selling price of £33.00 comprises £27 added in value during the three stages of production and £6 in tax.

If the three companies merge to form a single company M which undertakes the entire production process from start to finish, so that there is in effect a single stage of production, then the tax liability is lowered. The total value

Table 4.1 Cascade tax systems

Company/ product	Purchase price from previous stage	Value added	Price at end of stage	Tax due	Final price
	A. An example of cascade tax multi-stage production				
R Raw materials	0.00 +	10.00 =	10.00 +	1.00 =	11.00
S Semi finished	11.00 +	9.00 =	20.00 +	2.00 =	22.00
F Final product	22.00 +	8.00 =	30.00 +	3.00 =	33.00
TOTAL		27.00		6.00	33.00

Company/ product	Purchase price from previous stage	Value added		Tax due	Final price
	B. An example of cascade tax single-stage production				
M Single stage	0.00 +	27.00 =	27.00 +	2.70 =	29.70

added during the production process is still £27.00 per unit to which is now added £2.70 or 10 per cent in tax. Thus the final selling price is £29.70 giving company M a clear market advantage. Clearly the multi-cascade tax system discriminates against multi-stage production processes and encourages mergers.

In contrast, Belgium and Italy operated a mixed system of turnover taxes. The multi-stage or cascade system was applied down to the wholesale stage on most goods with a single tax paid at a single stage on others. France,[6] on the other hand, utilized a non-cumulative, multi-stage tax which was based on the value added at each stage of the production process. This was referred to as Tax sur la Valeur Ajoutée or VAT. The main advantage of this system of taxation was that it did not discriminate between different stages of vertical integration. As can be seen from Table 4.2, there is no difference in tax paid between the multi-stage and the single stage production processes. The two sets of companies are therefore able to compete equally regardless of the level of vertical integration. Thus a potential source of market distortion, prevalent in cumulative cascade systems, is overcome. Any decisions about mergers will be taken on grounds of economic efficiency rather than tax minimization.

In practice, VAT is calculated using an invoice approach rather than the value added approach shown in Table 4.2. Thus in the scenario quoted above, the final producer pays VAT on £27, the total invoiced value of

Table 4.2 Value added tax

Company/ product	Purchase price from previous stage		Value added		Tax due		Final price
			A. An example of VAT multi-stage production				
R Raw materials	0.00	+	10.00	+	1.00	=	11.00
S Semi finished	11.00	+	9.00	+	0.90	=	20.90
F Final product	20.90	+	8.00	+	0.80	=	29.70
TOTAL			27.00	+	2.70	=	29.70

Company/ product	Purchase price from previous stage		Value added		Tax due		Final price
			B. An example of VAT single-stage production				
M Single stage	0.00	+	27.00	+	2.70	=	29.70

production (including previous stages in the production process) and then reclaims VAT that has already been paid by the other manufacturers, from whom components and raw materials had been purchased. In our example company F will pay VAT of £2.70 per unit of good manufactured but reclaim the £1 paid by company R and the 90p paid by company S.

The adoption of a VAT system thus disallows one potential source of market distortion. However, it would be wrong to assume that simply adopting the same tax system throughout member states will eliminate all of the potential sources of market distortion.

The origin versus destination principle

Currently VAT is levied at the point of destination (consumption) rather than origin (production) although the Commission has made it clear that it sees this as a temporary situation and has proposed switching to the origin principle by December 1996 at the latest. This distinction between the two approaches is important when considering the problem of fiscal harmonization. The causes of potential problems are illustrated by reference to Figures 4.1 – 4.3.

We start by assuming that a product with similar characteristics is produced in Holland for 100 guilders and in Spain for 5,500 pesetas, which with an exchange rate of 1 guilder to 55 pesetas means that the production costs are

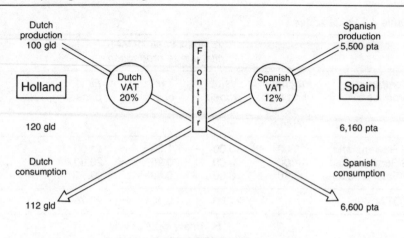

1 guilder = 55 pesetas

Figure 4.1 The origin principle

identical. (We are ignoring transport costs in of this example.) Under the origin principle, VAT is applied at the country of origin which for standard goods, in March 1989, was 20 per cent in The Netherlands and 12 per cent in Spain.

The Dutch-produced item requires 20 per cent VAT to be added in both the home and overseas markets. Following the solid arrows in Figure 4.1 we can see that it sells on the Dutch market for 112 guilders and on the Spanish market for 6,600 pesetas. On the other hand, the Spanish-produced item has had 12 per cent VAT added and thus following the unfilled arrows sells for 120 guilders in Holland and 6,160 pesetas in Spain.

This clearly gives the Spanish producer a competitive advantage in both markets which reflects tax differences rather than differences in productive efficiency. Under the origin system of VAT, international companies would choose to site their factories in those member states that imposed the lowest rate of VAT. Clearly if the rates of VAT were the same in all member states then this problem would no longer exist.

Figure 4.2 illustrates the destination principle of VAT which was the system of tax adopted by the EC in 1967. Under this system goods are exported tax free and VAT is paid by the importer in the country of destination when the goods cross the frontier. As can be seen the goods are now sold at the same price in both markets. However, the removal of fiscal frontiers has formed the centrepiece of the debate on taxation and the completion of the internal market.

As we have seen frontier controls are seen as a hindrance to trade: though they do not actually prevent a company from exporting, the extra paperwork they create and the costs they impose place additional burdens on exporters. The smaller the exporting company the larger the burden this is likely to

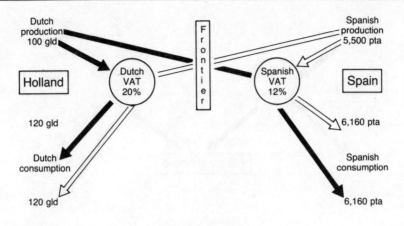

1 guilder = 55 pesetas

Figure 4.2 The destination principle

cause,[7] and because of this the continued existence of frontier controls clearly gives a market advantage to large companies.[8]

What then are the alternatives once frontiers have been removed? The first is to change to an origin-based system of VAT, such that it is applied to exports at the same rate as to goods for domestic consumption. Importing producers, wholesalers and retailers then add VAT at the importing country's rate to their part of the value added.[9] This, as we have seen, requires rates of tax to be harmonized throughout the Community, if market distortion and problems of cross-border shopping are to be avoided.

However, this is not the end of the story. Changing the VAT system in this way will also affect the allocation of tax revenues within the Community. At present member states receive VAT payments on the total value of taxable imported goods but not on taxable exports. If the above alternative is chosen then this will be reversed with VAT payments being received on taxable exports but not on imports. Thus a country with a large trade surplus with the rest of the EEC, such as Germany, will gain whilst those with a trade deficit, such as the UK, will lose.

An alternative is to allow importers to reclaim the VAT paid in the exporting country and apply the importing country's rate of VAT to the total value of the good. This is in effect an alternative way of applying the destination principle and is the approach suggested in the Cockfield Report. The sale would be taxable in the hands of the vendor and the VAT incurred by the purchaser would be deductible irrespective of the member state in which it had been charged. It would then be necessary to set up a 'clearing house' system to ensure that VAT collected by the exporting member state and deducted by the importing member state was reimbursed to the latter.[10]

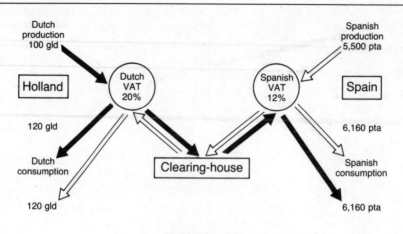

Figure 4.3 The Cockfield Report proposal

This system, which is illustrated in Figure 4.3, has attracted considerable criticism for two main reasons. First, the clearing house system was seen to be unnecessarily bureaucratic and costly. Second, some purchasers and institutions are currently exempt, or partially exempt, from VAT payments. These institutions would be required to pay VAT on their imports from other member states but would not be able to offset this against domestic VAT payments, because they have none or little by way of domestic VAT payments to set it against.

Georges Egret, the Secretary General of the French Internal Revenue Association, suggested a solution to these problems in April 1990.[11] The proposal was for the current system to remain in operation with goods being exported free of VAT. However, rather than VAT being added at the frontier it would, after 1992, be added by the purchaser. On 8 May 1990 the European Commission announced that it found this system acceptable but only on an interim basis; it would thus be in force from the beginning of 1993 and is due to expire on 31 December 1996 at the latest.

Purchases by non-taxable institutions and exempt entities

Non-taxable institutions and exempt entities (such as banks, insurance companies and public administrations) would be allowed VAT-free purchases to an annual maximum of 35,000 ECUs per year, beyond which they will be subject to VAT as with any other company. This was the interim measure accepted by the European Commission on 8 May 1990. However, Mme Scrivener, European Commissioner with special responsibility for taxation and the customs union, made it clear that:

the Commission found this system acceptable provided three conditions are fulfilled: a) it must be temporary, the final system being VAT payment in the country of origin of the goods; b) it must follow elimination of all border controls; c) it must include true simplification of administrative procedures for companies.[12]

Thus, before the end of 1996 the functioning of this system was to be examined and the terms of the change to a definitive system of taxation in the country of origin are to be set.

Cross-border shopping and alignment of VAT rates

A major consequence of the removal of fiscal barriers was that by January 1993 individual consumers would be free to purchase goods, for their own use and not commercial in nature, in any of the member states, provided that VAT is paid at the rate operated in the country in which the goods are purchased. This means, therefore, that limits on travellers' purchases will be eliminated and as a result cross-border shopping is likely to increase. The Commission also proposed that the ceiling on travellers' purchasing be increased from ECU 390 to ECU 800 in 1991 and further to ECU 1,600 in 1992 before being abolished altogether.

There were two important exceptions to this general rule. The first applied to purchases of new passenger vehicles which would be taxed in the country in which their license plates were registered; and the second to purchases from companies specializing in mail order sales which will be taxed in the country in which the goods arrive.

In effect, as far as individual consumers were concerned, a dual VAT system would operate after 1992. Consumers could choose whether to purchase goods in their own countries to which a domestic rate of VAT has been applied or travel to another member state and purchase the goods at a different rate of VAT with consequent market distortion. To avoid these distortionary effects, the Cockfield Report proposed that the VAT rates of the twelve member states should be brought closer together so that they were approximately equal. It was argued that experience in the USA where an absence of fiscal frontiers is combined with interstate differences in tax rates shows that complete harmonization of rates is unnecessary. Thus the Cockfield Report suggested that the target range for the standard rate of VAT should be 14–19 per cent with a norm of 16.5 per cent. (The upper limit was raised to 20 per cent in 1987.)[13] As Table 4.3 shows this band encompassed the standard rate for most member states.

This approach was finally accepted in December 1989 when member states agreed on guidelines concerning the narrowing of VAT tax bands; in particular, that the normal rate applicable to most goods and services would not, between the date of agreement and 1 January 1993, be reduced if it was

Table 4.3 VAT levels in Community member states (%)
(1 March 1990)

	Lower rates	Standard rate	Upper rates
Belgium	1 and 6	19	25 and 33
Denmark		22	
France	2.1 and 5.5	18.6	25
Germany	7	14	
Greece	3 and 6	16	36
Ireland	0 and 10	23	
Italy	4 and 9	19	38
Luxembourg	3 and 6	12	
Netherlands	6	18.5	
Portugal	0 and 8	17	30
Spain	6	12	33
United Kingdom	0	15	

Source: European Communities Commission, *Taxation in the Single Market*, Luxembourg,
   OOPEC, 1990.

lower than 14 per cent, increased if it was above 20 per cent or moved outside of the 14–20 per cent band if it was currently in that range.

Two subsequent refinements have occurred. First, it has been argued that there is no need to add an upper limit to the 14–20 per cent band as any state charging above 20 per cent would lose out through competition from other members. Second, on 24 June 1991, the twelve EC finance ministers reached political agreement that the normal minimum VAT rate should be raised to 15 per cent – requiring Germany, Luxembourg and Spain to increase their rates. Eleven countries accepted that the political agreement must be enshrined in a directive whilst the UK, on the grounds of sovereignty, refused to be tightly bound in this matter. In addition, the Commission proposed that member states would be free to set a reduced rate of VAT in the range 4–9 per cent which will apply to six product groups: foodstuffs (excluding alcoholic beverages); energy products for heating and lighting; water supplies; pharmaceutical products; books, newspapers and periodicals; and passenger transport.

Interestingly on 24 June 1991 the Commission accepted the retention of zero-rating for a limited number of goods included in the list of products above, provided there was no risk of competition being distorted. Thus, member states would be free to set two rates of VAT with the reduced-rate band being applied to about one-third of the common VAT base.

There has however been some disenchantment with these proposals. Denmark has opposed the introduction of unlimited tax allowances for travellers. Ireland has only recently withdrawn its reservation on this issue, following an understanding that the Commission will carry out a thorough study of the budgetary implications that unlimited tax allowances would have – in particular implications that the lowering of tax bands allied to cross-border shopping would lead to a potential loss of tax revenue. Both Denmark and Ireland have had relatively high standard rates of VAT and have argued that they would face a substantial fall in tax revenues in consequence of these changes.

The EC has congratulated itself on the progress that has been made but there is still a considerable way to go before the approximation of VAT can be said to have been achieved. The major sticking point will undoubtedly be the proposed switch to the origin system of taxation and it is clear that the redistribution of tax revenue likely to follow such a switch will ensure that the debate will continue up to the 1996 deadline, and probably beyond. In addition there is continued dispute over the use of zero-rated and lower tax bands. It also seems unlikely that this will be resolved before the start of 1993 unless a compromise based on a timetable for the phasing out of these zero-rated goods is agreed upon.

Excise duties

The problem

Excise duties are, in the main, applied to three general categories of goods – tobacco, alcoholic beverages and hydrocarbon oils. However, each of these can be subdivided into a large number of excisable products – for example twenty-eight types of alcoholic beverages and seven types of mineral oil. For ease of illustration we shall concentrate on the classic five products, cigarettes, beer, wine, spirits and petrol and take a standard case to illustrate the operation of excise duties for each product group.

Traditionally excise duties have taken several forms. They may be levied as a specific tax, i.e. an amount per unit of the product, regardless of price, or as an *ad valorem* tax i.e. a tax proportional to the selling price or as a combination of the two methods. Taking the case of cigarette taxation, all member states use the latter method – a combination of the two methods with a specific excise duty being added to an *ad valorem* element which probably includes the standard VAT. However, as Table 4.4 shows, the balance between the two differs: specific taxes tend to be favoured in northern member states whilst *ad valorem* taxes tend to be favoured by southern member states.

A further complication arises because there are several ways of applying a specific tax. For example, some countries add a specific tax per cigarette meaning that large and small cigarettes have the same amount of tax imposed on them, while for others it is a specific tax per gram of tobacco content resulting in a higher tax on large cigarettes than on small ones. The differences do not end there. The system of enforcing and receiving payment of duties also differs between member states. Unlike VAT payments, which are

Table 4.4 Excise duty rates

	Beer	Wine	Spirits	Petrol	Cigarettes
Belgium	0.13	0.33	3.76	0.25	0.15 + 66%
Denmark	0.71	1.57	10.50	0.46	1.52 + 39%
France	0.03	0.03	3.45	0.39	0.03 + 71%
Germany	0.07	0	3.52	0.24	0.52 + 44%
Greece	0.10	0	0.14	0.42	0.01 + 58%
Ireland	1.13	2.79	8.17	0.38	1.00 + 35%
Italy	0.17	0	0.69	0.53	0.03 + 69%
Luxembourg	0.06	0.13	2.53	0.20	0.03 + 64%
Netherlands	0.23	0.34	3.89	0.29	0.24 + 54%
Portugal	0.09	0	0.74	0.41	0.04 + 63%
Spain	0.03	0	0.93	0.20	0.01 + 35%
U K	0.68	1.54	7.45	0.31	0.96 + 34%
Commission proposal as at 19/12/89					
Basic	0.0935	0.0935	3.36	0.337	0.30 + 45%
Target	0.1870	0.1870	4.21	n.a.	0.43 + 54%

Source: European Communities Commission, COM (89) 525 final; COM (89) 526 final; COM (89) 527 final; S. Smith, 'Excise Duties and the Internal Market', *Journal of Common Market Studies*, vol. 27, no. 2, pp. 147–60, 1988.

Notes: All figures in ECUs.
Beer: based on 1 litre of beer of average strength (original gravity 1050)
Wine: based on 1 litre of still wine
Spirit: based on a 0.75 litre bottle of 40% spirits.
Petrol: based on 1 litre of leaded petrol. Unleaded petrol will be charged at 0.287 ECU per litre.
Cigarettes: based on a packet of 20 cigarettes.

made throughout the production and retailing process, excise duties are single-stage taxes. The timing of the stage at which these duties become due for payment, and hence the difference between taxed and untaxed goods, becomes important. In addition, excise duties are levied at a considerably higher rate than VAT and hence the potential gains from duty evasion or delays in tax payments are relatively high.

Most member states, including the Benelux countries, plus Denmark, Germany and Greece, enforce duty payment through tax stamps or 'banderoles'. This requires the physical stamping of goods on which duty has been paid: thus taxed and untaxed goods are easily distinguished. To prevent forgery these stamps are usually attached during the manufacturing stage. This has the advantage that it does not require close supervision of the production process, as untaxed goods can be easily identified at the retailing stage.

There are advantages and disadvantages for internationally traded goods in this banderole system. Exported goods do not need to bear the banderole allowing them to be easily exported duty-free. This advantage is counterbalanced by the disadvantage that, for imported goods, duty has to be paid immediately upon entry to the country. A further disadvantage of this approach is that the domestic manufacturers bear the costs of meeting the duty payments at an early stage in the manufacture and selling process with a clear incentive to minimize the time between duty payment and retail sale.[14] In addition, when the rate of duty changes there is difficulty for the authorities in ensuring that recently produced goods pay the newest rate of tax.

The UK, on the other hand, uses a system of bonded warehouses, whereby goods are stored in a bonded warehouse or other approved store without payment of duty, which is suspended until they leave the warehouse. The main disadvantage of this system is that it requires close supervision of the production process, including movement of the goods up to the point where duty is paid, with the consequent costs of administration and loss of revenue to the tax authorities. A major advantage of the system, from the manufacturers' point of view, is that payment of the duty can be delayed until the goods leave the bonded warehouse. However, goods designated for export need to be closely monitored until they leave the country and imported goods also need to enter a bonded warehouse under close control if tax evasion is to be avoided.

Progress to date

Progress in the area of excise duties was relatively slow until recent years. The initial stages were directed towards the structure rather than the rates of excise duties. However, more recently attention has been paid to the rate structure and on the 25 October 1989 the European Commission adopted the following proposal. However, to date, several questions still need to be addressed if the move towards the approximation of excise duties is to be achieved by 31 December 1992.

Under the proposal it has now been recognized that the imposition of a single rate of excise duty per product throughout all of the member states, as proposed in 1987, is unrealistic given the large differences in duties that currently exist. Thus, the new approach is to set minimum rates for all products and as an illustration, some of these are presented in Table 4.4. These minimum rates should be applied in all member states effective from 1 January 1993 at the latest.[15] In addition, the European Commission has also set objective or target rates to which member states are expected to converge in the medium to long run. No date has been set but the Commission's proposal envisages a revision procedure for minimum and target rates after 1992, taking into account transport, health, energy, environmental and fiscal policies. Both these rates are to be reviewed once every two years.

As can be seen from Table 4.4, the rates of duty are based on a variety of factors determined by the characteristics of each of the products. With regard to cigarettes, an allowance has been made for the differences in approach to the structure of taxation of this product. This is the only product for which the minimum rates are not set purely in terms of a specific duty. Thus minimum values have been set for both the specific and *ad valorem* or value added aspects of the excise duty which incidentally also includes VAT payments.

For other goods on which excise duties can be levied the situation is easier.[16] For beer the rate is per hectolitre/degree Plato and hence allowance is made for different strength beers. Translated to an average strength beer it can be seen that the rate per litre is the same as for still wine. The duty on spirits is calculated according to the pure alcohol content of the drink and thus spirits with a higher alcohol content have a higher rate of duty. Finally, because of environmental considerations there are differences in duty on unleaded and leaded petrol.

It should also be recognized that all of these products also have VAT applied to the final price, thus differences in VAT rates (with the exception of cigarettes) would further distort retail price differences. Member states have frequently argued that a low VAT rate has often been applied in combination with high excise duties and vice versa and so the Commission should consider the combined taxes rather than excise duties separately from VAT.

Clearly large differences still remain but as with VAT the Commission hopes that market forces will gradually bring rates of duty into line. Travellers' purchases are expected to be duty free and thus in the absence of approximation of rates of duty, there would be considerable scope for cross-border shopping by both traders and consumers alike.

Finally, there remains the problem of administration and control of payment of these duties, to which end the Community has proposed a system of linked warehouses. Goods would be transferred to and between warehouses without the application of excise duties, but once goods leave these warehouses then duty will be applied, and once applied, goods would be allowed to move freely within the Community. If this happens producers could be expected to choose to send their goods to the warehouse and hence pay tax in the country with the lowest duty payable, selling the goods in the country with the highest duty, a problem which is still to be resolved.

How then can the Community ensure that the duty paid is remitted to the country in which the goods are consumed, as at present? The linked bonded warehouse system could be combined with the 'banderole' system to obtain the benefits of both approaches. Goods could be tax-stamped when they reach their destination or as they leave the warehouse, if the warehouse is sited in the country of destination. Alternatively, tax could be paid when the goods leave the bonded warehouse and reclaimed or allowed against the excise duty payments due in the country of destination, if different to the country in which the warehouse is sited, so the excise duty of the country of destination is thus applied. Either way introduces administrative complications.

The use of a single stage tax such as excise duty thus highlights the problem of applying the destination principle. As can be seen applying the destination principle or a consumption-based tax requires a complicated system of rebates and administrative checks on tax payment. However, it can be argued that with a production tax (a tax at origin), administration becomes relatively easy. As with VAT, the Commission would like the Community to accept the origin principle, but the same problems arise with large revenue reallocations between member states following the change.

Corporate taxation[17]

Introduction

The European Commission has made very limited progress in the thorny area of company taxation, though recently momentum has gathered peace in this area. For example, in 18 April 1990, Mme Scrivener presented a new strategy for company taxation schemes.

Devereux and Pearson[18] have identified three possible reasons for wanting to harmonize these forms of tax. First, that the distribution of corporate tax revenues between member states is seen as 'unfair', second, that it causes administrative difficulties for both governments and business and, third, that it distorts competition within the Community.

Current corporate tax strategy may lead to multiple taxation of some company income. The profits a company is deemed to make are currently taxed in the country of production. However, if the company sends these profits to another country (say from a subsidiary to the parent) then a non-recoverable withholding tax maybe imposed. The country of residence of the parent company may then apply a further tax on these profits if the tax already applied is deemed to be too low. Finally, if the profits are distributed to shareholders, yet more tax may be levied, though this depends on the type of tax system in operation.

Thus it is with corporate taxes that the thorny question of jurisdiction becomes particularly relevant. Location of parent companies, their subsidiaries, where the products are sold and where their shareholders live will affect the amount of total tax paid, the shares of this revenue going to which country and hence the allocation of the tax burden. There is no obvious solution to who has jurisdiction or who has a just claim to a particular share of these revenues under the current system.

An equally important problem is the potential distortion of a company's decision of where to invest, produce and sell their products. A tax that does not influence this decision is referred to as a neutral tax. Economic efficiency

– the condition that goods should be produced in the country most efficient at making them – requires a neutral tax system. However, the problems of applying this apparently simple objective are far from trivial as can be illustrated by use of two simple examples.

Let us assume that a multinational Belgian company is considering where to set up its new production plant, and the cost of production and the potential profits for the new product are identical in both Spain and Belgium. However, as can be seen from Table 4.5 corporation tax is 43 per cent in Belgium and 35 per cent in Spain. If tax was raised on a residence basis, according to the country of residence of the parent company, the company would pay a rate of 43 per cent in both countries and the question of location would not be influenced by tax structures. However, if tax were paid in the country where the goods were actually produced then the lower Spanish tax rate would make production in Spain more attractive. This is referred to as taxing at source – of production in this case. A tax that does not distort the decision of where to invest in this way is referred to as capital export neutral (CEN). Capital export neutrality will ensure that the Belgian producer will invest and hence produce in the most efficient location.

Table 4.5 Company taxation

	Tax rate	Type of tax system	Local taxes[1]	Imputation rate[2]
Belgium	43	Imputation		33.3
Denmark	50	Imputation		20
France	42	Imputation		33.3
Germany	36/52	Imputation/ split rate	15	36
Greece	44	Imputation		44
Ireland	10 to 50[3]	Imputation		5.3
Italy	36	Imputation	16.2	36
Luxembourg	36 + 0.72[4]	Classical	6	
Netherlands	35	Classical		
Portugal	35/47	Split rate		
Spain	35	Imputation		9.1
U K	35	Imputation		25

Source: Adapted from OECD information reported to M. Devereux and M. Pearson, *Corporate Tax Harmonization and Economic Efficiency*, Institute for Fiscal Studies, Report Series no. 35, 1989 and A. Giovannini, 'Capital Taxation', *Economic Policy*, October 1989.

Notes: [1]Typical rates: German and Italian are tax deductible whereas the rates given for Luxembourg are not.
[2]Percentage of gross dividend.
[3]Until 31.12 2000, for manufacturing companies only. Under bilateral treaties, other countries sometimes assume that a higher rate of tax has been paid by companies investing in Ireland. Ireland operates a top rate of 50%.
[4]2% levy (deductible for Unemployment Fund).

The second example illustrates a further problem. Some goods such as roads, bridges and buildings can not be transported. Thus production, at least in part, takes place in the country in which the item is sold. Let us assume that Greek authorities invite tenders for the construction of a new bridge, which are then received from a Belgian and Spanish construction company. On the residence basis, if both companies are equally efficient producers, the lower rate of corporation tax in Spain will allow the Spanish construction company to tender at a lower price and make the same after tax profit as the Belgium company, even though all other costs etc are identical.

Under the residence approach to corporate taxation, these multinational construction companies will be attracted to the country with the lowest rates of tax. Musgrave[19] refers to taxes that do not distort choice as to where to invest for these reasons as capital import neutral (CIN). In this case, taxing at the source of production and sale would not distort competition and the companies from both Belgium and Spain could compete on equal terms as they will both pay the 44 per cent corporation tax rate applied in Greece.

This definition has been redefined by Devereux and Pearson to make CIN mean that all producers selling in the same market should face the same rate of tax, regardless of the country in which the good was produced. It now also includes goods produced outside of the country in which they were consumed. Thus CEN refers to the decision of where to produce and CIN to the decision of where to sell. For construction companies the country of construction, production and selling would be the same but the parent company may be based elsewhere.

In the absence of complete harmonization of fiscal tax systems, these two concepts lead to conflicts in the design of tax systems. Taxing companies on the basis of residence will guarantee CEN, thus an Italian company pays Italian tax regardless of where it invests. The achievement of CIN is more problematic but taxing companies only in the source country where the good is produced or sold, would move someway towards it.[20]

The current situation

Table 4.5 shows the large differences that currently exist in the rates of corporation tax paid throughout the Community. This is further complicated by the fact that some countries also impose local taxes on company income and more importantly because three different corporate tax systems operate throughout the Community.

A classical or separate tax system requires that the taxing of corporate and personal incomes are completely separated. Thus profits distributed to shareholders will first be taxed as company income and then separately as shareholders' personal income. Thus distributed profits are in effect taxed twice while profits retained by the company are only taxed once. In contrast, in the split-rate system retained profits are taxed at a higher rate than distributed profits to allow for the extra tax paid on them by shareholders.

The final system is called the imputation or tax credit system and was first adopted by France in 1953, and is now used, at least partially, by nine of the twelve member states. Basically the system allows all or part of the corporation tax paid on distributed profits as a tax credit against personal income-tax liability. A major problem with the imputation system concerns the treatment of the tax credit. Should a Dutch shareholder in a British company residing in The Netherlands receive a personal tax credit against Dutch income tax when corporation tax has been paid in Britain?

Corporation tax is currently charged at a standard rate on all operations within a member state regardless of who owns the company, i.e. on a source basis. In addition, most countries also charge a withholding tax on all dividends or interest payments that are distributed to either shareholders or a parent company in another country,[21] which can distort a company's decision of where to invest and so is incompatible with CIN.

Harmonization progress to date

As mentioned earlier, progress on reforming corporation taxation to move towards a harmonized tax structure has been very limited. The Neumark Committee Report of 1963 proposed the introduction of a split rate system whilst the Van den Tempel report of 1971[22] recommended the adoption of a classical system, but this was not the end of the story. A draft directive in 1975 advocated the adoption of the imputation system following the adoption of that system by the majority of member states and the draft directive further proposed harmonization of tax rates within a 45–55 per cent band.[23]

The 1975 proposals were concerned with the system of tax and the rates but not the tax base and so a further preliminary draft proposal was made in 1988. This deals with aspects such as allowances for depreciation and the methods of calculating commercial profits. If adopted it would have allowed for little difference between corporate tax systems in member states.

However, apparently in the spirit of the new approach to Community integration, the 1975 proposal for fiscal harmonization was withdrawn on 20 April 1990. The harmonization route has thus been abandoned in preference to 'a reliance on the coordination and approximation of national policies', which is a euphemism for a market-led approach. This approach has been most closely linked with that supported by the British government and is based on the belief that after 1992, market forces will operate to bring corporate tax systems into line since otherwise high-tax countries will lose their competitive position.

The 1990 proposals include the establishment of a committee to make a report within a year with a view to answering the following questions: do the current systems result in distortions in investment decisions now and potentially post-1992?; and can market forces alone can be expected to remove any perceived distortions should they be seen to exist? If not will the Community need to devise measures to remove them?

Cross-frontier business arrangements

As we indicated in chapter 1 the Community, as part of its industrial policy, has for a long time been endeavouring to create the legal and fiscal conditions to enable companies to conduct their affairs on a Community-wide basis without discrimmination or inhibition. On the legal front the Commission's approach has been to seek approval for a company law directive which would harmonize national company laws so that international mergers are possible; and for a regulation which would set up a system of European company law (hence the *Societas Europea*) alongside national company laws. Both these measures were identified in the Cockfield Report.

However, these legal measures are not of immediate relevance: what is of relevance is that the Commission has for a long period also been endeavouring to eliminate fiscal barriers which have discriminated against cross-frontier operations and these particular aims have been at the forefront of the Commission's proposals. First, companies should be able to organize themselves so that the parent might be located in one member state and the subsidiary (or subsidiaries) might be located in another (or others) without fiscal discrimination. This has not been the case since, as we have seen, subsidiaries have been required to deduct withholding tax when making payments to parents. Second, the Commission has sought to sweep away fiscal inhibitions which arise when a company in one member state acquires a company in another member state. In practice and in comparison with domestic transactions such acquisitions have been discriminated against, since the fiscal authorities have tended to demand immediate payment of capital-gains tax arising at the time of the transaction. If the tax liability was substantial it could make the cost of the amalgamation prohibitive.

Proposals to counter these problems were put forward as early as 1969, an interesting example of the degree to which the SEM had stagnated, and the Cockfield Report singled out these issues for action. They were dealt with in 1990 when the Council of Ministers adopted two directives whereby subsidiaries would no longer be required to deduct withholding tax when making payments to parents. Germany has until 1996 to comply with this directive.[24] Another directive provided that capital-gains tax arising in connection with cross-border acquisitions would no longer immediately attract capital gains in the country of the target – the tax could be deferred provided certain conditions were fulfilled.[25] In addition a Convention was also signed establishing a body to arbitrate in respect of transfer payments disputes concerning companies operating in more than one member state.[26]

This had first been proposed in 1976 and was also identified as as area for action in the Cockfield Report.

Assessment

As with many areas of taxation reform, it is not possible to achieve all desirable characteristics, namely economic efficiency, administrative simplicity and political acceptability which in this case means a degree of fiscal sovereignty. Complete harmonization achieves the former but means that sovereignty has to be foregone, while a residence-based or world-wide tax system achieves sovereignty but not efficiency.

The world-wide tax system requires domestic residents to be taxed on all of their investment income irrespective of the country of origin of that income. However, the 1990 proposals removed the worst aspects of double taxation but still left the problems of disparate tax rates and so forth. It remains to be seen whether rates become more closely aligned after 1992: if, following the introduction of the Commission's proposals, distortions still exist, a range of alternative reforms which may deal with the problem have been suggested by Devereux and Pearson[27] or Giovannini.[28]

Conclusions

During the late 1980s there was a noticeable shift in emphasis in the Commission's approach to fiscal matters. The earlier approach was to attempt to push the Community towards a system of complete fiscal harmonization. The Cockfield Report changed this to fiscal approximation and then, as the actual date for completion of the internal market approached, the expediency approach has changed the emphasis yet again towards the less rigid desire to simply remove fiscal frontiers and allow market forces to force competing nations to move their fiscal systems closer together.

One could argue that any move towards harmonization of disparate, well-established and jealously guarded fiscal structures was a major achievement and thus the Commission could rightly congratulate itself on progress to date. On the other hand the Community is still a long way from achieving the fiscal neutrality that will allow the free movement of goods and services required for completion of the internal market. Even if the much simpler desire of changing indirect taxes from the destination to the origin principle is considered we can see that this is unlikely to be achieved, even by December 1996, given the large amount of revenue reallocation it is likely to cause.

Large differences still exist in the key areas (from the Commission's viewpoint) of VAT and excise duty. However, most public finance commentators argue that differences in direct tax systems are more likely to cause market distortion than indirect taxes and that this is particularly relevant for company taxation as people are less mobile than companies. As we have seen progress in this area has been poor, in part because current systems of raising corporate taxation seem outdated in the modern world of multinational companies and international mergers. It is difficult to see what can be done in this area unless a totally new approach to taxing company profits is found. More importantly the Commission appears to have almost totally ignored local taxation together with income taxation and social security contributions. In the words of the Commission itself:

> Taxation is an important and, at the same time, difficult aspect of the programme for completing the internal market: important because, without proper rules governing the tax treatment of cross-frontier transactions, tax barriers would remain in place, and difficult because any decision relating to taxation has immediate repercussions for national budgets. The unanimity required by the Council of Ministers compounds the difficulty.[29]

Recently, there have been limited signs that finance ministers are beginning to accept the need to accept fiscal changes which will enable the internal market to work more efficiently. The Commission has pointed to agreements made in 1990 concerning the tax arrangements for transnational cooperation between firms. There is still a long way to go and it is difficult to see how complete agreement on fiscal matters can be achieved while member states are allowed to retain significant amounts of fiscal sovereignty.

Chapter 5

Banking and financial services

David T. Llewellyn

Introduction

In this chapter and the next the focus is upon services and the impact of the SEA in liberalizing their provision as part of the 1992 programme.

The basic elements of a common market for financial services were contained in the Rome Treaty: the right of establishment, Article 52; the freedom to supply services across borders, Article 59; and the free movement of capital, Article 67. However, the financial services sector (banking, insurance, fund management and investment services) has been one of the areas where in practice progress has been slowest; despite the treaty provisions, a comprehensive common market for such services did not emerge. The three main impediments have been exchange control limiting the free movement of capital, limitations on cross-border trade in financial services, and various barriers to the free location of financial institutions and other suppliers of financial services.

It needs to be established at the outset, however, that the freedom to provide services (Article 59) has always been a limited one. The treaty itself contained some general exceptions. In addition, the European Court of Justice formulated and developed an exception to the freedom to provide services. The judicial exception (first formulated in the *Van Binsbergen* case, and as subsequently applied and developed) established that specific regulatory requirements imposed on a cross-border supplier of services were allowed, provided four conditions were fulfilled. These included that the rules were objectively justified by the general interest; that such rules were also applied to domestic suppliers of the service; that the cross-border supplier would not be subject to comparable rules in its home country; and that the host country would be unable to apply other, less restrictive, measures to achieve the same end (the principle of proportionality). The purpose of the judicial exception was to submit, where necessary in the public interest, the cross-frontier suppliers of services to the same regulatory system as that imposed on domestic suppliers.

In the 1985 Cockfield Report[1] high priority was given to the freeing of international capital movements. This was viewed not only as an integral part of the full development of a common market in financial services but also as essential for the completion of the internal market in all its dimensions, and was argued on three grounds. First, freedom of capital movements was viewed as a necessary condition for the achievement of a totally integrated market for all goods and services and for promoting the free movement of labour across borders. Second, it was seen as a powerful incentive for governments to adopt economic policies conducive to price and exchange rate stability, which in turn were viewed as prerequisites for the eventual achievement of full EMU. Third, opening up the EC's capital market was seen as widening the freedom of choice for European investors and as contributing to a more efficient allocation of savings and hence greater welfare. In the Cockfield Report the role of financial services in the overall plan for the completion of the internal market was emphasized: 'the liberalization of financial services, linked to that of capital movements, will represent a major step towards Community financial integration and the widening of the Internal Market. The accent is now put increasingly on the free circulation of "financial products", made ever easier by developments of technology'.[2] The Cockfield Report outlined detailed legislative requirements which initially included around 300 specific proposals to remove obstacles to the development of a true internal market in the EC.

In the following section an outline is made of the special characteristics of finance which distinguish it from other industries, some of which have in the past impeded the evolution of an internal market in financial services. Existing barriers to intra-EC trade in financial services have mainly taken the form of restrictions on entry and access together with specific regulations inhibiting cross-border trade (such as in insurance). Compared with markets in goods, freedom to supply financial services, most especially to the personal sector, requires freedom of location as a more important condition than freedom of trade. A UK resident can easily buy a German car without the producer locating in the UK; on the other hand, if he plans to conduct his normal day-to-day banking business with a German bank, the branch needs in practice to be located in the UK. Though technology is undermining this requirement, it still remains the case that for many retail financial services the supplier needs to be physically located near to the customer. This is why much of the following discussion emphasizes freedom to locate.

In all countries finance is more highly regulated than most other industries, for consumer protection and systemic reasons. In practice such regulation can have the effect of impeding both free location and cross-border trade in financial services, and differences in regulation can create competitive distortions between different nationalities of banks.[3] In general, more lightly regulated banks have a competitive advantage over more stringently regulated institutions. Nevertheless, as emphasized by a former member of the Commission,[4] there is no prospect that banks will cease to be regulated, or that national regulatory and supervisory authorities will be replaced by a central agency. The new strategy contained in the Cockfield Report implied such an approach.

Although the focus of this chapter is upon the specific EC dimension of integration in financial services, the discussion must be set in the context of important global trends in finance. A major aspect of this is that competitive pressures in many aspects of finance, most especially related to wholesale banking and securities trading, have become global, and the factors underlying this trend – financial innovation, technology, securitization, competitive pressures, changes in regulation, and so on – do not have a specifically EC dimension.[5] The domain of competition in some aspects of finance has already become greater than the EC and, as discussed in a later section, this has implications for the extent of the changes which might be expected to emerge after 1992.

A second global dimension is regulation. In many countries regulation in finance has been changing substantially,[6] with a major shift in emphasis towards encouraging more competition and enhancing the role of market mechanisms. A higher priority has been given to raising efficiency in the financial sector and accepting that this requires more competitive conditions. In many countries deregulation has allowed financial institutions to diversify; regulatory attitudes to competition in finance have changed, as there is a strand in the history of regulation based upon the alleged dangers of excessive competition.[7] Almost universally, regulators have moved in the direction of encouraging and allowing more competition in finance: the emphasis has switched away from imposing anti-competitive mechanisms and condoning restrictive practices, cartels, and collusive agreements, towards the benefits of efficiency in finance via competition and the free play of market mechanisms. Competitive pressures have intensified almost universally in national financial systems.

A third, and related aspect is that, most especially in banking, regulation coordination has become global rather than Community-wide. The Basle capital convergence arrangements to be applied to banks, (by coincidence by 1992), relate to banks in all major industrial countries.[8] The EC requirements for bank capital have been based upon this global agreement. This again emphasizes that in many aspects of finance competitive pressures, and hence the regulatory implications, have become global in nature and not specifically European.

It is also evident that many national financial systems, including many in the EC, have been experiencing major structural changes induced by the combined pressures of competition, changes in regulation, technology and new strategic objectives of financial institutions. A universal trend has been towards diversification in the range of financial services offered by banks and other institutions,[9] and a particular feature evident in many countries has been the merging of banking and insurance. These trends have major significance for the EC because many of the directives focused on specific aspects of finance (banking, insurance) now relate not to exclusively specialist financial institutions but to financial conglomerates. The issue therefore arises as to whether competitive distortions can arise, because in some cases the services are provided by specialists and in others by highly diversified financial institutions. This complicates the regulatory process and the formulation of consistent directives because some countries adopt the institutional approach, whereby a bank regulator regulates everything that a bank does; while in others the functional approach predominates, where the focus is upon each function with a common regime and agency established for all institutions supplying each service. This has become a controversial issue in the Investment Services Directive where in some countries securities trading is conducted by specialist, separately capitalized institutions, whereas in others it is part of the business of universal banks.

The central role of finance

Care should be applied when considering data on the size of the financial sector. Financial services are different from most goods and services in that they are not demanded for their own sake and in this they are analogous to medical services.[10] Thus a high proportion of GNP devoted to banking or insurance may reflect either a strong demand for such services or an

Table 5.1 Economic dimensions of the financial services sector (1985)[1]

	Gross value-added as a % of GDP[2]	Employment as a % of total employment[3]	Compensation of employees as a % of total for the economy
B	5.7	3.8	6.3
D	5.4	3.0	4.4
E	6.4	2.8	6.7
F	4.3	2.8	3.8
I	4.9	1.8	5.6
L[4]	14.9	5.7	12.2
NL	5.2	3.7	4.9
UK	11.8	3.7	8.5
EUR 8[5]	6.4	2.9	6.2

Source: M. Emerson et al., 'The Economics of 1992', European Economy, no. 35, 1988, p. 87.
Notes: [1] Defined in the narrow sense as credit and insurance institutions.
         [2] Including net interest payments.
         [3] Employees in employment plus the self-employed.
         [4] 1982.
         [5] This aggregate accounted for 95 per cent of total Community GDP in 1985.

inefficient banking or insurance industry. Nevertheless, the data in Table 5.1 indicate that the financial sectors are significant both in terms of employment and their contribution to the economy. As the financial sector is used by all agents in the economy, and has an input into all industries, its efficiency has a potentially significant impact on overall economic performance. If the financial sector is inefficient in the provision of its basic services – such as financial intermediation, insurance, the payments system, fund management, facilities for changing the composition of financial portfolios, the pricing and redistribution of risks – substantial costs can be imposed upon the economy in absorption of resources, inefficient allocation of savings and investment, and suboptimal allocation of resources. Llewellyn[11] has considered the requirements of an efficient financial system and the role of competition in determining efficiency. If, as argued here, finance has been relatively protected, either by regulation or limits to competition, then the 1992 arrangements could have particular significance in finance. The Cecchini Report[12] noted that though financial services account on average for only 7 per cent of GNP, they could produce up to half the overall benefits to be derived from the completion of the internal market (see Table 5.2). A later section of the report casts doubt on the size of these benefits.

There are several particular characteristics of financial services in general, and banking in particular, which are not relevant for other industries and which have both impeded the development of the internal market in financial

Table 5.2 Macro-economic consequences of EC market integration for the community in the medium term. (This table shows the positive or negative effects on GDP, consumer prices etc., of a number of measures connected with the single market: abolition of customs formalities, open public procurement, liberalization of financial services, and supply-side effects.)

	Abolition of customs formalities	Open public procurement	Liberalization of financial services	Supply-side[1] effects	Total
GDP (%)	0.4	0.5	1.5	2.1	4.5
Consumer prices (%)	−1.0	−1.4	−1.4	−2.3	−6.1
Employment (thousands)	200	350	400	850	1800
Budgetary balance (% of GDP)	0.2	0.3	1.1	0.6	2.2
External balance (% of GDP)	0.2	0.1	0.3	0.4	1.0

Source: European Communities Commission, *The European Financial Common Market*, OOPEC, Luxembourg, 1989, p. 8.
Notes: [1] Economies of scale, increased competition, etc.

services, and also influenced the approach to its future evolution. These include:

(a) The central role of financial services in the economy which means that governments and regulatory authorities are reluctant to allow domination by foreign institutions.

(b) Finance is more regulated than other industries for systemic and consumer protection reasons. This has three immediate implications for the EC internal market: regulatory arrangements vary substantially between members; regulation has implications for competitiveness; and the issue arises as to which regulatory regime applies if an institution opens branches in another country or sells services across borders. Regulatory authorities will need to be assured that services are provided under suitable prudential standards irrespective of the nationality of the supplier.

(c) There is a powerful systemic dimension to finance and its regulation. Because of the central importance of confidence and the danger of contagion, the costs of failure of a bank (and some other financial firms) may exceed the costs to the firm itself.[13] Thus the efficient and acceptable regulation of all financial institutions in a country, irrespective of their nationality, is systemic. The French authorities would be concerned at the failure of an Italian bank in France because of its wider systemic implications as well as the interests of the bank's customers. This systemic dimension means that a regulatory or supervisory authority has an interest in the regulatory standards of other member countries, and may wish to impose its own requirements on foreign institutions located within its jurisdiction.

(d) Attitudes to competition are frequently different in finance for reasons noted earlier. Regulation may be directly anti-competitive in nature, and restrictive practices and other anti-competitive mechanisms may be condoned more readily in finance than in other areas of the economy. Mitchell[14] notes that, in a number of Community countries, banks and insurance companies do not fall within normal competition policy law and procedures.

(e) Location rather than cross-border trade is relatively more important in (especially retail) financial services than in most other industries. Thus, all countries (irrespective of size and any economies-of-scale that might exist) have banks and insurance companies whereas not all countries in the EC have a motor industry. The significance of this is considered in a later section.

(f) The reputation and information advantages of financial institutions are an important and overwhelming aspect of their business which may create a bias in favour of indigenous institutions.

Central to many of these special characteristics is regulation. Given that the requirement for regulation and supervision is not in dispute, two immediate issues arise. Does a common market in finance require a single regulatory authority? And if national authorities are to be retained, which regulatory authority's jurisdiction applies when services are sold cross-border, or when a foreign institution is located in the domestic economy: should it be the host (i.e. where the branch or customer is located) or home (where the institution is registered or licenced) country regulator, and what should be the division of responsibility?

It is to be expected that governments would, for both systemic and consumer protection reasons, be hesitant to allow cross-border imports of financial services or for foreign firms to operate in their markets if there were doubts about the regulatory arrangements of the home regulator. The question over the division of responsibility arises because some aspects of regulation are more efficiently conducted by the host while others by the home regulator. It is immediately apparent that there is ample scope for demarcation disputes and this is one reason why progress has been slow in evolving a common market in finance. Thus questions related to the fitness and properness of managers, capital adequacy of institutions, and ownership rules (such as whether a bank can be owned by a non-finance company, or an insurance company by a bank) – are more appropriately conducted on a home country principle (by the regulatory arrangements of the country in which institutions are incorporated). There is less certainty about 'conduct of business' rules where some are probably most efficiently imposed by the home country. While others, such as those related to the internal structure and systems of a firm, such as business rules with respect to how it conducts business with its customers, might more appropriately be put under the jurisdiction of the host authority. As noted by Clark[15] 'For all these reasons, the implementation of Community-wide regulatory arrangements in practice has come to depend first, on securing an acceptable minimum degree of harmonization between home country regimes and second, on understandings that certain aspects of regulation will, at least for the time being, remain the responsibility of host country authorities'.

A common market

A common market implies both freedom to trade (free of imposed and regulatory barriers) and freedom of location in member states. There should be no government regulations obstructing neutrality between buying financial services from domestic institutions, foreign institutions located in the consumer's country, or on a cross-border basis. This does not mean that other economic or market barriers do not exist to either trade or location and, as discussed below, these may be significant in finance. There are five main elements to a common market in finance: freedom to locate anywhere in the market area whether by branches or incorporated subsidiaries; freedom to supply services anywhere in the market without the necessity of specific authorisation; freedom of consumers to buy financial services from anywhere in the market and from any nationality of suppliers; the absence of exchange controls limiting the free movement of capital; and a single securities market, in that investors can issue and trade securities across national frontiers freely and without imposed hindrances.

Substantial imposed barriers have existed in financial services and some are given in Tables 5.3 and 5.4. In some areas the barriers may in practice be greater than indicated: first, though only Spain imposes any limits on the establishment of branches, formal authorization has been needed, dedicated capital has had to be provided (except in the UK), and branching has been on the basis of host-country regulation applying 'national treatment'. In other words a foreign institution has been able to undertake only that business in a country that the indigenous institutions have been lawfully able to conduct even if the home country has allowed a wider range of business. Second, while participation and acquisition seems to have been reasonably free, in practice regulators and governments have placed impediments to such purchases, especially if major domestic banks and other institutions are the target of foreign purchase, and if a major part of a financial sector would thereby pass into foreign control. Most countries require shareholdings in banks above a certain level to be notified, and in practice there may be substantial resistance to the foreign domination of key areas of finance. A Price Waterhouse study[16] concluded that there is control over the acquisition of domestic banks by foreign entities in all EC countries. The Governor of the Bank of England[17] has argued: 'It is not to be contemplated that one of the clearing banks should fall into foreign hands'. It is also the case in practice that it is as much the margin of discretion with which detailed regulations are applied that determines competitive standing of a foreign institution as the regulations *per se*.

Any limits on location and cross-border trade in financial services have the effect of limiting competition. The lower degree of competition that this implies might sustain several sub optimum market characteristics such

Table 5.3 Summary of restrictions in financial markets between EEC countries

	Establishment of branches	Participation and acquisition	Exchange controls
Belgium	none	none	yes
France	none	>20%	yes
Germany	none	none	none
Italy	none	none	yes
Luxembourg	none	none	yes
Netherlands	none	none	none
Spain	yes	>50%	yes
UK	none	none	none

Source: V. Grilli, 'Europe 1992: Issues and Prospects for the Financial Markets, *Economic Policy*, October 1989, p. 395.

Table 5.4 Barriers to integration in financial markets

Barriers to establishment in banking:
1   Restrictions on the legal form banks may adopt.
2   Limitations on the number of branches that may be established.
3   Restrictions on the take-over of domestic banks.
4   Restrictions of equity or other control of domestic banks.

Barriers to operating conditions in banking:
1   The need to maintain separate capital funds.
2   Differences in the definition of 'own capital' funds.
3   The need to maintain certain capital-asset ratios.
4   Exchange controls.

Barriers to competing for business in banking:
1   Limitations on services offered.
2   Restrictions on local retail banking.
3   Restrictions on acquisition of securities and other assets.

Barriers to establishment in insurance:
1   Lack of harmonization of licensing procedures.
2   Lack of harmonization in the constitution of technical reserves.

Barriers to operating conditions and competing for business in insurance:
1   Direct insurance: restrictions on the placement of contracts with non-established insurers.
2   Co insurance: establishment of a permanent presence imposed on lead-insurers.
3   Custom and practice in government procurement policies.
4   Lack of harmonization in the supervision of insurance concerns.
5   Reinsurance: compulsory or voluntary cessation of a percentage of contracts to a central pool or prescribed establishment.
6   Lack of harmonization in the fiscal treatment of insurance contracts and premiums.

Barriers to establishment in securities:
1   Membership of some stock exchanges limited to national citizens.
2   Constraints on the establishment of offices to solicit and carry out business in secondary markets.
3   Restrictions on the take-over of or equity participation in domestic institutions.
4   Limitations on the establishment of securities firms in a universal banking system.

Barriers to operating conditions in securities:
1   Exchange controls and other equivalent measures which prevent or limit the purchase of foreign securities.
2   Conflicting national prudential requirements for investors' protection.
3   Discriminatory taxes on the purchase of foreign securities.

Barriers to competing for business in securities:
1   Limited access to primary markets in terms of lead management of domestic issues.
2   Restricted access to secondary markets because of national stockbroker monopolies on some stock exchanges.
3   Restrictions on dealing with investing public.

Source: European Communities Commission, *Research on the 'Cost of Non-Europe', Basic Findings, The Cost of 'Non-Europe' in Financial Services* (Price Waterhouse), vol. 9, Luxembourg, 1988, p. 62.

as: non-market clearing price structures in credit markets; cross-subsidies; costs and profits which are higher than the competitive or contestable bench-mark; restrictive practices, cartels and collusive agreements; X-inefficiencies, etc. The evidence indicates that several of these characteristics of limited competition are evident in some EC countries. If such competitive impediments are removed some, if not all, of these features should be competed away and as such might be viewed as the consumers' benefit from competition.[18] In practice the effects in finance are likely to be less because there are several economic barriers to contestability and the emergence of a perfectly competitive outcome.

The Cecchini Report and the absence of a financial common market

A distinction can be drawn between wholesale and retail banking. In practice the competitive environment in wholesale and corporate sector banking has intensified more than in retail banking though the latter has not been immune. The net result is that market conditions in much wholesale and corporate banking business have become extremely competitive and profit margins in general are wider in retail than in wholesale business. There are two main reasons for this: the corporate sector has access to a larger number of banks than the personal sector; and for corporate business, the capital market is a potential competitor to banks. The corporate sector also has international banking and capital market options which further intensify competitive pressures on the banks' corporate sector business. In the process, a two-tier structure of banking has emerged in which the corporate sector increasingly has global options while the financial mediation of the retail and personal sector is still limited mainly within national financial systems. This is partly because, despite developments in technology, servicing the retail sector frequently still requires a branch network, and the size of individual transactions is small; thus while competition and integration in wholesale banking has effectively become global in nature, retail banking remains fragmented.

Even for corporate business, but especially in the provision of retail financial services, EC national financial systems are far from totally integrated, as there remain factors which maintain significant differences between them – including differences in regulation, taxation, the competitive environment, exchange control and the role of the state. The Cecchini Report attempted to quantify the possible impact on prices of measures to complete the internal market in financial services and these are summarized in Table 5.5, though qualified later. On the face of it, prices seem set to fall furthest in Belgium, France, Italy and Spain. The potential gains in the financial sector seem to be substantial given the wide disparities in prices for apparently standardized financial products between member states. Estimates of the potential gains based on price convergence, are given in Table 5.6.

The evidence seems to indicate wide differences in the price of standardized financial services between the EC countries. The differences vary between both products and countries. In general, the differences are greater in retail financial services than in wholesale services for reasons suggested earlier. There are particularly wide price differences for motor insurance, home

Table 5.5 Estimate of potential falls in financial product prices as a result of completing the internal market

%

	B	D	E	F	I	L	NL	UK
1. Percentage differences in prices of financial products compared with the average of the four lowest observations[1]								
Banking								
Consumer credit	−41	136	39	105	:3	−26	31	121
Credit cards	79	60	26	−30	89	−12	43	16
Mortgages	31	57	118	78	−4	:3	6	−20
Letters of credit	22	−10	59	−7	9	27	17	8
Foreign exchange	6	31	196	56	23	33	−46	16
Travellers cheques	35	−7	30	39	22	−7	33	−7
Commercial loans	−5	6	19	−7	9	6	43	46
Insurance								
Life	78	5	37	33	83	66	−9	−30
Home	−16	3	−4	39	81	57	17	90
Motor	30	15	100	9	148	77	−7	−17
Commercial, fire, theft	−9	43	24	153	245	−15	−1	27
Public liability	13	47	60	117	77	9	−16	−7
Securities								
Private equity	36	7	65	−13	− 3	7	114	123
Private gilts	14	90	217	21	−63	27	161	36
Institutional equity	26	69	153	−5	47	68	26	−47
Institutional gilts	284	−4	60	57	92	−36	21	:3
2 Theoretical, potential price reductions[1]								
Banking	15	33	34	25	18	16	10	18
Insurance	31	10	32	24	51	37	1	4
Securities	52	11	44	23	33	9	18	12
Total	23	25	34	24	29	17	9	13
3. Indicative price reductions[2]								
All financial services								
Range	6–16	5–15	16–26	7–17	9–19	3–13	0–9	2–12
Centre of range	11	10	21	12	14	8	4	7

Source: M. Emerson *et. al*, 'The Economics of 1992', *European Economy*, no. 35, 1988, p. 91.

Notes: 1 The figures in part 1 of the table show the extent to which financial product prices, in each country, are above a low reference level. Each of these price differences implies a theoretical potential price fall from existing price levels to the low reference level. Part 2 sets down the weighted averages of the theoretical potential falls for each sub-sector.

2 Indicative price falls are based upon a scaling down of the theoretical potential price reductions, taking into account roughly the extent to which perfectly competitive and integrated conditions will not be attained, plus other information for each financial services sub-sector, such as gross margins and administrative costs as a proportion of total costs.

3 Observations for consumer credit in Italy and mortgages in Luxembourg were not obtained, and have been represented by mechanical estimates in the calculations of the larger aggregates. The data for institutional gilts transactions in the UK were not available on a comparable basis, and so the figures for institutional equity transactions were used in the calculations.

Table 5.6 Estimated gains resulting from the indicative price reductions for financial services

	Average indicative price reduction %	Direct impact on value-added for financial services (million ECU and as % of GDP)		Gain in consumer surplus as a result of average indicative price reduction[1] (million ECU and as % GDP)	
B	11	656	0.6	685	0.7
D	10	4 442	0.5	4 619	0.6
E	21	2 925	1.4	3 189	1.5
F	12	3 513	0.5	3 683	0.5
I	14	3 780	0.7	3 996	0.7
L	8	43	1.2	44	1.2
NL	4	341	0.2	347	0.2
UK	7	4 917	0.8	5 051	0.8
EUR 8	10	20 617	0.7	21614	0.7

Source: M. Emerson *et al.*, 'The Economics of 1992', *European Economy*, no. 35, 1988, p. 92.
Notes: 1   Based on the assumption that the elasticity of demand for financial services is 0.75.

loans, consumer credit and some securities. Notable in consumer credit is the UK where, although in general the there are comparatively low prices for financial services, the price of consumer credit, abstracting from the level of interest rates, is exceptionally high.

This suggests there are significant gains to be secured through further integration and competition in finance. However, wide price differences are only in part due to a lack of integration and an indication of the scope for competition to eliminate differences in the prices of financial services between countries. Prices in financial services can vary for five general reasons:

(a) differences in efficiency in different financial systems;
(b) different regulatory taxes imposed in different countries;
(c) differences in the competitive environment, enabling a higher level of costs and semi-monopoly profits or rents in one system compared with another to be sustained;
(d) different structures of cross-subsidies within banks and other financial institutions;
(e) unexploited economies of scale.

In principle a high price of financial services in one national system should be competed away either through the entry into the domestic system of foreign firms, or by the users of financial services using foreign markets and institutions. This normal competitive process could be impeded, however, by exchange control, location costs, regulation and entry barriers together with information and transaction costs.

The Cecchini study predicted substantial benefits to be derived from more EC integration of banking and financial markets. It simulates the impact on consumer surplus of the reduction in prices to the lowest level in the EC. There are three major reservations to the Cecchini calculations. First, the accuracy of the methodology of measuring true price differences is questionable, and second, it contains an implicit assumption that it is predominantly lack of competition that accounts for the observed price differences. Third, it assumes that the 1992 arrangements will in fact raise competitive pressures in financial systems and that these will equalize prices. For the first point the calculations are based upon identifying standardized financial products and comparing each country's prices with the average of the lowest four prices for the product, making a comparison with a bench-mark that no consumer is actually paying. In practice, products cannot be standardized and so comparison is not made precisely for identical products. For instance, in insurance markets price differences will also reflect differences in risk. In addition, for many products, banks and other institutions adopt relationship pricing where prices are set with reference to the customer's total business with the firm; also, there are many cross-subsidies in pricing and many specific financial products cannot be unbundled from packages. Thus the rate of interest received on current accounts may be determined by the average amount held in the account and the existence or level of charges may also be related to the average or minimum size of balances.

As for the second point in the critique of the Cecchini methodology, there are many factors other than lack of competition or financial integration that may account for price differences. Given the major differences in institutional structure, price differences may reflect factors other than lack of competition, contestibility or differences in basic efficiency. Thus products may be bundled together and extensive cross-subsidies applied by a multi-product financial institution operating in markets with different cohorts of customers. In this case, although some cross-subsidies reflect differences in competitive conditions between markets[19] it would be misleading to ascribe differences in prices of individual products or services as evidence of the general lack of competition in certain markets, or to assume that competition would produce an equalization of prices between member countries. As there are also significant differences in prices for specific financial products within countries, it is unlikely that removal of regulatory and other imposed barriers would result in a single price throughout the EC.

Third, even if price differences do reflect differences in the competitive environment, because of economic barriers they may not be competed away by foreign entry. Liberalization does not necessarily increase competition enough to force price equalization, and does not in itself guarantee that competitive conditions will be equalized between member states. For economic reasons (entry costs, scale constraints,) financial and banking markets may remain partially segmented (as in the retail sector) without formal controls, regulation barriers, or imposed entry restrictions – such barriers clearly act as a competitive advantage to incumbents.

Overall, the Cecchini Report calculations set an upper limit to the benefits of a common market in financial services and the implied equalization of competitive conditions. Regulation and the lack of integration were not the only sources of price differences, which, even for standardized products, would not be eliminated. Calculated welfare gains based on the assumption that they will be eliminated overstate the potential gains. In a common market potential competition tends to discipline established firms since they are vulnerable to hit and run strategies – though this discipline, to be effective, requires that there are no sunk costs. In practice contestability may be limited in retail banking because of the high cost of developing a branch network (access to consumers), economies of scale, and technology costs of developing competitive networks such as Automatic Teller Machines (ATMs) which have become a standard feature of retail banking. Also the high costs and inconvenience of customers switching their banks (changing standing order arrangements, etc.), and the reputation and information advantages of incumbents all limit contestability.

The benefits

This is not to deny the potential benefits of the 1992 arrangements. It is well established that some aspects of some EC financial systems are inefficient; lack competition; have a bias against price competition; have a structure of cartels, restrictive practices and collusive agreements (often condoned by the regulatory authorities); have been subject to 'regulatory capture'; have protective regulatory arrangements, high costs and profits; and maintain pricing structures which sustain excess demand for credit. It is to be expected that, notwithstanding the economic barriers to entry and trade noted earlier, several of these should be competed away as a result of the 1992 arrangements, either by actual entry, cross-border trade, or by enhanced contestability. In a study of banking in the US, Fraser and Rose[20] found that despite consumer loyalty the entry of a new independent bank brings about significant changes in the nature of banking services offered to the local community by established banks.

The Cecchini Report indicated a wider range of benefits other than the immediate gain to the consumer through lower prices. General efficiency in the economy should benefit as financial services are a major input into industry. It was estimated that 50 per cent of the output of banking and insurance services represented intermediate purchases, and credit and insurance services accounted for about 6 per cent of all intermediate inputs into industry (abstracting from the level of interest rates). A further beneficial effect of more EC competition in financial services was through increased access to a wider range of markets, instruments and services. Enhanced possibilities of portfolio diversification, both for assets and liabilities should have the general effect of lowering the overall level of risk at each rate of return, and in the process should lower some risk premia, and exchange controls inhibit the selection of an optimum investment portfolio. The Price Waterhouse study suggested that EC capital markets are not fully integrated, in the sense that rates of return do not fully reflect all diversification possibilities, and Cho, Eun and Senbet[21] came to the same conclusion. If risks on different assets are less than perfectly correlated, the wider the range of investment options available, the better is the risk-reward trade-off. Further integration should, therefore, raise welfare either by reducing risk for each expected rate of return or raise the latter for any chosen degree of risk. As the correlation between stock markets is low, it is possible to gain a significant advantage from international portfolio diversification, to the extent that, as a result of the completion of the internal market, capital would be allocated more efficiently and there should be further generalized benefits to the economy as a whole.

Competitive structures, the structure of financial systems and regulatory arrangements in EC member states are less homogeneous in finance than most other industries. The impact of 1992 is likely, therefore, to vary considerably between member countries, and the general impact is likely to be greatest in those countries where internal regulation is most constraining, where internal competitive pressures are weakest, and where entry barriers have been most substantial. On this basis the greatest impact within the EEC is likely to be experienced in Spain where prices are particularly high due to a combination of restrictive regulation and a generally uncompetitive market environment. Italy, France, Belgium and Germany are intermediate cases, while prices are generally most competitive in Luxembourg, the UK and The Netherlands.

In the final analysis, 1992 is essentially about competition. Competitive pressures may be weak within a financial system for several reasons. First, regulation (especially when it imposes restrictions on the range of business) is frequently anti-competitive in nature, either by design or effect. Second, self-imposed regulation (via cartels and other restrictive practices) has the same effect. Third, the persuasive manner in which moral influence is exercised by the policy authorities may also have the effect of inhibiting competition and innovation. Fourth, the inefficiencies and profits secured through these routes are frequently not competed away by foreign competition, again due to entry barriers. Llewellyn[22] considers what would normally be predicted in an industry subject to more competition.

If the same applies to the finance industry, and the 1992 arrangements imply more competition, the analysis indicates what should be expected in banking and financial services as a result of further European integration. In this sense these are indications of what is likely to happen in the EC following the moves towards the completion of the internal market by 1992, and how the consumer might be expected to benefit.

When an industry is subject to more competition several changes are likely:

(a) Firms would tend to become more efficient, the average efficiency of the industry rises, and this is reflected in prices.

(b) The pricing of the product would tend to eliminate any excess demand due to prices being set below the market clearing level. Competitors compete away the excess demand.

(c) Internal cross-subsidies, and all pricing structures not based on cost or risk considerations, would tend to disappear under the pressure of competition. This is because new competitors target the subsidizing parts of the business (where prices and profits are uncompetitively high) and ignore the subsidized business. This competition normally forces a change in pricing between the two parts of the business.

(d) The industry often experiences more mergers as the less efficient firms find the competitive environment too demanding.

(e) There is pressure towards the elimination of any cartel that might exist over the fixing of the industry's prices. Cartels are effective only if the industry is cohesive and not subject to external competition.

(f) Overall profitability tends to decline.

(g) Restrictive practices tend to be competed away through circumvention as new competitors do not enforce traditional restrictive practices. There are many restrictive practices or uncompetitive mechanisms in many European financial systems. They can be very profitable for those practising them which is why they exist, and many are condoned and even encouraged by regulatory authorities.

(h) Firms seek to diversify the range of business as competition becomes more intense in traditional business areas.

(i) The overall risk of the industry is likely to increase.

(j) At some stage competition forces firms to leave the industry though, for systemic reasons, this is more problematic in finance than most other industries.

Llewellyn[23] gives examples of how each of these emerged during the 1980s due to enhanced internal competition in the British financial system most especially in banking, securities trading and the mortgage market. In the mortgage market, for instance, with the entry for the first time of banks into the mortgage market in the early 1980s cross-subsidies were competed away within months;[24] excess demand for mortgages was eliminated by market-clearing pricing policies as opposed to the previous policy of the building society cartel, which set mortgage rates below the market clearing level;[25] the cartel was abandoned as banks competed outside it; cost pressures on building societies evidently increased; and the pace of mergers accelerated, and a wider variety of mortgage products became on offer.

An alternative approach is given by Vives.[26] Noting that banking in many EC countries is characterized by lack of rigorous competition (particularly price competition), by regulatory capture, concerted action and collusive agreements, the prediction is that banking strategy will change as a response to more competition. However, as indicated in the analysis of an earlier section, Vives suggests that competition will remain imperfect due to the presence of significant economic barriers to entry and that the Cecchini Report estimates overstated the potential benefits of 1992. He concludes that while competition in banking will increase, it will not result in the perfectly competitive market for financial services which was assumed in the Cecchini Report. Banking seems not to fit the model of contestable markets. The Vives study[27] also suggests, along with Llewellyn[28], that European banks will seek to offset the increased competition brought about by 1992 by engaging in mergers, acquisitions and cross-participation agreements. Further, because of the nature of entry barriers, different degrees of competition will coexist in a segmented market and the benefits of increased integration are likely to be unevenly distributed within and between countries.

The Cockfield Report: a new strategy

The two major landmarks in the evolution of the single internal market were the Cockfield Report of 1985 and the SEA of 1986. Their significance derives from the fundamentally new strategy they outlined. The Cockfield Report set out the essential consequences, in terms of an action programme, of accepting commitment to the internal market by 1992. Given the central importance of regulation, and the competitive distortions that can arise with differences in regulation between countries, the old strategy was based on two principles. The first was a proposition that a commitment to a common market in financial services could not be made until regulatory arrangements had been harmonized between members. Only after a high degree of harmonization had been achieved would a common market be feasible or acceptable. The second element was that regulation was to be based on host country and national principles.

There were several problems with this original strategy. The most obvious, which delayed the evolution of a common market in finance, were the bureaucratic and political problems of negotiating a harmonized set of regulations in the context of substantial national differences. National authorities sought both to impose their regulation on other member states and resisted accepting compromises of their own arrangements. This was almost inevitably doomed to failure given the political and bureaucratic barriers to achieving a high degree of prior harmonization. While this principle was retained, progress towards a common market in financial services would be slow. The Cockfield Report stated that: 'experience has shown that relying on a strategy based totally on harmonization would be over-regulatory, would take a long time to implement, would be inflexible, and could stifle innovation'[29]. The conclusion was that 'a genuine common market cannot be realized by 1992 if the Community relies exclusively on Article 100 of the Rome Treaty'.[30]

By the mid-1980s prior harmonization was no longer seen as the best way of achieving the internal market ambitions. The new strategy meant alternatively that a clear distinction needed to be drawn in future internal market initiatives between what it is essential to harmonize, and what may be left to mutual recognition of national regulations and standards; this implied that, on the occasion of each harmonization initiative, the Commission would determine whether national regulations are excessive in relation to the mandatory requirements pursued, thus constituting unjustified barriers to trade according to Articles 30–6 of the EEC Treaty.[31] The new strategy represented a radical alternative approach and was based on three key principles:

(a) there would be an agreed set of minimum harmonized regulations;
(b) outside this set there would be mutual recognition of the regulatory arrangements of other member states; and
(c) regulation would be based upon home-country requirements i.e. the regulatory arrangements of the home country would apply for any institution in whatever member state it conducts business irrespective of the regulatory requirements the host country applied to its own institutions.

It was agreed that no longer would it be necessary to harmonize all regulatory requirements. In effect, an attempt had been made to secure the best of both worlds: combining what is essential to harmonize, and what can best be left to national authorities, but on the basis of mutual recognition. In the banking sector, for instance, the agreed common and harmonized regulation would relate to: authorization criteria; minimum capital requirements (in practice almost identical to the Basle rules); the definition of own funds (equity capital); large exposure limits; deposit-protection arrangements; control of the major share-holdings in banks; limits on banks' involvement in non-bank sectors; and a requirement that sound accountancy and internal control mechanisms must exist. With an agreement to accept the three basic principles, existing barriers to establishment and the free movement of financial services could be removed.

All this represented a major change for it established the principle of freedom of establishment and the cross-border provision of services within the Community. The overriding principle is the mutual recognition of each member state's regulatory and supervisory systems. If an institution is authorized in one country it is deemed to be similarly authorized in all other member states – in other words, an institution wishing to provide services in another member state does not need separate authorization whether the provision of services is via location in other countries or via cross-frontier trade. In principle this means that a bank with its headquarters in Rome will be as free to conduct business in Manchester, Paris or Frankfurt as it is in Milan. Thus a common passport has been provided.

The new approach also implies, however, (and this could become a major problem), that a bank operating a branch (rather than an incorporated subsidiary) in another member state may not be allowed to conduct the same range of business as home banks in that country because some activities may be allowed by the host country regulator but not by the home country regulator. Clearly there are several anomalies that can arise because the principle of a high degree of prior harmonization has been suspended. It is for this reason that further regulatory changes will almost certainly be made in many countries, and this will create further pressure for harmonization of regulation. This in effect reverses the causation of the old strategy. In the former strategy a common market followed prior harmonization. In the new strategy mutual recognition would pave the way for a common market and the resultant competitive anomalies created are likely to induce subsequent harmonization, which is likely to emerge for several reasons: the absence of prior harmonization will inevitably create competitive distortions which regulated institutions will seek to remove if they work to their disadvantage. Also, in some areas, foreign institutions will be able to conduct in member countries business that is prohibited to indigenous institutions. By the same token institutions incorporated under more restrictive regulatory regimes will be hampered in competing outside their own country. Vives[32] goes further arguing that, the Second Banking Directive, for instance, will prepare the ground for a contest among national regulators which will not necessarily yield an efficient outcome; incentives may be created for national authorities to set liberal standards giving national banks a competitive edge abroad. However, it is precisely the purpose of common minimum standards to prevent such competition in laxity.

The three key elements in the plans for a common market in finance are freedom of capital movements, the removal of impediments to cross-border trade in financial services, and freedom of location, each of which is distinct and involves different issues. As in the US, there may be freedom of capital movements while laws and regulatory barriers prevent banks locating freely throughout the monetary area. Similarly, there can be freedom of location for banks and international trade in some services even with exchange control, as was the case with the UK prior to 1979. In what follows, consideration is given to the evolution of a common market in the four major sectors of finance: capital movements, banking, insurance and investment services.

Freedom of capital movements

The full benefits of a common market in financial services cannot be achieved without freedom of capital movements. First, capital controls impede the optimum distribution of savings and investment as they limit the extent to which savers can invest in other countries and borrowers finance their investment by gaining access to the savings of residents in countries with exchange control. Second, in some areas, such as bank deposits, exchange controls prevent consumers taking advantage of more efficient services offered in other countries. Exchange control not only prevents, say, a French resident owning a foreign or French franc deposit at a bank in the UK, it also prevents him holding a foreign currency (or Euro-currency) deposit at a bank in France. Third, while this is seldom the explicit objective of exchange control, it has the effect of conferring competitive advantages on domestic institutions. A fourth reason why freedom of capital movements is an important part of the internal market strategy is that in practice, cross-border trade in some financial services such as life assurance is impeded by exchange control. Services which require funds to be transferred overseas will be monitored and checked carefully by the exchange control authorities to ensure they are not being used as a means to circumvent exchange control. Such monitoring is likely to add to the costs and administrative inconvenience of cross-border trade in these financial services.

While many countries have, or have had, exchange control for monetary policy and exchange rate management reasons, they have the effect (not necessarily intended) of imposing barriers on the free flow of cross-border trade in financial services. Their abolition, as envisaged in the SEA, is thus a fundamental element in the fulfilment of the 1992 ambitions in finance.

All member countries had various degrees of exchange control after 1945 which, at different rates, and with various degrees of commitment, they began to dismantle during the 1960s. The Commission's first directive aiming at freeing capital movements within the EC was issued in May 1960 and its scope was widened by another directive in December 1962. The approach chosen was to divide capital transactions among member states into a few broad categories. Those appearing under so-called lists A and B were transactions that either were ancillary to foreign trade or were related to operations in listed securities or to the flow of direct investments. With respect to them, these directives required unconditional freedom from restrictions imposed by member governments. As to the other operations, grouped under lists C and D, in particular dealings in money market instruments and transactions in bank deposits, the directives left European governments free to decide what kind of regime to adopt, whether complete or partial freedom or heavy restrictions. The turbulence experienced in the currency markets during the 1970s and the wide-ranging repercussions of the increases in the price of oil in that decade, led some member states to invoke Article 108 of the Rome Treaty. This, together with Articles 109 and 73, left open the possibility of making use of measures of safeguard to protect a country's external position. Therefore even the modest liberalizing requirements contained in these directives did not, in some member countries, notably, France and Italy, find practical application. As a result, the liberalization programme faltered during the 1970s and early 1980s more because of the instabilities in the international economic environment than any changes in longer-term objectives.

After 1984 there was a gradual easing of exchange controls in most EC member states and most had been eliminated by the end of 1989. A new Capital Liberalization Directive[33] was adopted in June 1988, to take effect by mid-1990. The aim of the first phase outlined in this directive was a complete and unconditional liberalization of all those capital movements most directly affecting trade in goods and non-financial services including long-term credits, transactions in publicly quoted securities and the issuing, placing and admission to the stock exchange of securities. At this time (see Table 5.7) four countries had no exchange controls (the UK, The Netherlands, Germany and Luxembourg). Belgium had no formal controls,

Table 5.7 Exchange controls and equivalent measures affecting cross-border operations in securities in the EC

| | Operations in foreign securities | | | | Operations in domestic securities | | |
| | Introduction of securities | | | | Introduction of securities | | |
Country	Primary market	Secondary market	Purchase or sale	Collective investments	Primary market	Secondary market	Purchase or sale
Belgium	O	O	O	O	O	O	O
Denmark	X[a]	O	O	O	X[b]	O	O
France	X	O	X[c]	O	X	O	O
Germany	O	O	O	O	O	O	O
Greece	X	X	X	X	X	O	O
Ireland	X	X	X	X	X	O	O
Italy	X	O	X[d]	X[d]	X	O	O
Luxembourg	O	O	O	O	O	O	O
Netherlands	O	O	O	O	O	O	O
Portugal	X	X	X	X	X	O	O
Spain	X	X	X	X	O	O	O
United Kingdom	O	O	O	O	O	O	O

Source: OECD, *Restrictions on Capital Movements*, Paris, 1987.
Notes: Countries with exchange controls are indicated by X; those without controls are indicated by O.
  [a] Bonds are restricted only
  [b] Partial restriction
  [c] Only securities traded on recognized markets are permitted
  [d] Deposit requirement

but still maintained a dual exchange market with some financial and capital transactions being directed through a different market than trade transactions (and at a slightly different exchange rate). All other countries had some form of exchange control, though they were gradually being liberalized.

The second phase of the liberalization process in the 1988 directive aimed at the complete and unconditional liberalization of capital movements classified under new lists B and C. Short-term capital movements linked to the acquisition and trading of monetary instruments or to short-term financial credits, the opening and use of bank deposit accounts and the placing of shares of mutual funds, were all the target of liberalization. Well-specified, temporary safeguard clauses for countries experiencing heavy capital outflows were allowed, while Spain, Ireland, Greece and Portugal were granted delays of implementation of two and four years respectively.

During the first half of 1990 the remaining restrictions on capital movements were dismantled in France and Italy and as a result, the deadline of 1 July 1990 set by the 1988 directive for complete liberalization of capital movements in eight countries was met. By the end of 1990 most member countries had virtually complete freedom in cross-border capital transactions, and a major basis for the completion of the internal market in financial services was in place. However, the 1988 directive also contained a safeguard clause allowing some temporary reinstatement (up to six months) of some measures for the purposes of monetary policy exigencies.

Banking

In general, barriers to the supply of cross-border banking have been more onerous than those related to location. In some countries laws and regulations have restricted the right of non-resident banks and financial institutions to conduct business with residents. The French banking law of 1984, for instance, required foreign banks to have an establishment in France before they could provide services to French residents. In The Netherlands foreign banks are not permitted to advertise their products to residents within the Netherlands.

Lamb[34] provides an excellent account of the evolution of EC arrangements with respect to banking. Several directives have been proposed in this sector; the major landmarks are as follows, all of which are planned to be operative by the end of 1992:

(a) The First Banking Directive on Coordination of Regulations Governing Credit Institutions, 1977;[35] this related to the coordination of national laws, regulation and administrative provisions relating to the establishment of branches and required such institutions to be licensed, and that they be permitted to conduct business in other member countries subject to host-country authorization. The key is that authorization could not lawfully be withheld if the sole ground was that the establishment of the head office was in another member state. However, the principle of host country authorization and regulation was firmly established. This meant that a French bank in Italy could only do what Italian regulation allowed Italian banks to do in their own country.

(b) The Directive on the Supervision of Credit Institutions on a Consolidated Basis, 1983[36] established the common principle that bank activities were to be supervised on the basis of their world-wide activities. For example capital requirements were to relate to their global balance sheet position thus preventing banks seeking to avoid capital requirements by booking business through less onerously regulated financial centres.

(c) The Directive on Bank Accounts was an attempt at a common system of presenting accounts of banks.

(d) The Directive on the Harmonization of the Concept of Own Funds.

(e) The Recommendation on Large Exposures.

(f) The Recommendation on Deposit Guarantees.

The major breakthrough, however, came in 1989 with the adoption by the Council of Ministers of the Second Banking Directive.[37] This was based on the new strategy principles outlined in the 1985 Cockfield Report of home country regulation, and mutual recognition. As stated in the directive:

> Member States shall ensure that at least the activities set out on the list in the Annex may be pursued in any Member State ... either by the establishment of a branch or by way of the provision of services, by any credit institution authorized and supervized by the competent authorities of the home Member State ...

Apart from the general principles implicit in the new strategy the major elements of the Second Banking Directive were:

(a) a comprehensive list (see Table 5.8), based on universal banking modes of bank activities to which the directive applied;

(b) minimum requirements as to the size of own-funds (equity capital) of credit institutions;

(c) the elimination of the requirement, previously imposed by all member governments except the UK, for branches of foreign banks to maintain dedicated capital for their operations;

(d) a requirement of disclosure of the identity of a bank's most important shareholders;

(e) disciplining banks' holdings of shares in other financial and non-financial companies; and

(f) regulating the exchange of information between home and host country regulators.

Table 5.8 List of banking activities subject to mutual recognition in the Second
Banking Directive

1. Acceptance of deposits and other repayable funds from the public
2. Lending[1]
3. Financial leasing
4. Money transmission services
5. Issuing and administering means of payment (e.g. credit cards, travellers' cheques and bankers' drafts)
6. Guarantees and commitments
7. Trading for own account or for account of customers in:
   (a) money market instruments (cheques, bills, certificates of deposit, etc.)
   (b) foreign exchange
   (c) financial futures and options
   (d) exchange and interest rate instruments
   (e) transferable securities
8. Participation in share issues and the provision of services related to such issues
9. Advice to undertakings on capital structure, industrial strategy and related questions and advice and services relating to mergers and the purchase of undertakings
10. Money broking
11. Portfolio management and advice
12. Safekeeping and administration of securities
13. Credit reference services
14. Safe custody services

Source: Second Banking Directive, 1989.
Notes: [1] Including inter alia   – consumer credit
                                      – mortgage credit
                                      – factoring, with or without recourse
                                      – financing of commercial transactions
                                      – (including forfaiting)

The Second Banking Directive will prove to be a milestone in the evolution of a genuine common market in banking. The directive focuses upon financial products rather than institutions and the range of products on the official list to which the directive applies is very comprehensive: all forms of lending, leasing, foreign exchange services, financial futures, credit cards, fund management and securities trading. The directive is about the provision of banking services either by trade or by locating to other countries and its main implications are:

(a) cross-border banking business should become easier;
(b) international expansion via location would be less obstructed in some EC countries though in others the impact would be small given the already easy access;
(c) location in other member states should become cheaper to the extent that dedicated capital will no longer be required for foreign branches of EC institutions. This means that a more efficient use could be made of capital

because less is earmarked for specific (foreign branch) purposes;
(d) there will be no specific solvency ratios or large exposure limits on foreign branches as is the case now in some member countries; and
(e) institutions would be free of restrictions on the business activities imposed by host regulatory authorities. In principle a bank will be able to undertake in any EC country what it is able to undertake in its own country.

Combined, these represent a substantial package and will undoubtedly make a significant contribution to the development of the common market in financial services.

The principle of home country regulation and mutual recognition is not total in two respects. The directive acknowledged the primacy of host country rules designed to protect the consumer:

> If the competent authority of the host Member State ascertains that an institution having a branch or providing services in its territory is not complying with the legal provisions in force in that Member State which are justified on the grounds of the public good, or pursuant to the provisions of this Directive on the powers of the host Member State, that authority shall request the institution concerned to put an end to the irregular situation. (Article 19(3))

Lamb[38] records that the ultimate sanction for failure to respect such host country rules is suspension of all activities in the host country (Article 5). A problem arises in defining the scope of this qualification. The Commission has taken the view that it applies only with respect to activities not included on the list of mutually recognized activities, but as the list is very wide this interpretation would limit the scope of the exception and the ability of host countries to impose their own rules.

One immediate example, which Davis and Smales[39] highlight as demonstrating the ambiguity of the scope, relates to variable rate mortgage lending, which is the norm in the UK, but is illegal in Belgium. The question is whether this is to be regarded as a technique or a function. While mortgage lending is one of the listed banking activities, variable-rate mortgage lending is not specifically mentioned, thus though there is no doubt that UK institutions can offer and market mortgage loans in Belgium there is some doubt whether they could offer variable rate loans while Belgian institutions cannot. If floating-rate lending is a technique it would be allowed and implicitly covered in the generic term mortgage lending. If it is a basic activity, and whether or not on grounds of consumer protection, the Belgian authorities could prohibit floating-rate mortgages within their country by all nationalities of banks. Neven[40] argues that the directive applies to the way activities are performed as well as the definition of the activity; there is nevertheless a grey area between the operating and the licensing rules. This particular example is clouded yet further by the fact that originally there was to be a specific directive for mortgage lending and the draft stated explicitly, 'mutual recognition of technique' (though in the author's view this reinforces the claim that it was the intention not to allow such loans to be exempted from the directive's principles). This directive has been withdrawn and superseded by the Second Banking Directive but that specific requirement was not included.

A second qualification to the principle of home country regulation related to activities not on the list of the Second Banking Directive. If a bank is able to conduct business in its own country in an area not specifically included on the list, it has no automatic authority to conduct the business in other member countries. Such activities can be conducted only with the express authorization of the host country. If, on the other hand, the home country authorization allows less than the full listed range in the home country, then only the authorized activities will benefit from the freedoms as in Article 16(1). Lamb summarizes the position: 'The clear intention is that it shall be only those activities available in the credit institutions's home market which may automatically be undertaken elsewhere, although the host countries may, as at present, allow a greater number of activities to be undertaken'.[41]

Insurance

In contrast to the banking and securities sector, and with the exception of reinsurance, the insurance industry in the EC, with the notable exception of the UK, has been relatively protected from outside competition and has not been part of any general globalization process. In addition to barriers created by exchange control, a series of legal barriers to trade in insurance have resulted in a situation where, except for major risks, insurance is fragmented into comparatively isolated national markets. In general the member states have imposed a multitude of restrictions on insurance services provided through branches or agencies and on services provided across borders. In many EC countries there are legally-imposed constraints on taking out insurance policies with a foreign insurer. Several countries retain strict systems of prior host-country authorization and control over foreign insurance companies, and their soliciting of business, and many require a foreign assurance company to establish a branch before offering services. Most EC countries require life insurance companies to set up permanent subsidiaries in order to conduct business with host-country residents, and six of the member states either prohibit or require special approval for insurance policies in foreign currencies. In general, the UK is the only member state in which foreign life insurance companies are allowed to compete freely, that is, without being required to establish a subsidiary as well as without being subject to any restriction on the currency in which the contract is denominated. Partly because of the multitude of these existing barriers, the extent of harmonization adopted or proposed by the European Community in insurance is considerably less than that in the area of banking.

The EC arrangements in the insurance sector are complex. In the first place, insurance is not a homogeneous product and there are important differences between the different types of insurance such as life or general insurance. Second, because of the complexity of the contracts, and in many cases their very long-term nature, issues of consumer protection are particularly powerful; a distinction must be made between different types of client, and in particular between those that regulators believe need a high degree of protection as opposed to those who are presumed to be well-informed. A third complication is that a distinction is traditionally made between the status of insurance companies and agents or brokers that sell and advise on insurance. It is also the case that in all countries insurance is a highly regulated sector in finance and there are substantial differences in regulation between member states which makes the process of harmonization more difficult and the principles of the new strategy more difficult to accept. There is no existing mechanism for the international regulation coordination comparable to that which exists in banking, and also, as in retail banking, there is comparatively little cross-border trade in retail insurance business.

In general, progress has been more substantial and faster in non-life insurance business than in life assurance, and for presumed sophisticated or larger-risk customers than for standard small-risk customers. The Freedom of Services Directive for Non-Life Insurance (adopted in 1988)[42] distinguished between such large risks, including all marine, aviation and transport risks and mass risks including small commercial risks and personal insurance. In the former, the home-country principle was applied, whereas in the latter the rules of the country in which the policy-holder resides applied. Though the 1988 directives were based on principles of mutual recognition and home country regulation, this was only for policy-holders deemed not to require the high degree of protection implied in host country control. A similar principle was applied in the Second Life Directive of 1988[43] in that customers could purchase at their own initiative life assurance on a cross-border basis, but had to accept the degree of protection and supervision prevailing in that country, in other words the home-country principle would apply in such unsolicited cross-border trade. If, on the other hand, an agreement were concluded outside the country of residence at the initiative of the insurance company, the provisions applicable would be those of the country where the risk was situated.

While both life and non-life directives dealt with cross-border trade in insurance, they have not to date provided for EC-wide branching under the home-country principle of authorization and control. It is still host countries that are responsible for the regulation of branches of foreign companies.

Efforts to achieve a common market for insurance services began with a directive, which came into force in August 1964, for the abolition of restrictions on freedom of establishment, and freedom to provide services in respect of reinsurance.[44] Basically this directive did little more than confirm the existing situation, since this activity (the insurance of insurers) was subject to only limited restrictions in the member states. This was followed by two further directives on property insurance. The First Non-Life Insurance Directive, adopted in 1973,[45] and the First Life Insurance Directive, adopted in 1979,[46] were designed to harmonize general conditions governing authorization, some of the financial requirements to be met and to facilitate the establishment of branches and agencies in other member states by abolishing various restrictions. The directives set out insurance companies' rights of establishment throughout the EC and under them, insurance companies' agencies and branches are subject to host-country control with regard to authorization and other requirements, although the home-country has responsibility for ensuring a firm's overall solvency. Above all, the right of insurers was firmly established to take up establishment in a host country under the same conditions and with the same rights as resident insurance companies.

In determining whether host-country rules could be applied to the cross-border provision of insurance services, the European Court of Justice considered the degree of protection required by policy-holders and insured persons, and distinguished between the needs of small policy-holders and those of large, commercial risks. The insurance directives adopted or proposed in 1988 used such distinctions to determine whether home or host-country control would apply. The non-life insurance and motor-vehicle insurance directives distinguished between large risks, defined primarily in terms of the number of employees, sales, and assets of the policy-holder, and mass risks. Similarly, the life insurance directive distinguished between those who take the initiative in seeking life insurance from a company in another member state, and those who do not take such an initiative. The directives applied the principle of home-country control only to the large risks and to those individuals who take the initiative in purchasing life insurance across borders. The rationale was that these categories of policy-holders had adequate knowledge to be able to buy insurance that was regulated and supervised only by the insurer's home country.

None of the early directives (1970s) provided for the freedom to supply insurance on a cross-border basis, and there have been long delays in developing a common market in insurance. In 1988 the Emerson Report[47] noted that the second directive on insurance services had been awaiting adoption for ten years. Some EC members maintained that, in the absence of a high degree of prior harmonization between all the member countries, they could only give proper protection to policy-holders if all insurers established in their respective countries came under the direct control of the host regulatory authorities. Given the lack of progress, the Commission took a test case against Germany (known as the *Schleicher* case) to the Court of Justice in the early 1980s, and similar cases were taken against Denmark, France and Ireland. The key issue was the extent to which a country was permitted to impose authorization and other regulatory requirements on insurance companies, based in other member states and wishing to offer cross-border services.

The Court found that 'the insurance sector is a particularly sensitive area from the point of view of the protection of the consumer both as a policy-holder and as an insured person'. As a result, the Court upheld that, in the field of insurance, there existed 'imperative reasons relating to the public interest' that might justify restrictions on the freedom to provide services. Host countries, though not entitled to require insurance companies to be established in their country, might be justified in imposing their own authorization procedures; however, any conditions attached to authorization had to both be objectively justified, and not duplicate the home country's supervisory control. The Court also emphasized that any such restrictions must be applied equally to foreign and domestic companies, which is consistent with the judicial exception to Article 59 first established by the European Court in the *Van Binsbergen* case, (see page 106). As one of the two exceptions to these general requirements, the Court said that strict controls might be exercised by the host state on policy-holder protection grounds, which might well be justified for mass risks, because of an individual consumer's difficulty in judging whether the insurer would be able to meet its long-term obligations.

Although some considerable progress has been made, there is as yet no universal adoption of the basic principles of the new strategy in all aspects of insurance. Nevertheless, it remains the ambition of the Commission to achieve a single EC insurance market with insurance companies, as with banks, able to provide their services on the basis of a single authorization.

This was the subject of the next or third generation of directives in the insurance sector. The first generation of the 1970s provided for the freedom of establishment of insurance companies; the second generation in the late 1980s opened the way for the free provision of services and provided for host-country control. The third generation should provide for a single authorization for the EC as a whole, based on home-country principles, and conditions for granting authorization should be harmonized throughout the EC. New draft 'framework directives' were put forward in 1990 for both life- and non-life insurance which proposed that insurance companies should operate throughout the EC with a single licence; these directives would enable insurance companies to set up branches in all member states and to sell the full range of their products on the basis of a single home-country authorization and supervision.

In practice, however, even with the third generation it still seems that, while further harmonization will be achieved, widely differing national laws and regulatory frameworks might persist after 1992, and that competition in retail insurance markets would in practice continue to be restricted. Accepting the principles of the new strategy presupposes a reasonable degree of prior harmonization in regulation, and this has been achieved in banking though as much because of global pressures and mechanisms for regulatory convergence, as those existing solely within the EC. As the national differences in insurance are greater, progress is likely to be slower.

Investment services

The third, more heterogeneous, area of finance to consider is that of investment services including securities trading, unit trusts, securities broking, portfolio management, underwriting and investment advice. This category also includes issues related to the access of companies to foreign stock exchanges and the quotation of securities on foreign stock exchanges. In this sector in particular arrangements for completing the internal market are closely related to the broader issue of freedom of capital movements within the EC. Different types of risks and issues of consumer protection are involved in this area, than those involved with banking and insurance.

Table 5.9 gives the scope (as of 1987) of restrictions on non-resident firms' security-related activities. Clearly, a genuine EC financial common market requires either a single securities market; or free access to different markets where companies can freely issue securities across national borders, where securities are freely traded on different exchanges, where foreign institutions can become members of stock exchanges, and where investors are free to buy and sell securities on exchanges in different member states.

The EC made initial efforts at an early stage to harmonize (at least to a minimum degree) the different regulations of the member states on the admission of securities to stock-exchange listing and to harmonize the information to be provided to investors, so harmonizing their protection. In 1972, in a proposal for a first directive in this area, the Commission stated that the omissions and differences in the information provided to the public regarding securities constituted a second barrier to capital movements between member states. In addition to the provision of information for the public and the protection of investments, a second consideration was the operation of a single securities market. Since 1979 the Council of Ministers has adopted a series of directives in this area, the first stage being the adoption in 1979 of the Directive Coordinating the Conditions for the Admission of Securities to Official Stock Exchange Listing.[48] The directive set out conditions to be met by issuers of securities, including minimum issue price, a company's period of existence, free negotiability, sufficient distribution, and the provision of appropriate information for investors. Member states were however free to impose stricter requirements.

Closely connected with this was the directive adopted in 1980 coordinating

Table 5.9 Restrictions on non-resident firms' security-related activities, EC and other selected OECD countries[a]

Country	Primary markets	Secondary markets
European Community		
Belgium	0	III, IV
Denmark	0	III
France	0	III, V
Germany	I	0
Greece	0	II
Ireland	0	0
Italy	0	II, VI
Luxembourg	0	0
Netherlands	I	0
Portugal	0	II
Spain	0	II, V
United Kingdom	I	0
Selected OECD countries		
Australia	0	VI
Japan	VII	VII
Switzerland	0	0
United States	0	0

Source: OECD, *International Trade in Services: Securities'*, Paris, 1987.
Notes: a. Restrictions are indicated as follows:
0: No restrictions.
I: Foreign firm may lead new issue only if reciprocity holds.
II: Broker licence forbidden to foreigners.
III: Broker licence limited to EC members.
IV: No direct sale to public, only to institutional investors.
V: Operations in exchange market must go through domestic local bank or broker.
VI: Limited foreign participation in domestic brokerage firms.
VII: Specific authorization needed.

requirements for the drawing up, scrutiny and distribution of the particulars published for the admission of securities to official stock-exchange listing.[49] The directive laid down the many items of information to be published when shares, debt securities and certificates representing shares were admitted to stock-exchange listing, dealing with the content, checking and publication of listing particulars prior to the official quotation of securities on an EC stock exchange.

The third stage in 1982 was a directive on the information that companies are required to publish (on a half-yearly basis) if their shares have been listed on an official EC stock exchange.[50] The directive required quoted companies to make publicly available on a half-yearly basis sufficient information to enable the public to evaluate the financial position of the company and the general progress of its business.

The new strategy has now since been applied to the marketing of unit trusts and investment funds based upon mutual recognition, minimum harmonization, and control by the country of registration or origin. A 1985 coordination directive provided for home-country authorization of unit trusts,[51] whereby any unit trust authorized by a member country may operate throughout the Community, but must comply with any relevant laws and regulations in force in the host country, even if these do not apply in the home country – including controls over advertising and marketing. For example, if the host country forbade doorstep selling of units, a unit trust must comply with this even if allowed in the home country. A significant consumer protection provision was that the management company of a unit trust must act 'solely in the interest of the unit holders'. It was also designed to set out a common set of legal provisions to achieve approximately equal conditions of competition and effective protection for investors in all EC countries. Under a second directive in 1985, member governments were required to remove all restrictions on the free marketing of units.[52]

The new strategy was also applied to earlier directives on listing requirements. The aim of a 1987 directive amending earlier directives on listing particulars[53] was to ensure that these listing particulars complied with earlier directives, and were approved in one of the EC countries, and so should be automatically recognized on the stock exchanges of other member states without the need for additional approval.

1989 saw the adoption of a directive coordinating the requirements for the drawing up, scrutiny and distribution of prospectuses to be published when transferable securities are offered to the public.[54]

The securities directive, which is the counterpart of the Second Banking Directive, was proposed by the Commission in December 1988. Like the Second Banking Directive, this proposed Investment Services Directive provided for removal of barriers to both the provision of cross-border services and the establishment of branches throughout the Community based on the principles of harmonization of essential standards, mutual recognition and home-country control. Investment firms would be able to establish branches throughout the Community without obtaining a licence from the host country for each branch. Once an investment services firm had been authorized in its home country, it would be able to operate throughout the EC. In order to ensure that such branches were able to compete effectively in the host country, the directive also provided for liberalization of rules governing access to stock exchanges, financial futures and options exchanges. In 1990, the Commission adopted a proposal for a directive on the capital adequacy of investment firms aimed at establishing minimum amounts of initial capital and defining a common framework for supervising market risks.

The Investment Services Directive also provided for liberalization of access to stock exchange membership in countries throughout the Community for investment firms authorized in their home member state. Price Waterhouse[55] suggested that the major obstacles to establishing a presence in a foreign securities market would appear to be regulations preventing foreigners being licensed as brokers. A host state is required to ensure that an investment firm that is authorized to provide brokerage, dealing, or market-making services in its home state, may 'enjoy the full range of trading privileges normally reserved to members of the stock exchanges and organized securities markets' of the host country. To meet this obligation, a host state is required to ensure that such an investment firm has the option to become a member of the host country's stock exchange or organized securities markets by setting up branches or subsidiaries in the host state or by the acquisition of an existing member firm.

Assessment of the impact

In this concluding section an attempt is made to guage the potential impact of the 1992 arrangements in the financial sector. Necessarily, the argument is uncertain and imprecise, especially compared with the somewhat exaggerated precision of the Cecchini Report. This was based on a questionable methodology, and suggested a precise quantification of potential benefits, based upon an analysis of price differences between member states. Much of the analysis to follow suggests that there are a series of market barriers indicating that the Cecchini methodology overstated the potential benefits to be derived directly from the various 1992 arrangements (what are termed the primary mechanisms) though what are termed secondary effects may not have been incorporated in the calculations. Indeed, it may be that, in the final analysis, the latter will prove to be more powerful and beneficial than the former.

One reason why it is difficult to judge the likely specific impact of 1992 is that the arrangements represent an accentuation of trends which are already apparent in many EC financial systems: increased competitive pressures and a general process of deregulation (see Baltensperger and Dermine for a discussion of general trends in European banking).[56] In the long run the greatest impact on financial systems and consumers of financial services will come from these two general trends and the specific role of the 1992 arrangements, which should be regarded as a continuum of the more fundamental factors in the evolution of EC financial systems, will be difficult to isolate.

The potential benefits of the 1992 arrangements in finance could emerge through six routes:

(a) Via enhanced competition either by more cross-border trade in financial services or through the entry of foreign institutions. Consumers should benefit as competition raises efficiency and less efficient suppliers of services are displaced.

(b) Through benefits to be derived from any economies of scale that might exist and to the extent that financial institutions successfully develop pan-EC strategies. Traditionally, gains to trade analyses are based on models of imperfect competition with either constant or declining economies of scale, tending to suggest only small gains to be derived from the easing of trade restrictions. Krugman,[57] on the other hand, suggests that the main benefits of trade between industrial countries are to be derived from exploiting potential economies of scale in the presence of imperfect competition; a similar approach is adopted by Harris[58] and Smith and Venables.[59] Thus increased competition can produce benefits through lower costs (economies of scale) and lower rents. In practice, however, the empirical evidence does not demonstrate the existence of economies of scale in banking – see Revell[60] for a survey of the evidence.

(c) The benefits to be derived from pooling risks – a reduction in risk for each expected rate of return – as the abolition of exchange control enables more efficiently diversified portfolios to be obtained. This is true for both individual investors and financial institutions. To the extent that risks in different countries are less than perfectly correlated, international diversification can improve the risk-return frontier.

(d) To the extent that barriers to foreign (EC) ownership are lowered, the potential threat of a take-over may act as a spur to efficiency in financial institutions.[61] Whether in general such pressure is invariably benign is, however, open to question.[62]

(e) Greater actual or potential competition may also alter the mode of competition. In many countries, price competition is weak in finance and non-price, often cost-raising, competition predominates. To the extent that external competition weakens existing formal or informal cartels – and in practice they are common in some EC countries – there is likely to be greater price competition.

(f) To the extent that regulation imposes competitive distortions, the prospect of greater competition may induce further easing of restrictive and protective regulation.

The first four mechanisms, to the extent that they follow directly from enhanced competitive pressures, would be included in the category of primary factors noted earlier. The last three factors are secondary in nature though not necessarily less powerful. Regulation arbitrage, potential regulatory competition and pressures from regulated institutions that are subject to competitive hurdles created by non-harmonized regulation between countries, are all likely to induce further deregulation in the finance sector. As argued in an earlier section, the new strategy is likely to produce a high degree of harmonization through the competitive pressures of the market place. In a different dimension, anticipation of greater competitive pressures has induced the regulatory authorities in Spain and Italy to sponsor consolidation and a series of mergers in their respective banking sectors, and in Italy this includes a change in regulation to allow more branching.

A useful focus is the Price Waterhouse study[63] which indicated the range of potential price reductions for standard financial services; overall, it indicated a gain in price convergence producing a change in consumer surplus in the region of 11–30 billion ECU. A critique of the study was outlined in an earlier section. Prices might vary for many reasons: differences in efficiency, monopoly rents in the form of high costs of profits, internal cross-subsidies, the non-exploitation of economies of scale and regulation. Thus not all are due to a lack of integration whereas the Price Waterhouse study was based on the questionable assumption that all prices would converge on the average of the four lowest prices identified for each product or service, with an adjustment of on average of one-half of such theoretical potential. In truth this is an entirely theoretical calculation of little practical significance and cannot justify any spurious precision in the measurement of the potential welfare gain.

An earlier section identified that, when considering the implications of the 1992 arrangements, a distinction should be made between wholesale and retail banking because the competitive conditions in these sectors vary both within and between countries. In the former, business tends to be large scale and an institution may have comparatively few, if large customers, and delivery can be made without the necessity of a network of branches. Retail banking, on the other hand, involves a large number of small accounts and access is usually through a branch network. An earlier section identified that the competitive environment in most countries is more intense in wholesale than retail banking, which is likely to mean that in some (though not all) EC countries, further integration in wholesale banking will be limited as integration has become in this sector global rather than European. However, in some EC countries where entry and access barriers have been formidable there will be scope for foreign competition in wholesale banking business as a result of the Second Directive.

In practice there are substantial economic barriers to trade in retail financial services and to entry into the retail sector in foreign countries by financial institutions. Thus even if the observed price differences were a reflection of a lack of integration it is not to be expected that prices would necessarily converge as suggested by the Price Waterhouse study. In view of the importance of these barriers they are considered in some detail:

(a) Entry costs are likely to be high whether they derive from establishing an own-delivery system (or branch network) or via acquisitions or mergers. For this reason it is frequently difficult for foreign banks and financial institutions to break into existing markets most especially if a branch network and high cost infrastructure are required which is frequently the case for delivery of retail financial services. It is not self-evident, therefore, that inefficiencies and monopoly rents can in practice be competed away through this route, as it may be inordinately expensive or risky to do so. Although retail banking tends to be the most profitable aspect of banking in most countries it is also the most difficult for foreign institutions to enter successfully.

(b) Scale requirements can be an effective barrier. The selling of retail services requires a minimum critical mass to be economic and effective. It is difficult to penetrate some retail services on a small-scale given that the fixed entry costs are high and profitability requires high volumes.

(c) Existing institutions have important reputation advantages which are a key element in the success of financial services in general and banking in particular. Consumers' perceptions, and even parochialism, may be an effective barrier to entry and reduce the contestability of financial markets. There is a natural tendency for consumers to focus upon familiar domestic banks whose name and reputation are well established, and who are known to provide a full range of services throughout the country.

(d) Information advantages are a powerful competitive advantage in finance. In fact, a powerful strand in the analysis of banking emphasizes information advantages[64] and well established, indigenous institutions are likely to have powerful information advantages in two respects. Firstly, local institutions will have superior knowledge about demand, the markets and the risks involved; Branson[65] argues that the existence of imperfect information (which is costly to acquire and analyse) is a rationale for local intermediaries. The second information advantage is that gained through existing, sometimes long-standing, customer relationships; a bank, for instance, gains enormous information from administering a customer's basic bank account through which income and payment transactions are made, and apart from the intrinsic value of such information, it also offers potentially powerful cross-selling opportunities.

(e) There are also substantial cultural differences between countries, which may impede the evolution of pan-EC products. The Bank of England suggests:[66] 'anything approaching a true single market in retail financial services is expected to be limited to a small range of items (e.g. credit-card based products) which can be offered on a common basis'. For instance, the use of cheques varies considerably between countries (high in France, Italy and the UK, but low in Germany and The Netherlands) as does the use of bank transfers. Similarly, there are major differences in the use of credit cards, and housing finance arrangements also vary considerably between countries according to Boleat.[67]

(f) Customer relationships are powerful most especially in banking and the incidence of switching banks is low even within a country; the transfer costs and inconvenience (changing standing orders, for example) can be powerful – see Neven,[68] Vives[69] and Grilli.[70]

(g) In many countries there is evidence of excess capacity in some financial services, including banking especially with the volume of existing branches. This is also likely to be an impediment to entry.

(h) With respect to cross-border trade in financial services two immediate problems emerge: the high transaction costs and inconvenience, and the foreign currency risk if the transactions are not conducted in the consumer's domestic currency. The latter does not apply with Euro-currency transactions (for example sterling business conducted by a bank in Germany) though to date, and for the first reason noted, Euro-currency markets have not developed at the retail level.

There are, therefore, substantial potential barriers likely to be faced by institutions with ambitions to develop retail financial institutions in countries other than their own. It is also important not to exaggerate the implications of 1992 as, even under the old strategy, banks and financial institutions have been largely free for many years both to establish in other EC countries and to offer some cross-border services. The new strategy, while a significant change, has not involved the creation of freedoms that have hitherto been totally absent, but it has, however, changed the terms of access such as home country regulation.

None of this is to suggest that there will be no benefits nor that the new strategy is of secondary importance. Benefits will emerge partly because the identified barriers are not total, instead varying between countries, given the existing differences in the competitive environment in which financial services are provided, and because institutions and regulators are likely to respond to potential competition. In this sense, 1992 might be said to raise the contestability of financial services. As already noted, many EC financial systems have high costs and rents, restrictive practices and cartels and pricing policies which involve cross-subsidies and excess demand for credit (non-market-clearing-pricing policies). Actual or potential competition might be expected to compete these away to some extent, and it may be that the real benefits will derive from this rather than entry or the development of cross-border services. The position has been put well by Davis and Smales:[71]

Either way, two outcomes are possible. Either entry does occur, and the local market improves as a result; or the local suppliers improve performance enough to keep potential entrants away. The amount by which a local bank has to improve its performance to avoid foreign incursion is to the point at which the advantages of its local presence just outweigh its inefficiency.

The greatest potential impact for both outcomes is likely to be felt in those countries where internal regulation is most constraining, where internal competitive pressures are weakest (perhaps because of cartels or restrictive practices) and where entry barriers have been most formidable. For instance, the impact within the British financial system may not be substantial as competitive conditions are already demanding, there is no exchange control, all major EC banks already have a presence in London, and there are no restrictions on the range of allowable business and foreign branches are not required to have dedicated capital. But British institutions will gain through enhanced access to other EC markets. In Spain, on the other hand, the impact is likely to be greater for opposite reasons.

Access routes

In the final analysis, the key issues are access – the method of accessing customers; and delivery systems – the methods by which services are provided. The central issues for competing banks are access to potential customers and the creation of effective delivery systems for financial services. Whatever the type of business being considered, for provision to be effective, an institution needs access to potential customers and this is likely to be secured differently for retail as opposed to wholesale banking services; and different banks will develop different approaches.

Access can be secured in five basic ways:

(a) by building a location, establishing a European network of branches;
(b) by mergers and acquisitions, where two institutions of different nationality merge so that a single institution has universal access in both countries;
(c) through the purchase of a company in another country which has ready access to customers;
(d) through developing business links with institutions in other countries so that the partner gives access to its customer base and acts in some cases as an agent; and
(e) via trade, though there has to be effective communication between the customer in one country and the supplier of a banking service in another.

The first method would be very expensive, would add to existing excess capacity, and would be subject to all the information and reputation barriers noted earlier. There are also problems with merger and acquisition strategies: the rationale is not self-evident if there are in fact no exploitable economies of scale, and Molyneux[72] observes that in practice there are not a substantial number of banks in the EC available to be purchased as many are mutual, some are very large and some others are in the public sector. Regulatory authorities may also impede the foreign ownership of key banks in a national financial system. It is also evident that there are likely to be formidable cultural problems in merging different nationalities of banks as was seen in the abortive merger between AMRO (a major Dutch bank) and the Generale Bank (Belgium). Nevertheless, acquisitions avoid the problem of creating more capacity; and several cross-border purchases of small- and medium-size banks have been made by, for instance, Barclays Bank, Commerzbank, Deutsche Bank, Midland Bank, Royal Bank of Scotland, and Abbey National and several others. There have also been several cases of equity exchanges with two banks in different countries each buying an ownership stake in the other; whether these proved in practice to be strategic alliances or defensive measures designed to discourage unfriendly take-overs has yet to be determined.

The link method is potentially powerful and is likely to emerge as a major business route because it enables different institutions to exploit their different comparative advantages. This has recently been used in the UK mortgage market and has enabled foreign institutions without an internal branch network to access retail customers. Any loan transaction has three stages: origination of the loan, administration of the loan, and the holding of the loan as an asset on the balance sheet. These are usually, but not necessarily, performed by the same institution. Foreign institutions have no advantage in origination of mortgages as they have no branch network to access the customer, but there are many British building societies which do have this facility. On the other hand, some foreign institutions have developed a comparative advantage in holding mortgage assets. The obvious strategy (and one that has been adopted) is for both to exploit their particular advantages with the foreign institution funding a loan that has been originated by a British institution which in turn is paid a fee for the origination. A recent example of this is where the Skipton Building Society markets mortgages in the UK for the Société Générale of France. The French bank raises the funds for the building society to sell mortgages through its UK branch network and the French bank pays the building society a fee and commissions.

In practice, and given the expense of developing a new branch network, this is likely to be a major implication of the second directive and its effect upon the future evolution of European financial institutions. Such links and joint ventures, designed to exploit different comparative advantages, are likely to become increasingly common between institutions in different countries. Foreign institutions will be holding assets which have been originated and administered by domestic institutions. This will prove to be a major way for foreign institutions to gain access to personal customers without incurring substantial costs through a branch network.

Most analysis of the potential impact of 1992 has concentrated on general benefits to consumers. There are, however, powerful potential distributional effects. Competition will not affect all consumers in the same way; the costs and benefits are likely to be unevenly distributed. This is already evident in the current structure of cross-subsidies and in the structure of wholesale and retail banking and financial services which have already been noted. An instructive case-study is found in the impact of deregulation on the UK securities industry in 1987 (during the so-called 'Big Bang') where evidence indicates that large, institutional customers gained, while securities trading costs rose for small customers. An analysis of banking markets by Grilli[73] again suggests that the benefits of competition are likely to be asymmetrically distributed, with larger depositors (attractive to new entrants) gaining in relation to small customers, because the market for deposits is segmented and subject to price discrimination. The evidence indicates that larger depositors have better information, are able to sustain the costs of acquiring information, have a greater potential to analyse it, have lower switching costs per unit of deposit and are more prone to take advantage of arbitrage possibilities. Similar conclusions are likely to apply to other financial services, with the possible exception of insurance where the role of brokers (who provide information and search advantages to consumers) is more evident, and where customer loyalty is known to be lower (partly because there is a less powerful bonding relationship between customers and their insurance companies than with their banks). Casual empiricism suggests that consumers are more likely to shop around, sometimes by utilizing the services of a broker, for car and life assurance than for banking services. It is evidently the case that consumers are more loyal to their bank, partly because of the wide-ranging relationship and costs of switching, than to their insurance companies.

Conclusion

The overall conclusion here is that the impact of the 1992 arrangements in finance should not be exaggerated. In wholesale banking there is no specifially European dimension to integration: competitive pressures are already global in nature. In much of the retail sector there remain substantial economic barriers to trade and location, and the existence of these and other market imperfections suggest that banking will remain imperfectly competitive. The evident market segmentation, lack of economies of scale and the advantages possessed by local institutions mean that inefficiencies can be sustained.

Chapter 6

The liberalization of transport services

Kenneth Button

In this chapter we continue to focus on those aspects of the SEM programme which relate to the liberalization of services. In this case the spotlight turns to transport, not only the traditional surface modes of road, rail and inland waterway, but also the previously neglected maritime and air passenger sectors.

The common transport policy

Transport forms an important element in modern economic systems. It is not simply that it is a major consumer of resources – it currently accounts for about 7 per cent of Community GDP and the United Nations Economic Commission for Europe[1] has forecast that 16.7 per cent of the Community budget will be going to transport by the year 2000; but it also provides a vital lubricating function for the entire productive system. Manipulation of transport markets, however, has the potential not only for achieving socially desirable objectives such as enhancing equity and stimulating economic development but also for distorting trade and wasting resources.

In these circumstances there are clear, potential, aggregate economic gains for any form of European union if transport markets can be made to function effectively and without distortion. This theoretical point has most eloquently been made by Gwilliam:

> A global reduction in transport costs has the same effect as a bilateral tariff reduction in increasing the market area for efficient producers, like tariff reductions, transport cost reductions may increase total welfare without necessarily increasing the welfare of all parties concerned. Also, like tariff structures, transport cost structures, if consciously managed, can have the effect of protecting selected groups.[2]

The founders of the ECSC in 1951 were well aware of the damage which manipulation of railway freight rates in particular could do in the market for steel and coal.[3] Indeed, considerable efforts were made in the 1950s to eliminate distortions which could bias the working of markets in these products.[4]

Equally, with the foundation of the EEC in 1957 the Rome Treaty highlighted the importance of developing a coherent transport strategy by establishing the creation of a Common Transport Policy (CTP) as one of only two specific sectoral common policies to be pursued. More specifically, Article 3 of the Rome Treaty stated that, 'the activities of the Community shall include ... the adoption of a common policy in the sphere of transport'. Unfortunately, the actual nature of this common policy, while revealed in general terms, was not laid out in specific detail and has been open to a variety of different, detailed interpretations. Articles 74 – 84 gave the Council of Ministers and other Community institutions powers to formulate policy and set down general principles upon which such policy was to be based; but as we have pointed out, the specifics were lacking and this exacerbated many of the problems of the CTP in ensuing years.[5]

In addition to the shortcomings of the Rome Treaty with regard to the establishment of a CTP, the very concept itself poses serious problems which have proved difficult to surmount in the intervening years.[6] The original EEC area and even that of the enlarged European Community, is not, for example, a natural transport market, and the exclusion of countries such as Yugoslavia, Austria and Switzerland poses problems.[7] Further, there are very divergent views between members as to how transport should be treated: countries such as the UK view it as simply another sector which should have its internal efficiency maximized while France, Germany and some other states treat transport as a tool for achieving wider social, regional and political objectives and adopt policies accordingly. The legacy of diverse infrastructures, administrations and operational policies inherited by the Community policy-makers have added to the problems of formulating a common approach.

Given these, and other problems, the creation of a CTP has proved rather elusive – indeed until the late 1980s it was really little more than a 'will-o-the-wisp'. Initial efforts to draw up a blueprint[8] for Community-wide harmonization of approach prior to progression towards liberalization of transport markets, brought little more than agreements on technical matters. These included working hours for drivers and minor liberalizations such as a small quota of Community-wide road haulage licences and forked tariffs, rather than fixed rates, for the international carriage of goods by lorry.

Even though these early efforts were subsequently subjected to severe criticism they really need to be set in the context of the previous institutional arrangements in Europe. The Community agreement whereby each country could designate a number of its road hauliers to carry goods to and from any other Community state, represented one of the first shifts away from the notion that a member state was the sole authority which could give access to another country's transport. The forked tariff system, which allowed international road hauliers to negotiate rates within Community-established maximum and minimum levels, initiated a limited form of market flexibility into what had previously been a generally heavily regulated sector.[9] Equally, from a pragmatic perspective, it seems unlikely that any subsequent progress would have been forthcoming if early agreements on nitty-gritty questions such as driving hours had not been achieved. Without harmonization of such matters there would always be the fear that one country's haulage or other transport industries would enjoy an unfair advantage.

One of the reasons for the relatively slow progress beyond these initial measures was undoubtedly the Commission's idealistic approach at the time and its policy of trying to pursue a blueprint strategy, which latter was particularly inappropriate in several ways. First, the rigidity of some of the measures contrasted sharply with the needs of sectors such as road haulage which rely largely on flexibility for their efficiency. Second, many of the ideas underlying these early measures were based upon notions, such as the potential instability of road haulage markets, which had been little researched and subsequently proved to be incorrect. Last, many of the measures, such as the forked tariff system and quota licences, offered compromise moves towards greater liberalization, but provided no further incremental way forward.

Criticisms by the EEC Commission[10] of the progress being made, coupled with the first enlargement of the Community in 1973, did lead to a new impetus in the mid-1970s and some reorientation of effort on the part of policy-makers. Greater focus, for example, was placed on liberalization of markets, the role of infrastructure policy and more attention was paid to the integration of transport matters into broader policy issues concerning regional matters, such as energy and the environment. Nevertheless, once again, the hoped for common policy proved elusive and progress was fragmented and slow. Reference tariffs, whereby the Community published non-binding rate guidelines for road hauliers and their customers became an alternative to forked tariffs for road haulage; the quota system was enlarged; bilateral licensing arrangements between members were standardized; and new consultation procedures concerning transport infrastructure investments were investigated. But in total the impact was not generally impressive.[11]

Perhaps the only area where real progress could be observed related to shipping policy, which until 1977 had been a barren area for policy-makers. Between that time and the mid-1980s, however, a skeleton policy was developed, beginning in 1977 with the adoption of the Brussels package which enabled member states to adopt the UN Code of Conduct for Liner Conferences (cartels of merchant ships providing regular services over specified routes). In the same year the Community agreed on a consultation procedure for shipping. Perhaps the most potentially important change, however, was the adoption of a memorandum[12] in 1984 which provided the mechanism for further development of a more complete policy – the subsequent uptake of the initiative was, however, slow.

By the 1980s, the major developments towards a CTP were in fact coming from outside the Community's institutions with an idea for so-called 'E-roads' originating with the UN Economic Commission for Europe, the European joint air traffic control being run by Euro control and plans for high speed rail links being developed by the Community of European Railways.[13] Effectively the EC had lost the initiative.

Two factors have been instrumental in bringing forth rather more substantive changes in the late 1980s. First, there were legal pressures exerted both within the administrative structure of the Community (especially by the European Parliament which took the Council of Ministers to the European Court of Justice in 1983 for failure to implement the CTP); and by outside agencies (for example by transport service suppliers such as the travel firm Nouvelles Frontières) for more rapid progress to be made in the liberalization of European transport markets. Second, and of more long-term significance, the decision to move towards a SEM automatically brought with it a need to rethink the direction and pace of implementation of the CTP.[14]

The Cockfield Report

The document setting the scene for the creation of a SEM – the Cockfield Report[15] – drew attention to a number of barriers to trade which required removal before a single integrated internal market could be realized. These physical, technical and fiscal barriers extend as much to transport as other sectors of economic activity. The Cockfield Report touched upon a number of specific issues regarding the CTP and made recommendations regarding each of them. These were seen as unfinished issues but, in retrospect, were rather limited in their focus and underplayed the difficulties of rapid progress after such a long period of effective inertia on the part of decision-makers. They were also rather narrow in terms of the modes of transport considered.

In detail the Cockfield Report declared that the elimination of frontier checks for road haulage traffic was required together with:

(a) for the international transport of goods by road between member states, the phasing-out of quantitative restrictions (quotas) and the establishment of conditions under which non-resident carriers could operate transport services in another member state (cabotage) was to be completed by 1988 at the latest;

(b) for the transport of passengers by road, freedom to provide services was to be introduced by 1989;

(c) for the international transport of goods by inland waterway, freedom to provide services where this was not yet the case was to be introduced. Where necessary, conditions would be established under which non-resident carriers could operate inland navigation services in another

member state (cabotage). Both measures were to come into effect by 1989;
(d) the freedom to provide sea transport services between member states should be established by the end of 1986 at the latest, though with the possibility of a limited period for phasing out certain types of restrictions; and
(e) greater freedom in air transport services between member states to be provided by 1987. This would involve in particular changing the system for the setting and approval of tariffs, and limiting the rights of governments to restrict capacity and access to the market.

These requirements represented both a deepening and widening of existing transport policy. Cabotage, liberalization of market entry and easing of frontier crossing, for instance, extended policy in an area where considerable efforts had already been expended. The introduction of freer maritime markets and the liberalization of air passenger transport could be seen as a widening of the focus of transport policy into areas which had previously not been viewed as integral parts of the CTP. One should also note that the Cockfield proposals only related to certain aspects of the CTP which were seen as important from the perspective of creating a SEM. Developments outside this (for instance in railway financing, infrastructure provision, state aid policy) while seen as important components of the CTP and in which advances had been made since 1985, were not thought to be of direct relevance.[16]

Late in 1985 the Council of Transport Ministers approved a document, 'Towards a Common Transport Policy'.[17] This reiterated the sector-specific objectives of the Cockfield Report and set down four basic principles to guide the liberalization process. Three of these – equality of treatment within and between different forms of transportation, freedom of competition and free choice of uses and coordination of infrastructure development – were well-established. But a fourth – the need to develop policies with respect to the environment based on the polluter-pays principle, attracted more emphasis than previously; it also conflicted potentially with traditional notions of equality of treatment of alternative modes in that it implied favouring environmentally-friendly transport.

Overall progress since the mid-1980s has not been so dramatic as was hoped for, in either the Cockfield Report or the 1985 policy statement. This is seen by reference to some of the key policy areas. As we noted earlier, in respect of international road transport it was envisaged that quantitative barriers in the international EC market would be removed by 1988 and, further, that conditions for cabotage would be established. The mechanism adopted for removing quantitative restrictions on international haulage has been the gradual, annual increase in the number of quota licences with the aim of full liberalization by 1993. Progress has not, however, been so speedy as the Cockfield Report envisaged, since members with less efficient haulage industries or those having concerns about the impact of such measures on rail transport have resisted rapid expansions in the number of licences. However, in 1988 the Council of Ministers approved increases of 40 per cent in the quota for both 1988 and 1989 and in March 1990 it was agreed, against the wishes of Italy and Germany (which objected mainly to the linear nature of the increase across countries) to expand the quota by a further 40 per cent for 1990. Subsequent expansions, however, are to be taken on a step-by-step basis.[18]

With respect to cabotage, the aim was to have total freedom within the Community market by 1993, but with the possibility of short term safeguards if, for example, unstable competitive conditions emerged. While the Cockfield Report hoped for cabotage by 1988, the reality has been that the first tranche of 15,000 cabotage licences (agreed by a qualified majority) were only shared out in 1990, with a 10 per cent increase planned for each of the two subsequent years. Under the legislation road hauliers holding such licences are able to establish operations throughout the Community based on the laws and rules of the states in which they exercise cabotage (i.e. they must conform to local weight limits, VAT laws and so on). Even with these licences, restrictions insisted upon by France and Germany still apply and the Commission can intervene if more than 30 per cent of the authorizations are found to be used in any given area – which may or may not be a single country.

With respect to international maritime transport, the Cockfield Report proposed that the freedom to provide sea transport services between member states should be established by the end of 1986, at the latest. What actually happened was that by the end of 1986 some movement based on the 1984 memorandum had been achieved although it hardly met the objectives set out in the Cockfield Report.[19] The 1986 package broadly achieved four things. First, it applied the principle of freedom to provide services between member states and between member states and third countries, although one must remember that this freedom in EC terms did not mean liberalization of the market, but rather embodied the notion of non-discrimination. Its aim was essentially to prevent member states favouring their own shipping companies to the disadvantage of other members' mercantile marine. Second, it set out conditions under which the Community could impose compensatory duty on non-EC shipowners if they were found to be pursuing unfair pricing practices (e.g. being subsidized), causing injury or acting in ways contrary to the Community's interest. Third, it indicated what was meant by fair competition in the maritime context and established the situations (such as liner cargo conferences) where *en bloc* exemptions to Articles 85 and 86 were granted. However, it also laid down conditions for consultation with shippers over rates, quality of service and so forth, to which liner conferences should adhere. Finally, it provided for coordinated Community action through diplomatic initiatives and counter-measures where access of EC shipping companies to ocean trades was restricted by a third country.

The draft proposals for reform aimed at actually freeing the internal shipping market only appeared in 1987 and have made little subsequent headway. The notions of a 'Community Fleet' for flagging purposes (the EUROS scheme whereby ships could keep national flags but, provided they conformed with certain technical requirements, would also fly a Community flag), and the introduction of cabotage rights for all EC shipping within the Community's area of operations, have met with opposition. Greece, in particular, questioned the necessity of the flagging proposal and drew attention to the potentially adverse effects of maritime cabotage on the mercantile marine of other states where shipping is also currently a major element in the national transport system.[20]

Equally, very little progress has been made with regard to the liberalization of public passenger transport (international coach services) and inland water transport. In particular, with the former there have been problems in initiating a system of cabotage rights with strong opposition being voiced by countries currently affected by through coach traffic and which fear that cabotage arrangements would also ultimately adversely affect their own road passenger transport industries. While the Community has stated its intention to devote considerable efforts to overcome the current impasse in international coach transport before 1993, there is a considerable way to go if current restrictions are to be removed which give the country of origin sole province over traffic originating within its borders. Equally, with inland waterways, a succession of multinational treaties have grown up over the past two centuries and those benefiting from them are reluctant to accept notions of cabotage.

As mentioned above, transport infrastructure policy was not seen in the Cockfield Report to be of direct relevance to the creation of an internal European market. However, some progress has been made since the mid-1980s towards the creation of an infrastructure programme designed to bridge the missing links. While this may not be seen strictly as an element in the move to a SEM, it does nevertheless represent something of a policy-deepening following on from agreements amongst Community members in the 1960s to consult over infrastructure plans. The developments have not been as great as the Commission had hoped in 1986 when it set out a list of priorities for transport investments which should receive Community support,[21] and though the programme was endorsed by the Council, no independent transport infrastructure budget was established. Monies have, however, been channelled into several of the priority projects – such as the Scanlink road and rail link between Denmark and Sweden, motorway standard links between Greece and Italy across Yugoslavia and the North Wales coast road as a transit link to Ireland – through the European Investment Bank and the European Regional Development Fund.

A further element of infrastructure policy has been the efforts of the Commission to improve commercial aviation facilities, especially with respect to air traffic control.[22] While the Council has rejected ideas of a single Community air-traffic control system, steps have been taken to bring Denmark, Italy and Spain within the existing Euro-control arrangement and to create a central flow management system to coordinate national air traffic control systems. Further, given that air traffic control is only as effective as its weakest link, monies are being made available (for example to Greece) to upgrade the less sophisticated national systems. The gradual ending of the cold war suggests that further activity in this area could well be expected in the next decade as more military air space is freed for commercial use and adjustments to air traffic control arrangements become necessary.

Linked with the initiatives in infrastructure expansion have been moves to make more efficient and equitable use of the Community's transport infrastructure. By 1990, however, these had still to be implemented but the Commission was active in seeking ways of ensuring that road track is charged for in a consistent manner across countries and that port users pay the full costs of their activities. The key notion, yet to be fully operationalized, is that infrastructure financing will be on a 'pay-as-you-use' basis (featuring road tolls or fuel tax rather than flat rate vehicle taxes on road users).

The aviation sector

The liberalization of the Community's aviation market is singled out for particular attention both because it provides an interesting case-study of the difficulties which can be encountered in moving towards a freer market situation and because it represents an important widening out of the development of a common transport policy.

International aviation within Europe grew up under a system of bilateral agreements between national governments which, as a rule, involved fare-setting, capacity controls, scheduling and other restrictions. In many cases routes had only a single designated carrier from each of the countries involved. Overall this neither stimulated efficiency among the carriers of each country nor, on a route-by-route basis, did it encourage efficiency on the part of the two designated carriers. Even in the limited cases where there was multiple designation, and more than one carrier from each country was allowed to operate, this was usually restricted in nature (often only two airlines from each country being involved) and did little to generate real competition. The situation was made worse on many routes where revenue pooling was part of the bilateral arrangement, since this virtually eliminated the incentive to attract additional passengers.

Additionally, many European airlines were state-owned and as such were seen as vehicles of national prestige as well as modes of transport; subsidies were the norm; further, given national sovereignty over airspace, cabotage was not permitted and national domestic aviation was heavily controlled, which was not consistent with the idea of a common air transport market.

The Rome Treaty, however, did not define transport; the liberalizing provisions of Article 3 of the treaty were only to apply to road, rail and inland waterways initially, with air and maritime transport to be left until such time as unanimous agreement was reached by the Council of Ministers. This was a pragmatic decision based mainly on the small scale of intra-EEC aviation in 1957, coupled with the complex nature of the intergovernmental agreements regulating it. What was not immediately clear, however, was the extent to which certain general treaty provisions, such as those governing anti-trust activities, and discrimination, applied to aviation.[23]

The Commission had been active in the 1970s[24] in trying to develop an aviation policy but viewed liberalization of fares and market entry as a long-term prospect. It was not really until 1984 that the Commission moved from looking at what it thought to be desirable to setting out actual liberalizing proposals.[25] The proposals put forward at that time were hardly revolutionary: fares were still to be regulated but only so that they fell within 'zones of reasonableness' (to ensure that excess profits were not earned by the airlines but at the same time enabling an acceptable return to be earned on assets). Further, there would be greater flexibility in terms of how traffic on routes would be allocated to different carriers and there would be controls over the agreements made by the airlines (for example in terms of revenue pooling).

Such initiatives, however, achieved little, and the progress which was made in the early 1980s took the form of relaxation of domestic aviation in some countries like the UK and of the introduction of more liberal bilateral agreements as between the UK and The Netherlands. In part these were spurred on by the demonstration effects of the deregulation of the US domestic aviation market, where fare-setting and market entry had been liberalized under the 1978 Airline Deregulation Act[26] and by the knock-on effects of the US pressure for an open skies policy in transatlantic air services.[27] The impetus for action at the Community level can be traced to the success of the French travel agent Nouvelles Frontières in gaining a ruling from the European Court of Justice regarding its air-fare cutting activities.[28] The key outcome of this was that it showed the Commission that despite the fact that the Council of Ministers had not granted it powers to implement Articles 85 and 86 in respect of airlines, its powers to attack collusive fare-setting were stronger than some had anticipated. It could still rule adversely on an airline restriction and national courts would subsequently take note of this. On this basis, the Commission began in 1987 to instigate proceedings against airlines with the underlying intention of forcing the Council of Ministers to respond by initiating wider reforms. The point of all this was that if court cases were successful full-scale competition could ensue. If the Council of Ministers wished to control the speed and intensity of competition it was in their power to do so by introducing appropriate deregulatory measures.

The response of the ministers, which also subsequently resulted in the withdrawal of legal actions by the Commission, was indeed to agree to introduce a relatively radical package of measures in 1987.[29] A permanent measure allowing the Commission to apply the Article 85 and 86 rules relating to competition directly to aviation, excluding intra-state operations and operations to third countries was adopted (see chapter 3).[30] Enabling legislation in 1988, however, did allow the Commission to exempt for a limited duration (to expire by 1991) *en bloc* three categories of agreement: those concerning joint planning and coordination of capacity, revenue sharing, consultations on tariffs and aircraft parking slot allocation; those relating to computer reservation systems (CRSs); and those concerning ground-handling services.

Whether these exemptions were likely to lead to airlines pursuing anti-competitive activities in practice is difficult to say;[31] in some areas it does seem unlikely. The European Civil Aviation Commission and the EC Commission have already drawn up codes of conduct designed to reduce the most blatant forms of abuse of CRSs. The main problem with CRSs in the USA is that they are often owned by a large airline with access sold to other airlines. This has in the past led to the owning company presenting flight information which is biased in its favour and, in addition, it was in a position to gain access to information about other airlines' bookings, load factors, and so on which could give it a commercial advantage in its own fare-setting, scheduling and marketing. Moreover, the form of owner-ship used in Europe, with joint ownership by a number of carriers, is different from that found in the USA, where one or two larger systems each owned by a single carrier dominate the market; the ability to abuse the system is therefore reduced,[32] indeed, even under the block exemption, should vendors abuse their position, the exemption could be revoked and the Council could ultimately divest the systems.

In many ways the rules governing CRSs in the Community are more satisfactory than those which have been in place in the US for a number of years. While the US regulations are designed to ensure information regarding services offered by different airlines is presented in an impartial way, the EC rules also ensure that there is so-called market neutrality. This means that information regarding different flight options (such as non-stop, stopping but with no change of aircraft and stopping with a change of aircraft required) for a particular route are also displayed in an unbiased manner. What has not really been tackled directly is the issue of halo effects – the distortions which can result from the way travel agents actually convey unbiased information on CRS screens to potential travellers. These effects have been found to bias systems in favour of airlines owning CRS systems in the USA because of the various incentives which influence agents in the advice they offer clients (often not overt, and including such things as ease of booking particular airline services from the CRS). Multiple ownership of European systems may reduce this problem, but it is still likely to remain to some extent.

The Council also adopted a directive in 1987 designed to provide airlines with greater pricing freedom,[33] and the enabling legislation allowed for collusion in the short term but individual airlines could act individually when applying for approval of air fares. A state authority was directed to accept a fare application if it was reasonably related to economic costs – i.e. it could not reject a fare simply because it undercut another operator. The Civil Aviation Authority in the UK, for instance, could not reject a fare proposal from Air France on the London–Paris route simply because it is lower than British Airways' fare. Disputes over a fare went to arbitration. While the fare-setting procedure applied primarily to economy scheduled fares, the directive also provided scope for discounts. Provided certain conditions were met, fares could be reduced by varying amounts. Fifth freedom operators (i.e. third party airlines carrying passengers between two other states) were allowed to match any discounts.

A phased policy of liberalizing market access over three years was also initiated by a decision of Council in 1987.[34] The traditional 50–50 division of traffic common in most bilateral pooling agreements was relaxed so that, in the period to October 1989, where competition existed the share could change up to a 55–45 split and state authorities were not permitted to intervene. The split could become as wide as 60–40 thereafter. This meant that countries such as Italy, Greece, Denmark and France which traditionally rigidly controlled capacity had to liberalize to a considerable extent.

Further, over a period of time member states gradually lost the right to refuse multiple designation by other member states on a city pair basis. This has the effect of widening the scope for national authorities to designate more than one carrier to each route. Automatic fifth freedom rights were also extended but effective competition from such activities was constrained by specific stipulations about the nature of services which could be offered and the types of airport which had to be used. Additional to all this, the Commission reminded member states of their obligation to open ownership of air carriers to nationals of other member states.

Regulation of European aviation is an ongoing process and the trend is towards further liberalization. While the above package of measures (now commonly called phase one) was being implemented within the Community, the Commission developed proposals for the next phase of policy reform. As a pragmatic measure, during a second phase of liberalization, the EC Commission proposed in 1989 the encouragement of greater use of regional airports as a priority. This was to meet the high levels of forecast demand for air travel at a time when there were going to be inevitable limits on infrastructure capacity at main airports. To cater for demand predictions, action was also needed to encourage the use of larger aircraft and, *ipso facto*, reduced air movements for a given volume of passengers.

The question of an appropriate mechanism for landing-slot allocation in this type of environment is a crucial one and the EC Commission seems uncertain as to the way forward. At present most airports have arrangements whereby the airlines themselves, and especially the incumbent carriers, decide on slot allocations. In the short term the Commission is still developing strategies in order to make better use of this existing infrastructure until new capacity comes on-stream.[35] In 1990 the options being reviewed were reduced to three. First, the notion of landing-slot auctions as devices to employ the market directly so that those carriers which make the most efficient use of a slot are in a position to purchase that slot from incumbents. Airlines would effectively make bids to use slots for a predetermined period and those offering the most would gain them. This idea, for obvious reasons, was unpopular with the incumbent carriers. There was also the technical problem that if planes were delayed they would lose their slot. On the other hand it conformed with economic notions of competition.

The second option is to limit the use any airline can make of slots and to reallocate the surplus generated to new carriers or to carriers which at present have few slots. This would increase competition by giving more airlines access to an airport but may well penalize very efficient carriers which, by virtue of their cost advantage, could make the most efficient use of a very large quota of slots. The third option, and the easiest to introduce in the short term, is for unused or little-used slots allocated to incumbent airlines to be transferred to new carriers which cannot at present operate at congested airports. This has the merit of both increasing overall effective capacity and introducing a greater degree of competition although, in practice, given the domination of incumbent airlines at many airports, the overall impact may be muted. Unfortunately political pressures may result in the third option being favoured.

Late 1989 saw a rather sudden and slightly unexpected movement forward in the liberalization process. An accord (a firm political agreement but still requiring facilitating legislation) was reached designed to move towards a SEM by the beginning of 1993. In part the rather sudden change may have been influenced by lobbying in Brussels on behalf of the French airline Union de Transports Aeriens (UTA) which was complaining about unfair discrimination against it in the allocation of European licences. UTA was refused European route licences by the French government on a number of routes currently served by the state owned Air France.[36] It was agreed by the Council in 1989 that by January 1993 the following would be completed:

(a) The removal of government-to-government capacity-sharing arrangements guaranteeing each country's airline a certain percentage of the market.
(b) The introduction of the principle of double disapproval for fares. This would remove the ability of just one country in a bilateral agreement to veto a change in airline fares – both would have to agree to block such a change. The measure would be introduced in a staggered fashion with fare zones being introduced allowing airlines to cut their prices to as low as 30 per cent of the standard economy tariff subject to the double disapproval rule until by 1993 they will be free to set the fares they wish subject to the rule.
(c) Governments would cease to discriminate against airlines provided that they met technical and safety standards and ran economically.

In addition to this accord, at the same meeting of the European Community Transport Ministers agreement was reached on ownership rules. Until then an airline had to prove that it was 'substantially owned' by one European nation or its nationals before it was allowed to fly from that country. The new rules abolish this requirement over a two-year period. This means that fifth freedom rights within the EC become automatic.[37]

Subsequent meetings of ministers in the summer of 1990 put some flesh on the final interim arrangements prior to the full implementation of the accord. From July 1990 this involved fare zones for normal, discount and deep-discount fares with restrictions planned for fares becoming tighter as the discounts increased. Double disapproval, in the intermediate phase would only apply to fares higher than the normal fares. To resolve the matter of conflict regarding fares, arbitration procedures were established; further, the share of markets reserved for any airline on a given route were to decline by 7.5 per cent a year to 25 per cent by 1992, and a member state would have to grant landing rights to more than one airline from another member state if a route represented more than 600 flights or 100,000 passengers annually. Fifth freedom rights could be exercised, with the exception of a very limited number of airports, for up to 50 per cent of an aircraft's capacity – it was 30 per cent up to 1990. More flexible agreements on the allocation of slots were accepted albeit with caveats linked to the containment of charter flights.

How significant will the new package ultimately be?[38] While the earlier package of measures essentially allowed airlines access to routes, it did nothing to compel a state to allow its own airlines access to routes. The *Ahmed Saeed*[39] case in 1989 effectively forced change in this respect with the European Court of Justice's judgement making it clear that EC competition rules apply to domestic air transport within a member state, and indeed to international air transport between a member and a non-member state. The new package would by 1993 compel states to allow their own airlines access to routes – it effectively allowed for the right of establishment of a company anywhere in the Community. The accord also means that cabotage will be permitted, subject to some limitations and conditions.

Progress towards meeting the requirements of a SEM with a strong market liberalizing orientation, has, therefore, gathered pace since 1985. Aviation is now part of this movement. In particular, there have been important moves to develop a structure of aviation regulation which will permit a high level of effective competition within the industry. What is equally clear, however, is that the existing system differs in many important ways from the open market approach which has been adopted in the US and, further, it seems clear that the American approach will never be fully embraced within Europe.[40]

Furthermore, it does not mean that problems do not remain within the framework which has emerged. Questions of cabotage rights and their role as links between domestic and intra-European international services are an obvious example. The long-term approach to mergers policy is equally still not completely clarified, and the Commission is seeking a way of ensuring that the European market does not become dominated by mega-carriers, but at the same time ensuring that in the larger international market European airlines are not disadvantaged by their size from competing efficiently with US and other major carriers.[41] Fostering a policy of allowing mergers where there exists complementarity but preventing those which reduce competition is, however, difficult to put into practice on a consistent basis. The situation is compounded by the expansion of such things as marketing agreements, minority share holdings of one airline in another and the growing practice of backing shares by equity capital. The hand of the Commission was strengthened in this respect in late 1989 when it was agreed that the EC merger policy would enable concentrations with a Community dimension to be investigated by the Commission (see chapter 3). In other words a proactive element was introduced into competition policy.

The takeover by Air France of UTA was one of the first to come under the new code. It may, therefore, offer some general insights as to how the competition directorate would actually view mergers and acquisitions in the aviation field. The decision of October 1990 was to allow the acquisition which, because of the previous joint ownership of Air Inter, would give Air France 97 per cent of French airline-operated domestic and international flights. However, state-owned Air France had to relinquish its 35 per cent stake in the airline Transport Aerien Transregional (TAT), and in addition some eight major domestic and 50 international routes had to be opened up to secondary French airlines and this was coupled with the acceptance of second carriers from other EC countries on routes into France.

Allowing the takeover but divestiture of routes and assets follows the pattern of a much earlier agreement reached prior to the introduction of the new competition policy, when British Airways took over British Caledonian and may well produce similar results. The enlarged company has increased market power and is thus in a better position to compete in international markets with the mega-carriers from the US and Asia, but the action to stimulate competition in domestic and EC aviation markets is not sufficient. The problem in the UK was that after 1988 there were few takers for the routes given up by the enlarged BA which subsequently moved back into them. In France it seems unlikely that TAT, Mineve, Air Littoral and Air Liberté combined with some local carriers will be able to fill the void left as Air France divests routes.

Progress towards liberalizing intra-EC aviation has unquestionably been gradual but there have nevertheless been significant steps forward over the past decade and further advances seem inescapable. Comparisons with the sudden, dramatic changes in the US are inevitable but the need to deal with each of the twelve countries has severely limited opportunities for rapid and planned transformation. Such speed may also have been undesirable for the EC, in the sense that the costs of being first in the field were borne by US carriers and their travelling public, whilst those concerned with EC policy have had the opportunity to wait and observe before acting. There is already evidence that this has happened with respect to such things as CRS controls and attitudes towards merger policy. The danger with this approach is that policy makers may wait too long and in seeking to ensure optimality in decision-making may actually miss important opportunities. Furthermore, the lack of a clear policy within the Community, coupled with the prospect of EC airlines not being fully attuned to the full rigours of competitive and contestable market conditions, could, in the long term, adversely affect the performance of European carriers in the world market. In particular, it could give US and Asian carriers greater scope to expand their international operations at the expense of European airlines.

Conclusion

It is undoubtedly true that the move towards the single market has concentrated the minds of transport policy-makers in the EC wonderfully. Progress towards creating a single liberalized market has been made, but much remains to be done. In terms of deepening, for example, still to be resolved are the issues of the eventual move to full cabotage in road haulage and in public passenger transport by road. Steps have been taken but the path still has potential pitfalls in it. Cabotage throughout Europe will inevitably have very different impacts upon the surface transport industries of member states and some degree of reaction from those with vested interests in the status quo is inevitable.

Where widening has occurred it has mainly been on the aviation front. Certainly, agreements on a more competitive ports policy coupled with plans for integrated port investment have emerged but maritime policy *per se* has made little progress. In particular, the lack of agreement on cabotage arrangements poses problems for intra-Community traffic, while lack of agreement to establish a European registry makes it difficult for a coordinated EC policy to be established regarding trade outside of the Community. Aviation policy has made very significant progress in the past four years but problems remain. While the lessons of the US, regarding the liberalizing of aviation within the Community have been learned and clear policies on such matters as CRSs have emerged, there still remain questions regarding the way in which mergers will be treated in the face of a world where aviation has become a global rather than regional policy matter. Linked with this is the issue of the extent to which the Commission can talk for the member states when negotiating traffic rights with non-member states. While it may be true that European aviation as a whole could enjoy advantages in the long term if world aviation markets were freer, there are significant differences in the efficiency of EC carriers and, for example, reciprocal agreements between the EC and US for mutual cabotage rights would mean many European airlines facing acquisition or extinction. National governments in the EC with a tradition of flag carriers as symbols of national virility are not all enthusiastic about giving over powers of negotiation to the Community.

Chapter 7

The external implications of 1992

Christopher Milner and David Allen

Introduction

The primary economic aim of completing the European internal market
was to benefit the member states of the EC, not to raise the welfare of
the world as a whole. It is, however, a matter of considerable diplomatic
sensitivity whether non-EC states, either individually or collectively, will
be better or worse off (absolutely or relatively) as a result of the 1992
programme. In any event the extent of any external gains or losses are,
and will remain, difficult to calculate precisely, which given the nature of
contemporary international relations, is likely to lead to external speculation
and apprehension as well as enthusiasm. The fact that the exact details
of the 1992 programme are not fixed but are constantly evolving serves
to exacerbate this process and encourages attempts by non-EC states to
influence that evolution. Furthermore the 1992 programme is inextricably
interwoven, via the SEA and IGCs on EMU and political union, with the
political objective of advancing the EC towards European union. The 1992
programme is therefore also an important factor in the general enhancement
of the EC's presence as both an economic and a political force in the
international system and this is also likely to provoke a variety of external
responses.

The naïvely optimistic view is that closer European integration will
result in gains for all countries. Immediate losses for non-members due
to any increase in trade diversion, or loss of priveleged access to previously
protected markets resulting from the lowering of internal barriers, can be
expected to be overshadowed by the dynamic effects of market expansion.
Baldwin[1] has estimated (probably rather optimistically) that this could lead
to the rate of economic growth increasing by up to 1 per cent a year. Similarly
increases in the competitiveness of European producers in the EC and foreign
export markets, resulting from the increased scale and integration of internal
markets, need not result in losses for non-members' export industries if there
are market growth effects, or if 1992 provides incentives and opportunities
for foreign firms to increase competitiveness. Non-EC firms located inside

and outside the EC can also benefit from the single market and the reduced costs of transacting across internal borders and of standardized technical requirements. Indeed some foreign producers can expect to gain directly from increased exports when discriminatory national bilateral trade measures are removed, such as the voluntary export restraints on the importation of Japanese cars into certain EC countries.

It is not naïve, of course, to point to the opportunities that 1992 will create for outside countries. An integrated market of 340 million consumers offers potential scale-advantages for outside producers. Economic growth within the EC induced by integration would increase the demand for products that are income-elastic. Reduced discrimination in EC commercial policy would benefit those countries previously discriminated against. It would be naïve, however, to overlook the fact that competitiveness is a relative concept, and that increases in competition within the EC may well favourably alter the competitive position of EC producers *vis-à-vis* non-member producers. Indeed 1992 provides a number of opportunities for the EC to ensure that EC members benefit relative to non-member competitors. The benefits of access to the completed market for non-members may be reduced by the need to pay an entry price. The price may be aquiescence to reciprocity demands for improved or preferential access for EC exports to non-members' markets. Alternatively the threat or actual existence of EC-wide protection may induce greater inward, direct investment and local content than would apply in the absence of such protection. Indeed the potential for such protection post-1992 may not only result from the increased opportunities associated with increased market power; but they may also arise from adjustment costs, associated with the market completion process, that provide internal incentives for greater protection against non-members. It is not difficult to understand how an appreciation of the considerations mentioned above can lead non-members to see 1992 more as threat than an opportunity and thus to believe that there is a need to counter the development of fortress Europe.

It is the aim of this chapter, therefore, to identify the nature of the external effects of 1992, to evaluate the balance of the threats and opportunities associated with these anticipated effects and to examine the responses to date of the major non-EC states and groupings of states. The emphasis of the analysis will be on the merchandise trade and trade policy implications of 1992, but attention will also be given to the related issues of services, factor mobility and development aid. In addition to the analysis of these specific issues, the aim is to investigate the wider implications of 1992 for the conduct of international economic policy both multi-laterally, as in the case of the GATT, and bilaterally, as in relations between the EC and the United States, Japan and EFTA.

The single market and external trade

Although tariffs and quotas on intra-EC trade have been largely removed over the years, important barriers to trade nevertheless remain and are the target of the 1992 programme. There are differences in technical regulations between members, delays at frontiers for customs purposes, restrictions on competition in the area of public procurement and restrictions on establishment in the area of financial and transport services. Individually many of these barriers impose only small additional costs to intra-EC trade and are probably easily overcome. Even if all these barriers are removed as a result of the 1992 legislation then natural sources of market segmentation, such as linguistic and cultural differences, would remain. Nevertheless when all removable internal market barriers are taken together, and when viewed in the context of the oligopolistic market structures that are pervasive in many of the industrial sectors of the EC, then there is substantial scope for reducing price divergence for comparable products and services between the member states.

Although significant progress has been made to date it is unlikely that the removal of technical, physical and fiscal differences between member states will be achieved immediately after 1992. However, the process of creating a European internal market after 1992 can be expected to gradually reduce constraints on the efficient use of resources within the Community and to create a more competitive environment. The specific sources of gain and of production and trade effects may be as follows; cost reductions resulting from the greater exploitation of scale effects, the stimulus to efficiency and rationalization resulting from increased competition, increased specialization in line with comparative advantage influences and induced product and process innovation.

The creation of the single market will affect both intra- and extra-EC trade. These changes can be expected to have both trade-creating and trade-diverting effects. Trade creation, or the increase in intra-EC exports and imports, will result from the reduction of barriers to trade between members. But there will also be trade diversion, in other words a reduction in extra-EC imports, as member states switch their source of supply from states outside to those within the EC.

Rough estimates of the magnitude of the effects discussed above have been produced by the EC Commission within the context of the 'Costs of Non-Europe' project[2]. The calculations are presented in the study in several stages: first, the direct cost-reduction effects of removing barriers affecting goods actually traded between EC members;[3] second, the direct and indirect production cost effects of removing barriers affecting goods produced in the EC, whether traded or not;[4] third, the dynamic effects of scale-economies associated with increased output and restructuring; and fourth, the dynamic effects of the elimination of X-inefficiencies and rents due to increased competition.

Stages one and two are concerned with the effects of removing barriers, while stages three and four are market integration effects. Estimates of the effects of stages one and two on extra-EC imports[5] for twenty-six primary and secondary sectors used in EC input–output tables are set out in Table 7.1. In two sectors (coal and coke) small increases in extra-EC imports are predicted: the elimination of some technical barriers for example will mean that the extra costs of meeting individual country specifications will be saved by external as well as internal producers and exporters. But clearly the static trade diversion effect is estimated to predominate. The net impact on extra-EC imports for five sectors is estimated to be zero, but falls are

Table 7.1 Estimated impact changes in extra-EC imports due to removal of internal barriers: EURO(7)

NACE	Industry groups	(bill. ECU) extra EC imports (1985)	(bill. ECU) Change in extra[1] EC imports		
		(a)	(b) Stage(i)	(c) Stage(ii)	(d) Combined
010	Agricultural products	101.33	−0.12	0.00	− 0.12
030	Coal	5.23		+0.15	+ 0.15
050	Coke	0.18		+0.01	+ 0.01
070	Petroleum+ natural gas	95.34	−0.27	−4.19	− 4.46
090	Electricity, gas, steam, water	0.58		−0.19	− 0.19
110	Nuclear fuels	1.67		0.00	0.00
130	Ferrous and non-ferrous	29.30		−9.08	− 9.08
150	Non-metallic minerals	4.31		−0.39	− 0.39
170	Chemical products	23.30	−0.34	−2.42	− 2.76
190	Metal products	4.44	−0.36	−0.55	− 0.91
210	Machines	17.51	−2.68	−1.47	− 4.15
230	Office machines etc.	19.47	−0.83	−1.30	− 2.13
250	Electrical goods	26.81	−1.73	−2.06	− 3.79
270	Motor vehicles	14.09	−1.46	−1.04	− 2.50
290	Other transp. equipm.	6.50	−0.32	−0.33	− 0.76
310	Metal, metal products	3.78		0.00	0.00
330	Milk, dairy products	0.67		0.00	0.00
350	Other food products	8.60		0.00	0.00
370	Beverages	0.69	−0.21	−0.02	− 0.23
390	Tobacco products	0.10		0.00	0.00
410	Textiles, clothing	20.44	−0.39	−1.19	− 1.58
430	Leather, footwear	4.98	−0.29	−0.32	− 0.61
450	Timber, wooden products	7.96	−0.27	−0.59	− 0.86
470	Paper and printing	12.73	−0.07	−0.85	− 0.92
490	Rubber and plastic	4.15	−0.04	−0.34	− 0.37
510	Other manufactures	12.13	−0.74	−0.73	− 1.47
	TOTAL	426.29			−37.16

Source: European Communities Commission, 'The Economics of 1992', *European Economy*, no. 35, 1988.
Notes: 1 Largest estimate for alternative cost assumptions.

predicted for the remaining nineteen sectors: the percentage fall due to the removal of barriers ranging from 0.12 per cent in the case of agricultural products to 33.33 per cent in the case of beverages. The significance of the percentage falls is, however, dependent on the extent of extra-EC imports in a particular sector. In these terms the most important changes are ferrous and non-ferrous ores and metals, chemical products, machines, office machines, electrical goods and motor vehicles.

Of course these estimates may be viewed as overestimates, to the extent that the costs of existing barriers are overstated or that the barriers are not fully eliminated after 1992. However it must be emphasized that these estimates relate only to seven of the twelve EC states[6] and that further trade diversion towards the new Mediterranean members of the EC can be anticipated. The longer-term or dynamic effects of market integration (stages three and four) are estimated (see Table 7.2) by the costs of non-Europe projects, comparable to those of stages one and two in terms of net welfare.[7] The time-scale for these effects is less predictable, and there have been criticisms of the over-optimistic growth scenarios suggested by the Commission.[8] There are, however, other independent studies that indicate a potentially substantial medium-term growth bonus from the 1992 programme. Baldwin's[9] most cautious estimates are for percentage increases in GDP (for combined static and medium-term effects) ranging from 4.5 per cent to 11.7 per cent in the case of France, to 5.9 per cent to 25.45 per cent in the case of Belgium.[10] But only fairly modest growth effects are in fact required overall to offset the type of impact-declines in extra-EC imports forecast in Table 7.1. The optimistic (and most unrealistic) end of the Baldwin growth phase estimates would imply substantial expansion of non-members' exports to the EC. It is probably not these direct trade effects of 1992, however, that are of interest to non-members, even though the

Table 7.2 Estimated dynamic consequences of the completion of the internal market on total GDP of EEC (% change)

		European Commission estimates		
		1 year	2 years	Medium term
(a)	Abolition of frontier controls	0.0	+0.1	+0.4
(b)	Liberalisation of public procurement	+0.2	+0.3	+0.4 → 0.8
(c)	Liberalisation of financial services	+0.4	+1.1	+0.8 → 2.1
(d)	'Supply effects' due to increased competition	+0.5	+0.9	+1.7 → 2.5
	TOTAL	+1.1	+2.3	+3.3 → 5.8

Source: European Communities Commission, 'The Economics of 1992', European Economy, no. 35, 1988.

compositional effects may be of significance to individual states. In any case the direct effects, if they do occur, do not require any specific reaction from non-members. There are however two potential indirect effects which are likely to be more important and which may spur non-members into some sort of response to the 1992 programme. First, the substantial increases in intra-EC trade predicted after 1992 will cause adjustment problems inside the EC, which may affect EC attitudes towards extra-EC imports. Second, increased competitiveness within the EC implies a new competitive threat from EC producers in non-members' own markets.

How specific third countries or blocs of countries are affected by the single market after 1992 depends therefore on the pattern and level of their trade with the EC, as well as upon the degree of market integration introduced by the programme. We return to the implications for specific countries and blocs later. For the present it is important to re-emphasize that the external implications will depend crucially on how both the EC and non-members react to the challenges and threats of specific elements of the single market programme. Let us elaborate this point with some specific examples.

Elimination of national restraints

National constraints on imported goods currently exist in the EC on both a legal and extra-legal basis. A recent GATT review of the EC's trade policies[11] criticized the EC for its propensity to strike bilateral agreements 'targeted against the most competitive foreign suppliers' among its trading partners. EC textile and clothing manufacturers are protected by eighteen bilateral agreements under the Multifibre Arrangements (MFA), maintained on a legal basis under Article 115 of the Rome Treaty. The best known extra-legal restraints are the voluntary export restraints (VERs) currently operated by the France, Italy, Portugal, Spain and the UK against specific imports. The most notorious concern exports of Japanese cars, machinery, electrical and electronic equipment to the EC but South Korea now appears to come a close second with agreements on frozen squid, footwear and video-tape recorders. The removal of these national restraints ought to be welcomed by non-EC states (and indeed by the European Commission which told the GATT that it was 'not aware' of some of these measures!) as liberalizing and pro-competitive. It has to be remembered, however, that these VERs and the specific source quotas of the MFA were introduced to appease specific industrial lobbies. The prize of greater internal and external competition is not likely to win many votes in these sectors. Inevitably there has been producer-pressure to have national restraints replaced by Euro-restraints, on the grounds that there is no reason why overseas producers should benefit from market completion to an equivalent degree to EC producers. Additionally, it has been claimed that transitional arrangements are required in order that EC firms can comfortably adapt to the new market conditions.

There is a danger that the Commission will find such arguments seductive, if only because they allow it to retain control of trade policy – control which has been lost as national VERs have proliferated. There is also a danger that pressure on the Commission from internal EC producers will be perceived outside the EC as part of a process designed to lead to fortress Europe.

An indication of this threat can be seen in the developments in the passenger car sector. Elimination of the VERs on Japanese cars would undoubtedly raise Japanese market shares in France, Italy, Portugal, Spain and the UK. While at present the Japanese car manufacturers together have about 11.6 per cent of the total western European market, the greater share they could achieve in unprotected European markets is already evident. In Germany they have 15.9 per cent, in The Netherlands 26.7 per cent, in Denmark 35.9 per cent and in Eire 42.2 per cent. Although Japanese car manufacturers captured only a 5.1 per cent share of the restricted (i.e those states protected by VERs) European markets in 1990, they already controlled more than 30 per cent of the open markets.[12] The Italian and French car industries have in particular led a well-orchestrated lobbying effort on the Commission. Until recently, however, the Commission's attempts to hammer out an agreed position among the member governments has been complicated by disunity among European car makers themselves. Now this seems to have been resolved by the isolation of Peugeot – Japan's most hardline opponent – and the newly formed Association des Constructeurs Européens d'Automobiles (ACEA) now have a united position, parts of which the Commission is likely to accept. The car manufacturers want to restrict the Japanese share of the EC market to around 15 per cent up until 1999 but accept that after that date all restraints should be removed. More controversially, the ACEA wants the 15 per cent ceiling to include all Japanese car makes irrespective of whether they are produced inside the EC or imported from Japan or the United States. This suggestion is likely to cause further internal wrangling between the UK (where Honda, Nissan and Toyota are already established) and France but more important for our purposes is the fact that in April 1991 for the first time, Honda started to ship cars to Europe from one of its US assembly plants. The US can be expected to react strongly to any perceived attempts by the EC to restrict the importation of what they would regard as American not Japanese cars. Although the Commission is unlikely to accept all the ACEA demands, the key point is that an agreement of sorts has been reached in a large, symbolically important, sector with a high political profile. A precedent has been established at an early stage in the 1992 process that potential adjustment problems can be used as a basis for securing special arrangements. Specific sectoral arrangements can and will be countenanced.

The question of specific sectoral arrangements was also highlighted in the recent GATT review[13] which raised several questions about the Community's institutional arrangements. It supplied additional fuel for those concerned about the democratic deficit (see also chapter 10) in the EC by pointing out the lack of a statutory independent body at the Community level to act as a watchdog in trade matters, now that national trade powers have been transferred to Brussels. The abolition of national VERs represents a further transfer or retransfer of powers from national governments, theoretically answerable to national parliaments, to the Commission and the Council, which are not effectively controlled by the European Parliament. The system under which the Commission proposes and the Council of Ministers disposes tends to favour sector-specific views against overall economic or trade considerations, and the 1992 programme is likely to continue this trend. Although cars, steel and coal are all cited as examples of the EC's enthusiasm for pursuing individual interests separately, the most glaring example of this is of course to be found in agriculture, where the decisions, or rather non-decisions, of the twelve farm ministers effectively contributed to the breakdown of the GATT Uruguay round of talks in December 1990.

Both the question of an EC replacement for national VERs, and the GATT Uruguay Round experience are good examples of the general problem that the EC has in coming to a common negotiating position in trade matters. The inflexibility of its decision-making machinery must put the EC at a disadvantage when attempting to negotiate as an equal partner with either Japan or the United States. As we have seen above, completion of the 1992 programme will inevitably require the EC to play an even greater role in world trade negotiations than before; the danger is that the current institutional arrangements will continue to prevent the EC from being able to punch its full economic weight in the contemporary international economic system.[14] This could lead to a shift of focus to the US–Japan axis; indeed, in the financial sphere this has already begun despite the promise of the 1992 programme for the EC's banking and financial institutions.

It is thus not entirely surprising that the EC stance in the run-up to 1992 has often seemed to stress the need for effective protection against dynamic American and Japanese forces, despite the protestations from Brussels that the Europe of the 1990s will be a 'world partner'.[15] In effect the Europeans find themselves in a double bind; the process of resolving or at least managing their internal problems is quite likely to lead to precisely the introspection and lack of responsiveness which in the outside world will be construed as a fortress Europe stance; while the need to react to outside pressures for openness will increase the penetration of the new Europe by outside forces with consequences for domestic and political structures in the EC itself and in its member states.

The Commission, on the other hand, might argue that these protectionist arrangements are only transitional and have the virtue of being limited to specific sectors and that protectionist barriers have not been raised overall. That is, however, precisely the argument which was made with the introduction of a short-term arrangement on cotton textiles in 1961 and its subsequent extension into a long-term arrangement and thence into the MFA. Thirty years later the restraints still exist (though Germany holds the current GATT record with a coal import safeguard restriction which dates back to 1958). In principle this provision should become redundant at the end of 1992 and transhipment across frontiers should be permissible. Again, however, there is pressure for some kind of transitional arrangement, especially from the southern European producers who have gained significantly from trade diversion. As yet no specific arrangements have been made because of two additional complications. First, the MFA is an agenda item on the GATT Uruguay Round and second, the EC is currently faced with growing demands from the emergent states of eastern Europe for a loosening of restrictions on their textile exports to the Community. The need to respond positively, or at least to appear to respond positively, to the aspirations of the east Europeans, both in terms of trade arrangements and potential membership, is an enormously complicating and unexpected external factor in the 1992 process.

If, as seems likely, an agreement is reached to extend the MFA, possibly with a commitment to phase it out over a transitional period, this could be used by the industry to argue for the maintenance of Article 115 restrictions for the transitional period. Again, from the standpoint of the credibility of 1992 commitments, this would be an important concession. In addition to accepting the existence of internal restraints in a so-called completed market, it may also provide encouragement to other sectors to seek similar arrangements. Whereas in the case of cars the principal external losers would be a single country (Japan), in the case of textiles and clothing it would be a wide range of industrializing and developing countries. This would be costly to the less developed countries, given the key role of textiles and clothing to their industrialization process and their narrow industrial base.

Standards and certification

About half of all the 1992 directives relate to standards and certification. Sweeping away the myriad of cross-national and cross-border regulations which currently exist could have a dramatic impact on internal competitiveness. The issue of standards is, however, one which probably causes greater anxiety than any other on the part of outside firms. There are a number of reasons for this. First, non-EC firms have no control over the actual standards agreed. Standard-setting could be manipulated to exclude non-EC firms. Second, mutual recognition does not apply to goods of non-EC origin. Thus protracted certification procedures could be applied to non-EC producers. Third, EC firms in certain sectors are excluded from mutual recognition requirements (specifically sanitary and phytosanitary standards and also, where public policy considerations are seen as being of vital interest, consumer protection and environmental regulation). This exclusion could be used to restrict access to the single market, and thereby to discourage penetration of the EC market.

We have to be careful not to exaggerate these fears, nor to allow them to hide the very real opportunities which common standards present to outside producers. Nevertheless, there exists real potential for market exclusion, not through the actual setting of standards *per se* but rather through their enforcement. Consider the case of high definition television (HDTV). At present, no decision has been taken on the industry standard. It is possible that this could be strategically delayed until other non-EC standards are agreed, for instance by Japanese or US manufacturers. In which case, the EC standard could be set to ensure it differs from others and this would offer a competitive advantage in the European market to local producers. However there is some evidence that the EC is in fact becoming more open to input from outside the Community prior to the drawing-up of such standards. At least one US manufacturers' association has begun a process of discussion on standards with the Commission; and in another sector, the European regulatory body sent proposed regulations to US suppliers for comment.[16] In any case once the details of a standard are known, overseas producers will be able to manufacture for the whole European market and there is some evidence to suggest that US and Japanese firms are in advance of their European rivals in terms of restructuring in order to deal with the European market as a whole.

Once a standard is established, enforcement could still be a problem for non-EC firms. It is by no means certain that the EC will recognize testing carried out in non-EC facilities and an insistence on either EC testing, or retesting, could be exploited to both raise the transaction costs of trading and to create uncertainty in the minds of exporters. Since the setting of standards is so pervasive, no single trading partner is particularly exposed here. Advanced industrialized economies like the US, Japan and those of EFTA are particularly concerned about high-technology products and all agricultural exporters, developed or developing, have some reason to be anxious about sanitary, phytosanitary and food processing standards. US interests were, for instance, damaged by uniformity, in the case of the EC-wide ban on meat from cattle fed with hormones, putting at risk all US meat exports; this replaced the previous varied pattern where some markets remained open to US products. Another interesting aspect of the hormone case, and one which is of relevance to future US negotiations with the EC on these matters, is the fact that Washington's tough Federal Government stance against the EC was somewhat undermined by the activities of a Texan delegation that arrived in Europe offering hormone-free Texan beef!

Government procurement

Contracts awarded by EC governments, which range from relatively low profile activities such as garbage collection and stationary orders, through to much higher-profile activities like telecommunications systems, airport construction and power-generating equipment are of considerable significance in many markets. Overall government procurement constitutes approximately 15 per cent of the Community's gross domestic product compared with about 5 per cent in the US. This is an area where there has long been controversy regarding discrimination in favour of local producers. In some instances this is transparent, as in the 1933 Buy-American Act; in most cases it is more opaque. Despite the conclusion of a GATT Code on Government Procurement in the Tokyo Round, there is still evidence of discrimination. According to the Cecchini Report, the potential gains from greater competition in the award of public sector contracts amount to around 11 per cent of the total potential gains of the single market programme.

The 1992 directives in this area are designed to make the procedures for the award of public procurement contracts more transparent, to make the process itself more open, to introduce an obligation for the details of successful tenders to be disclosed, to provide a mechanism for appeals against infringement and to review the position of currently-excluded sectors. If implemented, and adhered to, these provisions would make for more open procurement procedures and stimulate greater competition. While it would be ideal from a non-EC point of view for this projected opening of the EC market to take place on a global basis, the current arrangements would establish an EC public procurement market. The Community is under no international obligation to expand this regime beyond the EC and in any case, as Calingaert points out, 'it will be traumatic enough for the interests involved to expand the market to the other EC member states'.[17] Although there seems to be a presumption that EC firms and foreign firms based in the EC will all be treated on an equal basis when it comes to competing for these contracts, it remains to be seen whether or not this works out in practice. It is certainly the case that non-EC based foreign firms will be encouraged by these directives to increase their inward investment into the EC because of the local content provisions that will apply. At present the new arrangements would require 50 per cent EC content in competitive bidding procedures and would give a 3 per cent price preference for European goods.

For firms based outside the EC there are signs that the Community is prepared to consider opening up at least some of its public procurement market beyond its own frontiers but only on the basis of reciprocal agreements within the GATT. Indeed it is clear that in shaping its 1992 regime the Commission has inserted protective measures designed to bolster its negotiating position within the GATT – one of a number of examples of the confusing and sometimes contradictory overlap between the creation of the EC internal market and the EC's participation in the creation of a wider international trade system.

It is evident from the above discussion that full implementation of the single market programme could have a significant impact on, and long-term implications for, both intra-EC and extra-EC trade. Even if the aim of an increase in the relative competitiveness of EC producers is achieved, market growth can offer opportunities for non-EC producers to gain also from the creation of the single market. However the internal adjustment costs of the programme and the increased power to demand reciprocal benefits outside the EC may provide an incentive, combined with the strong influence of domestic politics on the EC decision making machinery,[18] to skew the benefits away from non-EC producers. The external implications of 1992 depend therefore on the way in which the single market programme is implemented, which in turn will be fashioned by the EC's external commercial policy relations after 1992.

EC commercial policy after 1992

In principle the EC, acting on a mandate provided by the Council of Ministers, has full and complete control of Community commercial policy. The Community has a Common External Tariff (CET); a Common Agricultural Policy (CAP), which relies in part on a range of border measures – most notably variable levies – and the Commission negotiates on behalf of all members in the GATT. Furthermore, the Community has set up a multilayered system of trade preferences towards non-members. The EC accords preferences under free trade agreements with the six EFTA countries and Israel; under association agreements with Turkey, Malta, Cyprus and sixty-nine African, Caribbean and Pacific countries (under the latest Lomé Convention); and under cooperation agreements with eight Mediterranean countries. Similar deals are under negotiation with east European countries and with members of the Gulf Cooperation Council – about 60 per cent of EC imports derive from countries participating in these preferential schemes which have recently been the target of criticism by the GATT secretariat and which have always been regarded with great suspicion by the US Congress.

In recent years Community control has been weakened somewhat by the proliferation of national restraints in various forms – we have already cited the cases of cars and textiles, but in 1988 it appears that EC member states maintained as many as 1,000 individual quotas or other measures restricting imports.[19] After 1992, with the abolition of national restraints, this particular source of freedom to national governments should disappear. Full and complete control at Community level would then be re-established. What will be the emphasis of Community commercial policy after 1992? This is a crucial question for the evolution of the multi-lateral trading system in the 1990s. It will be fashioned in large measure by the posture adopted by the Commission on behalf of the Community and by the impact of the 1992 process. As we have argued above, this posture will itself be significantly affected by bargaining between the EC member states who all have their own domestic concerns to satisfy. Broadly speaking, the potential exists for two extreme scenarios – a more protectionist fortress Europe or a more liberal 'free' Europe posture which in turn is likely to play its part in determining whether the world trading system remains globally open or descends into bloc politics.

We observed in the previous section that the potential instruments to effect a fortress Europe may exist after 1992: Community-wide restraints which replace national restraints; discriminatory use of certification and testing procedures; aggressive use of reciprocity provisions; more vigorous emphasis on rules of origin and local content requirements. In addition, EC anti-dumping provisions have in recent years offered more scope for protection and have been used more aggressively. In particular the EC has developed a firm posture towards Japan both on dumping and on the development of 'screwdriver' assembly plants within the EC. However Japan has already successfully challenged EC anti-dumping practices within the GATT.[20]

The probability of more extensive and more aggressive use depends upon several factors, in particular; the speed with which gains are realized and the distribution of those gains; the speed with which adjustment pressures arise and the distribution of adjustment costs; the strength and organization of protectionist lobbies; the trade policies of other states and the outcome of the GATT Uruguay Round.

The speed with which gains from 1992 are realized will have an important bearing on the pressures for protection, as will their distribution. These gains can not however be isolated and may well be offset by other adverse developments in the European and World economy. If gains are apparent and the more evenly they are dispersed, the lower the probability of protectionist pressures. One of the factors behind the impressive tariff liberalization conducted under GATT auspices between 1947 and 1967 was the fact that net benefits were clearly positive and widely dispersed. Most of the work conducted thus far suggests that the principal beneficiaries of the 1992 process will be the southern European states, because they are not as yet well integrated. However the benefits of these gains will be reaped only after an adjustment period. Adjustment costs are the price that must be paid for changes in resource allocation across industries and regions and this has already been recognized within the EC to the extent that one of the internal 'prices' of the 1992 programme has been the decision to double the structural funds over the five-year period to the start of 1993. However this may not prove to be enough for even the Cecchini Report acknowledges that transitional unemployment will increase by 250,000. Moreover this is likely to be geographically and industrially unevenly spread. This will be due in part to low wage, southern production displacing other European production in industries such as clothing and footwear.

The influence of national, industry lobbies on the Commission and trade policy ought to reduce. If, however, industry groups become coordinated Euro-lobbies they may be in a position to wield much greater influence. Again the success which the car industry, having created the ACEA, has realized, is salutory. There is no formal debate about creating EC industrial policies along the lines of the CAP nor is there much chance that Sir Leon Brittan, the competition commissioner, would go along with such an idea. However it is possible that protectionist EC-wide policies could emerge piecemeal to fan the fortress Europe fears of those outside the internal market. Specific ventures such as the Airbus project or the plan to develop a European standard for high-definition television spring to mind.

The actions of other states will be important, however, since the EC, acting as a unit should have more leverage and greater retaliatory potential than its constituent members acting in isolation. The most pressing issue here is the recent shift to bilateralism[21] by the US in its use of Super-301 provisions.[22] The EC was not cited by the US in either 1989 or 1990; if it were at any stage, retaliation could be expected to be swift and direct. Similar considerations apply to Japanese trade policy and EC pressures for market-opening while the evolution of both US and Japanese policy will also be influenced by the outcome of the GATT Uruguay Round. So too will that of the EC and in many respects it is from this source that potential defences for a 'Free Europe' could emanate.[23] As we have already suggested there are a number of overlapping issues across the GATT Uruguay Round and the 1992 agenda. Of the fifteen negotiating groups reporting to the Trade Negotiating Committee in the current round no less than nine are dealing with issues which figure in the 1992 programme. Many of these, like agriculture and services, are highly contentious with little scope for immediate or complete resolution. If we leave agriculture on one side – agriculture is crucial to the GATT but 1992 and the CAP do not really have much to do with one another – then 1992 and the GATT round affect each other in two distinct ways. First, as we shall see in the next section, any new rules for trade within the EC covering activities like intellectual property, financial services or government procurement are an example to the GATT of how things might work on a global scale. Second, in its behaviour towards the outside world the EC is exploring the extent to which such trade is amenable to global ordering via its anti-dumping practices and its demands for reciprocity in financial services.

The GATT Uruguay Round was due for completion in December 1990 but foundered mainly because the European Community came up with far too little, far too late in the way of proposed reforms of its agricultural policy.[24] If however agreements are eventually reached they could go some way towards containing bilateralism in trade policy and preventing the emergence of a world of trading blocs dominated by the EC, Japan and North and even South America. For example, disciplines on trade-related investment measures (TRIMs) could introduce important constraints on VERs; agreement to phase out MFA could eliminate the threat of EC restrictions and so on. This is a crucial issue for the external implications of 1992. Appropriate agreements would help to re-establish respect for the GATT and any constraints on the unilateral actions of the EC, as well as others in the international trading community. They would also help prevent a post-1992 drift of EC commercial policy towards the fortress Europe scenario. The irony, of course, is that the fate of the GATT Round itself seems, at the time of writing, to depend on the EC's ability to exert a significant leadership role at a time when it is distracted, both by the 1992 programme and the two IGCs and by the need to respond, both politically and economically, to the dramatic changes in eastern Europe.[25]

The outcome of multi-lateral trade negotiations should not be seen, however, as being independent of other policy issues. There are likely to be important linkages between the trade and other related aspects of 1992.

Trade-related issues and 1992

There are, no doubt, a large number of potential linkages between the external policy dimensions of 1992. We restrict ourselves here to a few of the more obvious ones.[26]

Market access in services

Trade in services was put on the GATT agenda for the first time during the Uruguay Round of talks: given the experience of trade in goods and the special problems of services, it is likely to stay on the global agenda for some time. 1992 has considerable significance therefore for the outcome of present and future multi-lateral and bilateral negotiations.

Within the EC the creation of a European financial common market is correctly seen as being central to the prospects for success of the whole 1992 programme. Without it, the wider objectives of the complete freedom of movement of goods and factors of production will not be realized. Indeed it can be argued that it was the failure to achieve financial deregulation between 1957 and 1985 that contributed to the fragmentation of goods markets which ultimately brought pressure for the 1992 programme.

Financial services include banking and credit provision, brokerage and securities services and insurance services. Together these account for around 7 per cent of EC GDP and over the last fifteen years the sector has grown faster than the EC economy as whole. In the global context European suppliers are major players. The EC financial services sector is, however, highly fragmented and in an integrated market these differentials would be arbitraged. The potential for gain is significant – around one-third of the total anticipated gains from the whole 1992 programme. As a result a large number of the 1992 directives cover this sector. The guiding principles behind these directives are mutual recognition and home country control. With capital movements completely liberalized, full rights of establishment and complete freedom to provide services would become effective.

What are the implications of all this for non-EC suppliers? An integrated European market is potentially lucrative to outside suppliers, in part due to the potential for arbitraging pre-integration price differentials; in part because of the growth potential of the market. Suppliers of financial services, especially those based in Japan and the US, already have considerable experience of offshore production and will be attracted by the larger European market. The key point is that these services are difficult to offer at arms length – direct investment and supply of a financial service tend to go hand in hand. On what terms can non-EC suppliers expect to gain access?

The issue which has emerged as central to the prospects for this sector is reciprocity in rights of establishment and national treatment. To take a specific example, when the Second Banking Directive was first accepted it was stated fairly directly by Delors that mirror-image reciprocity would be enforced. In other words, foreign banks would only be granted access to the EC on condition that EC banks gained access to their home markets on exactly the same terms. In the context of both US and Japanese banks this could have constituted an impossible obstacle to overcome. For example, the Pepper-McFadden Act of 1927 forbade US banks from operating outside their own state; and the Glass-Steagall Act of 1933 separated commercial and investment banking. US banks becoming established in the EC could thus engage in universal banking but demanding mirror-image reciprocity would amount to demanding treatment for EC banks in the US to which US banks are not entitled. This would clearly not be acceptable and would thus have constituted a serious barrier to entry. However both the US and Japan reacted sharply to this suggestion and proposed that the EC stick to national treatment and in this they were supported by the free traders within the EC. As a result the Commission has softened its attitude whilst preserving the right to seek national treatment that gives effective access. There nevertheless remains a potential for a return to a more aggressive interpretation by the EC and this will therefore remain a sensitive issue, with Congress ever alert to possible discrimination and Japan only too aware of the fact that eighteen of the world's largest banks are Japanese. Since reciprocity will not be applied retroactively the strategic reaction of these banks has been to enter the EC market ahead of 1992.

The markets for the provision of transport services in the Community are even more fragmented than those in financial services. This is a result of different national policies in road haulage, shipping and airline services which have not been harmonized and as a result 1992 directives are aimed at both harmonization and liberalization. If successfully implemented, these measures should ensure greater competition amongst, and greater market access for, EC operators. The future position of non-EC operators is uncertain and is likely to raise difficult issues of reciprocity and equivalent access. Airline services is the sector where this is likely to be most prominent. At present foreign carriers have made bilateral arrangements with individual EC governments. This has in turn allowed them access to extensive intra-EC transportation rights. Following the completion of the internal market, what is currently cross-border carriage would become cabotage. Because the US authorities have negotiated on a bilateral basis with individual EC members, no reciprocal rights to cabotage within the US have been granted. There would thus be a clear asymmetry of treatment. The Commission has announced its intention to assume responsibility for the future negotiation of bilateral agreements, rather than leaving these to the member states. It seems clear from this that appropriate pressure will be brought to bear on the US and Japan to extend equivalent access provisions on cabotage in those markets.[27]

Inward factor mobility

The pre-1992 EC is probably better viewed as a customs union than a common market and the 1992 programme is meant to change this. Free movement of capital, together with the reaffirmation of the rights of establishment and national treatment should clear the way for the free movement of investable resources across internal EC frontiers. The free movement of labour is also an objective but may prove to be more difficult to achieve. However, the extent to which it is achieved will inevitably have implications for the EC's attitude toward the inward movement of labour from outside the EC.

A great deal of the migration of labour in Europe has traditionally been from non-EC to EC states. From Turkey, Cyprus, Algeria, Tunisia, Libya, west and east Africa to Germany, France, Belgium, Italy, The Netherlands and the UK. The perceived differences in living standards which stimulate these flows are in fact likely to persist and, if the growth effects of 1992 materialize, are likely to widen. Furthermore the recent changes in eastern Europe and the Soviet Union are likely to add to this demand to migrate into the EC – in the case of eastern Europe it will be very difficult for the Community, which has been encouraging just such a migration for years, to deny access to newly-liberated fellow Europeans. Thus the demand for relocation will not only persist after 1992, it is likely to increase. Will non-EC labour be able to migrate, whether on a permanent or temporary basis, as readily after 1992 as for most of the post war period? There are a number of reasons for doubting this.

If there is a greater mobility of labour within the EC, the demand for relatively unskilled, low-wage labour may be more easily satisfied internally by migration from the Mediterranean. This is already a potential source of cheap labour but the removal of restrictions lowers the cost of migration for EC as opposed to non-EC workers and increases its attractiveness for the former group. Specifying rights of residence and movement for EC workers and their families discriminates them as a group from non-EC workers by highlighting the absence of rights for the latter. As a result a more significant implicit barrier will be erected after 1992 against non-EC workers. In addition, as we have seen, political pressures may result in a more liberal attitude being shown towards east–west as opposed to south–north migrants. All this suggests that the 1992 provisions will make migration, especially from the south, more difficult unless of course the completion of the internal market unleashes such a growth dynamic that the overall demand for unskilled labour rises significantly.

The story is quite different in the case of inward capital mobility. Given the nature of capital, one is likely to see greater flows than in the case of labour. This is very likely to facilitate capital accumulation within the EC and contribute positively to the growth effects of 1992 for the EC. As the 1992 programme has gained momentum the inflow of capital has increased. This is driven by a combination of offensive and defensive considerations; a desire to establish a market presence whilst directives are actually being drawn up and a desire to be inside the market prior to any barriers that might be erected to regulate further entry. Indicative of a growing interdependence between the US, Japan and the EC is the fact that while American and Japanese money has been pouring into Europe[28] as 1992 approaches, so Europeans have been heavily investing in the US. Thus in 1988 the UK spent $16 billion buying US assets and $2.9 billion in the EC while in West Germany in 1988–9 some DM22.5 billion was invested in the US against DM16 billion in the EC.[29]

What of the prospects for inward investment beyond 1992? Without restraints, one would expect to see further inward investment in order to establish a presence in a market of 340 million consumers. It is clear that a major factor in driving further investment is the fear that future market access might be impeded. In order to be in a position to circumvent these barriers, investment flows (especially from Japan and the Far East) can be expected to increase, if unimpeded. The mutual interdependence of investment noted above is likely act as a counter to extreme attempts to inhibit inward investment in the EC.

The price of entry on the other hand may increase. EC rules on local content already exist and a failure to meet them may expose firms to most favoured nation (MFN) duty or to anti-dumping provisions. Local content requirements may become more rather than less important because 1992 increases individual EC governments' leverage in pressing for local content commitments. In the recent past, both France and Italy have attempted to resist Japanese penetration of their national markets and have condemned the UK's enthusiastic welcome to the Japanese as a Trojan horse policy (not the first time that France has accused the UK of being a Trojan horse *vis-à-vis* the EC; the last time was in the 1960s when the UK was perceived to be providing a similar service for the US). However in April 1989 the French were obliged to abandon their attempts to block imports of Nissan cars assembled in the UK and the French government has since then embarked on a campaign to persuade more Japanese companies to invest in France.

There are clear output and employment benefits for the EC associated with increases in capital inflows and increased local content. Any switch of resources away from the investing countries is more of an ambiguous gain from the investing country's point of view. The growth effects of 1992 may maintain or even increase rates of return on investment, but returns might be even higher if the single market could be supplied at arms length or with lower local content. In any case the capital exporting countries will be concerned also about the employment effects as well as the geographical diversion of capital although these concerns will, to a certain extent, be offset by a continuation of outward investment from the EC to the US and Japan.

Development assistance

The EC states provide development assistance both on a bilateral and a multi-lateral basis. Development assistance comes in two forms, via aid disbursements and trade preferences. The bulk of the former is bilateral, with only 10 per cent of the total being multi-lateral; the bulk of the latter is multi-lateral, operating through the Community's general system of preferences (GSP) and the Lomé Conventions. Although there are no specific 1992 directives pertaining to development assistance, 1992 and related developments are likely to have consequences for both trade and aid provisions. The EC's GSP currently affects over 120 countries. Although the arrangement ostensibly gives preferential access to the EC, this is severely constrained by quotas, limitations and content requirements. As a result, the actual benefits of GSP are not generally very large.[30] Moreover, preference margins have been eroded by multi-lateral tariff reductions. Although none of the 1992 provisions directly affect these arrangements there is some evidence that the Commission is using them as a basis for increasing pressure on the more successful industrializing countries to graduate from the scheme. 1992 is likely to increase that pressure given the increased internal competition in labour-intensive manufactures from southern EC producers that is to be expected.

The Lomé Conventions are a series of agreements between the EC and currently sixty-nine African, Caribbean and Pacific (ACP) states. As with the GSP, the trade assistance component takes the form of a preferential tariff regime. Again, however, the actual preferences provided are constrained by limitations and rules of origin. Moreover, in the case of limitations, they are even more of a constraint than in the GSP. This is because the ACP countries as a group have lower per capita incomes and, even more importantly, are more heavily dependent on exports of foodstuffs – in many cases products which are covered by the CAP. The Fourth Lomé Convention, which was agreed in December 1989, provided for some easing of limitations and this will remain in force until 1999. If in the meantime significant adjustment pressures are experienced within the Community, these will no doubt be further reviewed. Many of the African delegates to the Lomé negotiations expressed concern that the free flow of goods between European states will make it more difficult for exporters to Europe to find markets – especially for the non-traditional commodities to which many African countries are trying to move. The export of manufactured goods from ACP countries to the EC, US and Japan has in fact fallen by more than half in each case since 1970.[31] African states are being told that they must make themselves more attractive to overseas investors in the run-up to 1992, but figures show that exactly the reverse has happened.

Each member state of the EC has aid programmes. These vary in magnitude from around 0.05 per cent of GNP (Eire) to around 0.4 per cent of GNP (The Netherlands). The programmes also vary in terms of geographical orientation and in the proportion of total aid which is tied. This varies from 10 per cent in the case of Denmark to 62 per cent in the case of Italy. On average about 50 per cent of total bilateral EC aid disbursements are tied in one way or another. After 1992 the EC will be one single trading bloc and any tied aid will be tied to the EC as a whole, rather than to specific donor member states. Such a development should turn out to the advantage of the recipient countries, in that it allows tied imports to be sourced from the lowest-cost EC producer. It remains to be seen, however, whether donors will be willing to give up tied aid without some sort of struggle.

The second way in which aid disbursements may be affected by the 1992 process is via internal aid diversion. The EC has already agreed to double its structural funds in the run-up to 1992 and this may result in downward pressure on aid budgets. It should also be noted that aid to eastern Europe is also likely to exert the same sort of pressure on the overall aid budgets for developing countries.

It has been estimated that completion of the single market will add only ECU 7 billion to the exports of developing countries.[32] The Overseas Development Institute has argued that increased exports of primary products and manufactured goods will be offset by losses through trade diversion, as the EC becomes more competitive and self sufficient in some of the goods that it now imports. The newly industrializing countries of South-east Asia are believed to be especially vulnerable and many are therefore having to invest inside the EC – as indeed are Latin American countries like Brazil.

Even if the aggregate trade effect is not that large it could have a significant impact on specific countries, especially those currently benefiting from bilateral preferential arrangements with individual member states. Thus, for example, the Windward Islands are likely to lose the protected UK market for their expensive bananas and Morocco could lose its special access to the French orange juice market. Developing countries may well be hit by EC-wide quota restrictions on products such as footwear, consumer electronics and ceramics and developing country exporters could also be hit by tougher standards after 1992. These would constitute trade barriers in some cases, applying especially to wood, cut flowers and fish and fish products, which are becoming important exports for many developing countries.

So far we have examined the external impact of the 1992 programme in rather general terms. In the next section we turn to examine that impact on three of the EC's most significant bilateral relationships.

Bilateral relations and the EC in 1992

Examination of each and every bilateral relationship is impossible. Indeed many states, individually or collectively, are better viewed as passive agents in the 1992 process. The developing countries are, for instance, unlikely to exert influence via reciprocity over the content and implementation of the programme. Though, as the earlier sections have shown, 1992 does have potentially wide ranging external effects, such as on aid and migration, which have implications for specific developing countries. Some of these bilateral relations have been investigated by other authors; Horovitz[33] and Nello[34] on EC-eastern Europe; Milner, Presley and Westaway[35] on the Middle East; Mayes[36] on Australia and New Zealand and Pelkmans[37] on Asia. Some specific relationships merit attention, however, because the states in question are able to actively respond to, or influence the outcome of, the 1992 programme.

The United States

The 1992 initiative and the revitalization of the process of European integration was generally welcomed by the Reagan administration but from the outset fears of potential European protectionism were expressed in the business community (the US business community based in Europe has tended, however, to be more relaxed about 1992) and in the Congress. Although concern about the economic effects has often been countered by strategic considerations in favour of greater European integration, US–EC relations at the start of the 1992 programme were notable for a whole series of trade disputes and internal market related squabbles. In fact detailed US interest in the 1992 programme only really developed in the spring of 1988. For approximately one year the fortress Europe scenario held sway in Washington but the combination of the arrival of the Bush administration and the realization of the political significance of events in eastern Europe meant that by mid-1989 a somewhat calmer vision of 1992 had emerged. According to the American Chamber of Commerce the perception of Europe in 1992 was not so much one of a fortress but of a series of potential 'miniforts providing selective protection'. American officials came to realize that EC policy was being put together on the run, with the pace being set by the 1992 deadline. Anticipating the problems that were to emerge in the GATT at the end of 1990 a State Department official commented 'the worry is that EC-92 is becoming a major actor in world trade without much capacity to think ahead. Its hard to find people in the Commission with a view to the future of the world trading system'. In other words the Americans worried about the capacity of the Europeans to handle a number of difficult issues at the same time. American policy shifted from a brief period of paranoia about 1992 to one of 'optimism tempered with vigilance'.

The shift in US policy was also marked by a determination to improve the institutional structures supporting the relationship between the US and the EC. Most of the initiatives for this came from the American side and were prompted by both an enthusiasm for, and a wariness of, the enhanced role that the EC seemed destined to play in the Europe that was likely to emerge in the 1990s. To this end an agreement was reached in March of 1990 that the US President and the President of the EC Council of Ministers would meet twice a year – once for each six-month EC presidency – and that the US Secretary of State would also meet, at the same time, with all the EC foreign ministers. In parallel, at the Commission level, it has been agreed that the US President and the Commission President will meet regularly (Bush and Delors met three times in 1989) and that there will be half-yearly meetings between commissioners and members of the US cabinet – already Mrs Carla Hills, the US trade representative and Frans Andriessen, the External Relations Commissioner, meet on a monthly basis. Finally, the US government increased the seniority of its inter-agency task force handling EC issues.

These arrangements reflect a US determination not to be left out, either by the moves towards EC integration, or by the changes in eastern Europe. Though the worst US fears of fortress Europe have abated, concerns about some of the details of 1992 remain and are regularly raised in the US Congress. Before we turn to an examination of some of these concerns it is worth noting that US–EC problems over the single market and over the future of the trading system pale into insignificance when compared with the mutual suspicion and lack of understanding that exists between the US and Japan.

There are in any case potential economic benefits for the US to be derived from 1992; if 1992 produces the anticipated growth effects then US-based companies can expect direct benefits from export growth. The gains to those already with a manufacturing presence inside the EC are more certain, and more important, for sales of US companies manufacturing in Europe are four times greater than US exports to Europe. The outsiders, often small US companies, have been more sceptical, even negative about the single market process and it was this constituency which raised so much fuss about fortress Europe in 1988. Although, as we have seen, this general fear is no longer the focus of attention, there remains concern about a number of specific issues of the 1992 programme; for example, reciprocity, forced investment and government procurement.[38]

On reciprocity the focus of US concern has been on the Second Banking Coordination Directive discussed earlier. It was feared that the reciprocity provisions in this case would significantly damage US interests since the relevant US legislation could only be changed with great difficulty. Subsequently the EC has revised and clarified the reciprocity provisions so as to reassure the US that they would not face demands for mirror-image legislation. This was seen by the US as a test of EC intentions and helped to defuse some of the fears of restricted access on a wider scale. However access does not necessarily mean equal treatment, and some US firms with no pre-existing presence have felt under pressure to make forced investments in the EC when they would not have done without 1992. The rules of origin provision for semi-conductors is an example of this type of US concern. The EC changed its rules of origin to relate to the 'last substantial transformation'. As a result INTEL was obliged to invest in plant in the EC in order to satisfy this new rule. Although the 'last substantial transformation' principle also underpins US rules of origin, it is the change of approach and lack of transparency about how and why the changes took place that has caused US-based firms to fear that such decisions may be used in future as a hidden trade policy instrument. It is understandable that firms not based in the EC should be concerned about the ways that decisions are taken within the EC – from a distance Brussels must seem very confusing and not a bit like Washington. However, US-based firms should perhaps take heart from the experience of US firms based within the EC who report that the Commission is open to lobbying and that within the Council of Ministers there exists a significant – in the context of majority voting – grouping of states who are keen to preserve the liberal, open trading credentials of the EC after 1992.

It may be that if the GATT Round is eventually concluded successfully and if it includes agreed principles for limiting the use of rules of origin as an instrument of commercial policy, these fears will be defused. However, the single market programme has highlighted the externally perceived link between administrative protection and the entry price issue. Forced investment is one way that the entry price may be extracted.

There are, of course, many aspects of the 1992 initiatives which have US support: ultimately the impact of 1992 on the US must be viewed in net terms. In advance of 1992 there is inevitable uncertainty, especially amongst US-based firms, about the nature of these net effects. Even when there is obvious US interest in the principle of a particular initiative, the actual outcome may produce tensions in the US–EC relationship. The US has long argued, for instance, that the European markets for government procurement have been closed when US markets are open. There is obvious US support, therefore, for the 1992 initiative to open up public procurement, and in particular interest in the EC's telecommunications and power plant sectors – 90 per cent of US telecommunications sales in Europe are to public authorities. But problems are likely to arise with the third party provisions of, for instance, the utilities directive. According to these provisions, purchasing utilities may decline to handle bids involving products containing less than 50 per cent EC content. Furthermore, there will also be a 3 per cent EC price preference. The EC argues that these provisions are justified because the GATT government procurement agreement covers only the national-federal level. The US feels subject to domestic constraints on its ability to extend GATT cover to state and private utility purchasing.[39] Again therefore there is a fear that local content provision will be used to keep the EC market for the Europeans. There is an additional fear here that the EC action is in fact designed to keep the Japanese out of the European market but that this could hit the US in two ways. First of all, the Japanese might, by rules of origin regulations, be prevented from exporting to Europe from their considerable manufacturing base in the US. Second, there is concern that Japanese exports might be diverted from the EC to the US. There has even been talk in the US of utilizing the 301 action against the EC; but here the US has to be careful for the EC single market will eventually come to represent a powerful bargaining tool and if necessary, retaliatory weapon.

The bargaining power of the European regional block is of concern to the US, especially given the EC's negotiations with EFTA to create a European Economic Area – not to mention the more recent possibility of extending this area into eastern Europe. Some of the expressed concern has been part of US bargaining for specific concessions in advance of 1992. Some has also been used no doubt by US politicians who seek to defend sectional interests through the strengthening of US trade legislation. But the US's concern about the EC commitment to multi-lateralism is not fashioned by the substance of the 1992 programme. The US shows signs itself of wishing to retain the option to negotiate bilateral regional trade arrangements. Following its free trade agreement with Canada there are efforts to negotiate similarly with Mexico. It is EC intent towards multi-lateralism, combined with their respective responses to the Japanese challenge, that will ultimately be the source of trade tensions between the US and the EC after 1992.

Japan

It is certainly the case that in the EC–Japan–US triangle the weakest relationships exists between the EC and Japan. It is also the case that the 1992 programe, along with the developments in eastern Europe, have given a new urgency to Japanese attempts to improve that relationship. The Japanese have followed the US through a period of exaggerated fear about 1992 to one of more cautious optimism. Nevertheless the Japanese, far more than the Americans, have reason to see 1992 as something aimed partly at them, and indeed as something that might encourage the US to join forces with the EC against Japan. The Japanese are therefore perhaps keener than the Americans to stress a desire that 1992 does not undermine the multi-lateral trading system ruled over by the GATT. It is this system that is Japan's best guarantee that it will not be made the target of protectionist measures either by the EC or the US.

The Japanese have therefore, like the Americans, paid some attention to improving the structural arrangements underpinning their relationship with the EC. First, the Japanese have taken steps to improve their relations with the EC in recognition of complaints made by Delors that they preferred to deal with individual member states on a divide-and-rule principle (given the great variations in their treatment by the French and the British, for example, it is hardly surprising that in the past the Japanese have seen advantage in dealing, not with the EC, but with its individual members). In January of 1990 the Commission and the Japanese agreed to hold more regular high level meetings to try and make their mutual relationship as strong as they both enjoy with the US. In May 1990 Japanese and European Community ministers agreed to develop further their political relations and to set up a new working group on bilateral trade. The reference to bilateral trade represents a concession from the Japanese, given their enthusiasm for preserving the sanctity of the GATT process but is itself a reflection of Japanese concern about the power of the EC single market. Japanese interest in the EC and its single market has of course been heightened by the links that are developing between the EC and EFTA and, more recently, between the EC and eastern Europe.

Japan is directly affected by the single market in many of the ways that the US is affected. Its major firms have pursued in general terms a strong global strategy, and as a result forced investment and local content provisions do not create an unfamiliar environment to Japanese firms. Though Japanese officials have successfully complained about the EC's use of its anti-dumping rules and echo US concerns about reciprocity and standards, they are less anxious than the Americans to resist pressure for inward investment (this gives them good reason to be astonished at earlier French attempts to negate their inward investment by restricting the sale of locally-made Japanese products). The Japanese see themselves as natural foreign investors as a result of both the 1992 programme and the strong yen. Like Americans before them they now talk of the necessity of becoming 'good corporate Europeans'! Thus while the Japanese have responded rapidly to 1992 by increasing their presence inside the single market, they have reason to remain worried about local content rules distorting their investments. They want to preserve the quality of their products and they do not want to be effectively barred from less developed EC states where local industry is unable to provide components of adequate quality.

Clearly Japan would prefer a more, rather than less, liberal application of the 1992 programme; less strategic use of standards and certification arrangements, or less restrictive local content provisions in the case of government procurement arrangements. Similarly, Japan would no doubt like to see less restrictive transitional arrangements for the replacement of national restraints, as in the cars example cited. However, given its concern to avoid the breakdown of the relatively open multi-lateral trading system, Japan has generally followed a relatively passive stance when restrictions have been imposed upon it. It has sought to accomodate restrictions rather than challenge them in a confrontational style;[40] and it has also sought to respond positively in recent years to EC demands for reciprocity in the opening-up of the Japanese internal market. The EC is interested in using the power of the internal market to do something about Japan's convoluted distribution system which is an impressive barrier to EC imports. The Community would also like to see changes in the distortive effect of land prices in Japan and on the extent of vertical integration in the Japanese economy. The Japanese are perhaps able to show willing over a number of these non-tariff barriers, safe in the knowledge that culture represents the most effective and hardest to overcome protector of the Japanese home market. Japan is more concerned therefore with whether the tendency on the part of the EC to be introspective towards trade policy is likely to become more pronounced after 1992 leading to a dimunition of the prospects of maintaining and strengthening the multi-lateral system. This worry is increased by the prospect of US-Japanese trade differences becoming greater.[41]

As was argued in an earlier section of this chapter, EC commercial policy after 1992 will be fashioned by the extent and speed of the adjustment pressures associated with 1992 itself and by the eventual outcome of the Uruguay Round. These are interrelated factors, which will in turn be influenced by the major players' assessments of how the GATT system has served their interests. There are signs of weak commitment to a multi-lateral system; non-compliance or weak enforcement of GATT disciplines; and gravitation towards regional trade arrangements. In this latter case, Japan's interest in the Association of South-East Asian Nations (ASEAN)[42] reflects its fear that a fragmentation scenario for the trading system and the GATT Uruguay Round is a possibility.

Either a very positive or a very negative outcome to the GATT Round seems unlikely given the complexity of the agenda and the desire to avoid the label of failure that is usually associated with international economic policy-making of this type. A two-tier system, with current GATT multi-lateral disciplines coexisting alongside regional arrangements, may well emerge. This is likely to lead Japan to believe that the risk of heightened trade conflict with the EC and the US will increase after 1992. The attraction to Japan of a powerful Pacific trading bloc will increase in these circumstances.

EFTA

In the case of the US and Japan, 1992 threatens to influence the balance of economic power, where reciprocity by the US and Japan is a significant consideration for the EC. In the case of EFTA this is not so. The EFTA countries are individually small and even together represent less than half the German economy. Thus the EC is far more important to EFTA countries than EFTA is to the EC. This was not of so much concern to the EFTA states before the internal market programme was developed in the mid-1980s. The EFTA states were not interested in the CAP or the structural funds and for reasons of both neutrality and political preference, did not wish to participate in the EC's institutional development. The 1992 programme however promised to transform the EC into a real common market and therefore EFTA was faced with a fundamental decision on how to react. This was given even greater urgency following the dramatic changes in eastern Europe which both removed neutrality as a barrier to EC entry and posed the threat of EFTA either being side-lined or used as a sort of kindergarten for east European states preparing for full membership of the EC.

At one extreme EFTA could do nothing and hope that the existing free trade arrangements with the EC would protect it from any adverse extra-EC trade effects and possibly allow it to benefit from any expected demand growth in the EC. At the other extreme EFTA states, collectively or individually, could try to participate in the single market either by seeking full EC membership or by reaching an agreement with the EC to create an internal market that spans both EFTA and the EC.

The economic assessments of the optimal reponse that EFTA could make to the 1992 programme have been fairly unanimous; EFTA states could gain significantly by becoming part of the internal market.[43] Indeed the gains resulting from integration may be greater for some EFTA states than some EC states. EFTA home markets are small, and the scope for benefits from increased scale and competition in the enlarged European market will be greater than for the larger EC states. The opportunity cost of staying outside is however unclear since the spill-over effects on EFTA are difficult to evaluate. The extent of the actual integration of the

EC market is uncertain and the nature of the reponses of EFTA producers to the new market conditions can not be forecast accurately. The judgement seems to be, however, that there would probably be net negative effects from remaining outside. It is likely that there would be positive effects associated with demand expansion in the EC and beneficial, spillover effects for EFTA consumers from increased competition in the EC and lower prices and profit margins in EFTA. On the other hand more aggressive competition in EC markets and lower transaction and production costs within the EC could reduce market shares and depress export prices of outside EFTA producers. Indeed increased competition in export markets and increased need to specialize in order to remain comparatively scale-efficient might force outside EFTA firms to restrict product range and with it domestic consumers' choices. Without the same access to the EC market as EC car manufacturers, for example, it is quite conceivable that Saab would be forced to abandon some models to remain competitive in home and export markets. More dramatically Saab might have to consider shifting its manufacturing plant from Sweden to a state within the EC market.

Given the greater economic interaction of EFTA states with the EC than between themselves, the economic assessment was generally supportive of the EFTA countries seeking to actively participate in the single market programme. As a result the EC and EFTA decided in 1989 to begin formal negotiations on establishing a European Economic Area (EEA) (previously known as European Economic Space). The EC was primarily motivated by a desire to ward off potential full membership bids from individual EFTA countries. However events in eastern Europe and a growing concern about the progress of the EFTA–EC talks, combined with a realization that in the two IGCs the EC could further enhance its integration, have ensured that Austria, Norway and Sweden are on the brink of full membership. The EEA is beginning to look more and more like a staging post on the way to a greater enlargement of the EC rather than an end in itself.

The negotiations for an EEA were held up by a dispute between EC and EFTA over the institutional arrangements for the EEA and the extent of EFTA's ability to influence EC decision-making. EC states were reluctant to allow states that are not fully paid up members of the Community to influence the operation of the single market; EFTA was founded in 1960 as a reaction to the creation of the EC, and the EEA can be viewed as a further enforced reaction by EFTA to the completion of the EC's internal market. Agreement over the creation of a European Economic Area was reached in the late autumn of 1991, with EFTA accepting the need to accommodate EC single market policies through the revision of its own policies. Bargaining power of course lay with the EC, but some EFTA states no doubt also have their eyes set on assimilation into an enlarged EC. Under pressure from Britain, the acceptance of further enlargement was reinforced in Maastricht, and the Community already has applications from Sweden and Austria to respond to once the internal market is completed at the end of 1992. With further enlargement, assimilation rather than reaction will become more difficult for the remnants of EFTA to avoid. At the time of writing, the current agreement for the European Economic Area is being challenged in the European Court of Justice on the grounds that the Court may not have jurisdiction over non-member states. The outcome of this jurisdiction issue is uncertain, but it is certain that the agenda for the EFTA countries will continue to be set by the evolution of the single market.

Conclusion

1992 is likely to have enormous implications for all European non-members of the single market. As can be seen by the reaction of the EFTA states, the east European states and the US and Japan, 1992 provides a very strong incentive to be within the market, *de jure* or *de facto*. This chapter has attempted to anticipate some of the external implications of the 1992 programme. The question that must remain unanswered for the present but which will be relevant for the rest of the 1990s is exactly how the responses of those presently outside the EC will shape the evolution of the single market after 1992. First of all will the EC, Japan and the US manage to preserve the global trading system or will they come to lead their respective blocs in an increasingly fragmented and regionalized system? Second, how will the EC react to the demands of all the present European non-EC members who are attracted by the magnet of the EC's internal market? Will the EC be able to accomodate them short of full membership or is further enlargement to a Community of over twenty states inevitable given the political circumstances of the new Europe? If enlargement becomes inevitable what will happen to the single market?

Part III

Beyond 1992: deepening and widening

Chapter 8

Onwards to EMU

Brian Tew

The Rome Treaty and the Werner Report

The Rome Treaty, which came into effect in January 1958 to establish the EEC, provided (in Article 106) for setting up consultative machinery, including a monetary committee, to enable the EEC Commission and the members of the Community to discuss and coordinate their policies and activities in respect of international monetary questions.

A monetary committee[1] was duly set up and in 1964 the Commission gained the consent of the Council of Ministers to widen its power and to establish a committee for short- and medium-term economic policy, a committee of central bank governors and also a budgetary committee. Of these, the important ones for monetary matters were the monetary committee and the committee of central bank governors; there were also periodic meetings of the finance ministers of the Community. These consultative arrangements are still in operation and there is no doubt that in consequence the member countries are prepared to discuss their affairs at Brussels in a more intimate and detailed fashion than is usual among sovereign states. It would, however, be premature to claim that they have yet reached the stage of being able to resolve differences arising between themselves in the field of monetary cooperation, and thus to present a common front to the rest of the world. Thus the role of the Community in international monetary negotiations is very much weaker than its role in trade negotiations. In the latter, the Commission presents a common front at GATT meetings, whereas Community members act independently with only rarely a common position agreed on in advance, at IMF meetings or at meetings of the so-called Group of Ten or G10 (the great powers' forum for monetary affairs).

The Rome Treaty envisaged something more than mere consultation on monetary matters between its signatories – one of the articles in chapter 2 (Article 108) provides for the possibility of a member of the Community being afforded 'mutual assistance' by 'the granting of limited credits by other member states, subject to the agreement of the latter'. Since the late 1960s the Community has in fact given a great deal of thought to plans for developing closer monetary integration. Two rival schools of thought had emerged by 1970: the monetarist school, reflecting the views of Raymond Barre, and the economist school, reflecting the views of Karl Schiller. In March 1970 the Council of Ministers set up a special group under Pierre Werner to study these rival proposals and as far as possible to reconcile them.

The conflict in the Werner group between monetarists and economists was essentially: 'a dispute over the ordering of events in the process of monetary integration. The "monetarists" called for the immediate adoption of irrevocably fixed exchange rates; the "economists" wanted coordination and harmonization before any rigidity in exchange rates was established.'[2] The final Report of the Werner group, published in October 1970,[3] attempted a compromise between the two schools of thought, but in fact leaned rather towards the monetarist approach. It envisaged the eventual achievement of complete monetary union, to be approached in stages by acting on the following recommendations:

(a) that the EEC countries should pool their reserves (of gold, dollars, IMF drawing rights, etc) and settle their individual deficits and surpluses by internal EEC financial arrangements;

(b) that the EEC members should agree a matrix of exchange-rate parities between their respective currencies and keep actual exchange rates very close to these parities (as in the Snake scheme – see page 195);

(c) that these parities should be adjusted less and less frequently, until finally as from the end of stage two (which the summit conference of October 1972 ruled should be in 1980) the parities should be fixed for ever; and

(d) that eventually the national currencies of the member countries, originally six in number, should preferably be replaced by a single Community currency.

Action to date has been confined to the first two of the above proposals, on which significant progress was achieved with the establishment in March 1979 of the European Monetary System (EMS). Prior to 1979, nothing had been done towards implementing the Werner reforms except the Snake scheme; even this had a chequered history in that defections from it were rather frequent.

The essential feature of the Schiller plan was that the first stage in the approach to monetary union should be 'almost completely devoted to the setting up of a concrete base for the coordination of economic policy'.[4] This was not insisted on in the Werner Report, and had not been acted on by 1991. There has none the less been a convergence of national policy and performance between those members of the EMS that opted in 1979 to participate in the exchange rate mechanism (ERM).[5] This has largely been achieved by Germany's fellow participants following Germany's lead (see below, page 201), rather than by coordination achieved under the auspices of the medium-term economic policy committee, as the Schiller plan had proposed.

The IMF

In the 1960s members of the EEC were also members of the International Monetary Fund (IMF) and as such operated what came to be known as an adjustable peg. Each member country agreed with the IMF Executive Board a par value of its national currency (adjustable from time to time with the Board's permission), the peg being denominated in principle in terms of gold, but *de facto* in terms of the US dollar. Each of the EEC members pegged on the dollar by undertaking to keep the market value of its currency within a tunnel, the ceiling of which was 1 per cent above its dollar parity and the floor 1 per cent below. The means by which this was implemented was left to individual members but one of the means adopted was official transactions in the foreign exchange market, almost always using the US dollar as the intervention currency.

At the Smithsonian conference of G10 finance ministers in December 1971, the tunnel was enlarged to 2.25 per cent above and below the dollar parity (or central value, as it was now termed). Hence a European country's currency could fluctuate, from ceiling to floor, or vice versa, by 4.5 per cent in relation to the dollar. But if one European currency rose from floor to ceiling while another fell from ceiling to floor, their relative fluctuation would be 9 per cent. Such a large fluctuation between two European currencies was unacceptable to the EEC in its aspiration to move by successive stages to eventual monetary union, as mapped out in the Werner Report. In this report, EEC central banks had been 'invited, from the beginning of the first stage [from January 1971] to restrict on an experimental basis the fluctuations of rates between Community currencies within narrower bands than those resulting from the application of the margins in force in relation to the dollar'.

The essentials of the Werner plan were adopted by the Community's Council of Ministers in February 1971. In the light of them the widening of the tunnel accepted by G10 at the Smithsonian conference was seen as a step backwards, and as a challenge to Community members to inaugurate specifically EEC arrangements for keeping within narrower limits fluctuations between member countries' currencies. This was the purpose of the 'snake in the tunnel': the dollar value of the member countries' currencies would be kept within the wide tunnel provided for in the Smithsonian agreement, and supervised by the IMF; at the same time they would have their relative movements confined within a narrower EEC Snake.

The Snake

The formal provisions of the Snake scheme, agreed in 1972, were that when the strongest Snake currency's percentage premium over its dollar parity, plus the weakest currency's discount on its dollar parity, reached a predetermined limit (2.25 per cent, or half the amount permitted by the Smithsonian tunnel)

– then one or other of the countries concerned had to buy the weakest currency with the strongest.[6] The country might be either the weak-currency country (debtor intervention) or the strong-currency country (creditor intervention) – or both together. With creditor intervention, the intervening country buys the weak currency in the exchange market with its own currency, which it can make available as required; hence the only problem which arises is what to do with the weak currency which has been purchased. With debtor intervention, the intervening country has first to borrow from its partner the strong currency needed for purchasing its own weak currency in the market: hence the need for the very-short-term credit facility which was incorporated into the EEC scheme.

Whether the intervention was by the creditor or by the debtor country, a settlement arrangement was needed; by which the creditor countries could periodically exchange their accumulation of weak currency for a more acceptable reserve asset, and at the same time obtain repayment of their very-short-term credits – likewise in terms of an acceptable reserve asset. The EEC scheme provided that the monthly settlements should be effected by the transfer by the debtors to the creditors of a mixed bag of reserve assets selected on an agreed formula.

However, the formal provisions of the Snake scheme played little part in the actual operation of the arrangement, since usually a weak-currency country chose to take remedial action before the value of its currency depreciated to its lower limit in relation to the hardest currency. This being so, it could (as under the IMF rules) choose its own remedial action, and when the action it chose was to support its currency in the foreign exchange market, the intervention currency it preferred usually remained the US dollar.

This was so even after the IMF exchange-rate arrangements collapsed, as they did early in 1973, and EEC members henceforth ceased to peg on the dollar. Instead of pegging on the dollar, the EEC members participating in the Snake now sought to keep market exchange rates close to their Deutsche Mark (DM) parities, since the DM was most of the time the hardest Snake currency. Thus membership of the Snake for Germany's partners amounted *de facto* to pegging on the DM, most frequently continuing to use the dollar as the intervention currency.

The Snake came into operation for the original six Community members in March 1972. Three new members (the UK, Denmark and Eire) joined in May 1972 but defected in June; Denmark rejoined in October 1972, but the UK and Eire remained outside the scheme. Italy left the Snake in February 1973; France left in January 1974, rejoined in July 1975, but left again in March 1976. On the other hand, two non-EEC countries joined: Norway in May 1972 and Sweden from March 1973 to August 1977. On the eve of the establishment of the EMS in 1979, the Snake membership comprised Germany, the Benelux countries, Denmark and Norway.

The EMS

The EMS came into operation in March 1979 as a successor to the Snake. All nine of the then members of the EEC joined the EMS, and all but one (the UK) became full members, participating as such in the new exchange rate mechanism (ERM), which incorporated the essential features of the old Snake.

As with the IMF exchange-rate arrangements of the 1960s and the Snake of the 1970s, the new formal ERM provisions, which were basically those of the Snake with several additional complications, turned out to be an imperfect guide to the arrangements which obtained in practice.

The ERM in practice

As with the Snake arrangement, participating countries in the ERM agreed on par values for each national currency in terms of any one of them, so that there were official exchange rate parities in respect of each pair of ERM currencies, and these parities, once agreed, could only be changed by consensus. (Parities have in fact been changed on twelve occasions). Again as with the Snake arrangements, the ERM agreement prescribed official transactions in member country currencies to keep market rates within 2.25 per cent (exceptionally 6 per cent) each side of the official bilateral parities. To take a specific example, if the French Franc (FF) should fall to a discount of 2.25 per cent against its DM parity, both France and Germany must buy FFs with DMs.

Usually, however, (though not invariably) the weak-currency partner in a bilateral relationship (France in the above example) feared the speculation which could be provoked by a fall in its exchange rate to a 2.25 per cent discount. The weak currency partner would then decide to take remedial action both before the 2.25 per cent threshold was reached and also before its strong-currency partner took remedial action. Since in practice the strongest ERM currency has hitherto usually been the DM, the action of Germany's partners has amounted in effect to pegging on the DM, just as under the preceding Snake regime.

When France takes *discretionary* remedial action to support the FF, this action need not comprise the purchase of FFs with DMs. France can decide for herself what action to take. So, what options are available? First, she can opt for an intervention currency other than the DM; for instance she can support the FF by selling dollars. Second, she can jack up short-term interest rates by undertaking appropriate transactions in the Paris money market and thereby induce an inflow of private sector capital. Third, prior to 1990, she could check a capital outflow by the use of exchange controls, though this instrument of policy has now been abandoned. Last, she could tighten her fiscal stance by increasing tax rates and reducing government expenditure, though the effect of this on her exchange rate is uncertain, now that she has no exchange controls to impede an outflow of capital.[7] Suppose France chooses not to opt for exchange control or fiscal policy, she will almost certainly adopt the following remedial action:

(a) The French authorities will intervene in the foreign exchange market to sell foreign currency (taken from the reserve or borrowed for the purpose) and then seek to insulate the French banking system from their transaction by buying FF-denominated securities in the money market or on the stock exchange. This procedure is known as 'sterilized intervention'.

(b) If sterilized intervention does not work, or gives rise to unacceptable side-effects, the Bank of France will jack up interest rates in the Paris money market, which it can always do by reducing its own lending in the market or increasing its own borrowing. This will in the short run attract a private sector capital inflow and in the longer run reduce private sector expenditure on goods and services, including those imported from abroad.

Unfortunately, however, both types of remedial action may run into difficulties. Take first sterilized intervention. Here the official sales of foreign currency typically need to be on a large scale to make any impression on the market, so the problem arises of whether the necessary foreign currency can be obtained on acceptable terms by drawing on reserves and by official borrowing?

There is additionally the problem that official purchases of FF-denominated securities, by which the French authorities seek to insulate the French banking system from their sales of foreign currency, do not sterilize completely. If the counter-parties to official French purchases of FF securities are *commercial banks*, the net effects of the official transactions in the two markets on the banks' total balances at the Bank of France will be zero, but bank deposits mopped up by the official sales of foreign currency would not be offset,[8] so that there would be a reduction in the money stock. Alternatively, if counter-parties to the official purchases of FF-denominated securities are *nonbanks*, the aggregate balance sheet of the commercial banks will then remain completely unchanged; however, the official purchases will tend to bid down the yields on FF-denominated securities, thereby encouraging a net private sector capital outflow into securities denominated in other currencies (which is counter-productive, given that the whole purpose of the official intervention in the foreign exchange market was to *support* the FF).

If, for the reasons spelt out above, official sales of foreign currency have to be discontinued or the side effects of official purchases of FF securities prove to be unacceptable, the Bank of France must have recourse to its other instrument of policy, the jacking-up of interest rates in the Paris money market. This technique for supporting the FF gives rise to no conflict of objectives if the French authorities fear that the French economy is over-heating and needs the curb of higher money market rates. But on the other hand a conflict of objectives occurs if the economy is already depressed and needs a stimulus rather than a curb.

According to economists of the Keynesian school, an escape from such a conflict of objectives can be achieved by adopting an appropriate adjustment to fiscal policy: unwanted deflationary consequences of higher interest rates could be offset by a cut in tax rates or an increase in government expenditure. In practice, however, the role of fiscal policy in demand management has hitherto been to reinforce the deflationary effect of higher interest rates, not to *offset* it (see below, page 205).

These considerations led the House of Commons Treasury and Civil Service Committee, in its report on the 1990 Budget, to the following conclusion (para 89):

> Entry of sterling into the ERM will have serious consequences for the Chancellor's conduct of economic policy. The interest rate . . . will need to be devoted to the maintenance of sterling's parity . . . it is clear that in future the Chancellor will have to rely more on fiscal policy . . . than has been envisaged in his Budget statement. Otherwise the authorities will have no choice but to exercise the option of currency revaluation, which, as the Chancellor pointed out, 'always exists'.

As we have already seen, in practice the option of currency revaluation has been exercised by members of the ERM on a number of occasions in 1979 and subsequently; altogether there have been twelve occasions when parities have been adjusted.

Intervention currencies

Since Germany's partners in the ERM have *de facto* pegged on the DM (as they had done previously under the Snake arrangements) it may seem surprising that they did not always use the DM as their intervention currency. However, the German authorities have been reluctant to see the DM used indiscriminately in this role, and in practice other currencies (especially the US dollar) have been used instead – though to a greatly diminishing proportionate extent, as Table 8.1 shows.

Other provisions in the EMS agreement

The Community acted on Article 108 of the Rome Treaty by providing no less than four credit facilities, all of which are available to participants in the ERM. However, very little use has been made of any of them. The very-short-term financing facility is available without challenge from the creditor country only for obligatory intervention at the weak currency's official floor, and

Table 8.1 Currency distribution of foreign exchange intervention[a] in the EMS

	1979–82[b] %	1983–5 %	1986–7[c] %
US dollars	71.5	53.7	26.3
Deutschmarks	23.7	39.4	59.0
Other EMS currencies	3.5	4.1	12.7
Other currencies	1.3	2.8	2.0
	100.0	100.0	100.0

Source: IMF, *Financial Development*, September 1990, p. 37.
Notes: a Intervention includes both purchases and sales.
            b From March 1979.
            c Up to June 1987.

hence has been rarely used. The short-term monetary support facility and the medium-term financial assistance facility were each used once (by Italy) in the 1970s, but neither has been activated since the establishment of the EMS. Finally, the Community loan mechanism has been used only twice, by France in 1983 and Greece in 1985.

The EMS agreement provided for a divergence indicator which would trigger changes in policies at an early stage. A warning light would flash when the market value of a member's currency deviated by more than a prescribed percentage from its par value in terms of the ECU basket of currencies (see below). In practice, however, the indicator has never been fully able, as its proponents had hoped, to assume the role of linking exchange rate developments to an increasing convergence of economic policy.

The European Currency Unit (ECU)

This brings us to the role of the European Currency Unit, or ECU. The origin of this unit dates back to 1975, when the Community decided to keep its books in terms of a European unit of account, defined as a basket of member countries' currencies. The EUA was subsequently renamed the ECU and serves both as the unit in which the Community's accounts and transactions are denominated and also, in the financial markets, as the unit in which negotiable securities, deposits and loans are denominated as an alternative to denomination in dollars or other national currencies.

In addition, the EMS agreement gives the ECU a role as an official reserve asset and as a means of official settlement (though it has been little used in the latter capacity). The ECU as a reserve asset comes into existence as the result of the deposit by EMS members[9] of gold and reserve currencies (especially US dollars) with the European Monetary Cooperation Fund (EMCF), an EEC agency established in 1973 in which EMS members temporarily deposit one-fifth of their official reserves. The legal form of this transaction is akin to a swap in the foreign exchange market, the spot part of the transaction being an exchange of dollars or other assets from the member country's official reserves, for ECUs of equivalent market value. The forward part is an obligation by the EMCF to repurchase its ECUs three months later at a predetermined exchange rate.

The ECUs issued by the EMCF can in principle be used for official settlements between member countries, but only subject to limitations (somewhat alleviated in July 1985) such that the use of ECUs for settlement purposes has been minimal. Moreover, the original intention that the EMCF should be replaced by a European Monetary Fund, empowered to introduce a fiduciary element into the issuance of ECUs, has so far not been implemented. Finally, the EMS does not provide for the use of ECUs in private transactions; the flourishing private market in ECU-denominated securities, deposits and loans is completely independent of the official ECU currency.

The same currency label has recently come into use to describe the single European currency originally envisaged in the Werner Report and more recently envisaged by the Delors Committee in 1989.[10] It would be a replacement for the present national currencies of Community members in stage three of the progress envisaged by the Committee towards economic and monetary union (EMU). This stage three currency, if and when it comes into existence, would be a completely different animal from the present ECU and to avoid confusion will in this chapter be labelled 'ecu' rather than 'ECU'. Whereas the value of the present ECU derives from the value of the national currencies in the ECU 'basket', the stage three ecu would have to stand on its own feet in the foreign exchange market when traded against non-Community currencies such as the dollar or yen.

Policy coordination

The various committees of the Community provide the appropriate machinery for the coordination of monetary policy. Though they have assured a free exchange of *ex post* information and a free discussion about issues of economic policy, there had up to 1991 been very little genuine policy coordination, except on the occasions when finance ministers have met to agree parity realignments.[11] There has over the years been a convergence of policy and of performance among ERM members, as shown by the fact that parity adjustments have become smaller and less frequent; but this convergence has been achieved very largely by Germany's partners converging on Germany. Germany's monetary policy has usually been guided by the Bundesbank's perception of the dollar exchange rate most appropriate to the circumstances of the German economy, not of the whole Community's economy and/or the optimum rate of growth of the German money stock, not the whole Community's money stock.

The Delors Report[12]

As we indicate in chapter 1, with the adoption of the SEA in 1986 the way forward to EMU was prepared (in particular the preamble and Article 102A). At the Hanover meeting in June 1988 the European Council entrusted a committee, chaired by Jacques Delors, President of the EC Commission, with 'the task of studying and proposing concrete stages leading towards this union'. The Delors Committee (comprising Delors, twelve central bank governors participating in a personal capacity, three experts and another member of the Commission) duly submitted its report to EC heads-of-state and government on 14 April 1989. The Report defined what EMU would entail and considered the institutional changes it would involve.

The Delors Report set out the principles which the Committee believed should govern step-by-step progress towards EMU, including the need for parallel progress in both economic and monetary fields. It described three separate stages that could be followed to EMU, claiming that each stage would represent a significant change in relation to the preceding one; but each would evolve gradually, so bringing about a change in economic circumstances which would pave the way for the next stage. It emphasized that the question of when each stage should be implemented was a matter for political decision, but suggested however that the decision to enter upon the first stage should be a decision to embark on the entire process. The report noted that the Rome Treaty, as amended by the SEA, was insufficient for the full realization of EMU and that a new political and legal basis would therefore be needed. To this end, the report recommended that by the time of transition to stage two, the necessary treaty change would have to be prepared and ratified.

The report made the proposal, which the Community duly adopted, that stage one, which did not involve any treaty amendment, should start on 1 July 1990. Stage one involved a greater convergence of economic performance through the strengthening of economic and monetary policy coordination within the existing institutional framework. The 1974 council decision on economic convergence was to be replaced by a new procedure to strengthen economic and fiscal policy coordination; in stage one this was to remain the primary responsibility of the Council of Economic and Finance Ministers, with the participation of the Chairman of the Committee for Central Bank Governors, as appropriate. Action was to centre on the completion of the single market and the full implementation of the already agreed reform of the structural funds.

In the monetary field, during stage one all Community currencies were to come to participate in the exchange rate mechanism of the EMS under the same rules. (At present Portugal and Greece have not yet joined the ERM while Spain, which joined in 1989, and the UK, which joined in 1990, are allowed a swing of 6 per cent each side of parity, instead of the usual 2.25

per cent.) At the same time, though realignments of exchange rates would still be possible, attention was to be focused on other adjustment mechanisms. In addition, all impediments to the private use of the ECU were to be removed and the Community was to implement fully its objective of a single financial area in which capital could move freely and the cross-border provision of financial services would be fully liberalized (see chapter 5).

In stage two the report suggested that the basic organs and structure of EMU would be established. During this transitional period, responsibility for economic and monetary policy would be transferred increasingly from national authorities to new institutional structures, including a European System of Central Banks (alias the Eurofed) which would start on the process of formulating and implementing a common monetary policy for the Community. A proportion of national foreign exchange reserves would be pooled and used to conduct exchange market intervention. Exchange rate realignments would not be ruled out but would be made only in exceptional circumstances. The procedures for determining macro-economic policy could be further strengthened and extended on the basis of the new treaty and policy guidelines would be adopted by majority decision – though the rules would not yet be binding on member states. In particular, the report suggested that the Community as a whole would set for individual member states precise (but not yet binding) rules relating to the size of annual budget deficits and their financing.

In stage three, the report suggested that exchange rates would be locked irrevocably and in due course the change to a single Community currency would take place. All official reserves would be pooled and managed by the ESCB which would take responsibility for the formulation and implementation of monetary policy and for official intervention in the foreign exchange markets. The report stated that the rules and procedures of the Community in the macro-economic field would become binding and that the Council would have authority to make discretionary changes in Community resources to supplement structural transfers to member states. The report also stated explicitly that there might need to be further strengthening of Community structural and regional policies, with the increase in resources that would imply.

Moreover, the Council, in cooperation with the European Parliament, would also have the authority to impose constraints on national budgets to the extent necessary to prevent an unduly lax fiscal policy in a member state from compromising the ESCB's control over the Community's monetary stance. The need for imposed constraints would arise in two ways. First, an unduly expansionary fiscal policy in a member state would attract additional imports into the Community and thereby depress the market value of the Community's currency in relation to foreign currencies, for example the dollar and yen. Second, the finance of budget deficits by the issue of national debt denominated in foreign currencies would have the opposite consequence, while if the debt were denominated in the Community's own currency this would bid up interest rates in that currency.

The budgetary constraints specifically recommended in the Delors Report would: first, impose effective upper limits on budget deficits of individual member countries of the Community, although in setting these limits the situation of each member country might have to be taken into consideration; second, exclude access to direct central bank credit and other forms of monetary financing while, however, permitting open market operations in government securities; third, limit recourse to external borrowing in non-Community currencies. Moreover, the arrangements in the budgetary field should enable the Community to conduct a coherent mix of fiscal and monetary policies.

The Delors Report: stage one

Agreement was reached at the Madrid summit of the European Council in June 1989 that stage one of the Delors Report should come into operation on 1 July 1990. This meant that the Community is now committed to extending membership of the ERM to include all Community members (in particular the UK, which duly joined in October 1990, and Portugal and Greece, which have yet to join); and to the abolition of all exchange controls and the improvement of policy coordination. In addition, we may plausibly foresee the following developments in the course of stage one:

(a) a diminished recourse to credit ceilings, reserve ratios, and other regulations hitherto imposed for the implementation of monetary policy, since such regulations will become virtually unenforceable with the abolition of exchange controls on capital transactions;
(b) a greater readiness to consider the possibility of increased use of fiscal policy for demand management purposes (given that monetary policy needs to be dedicated to the objective of pegging on the DM);
(c) the increased use of European currencies, and a diminished use of dollars, for official transactions in the foreign exchange market.

Pegging on the DM arrangements have operated in the Community since the establishment of the ERM in 1979 and have always been somewhat fragile, in that their undoubted success has owed a great deal to fortuitous events which have helped to prevent the DM from becoming too strong in relation to other ERM currencies. Will these arrangements be more robust or alternatively more fragile in the 1990s than in the 1980s? Some of the possible changes in the 1990s point to the former conclusion, but others caution against undue optimism.

In the first place, unless the market comes to discount completely any possibility of exchange-rate adjustments, the international flow of capital for speculative purposes[13] will be aggravated by dismantling all exchange controls on capital transactions. Second, the extension of ERM membership will mean that the participants in the system will include more inflation-prone countries in the 1990s than in the 1980s. Moreover these countries will no longer be able to combat their inflation by recourse to credit controls and such restrictions. So unless they are able to experiment successfully with fiscal deflation they will have no other recourse except deflationary official transactions in the financial markets, leading to a rise in interest rates and an appreciation of the currency. But the rules of the game in stage one requires member countries to dedicate their official transactions in the financial markets exclusively to a different (and possibly incompatible) objective, namely keeping exchange rates very close to their predetermined ERM parities. Faced with a conflict of objectives, the inflation-prone participants will be liable to demand a frequent revision of parities and to incur the displeasure of their fellow members by jacking up interest rates. A foretaste of problems to be faced in the future is the episode beginning in July 1990, when high interest rates in Italy and Spain, imposed to combat inflation, took the lira and peseta to the upper limit of their permitted swings in relation to the French franc, and thus appeared for a time to jeopardize France's ability to avoid an otherwise unnecessary and unwanted jacking up of French interest rates.[14]

What then can an inflation-prone country do to moderate inflationary pressure, given that monetary policy cannot hit conflicting external and domestic targets simultaneously? The *Financial Times* pointed to fiscal policy as the only recourse,[15] thus underwriting the conclusion of the House of Commons Treasury and Civil Service Committee (see page 199). However, it must not be too readily assumed that the use of fiscal policy for demand management purposes necessarily offers an effective and acceptable escape from the kind of dilemma faced by ERM participants suffering from inflationary pressure. Admittedly, economists of the Keynesian school have always advocated that any unwanted deflationary consequence of monetary policy could be offset by a more reflationary fiscal policy, and vice versa. But in practice the use of fiscal policy to offset the unwanted deflationary or reflationary consequences of a monetary policy aimed primarily at influencing the exchange rate has so far remained no more than a theoretical possibility. This is for three reasons:

(a) In many countries (though not in the UK) the law or convention prescribes a separation of executive responsibility such that monetary policy and fiscal policy are in different hands, so that coordination of the two is difficult to achieve.
(b) The adjustment of the stance of fiscal policy is normally an annual event, so that it is difficult to fine-tune fiscal policy in line with changes in monetary policy.

(c) Thanks to the influence of Professor Milton Friedman and his followers, monetary policy came in the 1980s to be regarded as much the most important instrument of policy for keeping an economy on course; hence the role of fiscal policy was seen as supporting monetary policy, not offsetting it.

The Delors Report: stage two

The Delors Report saw its proposed stage two 'as a period of transition to the final stage and would thus primarily constitute a training process leading to collective decision-making, while the ultimate responsibility for policy decisions would remain at this stage with national authorities.' In the monetary field, exchange rate realignments would not be excluded as an instrument of adjustment, but there would be an understanding that they would be made only in exceptional circumstances.

Subsequent to the Delors Report, various proposals have been made, initially by the UK and subsequently by Spain and France, for a revised version of the present ECU to be introduced in stage two. The Spanish and French proposals would simply provide for the modification of the composition of the present ECU basket of national currencies, so as to 'harden' the ECU; that is, prevent its parity value from depreciating (or from depreciating very much) in relation to the national currency of any Community member.

Fundamentally different from these proposals for a harder-basket was the UK's proposal for a so-called hard-ecu,[16] to be introduced in stage two as a parallel currency (alongside the existing national currencies) but with the possibility of eventually displacing them in stage three if it found so much favour in the market that in due course national currencies went out of widespread use.

The hard-ecu would be an additional currency in the ERM, managed by a new Community agency, the European Monetary Fund (EMF). Its initial central value in terms of the present national currencies would have to be negotiated, but thereafter its central value would never be devalued in relation to the national currency of any Community member. The instrument of policy by which the EMF would keep the hard-ecu sufficiently hard would be the level of the interest rate it would pay on its hard-ecu-denominated deposit liabilities.

The individual British citizen, or firm, would get hold of hard-ecus by asking his or her commercial bank (say Barclays) to convert his or her sterling deposit into a hard-ecu deposit, which the bank would be prepared to do on terms which reflected the terms on which the bank could lay off the risk by in its turn replacing a sterling asset by a hard-ecu asset. The EMF would be prepared to facilitate such an exchange of assets by Barclays by offering to take sterling Treasury bills from Barclays, in return for which Barclays would get a hard-ecu-denominated deposit at the EMF, remunerated by an interest rate determined by the EMF management board. The rate of interest received by Barclays on its deposit at the EMF would be reflected in the interest rate it would be prepared to pay its customer on his hard-ecu deposit.[17] An increase in the EMF's hard-ecu interest rate in relation to sterling interest rates would encourage the British public to switch out of sterling deposits into hard-ecu deposits, and vice versa for a reduction in the EMF's rate.

The EMF might jack up the interest rate it paid on its hard-ecu-denominated deposit liabilities for either of two motives: either to encourage the Bank of England (or other national central bank) to follow suit, and thereby combat inflation in a more resolute way; or in the hope that the Bank of England (or other national central bank) will not follow suit, thereby hastening the progressive replacement of national currencies by the Community's currency (the hard-ecu).

If the first rather than the second scenario were the EMF's motive, it would put pressure on the Bank of England by requiring the Bank to redeem the EMF's excess holdings of sterling Treasury bills in terms either of hard-ecus borrowed from the EMF at a penal rate or of some other acceptable reserve asset (say gold or US dollars). However, since as a participant in the ERM the Bank of England needs anyway to set sterling interest rates high enough to keep sterling attractive in relation to the hardest national currency (hitherto usually the DM) the EMF would probably conclude that this was discipline enough on the Bank of England, so the first motive would be unlikely to apply in practice. If on the other hand the EMF's motive was the second, most people would see its tactic as an exceptionally inefficient way of replacing national currencies by a single Community currency, since the high interest rate offered on hard-ecu deposits might well impose an excessively deflationary monetary policy on the whole Community and would incidentally leave the EMF with a large portfolio of assets denominated in more or less extinct national currencies.

Hence it is not surprising that the UK proposal for a hard-ecu has found little support among the eleven other Community members. There has also been only lukewarm support for the harder basket suggested as a possibility by Spain and France.

Despite the various reforms proposed for stage two, the likelihood is that the ECU will survive through stage two in its present basket form, with only minor adjustments in the currency-composition of the basket; nor in other respects will stage two witness very much progress along the road to monetary union. Hence the enthusiasts for monetary union advocate a swift transition to stage three, but it is yet to be seen whether they will get their way.

The Delors Report: stage three

The Delors Report envisaged that its proposed stage three would see a 'move to irrevocably locked exchange rates' and subsequently a change-over to a single currency, issued by the ESCB, which would itself comprise the present national central banks plus a new policy-making European Central Bank (ECB).

The Madrid summit of the European Council of Ministers not only decided to launch stage one on 1 July 1990 but also asked the competent bodies of the Community to carry out preparatory work for the organization of an IGC to lay down the subsequent stages of EMU. In this context, the Committee of Central Bank Governors, under the chairmanship of Karl Otto Pöhl, the Bundesbank President, embarked upon the task of drafting a Statute of the European System of Central Banks and of the European Central Bank. A draft was duly completed on 27 November 1990, together with a commentary on each of its articles. As the Chairman explained in his covering letter, 'The Statute addresses Stage Three of Economic and Monetary Union, i.e., a situation when it has been decided to fix irrevocably exchange rates between the Community Currencies and to introduce eventually a single Community Currency.'

As explained in a National Westminster Bank publication:

> The legal structure is that a European System of Central Banks will be created. This will consist of the national central banks (which of course already exist) and a European Central Bank. The national central banks will be the only shareholders of the European Central Bank (ECB), . . . [whose] management structure is a council, consisting of the national central bank governors and possibly one or two other representatives. Under this will be the executive board, which will consist of the Governor and Deputy Governor of the ECB, supported by four other people, who will be executives of the bank, and will not be members of the council. . . .
> The statute sets out that the ESCB shall be independent of outside influence, including from the Commission, the European parliament or national parliaments. There will, nevertheless, be forms of accountability to European institutions. . . .
> The key feature in relation to the independence of the central bank occurs as regards its advisory role in exchange rate policy. Exchange rate policy is taken to be the responsibility of other Community institutions, although the drafts do not say which ones, and the role of the ESCB (Article 4.3) is purely advisory. 'The ESCB is to be consulted, with a view to reaching consensus, consistent with the objective of price stability, prior to any decision relating to the exchange regime of the Community . . .'
> Stage 3, beginning at some date unspecified, is meant to include the irrevocable fixing of exchange rates, followed by a single currency. . . .

What is not brought out in the discussion about EMU is the enormous change between the two parts of Stage 3, from irrevocably fixed exchange rates to a single currency. As long as countries have their own currencies, even if irrevocably fixed, the key responsibility of national central banks will be to maintain exchange rates within the system. It does not matter a great deal if governments have different methods of conducting monetary policy, or if central banks have different constitutions. Whatever the institutional arrangements, and whatever instructions the ECB might wish to give national central banks, their overriding duty will be to maintain the exchange rate relationships. In this first part of Stage 3 there can be enormous freedom of policy within countries on a wide range of matters, provided that the overriding objective of exchange rate stability is maintained. . . . When one moves to the second part of Stage 3, to a single currency, then everything changes [quite contrary to the Delors Report's assumption of gradual evolution]. At that point there has to be one central monetary policy. The degree of latitude allowed national central banks and national governments will be extremely small.

The timing of institutional changes is uncertain. The broad consensus is that the ESCB should come into being at the beginning of Stage 3. Some might wish to see yet further delays, until greater convergence had been achieved.[18]

The summit meeting of the European Council in Rome in December 1990[19] formally inaugurated two IGCs, one on political union and the other on EMU. The latter IGC began its deliberations by working through the Rome Treaty (as amended by the SEA in 1986) article by article, to determine which articles will need to be amended to make possible the various proposals which have been tabled for stages two and three.[20] Once this preliminary task has been completed, the IGC will have to try to agree recommendations for monetary reforms to be introduced in stages two and three. It will then propose amendments to the treaty to provide for their implementation or at any rate to facilitate their implementation at a later date by delegated Community legislation. The main issues it will need to pronounce on are the possible introduction of a parallel currency (maybe on the lines of the hard-ecu proposed by the UK) in stage two and the possible transition to a single European currency in stage three.

Under the latter heading the IGC will need to consider whether a transition to a single European currency should occur only if it can replace all national currencies at one and the same time or whether, on the other hand, there is to be the possibility of a two-speed transition, with perhaps five or six countries leading the way and the rest following later. The laggards would presumably include the UK, which has objections in principle to a common currency, plus some of the Mediterranean member states, which do not object in principle but whose economic performance may be deemed to be inadequately convergent with that of the best performers and in particular of Germany.[21]

The UK's misgivings about the introduction of a single currency have been set out very clearly by Roger Bootle,[22] as follows:

> For the retention of exchange rates to make sense it has to be true both that domestic prices could not fall sufficiently in reaction to adverse shocks and that when the exchange rate is allowed to take the strain instead, domestic prices (and wages) will not rise sufficiently to offset the effects, that is to say that it is possible to change the *real* exchange rate by changing the nominal rate.
>
> This condition throws light on two questions – what sets the appropriate boundaries to a currency union and what explains the shifting of exchange rate regimes over time. Why shouldn't Newcastle have its own currency and permit exchange rate fluctuations between the Geordie and the Pound? Because as a separate currency area Newcastle would be so small economically that a huge proportion of its economic activity would involve cross currency trade. Accordingly, the exchange rate would be a price of overwhelming importance and Geordie prices would go up more or less commensurately with falls in the Geordie exchange rate, bringing no net gain in competitiveness. In general, it will not make sense for small countries to have their own currencies, unless for some reason they can demonstrate superior monetary management (as in the case of Switzerland).
>
> At the other extreme, it is clear that the three major trading blocs of the world, North America, Europe and Japan, are large enough to make serious use of exchange rates. Not even the European Commission is suggesting the evolution of a single *world* currency, abolishing all exchange rate movements between them.
>
> But where the appropriate currency boundaries should be set between these two extremes is far from clear. Some will want to draw on the experience of the United States to argue the case for a common currency for the European bloc. Doubtless the existence of a common currency for the various states of the union has been a factor helping to bind them together. Yet it is not obvious that it has brought economic advantages against the alternative of some states having their own currency. Moreover, the USA has been helped in making a comparative success of a single currency by two vital characteristics of its economy – a high degree of labour mobility and an extremely entrepreneurial and flexible business culture, assisted by low levels of unionisation. These characteristics have provided substitutes for the exchange rate as a means of adjustment to shocks.
>
> In the 19th century, however, virtually the whole developed world was on a fixed exchange rate system (the Gold Standard) which, although not quite a monetary union, shared some of the characteristics. Why was it so successful? Largely because economies exhibited such flexibility that

prices were able to fall in absolute terms, often by large amounts. With such flexibility *of prices* there was no pressing need for flexibility of exchange rates.

And it was precisely because such flexibility had been eroded that Keynes opposed a return to the Gold Standard at the old parity in 1925 and subsequently retained in his designs for the Bretton Woods exchange rate system (which served so well for 25 years after the war), provision for changes of exchange rate parities.

How does Europe come out on this issue? Firstly, there is little doubt that the major countries of Europe, including the UK, do retain a certain degree of influence over the *real* exchange rates. So that the freedom to vary the exchange rate does amount to something more than simply the freedom to choose your own inflation rate.

Secondly, it is clear that shocks affecting different European economies differently do still occur. German reunification provides a textbook case for currency re-adjustment. . . .

Thirdly, we cannot be optimistic that without the power to vary exchange rates domestic price flexibility would provide a substitute. The European economies are not flexible compared to the United States, labour mobility is lower and unionisation is higher. Moreover, the very act of monetary union might make matters worse. For the tendency for workers in Manchester to expect the same wage as workers in Munich would surely be greater when they were all paid in the same currency.

Furthermore, the omnipresent tendency of the bureaucrats in Brussels to want to set common standards for everything throughout the Community regardless of underlying economic forces would lead in the same direction. The current tendencies of the European crypto-state are precisely those *least* likely to make a success of Monetary Union.

Nor is this point mere theoretical surmise. You have only to look at East Germany. To minimize the adverse effect of monetary union upon East German production and employment, wages there have to be kept low in relation to West Germany. Yet wage levels have been pushed *up* by trade unions and generous social security benefits have made the problem worse.

'Regional transfers' provide the stock answer to the problems of sharply divergent performances of regions locked into a currency union. The idea is that advantaged areas make donations to the less advantaged, rather in the manner of transfers within the EC today. But in a full currency union encompassing Britain, Italy and Spain transfers would have to be on a much larger scale. Would they be feasible?

The potential loss of *sovereignty* from monetary union is many faceted. It starts with the obvious lack of control over exchange rates and interest rates. Since in practice British control over these is already circumscribed, the loss (although real) is limited. But it extends also to fiscal policy. With a European bank responsible for European monetary policy would it be possible to leave national governments to borrow and spend whatever they liked in that same national currency? Limits would have to be agreed centrally. And from there on to tax rates. Meanwhile, who would control the substantial regional transfers supposedly available to ameliorate the plight of the weaker areas (Britain)? He who pays the piper calls the tune. None of this is to say that such a loss of sovereignty would *necessarily* be a bad thing. On that there is room for reasonable men to disagree.

The case in favour of a single currency has been made at length by the Commission, in its report *One market, one money*,[23] and Roger Bootle fully accepts the force of this case. He writes:

The potential *benefits* of EMU are clear. At the basic level they consist of the saving of transactions costs associated with changing different European monies. This then may lead on to further economic advantages deriving from the greater integration of European economies and increased trade, and arguably to higher investment.

The Commission's report identified a variety of separate mechanisms by which EMU would benefit the European economy. The main ones are:

(a) An end to exchange rate variability and uncertainty.
(b) The reduction of foreign exchange transaction costs (and their complete disappearance with the eventual introduction of a single Community currency).
(c) The combination of 1992 and EMU should trigger an increase in the underlying rate of growth of the European economy, due to the reduced obstacles to cross-frontier trade and the resulting improvement in investment opportunities and in business confidence.
(d) The monetary policy pursued by the proposed independent Community central bank would combat inflation more effectively than the policies now pursued by the national monetary authorities of many of the member states.
(e) In particular the Community central bank would refuse to finance the budget deficits of member states.
(f) Since excessive wage increases could no longer be validated by a devaluation of the local currency, the temptation to advance excessive wage claims would be moderated.
(g) Under EMU a minimum standard of budget discipline would be imposed on all member states.
(h) In consequence of the elimination of high levels of inflation, the level of interest rates imposed throughout the Community would correspond broadly to those experienced in low-inflation member states such as Germany and Benelux; hence a reduction in the rates which now have to be imposed in inflation-prone states such as the UK, Italy and Spain.
(i) The reduction of interest rates in member states at present prone to

inflation would ease the budgetary burden of servicing their outstanding national debts.

(j) In the past, the need for exchange rate changes has often related to the incidence of country-specific shocks that cause losses of demand for a country's typical products. However, integration as a result of 1992 and EMU will lead to changes in industrial structures in the direction of deeper intra-industry trade and investment relations. This means that most countries become involved in both exporting and importing the products of many industries. Old-style comparative advantage, in which countries specialize their production in distinct commodities, becomes less important, and as a result sector-specific shocks become to a lesser degree country-specific in their impact. Moreover, EMU will eliminate an important category of country-specific shocks which originate in exchange rate movements themselves and in imperfectly coordinated monetary policy.

(k) Under EMU balance of payments constraints would disappear and private markets would finance all viable borrowers.

(l) Under EMU the ecu would probably become a major international currency, along with the dollar and yen.

(m) Moreover the Community would enjoy an important presence in international monetary fora, for example, in the IMF and the Group of Ten.

What is clear from Roger Bootle's analysis is that the disadvantages which may accompany the advantages of a single currency differ widely from one member state to another. At one extreme are the Benelux countries, whose economies are already so integrated with Germany's that their price levels (measured in local currency) may be expected to go up or down more or less commensurately with changes in their DM exchange rate. It is therefore not possible for them to change the real exchange rate by changing the nominal rate. For such countries, discarding the possibility of changing the nominal exchange rate amounts to abandoning an instrument of monetary management which has already lost its effectiveness. Hence for them the economic advantage of adopting a single currency in common with Germany is sheer gain, and the gain is potentially large. At the other extreme is the UK and other major EC countries, which 'do retain a certain degree of influence over their *real* exchange rates',[24] though this influence will be progressively eroded as the European economy becomes ever more closely integrated. This consideration, as well as the unequal degree of economic development in different parts of Europe, may well persuade the IGC to propose the amendment of the treaty in such a way that the progress in stage three to a common currency can if necessary proceed at unequal speed for different members of the Community.

Chapter 9

The Social Charter and other issues

Dennis Swann

Introduction

In our opening chapter we noted that the SEA directly or indirectly led to a deepening of the economic integration process. The words directly and indirectly are important because the role of the SEA in this respect was variable. Thus in the case of EMU, which was discussed in the previous chapter, it cannot be said that the Act was the immediate source of that development; rather it was the preamble's recollection of the 1972 commitment to EMU which was the inspiration which led the subsequent Hanover summit to set the Delors Committees' deliberations in motion. Much the same could be said in the case of the Social Charter: it was not expressly called for in the Act, but the preamble was again significant however. In it the contracting parties emphasized their determination to promote democracy on the basis of the fundamental rights contained in the Convention for the Protection of Human Rights and Freedoms and the European Social Charter – both of these being products of the quite separate Council of Europe. Again, this was the inspiration which led the heads-of-state and government at their 1988 Rhodes meeting to look to the Commission for suggestions as to the way forward; the result was the Social Charter and the associated action programmes. By contrast, provisions relating to the need to press ahead in respect of regional policy (economic and social cohesion), R&TD and the environment were provided for in the main body of the SEA – here it had a direct impact.

The regional issue

The Rome Treaty system

The original Rome Treaty contained no provisions relating to an active regional grant-giving policy at Community level. But the European Investment Bank (EIB), which was specifically provided for in Article 3, has consistently devoted the bulk of its resources to the backward regions of the Community. The bank is not in the business of making grants but it operates through the agency of loans. It does not follow from this that the original Rome Treaty was not concerned with regional grant issues; as we saw in chapter 3, the Commission has since the early days of the Community been actively engaged in policing regional state-aid giving in accordance with Articles 92–4.

Following the Paris summit of 1972 the role of the Community changed. The Commission continued to act as policeman but it was decided that the Community should play a more active role in regional aid-giving, and to this end a European Regional Development Fund (ERDF) was established which came into existence in 1975.

The SEA

The nature of Community regional policy was further developed following the SEA. The reader will recall from chapter 1 that it involved an element of bargaining between more developed and less developed members of the Community. In return for accepting the intensified industrial competition implied by the completion of the internal market, the poorer members of the Community demanded some form of compensation. In part this took the form of an amendment to the Rome Treaty, whereby a new title was inserted covering economic and social cohesion, and a series of supporting articles were also added. Whilst they did not in so many words call for the creation of a Community regional policy, they did declare that the aim of the Community should be to reduce disparities between various regions and reduce the backwardness of the less favoured regions. In the original Rome Treaty these were merely grand aspirations laid out in the preamble, but as a result of the SEA they have now been incorporated into the main body of the Rome Treaty. In parallel with this the Community budget settlement of 1988 laid down that the structural funds like the ERDF and ESF should grow, and indeed that structural spending in 1993 should be twice that of 1987; moreover this structural spending should be concentrated on the poorest regions.

This in turn led to a further redesign of the ERDF which came into effect in 1989, and which was concerned with the targeting and coordination of fund assistance. From its inception attempts had been made to focus fund spending on the areas most in need of help and to dovetail fund activity with other Community policies. The SEA gave further consideration to the issue of targeting and indicated that the fund should concentrate on the development and structural adjustment of regions whose development was lagging behind and on the conversion of declining industrial regions. It also called for a closer coordination between the work of the structural funds and that of the guidance section of the European Agricultural Guidance and Guarantee Fund (EAGGF).

The five priority objectives laid down for the three funds were as follows:[1]

(a) Objective 1 – the promotion of the development of those regions which are lagging behind: now entrusted to the ERDF and ESF and the EAGGF guidance section.

(b) Objective 2 – the conversion of regions affected by serious industrial decline: now entrusted to the ERDF and ESF.

(c) Objective 3 – the reduction of long term unemployment: now with the ESF.

(d) Objective 4 – the integration of young people into the labour force: also entrusted to the ESF.

(e) Objective 5 – the promotion of rural development in the light of the reform of the CAP: entrusted to the ESF.

The reader should note that recent lending by the EIB has reflected the objectives set for the ERDF.

The social issue

The development of Community policy on social issues is best treated in two phases. The first phase ran from 1958 until the negotiations leading up to the SEA, during which phase modest progress was made. The second phase ran from the SEA to the present, and during this period social policy assumed a higher and indeed controversial role.

The Rome Treaty and 1974 action programme

During the first phase Community social policy consisted of four elements. First of all Article 2 of the Rome Treaty laid down the tasks of the Community, and these included the promotion of: 'an harmonious development of economic activities, a continuous and balanced expansion, an increase in stability, an accelerated raising of the standard of living'. Thus a major preoccupation of the Community came to be the improvement of living standards, which had social as well as economic implications. However the question of how improved living standards would manifest themselves (whether private consumption or social protection) was largely left to member states in the first instance. In the longer term the harmonizing influence of the Community was expected to play a role.

The second element related to factor mobility and particularly to the free movement of labour and within the professions: the ability of individuals to move and better themselves was as much an act of social policy as the granting of social benefits. The Community also created conditions of free movement for labour, supplied information on job availability in other countries, provided for the recognition of professional qualifications, enabled social security benefit eligibility to be transferred from one state to another and allowed migrant workers to participate more generally in the social and economic life of the host country.

The third aspect of social policy was to be found in Articles 117–122 whose central concern was social improvement and social harmonization. Article 117 looked to the need to promote a better standard of living, the latter being broadly defined and including not only wages and salaries but many other social factors. Article 118 indicated that these social factors should encompass matters relating to employment, labour law and working conditions, basic and advanced vocational training, social security, occupational hygiene, prevention of occupational accidents and diseases, the right of association, and collective bargaining between employers and workers. The basic message of Articles 117 and 118 was that it is desirable that social standards should rise and that in the process they should be harmonized. For the most part no specific targets were set and no timetables were laid down. Nevertheless, it was assumed that harmonization would occur progressively, partly as an inevitable by-product of the creation of a common market, partly by virtue of the opinions produced by the Commission and partly by virtue of the Commission bringing the member states together to study social policy issues. Specific powers to act were conspicuous by their absence; but two qualifications are appropriate. First, issuing harmonizing directives under Article 100 might in certain cases occur since Article 101 declares that such directives can be adopted when discrepancies between the laws and practices of different member states distort competition. However, it has to be recognized that in the period prior to the SEA, Article 100-type harmonization was based on unanimous voting in the Council of Ministers. Second, as we shall see, equal treatment between men and women was a specific requirement under the treaty; here a basis for action was clearly provided.

Social security is one of the topics subject to improvement and harmonization under Articles 117 and 118, and harmonization of the social security contributions made by employers was a topic of keen debate in the negotiations which led up to both the Paris and Rome Treaties. The reason for this was that within the six the employers' burden was relatively heavy, most notably so in the case of France. The French in particular sought a commitment to harmonize such social charges in the negotiations leading up to the coal and steel treaty but they failed. In practice the old High Authority was not given a power to harmonize social conditions and the Paris Treaty merely referred to the general intention to harmonize conditions in an upwards direction. The French returned to the attack in the Rome Treaty negotiations, but again they failed.

In respect of equal-pay-for-equal-work matters were otherwise. Article 119 of the Rome Treaty required that during the first stage each member state would introduce the equal-pay-for-equal-work system. The reason why the French pressed the equal-pay-for-equal-work point is obvious enough: in industries where the wages of women were raised above their normal level, in the absence of the law governing equal pay French industry would be at a competitive disadvantage in relation to member states which did not have such a law. The general espousal of equal pay under the treaty therefore amounted to agreeing to the proposition that equalization would remedy distortions which would otherwise be caused by different legal provisions.

The fourth element of Community social policy was connected with the ESF which was expressly provided for in Article 3 of the Rome Treaty. Unlike the EIB it was and is still in the grant- rather than the loan-giving business, and its funds derive from Community budget revenues. Its initial task was to reimburse 50–5 per cent of national expenditures on the retraining and resettlement of the unemployed and on the maintenance of jobs whilst enterprises in difficulties converted to other activities. The detailed objectives of the ESF have been changed from time to time: in 1978 the scope of the fund was extended to include creating jobs for the unemployed under 25; and in 1983 it was decided that the bulk of the funds should be devoted to their training and employment. However other priorities were also identified in 1983 in connection with the long-term unemployed, with women wishing to return to work, with handicapped persons wishing to work, with workers needing to retrain because of technological change, with migrant workers and with persons working in the field of employment promotion.

The Paris summit of 1972 appeared to give a major impetus to social policy though in the event the results were rather modest. The summit noted that economic expansion was not an end in itself: social considerations were also important. Disparities in living conditions should be reduced, and this should be achieved with the participation of all the social partners. The quality of life as well as the standard of living should be improved, particular attention being given to intangible values. The summit called for an action programme, and the Commission subsequently obliged by publishing in 1973 its social action programme.[2] The document contained a long list of areas where action was needed, some being matters of priority, which we shall not attempt to list here. The action programme was accepted in a somewhat amended form by the Council of Ministers in January 1974. The detailed actions fell into three categories: those relating to the attainment of full and better employment; provisions concerning the improvement and upward harmonization of living and working conditions; and measures which would increase the involvement of management and labour in the economic and social decisions of the Community, and of workers in the running of their firms.

On the employment front, a good deal of attention was devoted to the problem of unemployment among young people. Recasting the rules of the ESF with a priority for the under 25s has already been mentioned. Education ministers also introduced a range of measures which in the broadest sense had implications for employment. These related to the educational needs of the children of migrants; to the need to prepare young people for work and to facilitate their transition from education to working life; to provision of equal access for boys and for girls to all forms of education; to the combating of illiteracy and to the teaching of Community languages. An important institutional development occurred in 1977 when the European Centre for the Development of Vocational Training was opened in Berlin.

The Community was quite active in respect of the improvement of living and working conditions. In 1977 the health ministers held their first meeting under the aegis of the Rome Treaty, and the Community became active in a limited way in the field of health and safety at work. Directives were adopted in respect of protection from ionising radiation, from the risks involved in the use of dangerous substances and from the hazards arising in connection with major structural accidents (the so-called Soveso Directive). The Community was quite active in respect of women's rights. In the case of equal-pay-for-equal-work the Commission found that the member states had been dragging their feet, and therefore in 1975 the Council issued a Directive requiring the principle to be adopted within one year. In 1976 there followed another directive on the principle of equal treatment for men and women regarding access to employment, vocational training and promotion and in respect of working conditions. In 1978 a directive was also adopted on the subject of equal treatment for men and women in matters of social security.

The Community has also sought to achieve a stronger protection of all workers' interests. In 1975 the Council adopted a directive on the approximation of laws concerning mass dismissals, and in 1977 it issued a directive on the approximation of laws relating to safeguarding rights of employees in the event of transfer of undertakings, or parts thereof; in 1980 a directive was also adopted on protecting employees in the event of an employer's insolvency. Important institutional developments included setting up the European Foundation for the Improvement of Living and Working Conditions in Dublin in 1976, and the decision of 1974 to establish the Advisory Committee for Industrial Safety, Hygiene and Health Protection.

There was much less to show on the participation and industrial-democracy fronts. The Commission put forward a proposal for a fifth directive on the approximation of national company law which sought to give workers a say in the running of companies. However it failed to find favour with the Council of Ministers. Long ago the Community proposed to establish side by side with national laws, a system of Community law which would enable a European Company or *Societas Europea* to be formed. This too envisaged worker representation but also failed to find favour with the Council of Ministers. Mention must also be made of the Vredeling initiative, named after the Commissioner who proposed it in 1980, which sought to set up formal employee information and consultation procedures in certain companies in the Community. It encountered strong opposition both in its original and subsequently watered down versions; employers objected to both; trade unions objected to the second version but liked the original one. It was not taken up.

The SEA and the Social Charter

The impression which emerges is that by about 1980 much of the steam had gone out of the social action programme except where it concerned unemployment. The unemployed now held the centre stage and a good deal of the work of the Council of Ministers was concerned with making recommendations on various possible approaches to the unemployment problem – implementation of actual policy being very much a matter for national governments.

However from about 1985 the pace of social policy change began to quicken. Several background influences can be detected: one was the concept of *L'Espace Sociale*, which literally means social space or social area. This was not new as the idea of a European social area had been put forward by the French President in 1981, and been taken up by the Commission President, Jacques Delors. He appears to have seen it as a natural complement to the idea of completing the internal market by 1992. He contended that some degree of equality in social standards was desirable – otherwise in an increasingly competitive environment those countries with lower standards of social protection would undercut those who sought to provide higher standards (Delors was of course drawing attention to the possible danger of 'social dumping'). Another influence was associated with the idea of social dialogue, a dialogue between the two sides of industry; here too Delors was much to the fore when in 1985 he organized at Val Duchesse, a chateau in Belgium, a series of discussions on socio-economic issues, in which the major participants were the European Trade Union Confederation, the Union of Industries of the European Communities and the European Centre of Public Enterprises. In addition there was the concept of a people's Europe: here the emphasis was on the need to develop the kind of policies which had real practical significance for the average citizen and would bring home the contribution which the European Community could make to their well-being. The task of developing these was assigned to the Adonnino Committee, referred to in chapters 1 and 2, when discussing the origins of the SEA. Its covered a variety of topics and high on its list for future action was the need to provide greater freedom of movement for individuals. Finally there was the SEM concept contained in the Cockfield Report. While many of these proposed measures were not social in character, those concerned with company law had a distinct bearing on the issue of employee-participation in industry.

The social measures which actually emerged during the second phase were as follows. First, as indicated in the discussion of regional policy, the SEA introduced into the Rome Treaty provisions concerned with economic and social cohesion which had implications for the ESF. As noted, these additions to the treaty stressed the need for a closer coordination of the activities of the ESF, the ERDF and the EAGGF guidance section. The Community budget agreement of 1988 shifted more resources to the ESF and ERDF structural funds requiring them to focus their aid on the poorer member states. The discussion of regional policy also showed that specific roles were identified for the various funds (see page 216) for the tasks assigned to the ESF.

Second, the SEA added two new articles to the section of the Rome Treaty concerned with social policy. The new Article 118A required member states to pay particular attention to encouraging improvements, especially in the working environment, in the health and safety of workers. Member states should aim to harmonize conditions but not at the expense of improvements already made: in other words the old upwards harmonization process should continue. The necessary harmonization directives would only require a qualified majority vote in the Council of Ministers. The new Article 118B emphasized the idea of social dialogue to which end the Commission was required to develop such dialogue at a European level, to lead, if the two sides considered it desirable, to relations based on agreement. The Val Duchesse talks have continued, though they have tended to produce joint opinions rather than binding agreements and legislative obligations; nevertheless they have served to improve industrial relations.

In committing the Community to complete the internal market by 1992, the SEA has also placed on the agenda a number of proposals which have social significance. Notable among these were measures relating to free movement of labour and the professions; the Commission also highlighted the need to make progress on the fifth company law directive and on the subject of the European Company Statute.

Significant as these developments were, they can hardly be said to constitute a revolution in Community social policy. By contrast the Social Charter, to which we now turn, was potentially altogether more significant. The Charter did not proceed directly from the SEA but it can be argued that the seeds were sown in the preamble to the Act which contained an important statement of principle, affirming that member states accept the fundamental rights of citizens contained in two important international conventions – the Convention for the Protection of Human Rights and Fundamental Freedoms and the European Social Charter. As we noted, these were products of the Council of Europe, but their contents, particularly those of the second document, provided a potential foundation upon which to build a whole series of rights under the Rome Treaty.

Signs that this could happen were increasingly apparent in subsequent summit communiqués. Thus the Hanover summit of June 1988 merely stressed 'the importance of the social aspects of progress towards the objectives of 1992'. But the Rhodes summit later that year went further in emphasizing that the completion of the internal market should not be regarded as an end in itself but as part of a larger design which involved maximizing the well-being of all within the European tradition of social progress. The summit communiqué also indicated that the heads-of-state and government should look to the Commission for proposals based on the social charter of the Council of Europe. At Madrid they went yet further by declaring that the same emphasis should be placed on the social as on the economic aspects of the single market and that they should be developed in a balanced manner; a preliminary draft of the Social Charter was also discussed. Matters came to a head at Strasbourg later that year, when the Social Charter was tabled and approved by eleven of the twelve member states though the UK declined to subscribe.

This is a convenient point to discuss the UK's position on this issue which could indeed be described as Margaret Thatcher's view on the matter. She had already made her feelings known when in September 1988 she addressed the College of Europe in Bruges: she made it clear that she was opposed to state interference and regulation: 'We have not successfully rolled back the frontiers of the state in Britain only to see them reimposed at a European level. . . .'[3] In her view the Community should not be contemplating more and more regulation but rather should be aiming to deregulate. New regulations would raise the cost of employment and make Europe's labour markets less flexible and less competitive against overseas suppliers. As for the European Company Statute, member states could do what they wanted within their own borders but the UK would resist the imposition of 'collectivism and corporatism' – this presumably referred to the idea of worker participation in company management. The Bruges Group, which came into existence shortly afterwards, echoed these views.[4] Thus well-meaning attempts to establish statutory minimum wages were counter-productive – jobs would be lost; then again attempts to penalize social dumping would impede the development of the poorer member states. The example of the rising standards of living in the Far East and South-east Asia was adduced in favour of allowing countries to exploit comparative advantages unimpeded by measures designed to prevent social dumping.

The Community Charter of Basic Social Rights for Workers[5] – to give it its full title – took the form of a solemn declaration which did not have the force of law. According to Commissioner Vasso Papandreou it seeks to establish a European social model which will guarantee that the search for greater competitiveness and efficiency is paralleled by simultaneous and equal advances in the social field.[6]

The Charter enshrines the following rights and freedoms for Community citizens – in particular for workers whether employed or self-employed:

(a) The right to freedom of movement. Here the emphasis is on the right to move to other countries and take up occupations on the same terms as nationals.
(b) The right to employment and to fair remuneration for that employment.
(c) The right to improved living and working conditions. Here the emphasis is on the idea that the completion of the internal market should be accompanied by harmonization of social conditions whilst the improvement is being maintained.
(d) The right to adequate social protection.
(e) The right to freedom of association and collective bargaining.
(f) The right to vocational training. Every worker has a right to continue vocational training right through his or her working life.
(g) The right of men and women to equal treatment. This extends beyond pay to access to jobs, education, training, career opportunities and social protection.
(h) The right to worker information, consultation and participation.
(i) The right to health and safety protection at the workplace.
(j) The right to the protection of children and adolescents. This includes a minimum working age of sixteen and rights to such things as vocational training after leaving school.
(k) The right of elderly persons to retirement pensions which provide a decent standard of living. Those not entitled to a pension should nevertheless be entitled to a minimum of social protection.
(l) The right of disabled persons to take advantage of specific measures especially in the fields of training and occupational and social integration and rehabilitation.

We have already noted that the Social Charter did not have the force of law, which at first glance would suggest that if it were to be implemented the initiative would have to come from each member state acting individually within its own legislature. However the situation is more complicated than that for two reasons. Some Charter topics do fall within the competence of the Community, or the Commission would endeavour to argue so. Also the principle of subsidiarity (see chapter 2) enables the Community to act when the aims to be achieved can be more effectively attained at Community as opposed to member state level. Having said that, it is necessary to recognize that the Commission in its proposals cannot exceed the powers which are laid down in the Rome Treaty as amended by the SEA.

Not surprisingly the Commission proceeded to produce an action programme[7] (to be followed by further such programmes) of measures designed to implement the Social Charter. For example, it put forward a list of draft directives relating to health and safety at work (as a result of Article 118A) – indeed a number of key directives in this field were approved in June 1989. Some proposals have not been controversial, but others undoubtedly have:

the Commission was apparently on safe ground when it produced draft directives relating to machinery and plant safety and so on; but it also noted that long working hours led to fatigue-related accidents, and therefore sought to introduce a directive relating to hours of work, rest periods, overtime and holidays. These ideas met with stiff opposition in the UK where it was maintained that these were matters properly covered by UK law. The UK was also in the vanguard protesting against a Commission proposal that employers should grant to part-time and temporary workers the same rights and benefits, on a pro rata basis, as to full-time workers. The UK argued that this would in fact price such workers out of jobs – as we have seen, Thatcher free-market economics predicts adverse employment outcomes from well-meaning attempts of this kind to do good. This particular proposal also gave rise to a difference of opinion as to which Council of Ministers voting-rule should apply. The Commission took the view that such differences in national rights and benefits led to distortions of competition; that being so they ought to be treated as a matter for harmonization under Article 100. However, Article 100 has been modified by the new Article 100A (after the SEA) and most harmonization now proceeds on a majority-voting basis – if the UK was alone in opposing the measure it could therefore be out-voted. The UK however argued that according to the SEA the shift to majority voting under Article 100A did not apply to topics relating to the rights and interests of employed persons! Subsequently in June 1991 the UK was again isolated, this time in its opposition to the proposal for a maximum forty-eight-hour working week and to a package which was designed to give working women the right to fourteen weeks maternity leave on full pay and would prevent them from being passed over for promotion on grounds of pregnancy. All this suggests that the Social Charter may not have a smooth passage (see also Maastricht details in chapter 12).

The Environment

The Rome Treaty

The original Rome Treaty contained no provisions calling explicitly for a Community policy on the environment and appeared not to provide the Community with powers to act in such matters. Nevertheless, the Community did go on to establish an environmental policy, following the extremely creative Paris summit of 1972 when the heads-of-state and government called for its introduction. But how were the directives which emerged justified in legal terms?

The basis of justification was twofold. The Community was from time to time forced to deal with environmental issues which arose in connection with the approximation or harmonization of national laws under Articles 100 and 101. For example, member states impose rules concerning the emission of exhaust gases by motor cars; to the extent that these differ from state to state, cross-frontier trade in cars could be inhibited. Inevitably in such cases the harmonization of national laws required the Community to make decisions on the question of pollution standards. In addition, Article 2 of the Rome Treaty outlined in a broad way the tasks of the Community including 'a continued and balanced expansion' and 'an accelerated raising of the standard of living'. It was therefore argued that action on environmental issues was a necessary part of such a programme; once this was accepted then Article 235 was at hand to enable the Community to take whatever additional powers were necessary to achieve environmental objectives. Not everyone was satisfied with this broad interpretation but it was never fundamentally challenged.

The SEA

All this has now been supplemented by the SEA which inserted a new title into the Rome Treaty expressly concerned with the environment. The new Article 130R declared that Community action in relation to the environment should seek to preserve, protect and improve the quality of the environment; contribute to the protection of human health; and ensure a prudent and rational utilization of natural resources. Environmental protection would also be a component of the Community's other policies. Article 130R went on to say that preventive action should be based on the principle that the polluter shall pay; and that in developing policies account should be taken of the potential benefits and costs of action, or inaction. Member states would not be precluded from introducing measures which were more stringent than those commonly agreed – provided they were otherwise compatible with the treaty. Article 130S provided for action on environmental matters on the basis of unanimity in the Council of Ministers. However harmonization activity concerning environmental protection was covered by the new Article 100A and this after the SEA merely required a majority vote in the Council of Ministers. The SEA did however hold out the possibility that the Council of Ministers might also decide certain environmental issues on the basis of majority voting. A subsequent attempt to do this was opposed by several countries including the UK and so the matter was left to the IGC on political union. The reader will not be surprised to learn that these voting arrangements have given rise to some conflict since some issues could arguably fall under either procedure. Incidentally Article 100A also declares that actions under it which relate to environmental protection 'will take as a base a high level of protection'.

Community environmental policy has given rise to some disputes both between member states and between individual member states and the Commission. A dedicated environmentalist would regard it as desirable that all pollution should be eliminated, but economists do not take such a view. Rather they aim for the optimum degree of pollution – in other words accepting that it may be necessary to live with some degree of pollution: beyond a certain point in the clean-up process the benefits to be derived from getting rid of a bit more pollution are less than the costs of getting rid of it. In the early days there appeared to be a possibility that some states were in favour of proceeding towards the extreme position of eliminating all the pollution that it was technically possible to eliminate. On the other hand the UK adopted a different approach, essentially the economist's view that the costs and benefits had to be weighed against each other. In the end, something like the economist's view prevailed at Community level and, following the SEA, a weighing of costs and benefits is now quite clearly the required approach.

When pollution is under consideration the economist's approach is to say that it should be dealt with by internalizing the externality. A logical way to do that is to impose an appropriate level of tax on the polluter – assuming that it is possible to place an appropriate monetary value on the negative effect sustained by the rest of society. In practice the imposition of taxes is not the approach normally adopted in the Community; rather the Community tends to proceed by imposing standards, in respect of emission levels or in terms of the effect on the environment. The Polluter-Pays Principle (PPP) was also enshrined in the SEA: it was not a new development in Community thinking – its adoption goes back to 1973–4. The adoption of PPP is often taken to imply an acceptance of a tax-based solution; however in the case of the Community it meant no more than that the costs of controlling the pollution were borne by the polluter, in other words the polluter would not receive subsidies to enable him to conform. The 1974 communiqué from the Commission on this subject did envisage some loopholes.[8] Such a general approach is not necessarily optimal.

National differences have also surfaced in the past in respect of standards to be attained by anti-pollution activity. One approach is to lay down uniform emission standards, but the alternative is to set standards by reference to the impact which pollution has on the quality of the environment. In the end the member states have usually been given a choice and the SEA has not changed the position on this issue.

The implications of the SEA for environmental policy are significant but should not be overestimated. It has to be admitted that even in the absence of a specific reference to environmental policy in the Rome Treaty a considerable amount of progress had been made. Up to 1990 more than 100 measures, mainly directives, relating to the environment had been introduced and the great bulk of them were agreed prior to the entry into force of the SEA in 1987. A considerable list of measures had been introduced which were designed to combat water pollution, adopting two main approaches. Minimum quality standards for receiving water were set depending on their final use such as drinking or bathing. Directives were also adopted to prevent the discharge of dangerous substances which because of their toxicity and persistence could pose a major threat to health and the environment – cadmium and mercury are just two of the dangerous products for which specific directives were introduced. The Community also produced a series of directives concerning noise levels in relation to household appliances, hydraulic diggers, tower cranes, lawn mowers and motor cycle exhausts. A significant programme of action was set in motion to curb air pollution; air quality standards have been set, including guide and limit values for sulphur dioxide, lead and nitrogen oxide. Rules were also introduced concerning product quality: a directive was issued which fixed the maximum sulphur content for gas oil, but not heavy fuel oil, and another set a limit to the lead content in petrol. The clean car initiative gave rise to a measure to encourage the use of lead-free petrol. Directives were also introduced controlling the marketing and use of dangerous chemicals and other substances; others were concerned with their classification, packaging and labelling. Standards were devised in relation to the management of waste and the transport of hazardous wastes.

Since the SEA, directives have continued to pour out on topics as diverse as the contained use and release into the atmosphere of genetically modified organisms; on jet aircraft noise; and on the depletion of the ozone layer. The Community was involved in international discussions concerning the depletion of the latter caused by the release of chlorofluorocarbons (CFCs) and halons together with other substances such as carbon tetrachloride and methyl chloroform which are also understood to have the same effect. It is a signatory to the Vienna Convention on the ozone layer and the Montreal Protocol on CFCs. The Protocol committed those signing to a 50 per cent reduction in CFCs by the end of the century – although in 1989 the Council of Ministers agreed to ban most CFCs by then; at the time of writing the Commission is proposing a phasing-out by 1997, with an 85 per cent cut by 1995.

The SEA, is, as we noted earlier, significant in that it modifies the Community's decision-making powers. Prior to it most decisions on environmental matters were made on the basis of Articles 100 and 101, but the unanimity principle was bound to lead to agreements which represented the lowest common denominator. Now that majority voting is possible, future measures should give rise to tighter controls. Unfortunately, environmental measures under new Article 130S are based on unanimity, and as we have seen, the Council of Ministers has so far resisted shifting the basis to majority voting.

A significant change which could easily be overlooked is a provision in the new Article 130R to the effect that environmental protection requirements shall be a component of the Community's other policies. The Commission in its fourth environmental action programme (1987–92)[9] has taken this on board. There is also evidence that the Court of Justice will take due account of environmental issues in its judgements. This was made apparent in the *Danish Bottle* case[10] which the Court ruled on in 1988. The Danish government had introduced rules which required returnable containers for beer and soft drinks together with licences for new types of container. The Commission had argued that this represented a barrier to trade but the Council decided in favour of the Danes on grounds of environmental protection.

The entrenching of environmental policy in the Rome Treaty will also presumably strengthen the Commission in its enforcement drive. The reference of the UK to the Court of Justice in relation to water standards may be one sign of this. In the context of enforcement, mention must be made of a decision in 1990 to set up the European Environment Agency to provide objective and comparative data on the environment in the member states and provide a firm basis for both the enforcement and the formulation of environmental policy.

Research and technological development

The Rome Treaty

As in the case of regional, social and environmental policy, the Paris summit of 1972 marked a significant turning point in Community policy towards R&TD. The summit communiqué expressly referred to the need for a common policy in the field of science and technology. The Commission duly produced a memorandum in 1973[11] and its general lines of action were enndorsed by the Council of Ministers in 1974. Subsequently limited Community budget resources were devoted to R&TD activity. Some of this took the form of direct action – i.e. research work within the Community's own Joint Research Centre. The rest consisted of indirect action – programmes of research identified by the Community but carried out by firms, universities, and other bodies with the Community paying a proportion of the cost.

By the early 1980s the Community began to realize that it was suffering a loss of competitiveness in world markets and that a more dynamic response was needed to the technological challenge posed by the US and Japan.

Alternative approaches

Two strategies were proposed. One was that protection was needed for a limited period if Europe's advanced technology industries were to attain international levels of competitiveness. The French government advocated such an approach in a memorandum issued in 1983. The alternative was to develop a more intensive collaborative approach to the technological challenge: it was this view which finally prevailed.

The approach which followed had the following characteristics: the areas in which the Community was at risk should be identified; having identified them, the Community should seek to meet them on a collaborative basis; more budget money would have to be devoted to R&TD and this was agreed at the Fontainebleau summit in 1984. Community efforts should be set within multi-annual framework programmes – which has been so since 1984. R&TD collaboration should be at the research end since otherwise competitors such as the US would cry foul on grounds of subsidization. R&TD collaboration should extend to states outside the Community – which is not new, as such collaboration goes back to 1970. The Rome Treaty should explicitly address itself to the R&TD issue.

It is only the latter which calls for further comment. The idea of injecting an explicit commitment into the treaty was aired in a memorandum which the EC Commission addressed to the Milan summit in 1985. The memorandum was entitled 'Towards a Technology Community'.[12] It was endorsed by the European Council and became one of the background documents which led to the SEA: as a result of the SEA, the Rome Treaty was amended. A new section was added, headed Research and Technological Development (R&TD). The ensuing articles state that the Community's aim should be to strengthen the scientific and technological base of European industry and to encourage it to become more competitive at the international level. To this end the Community would encourage firms, universities and research centres in their research and technological development activities. It would also help firms to exploit the Community's internal market through the opening up of public contracts, standardization and the removal of fiscal and legal barriers to cooperation. The treaty was also amended in respect of the decision-making process. Although the multi-annual R&TD framework programmes will be decided on the basis of unanimity, individual items within it will be decided on a majority basis. This latter should help to speed up the collaborative process.

Chapter 10

The European Community and the new Europe

David Allen

Even before the dramatic events in eastern Europe of 1989, it had become evident that the European Community had found, in the 1992 programme and the SEA, a new integrative dynamic that had lifted it out of the doldrums of the 1975–85 decade. Though the SEA disappointed many commentators at the time, who compared it unfavourably with the more extensive plans for a European union enshrined in the draft treaty drawn up by the European Parliament in 1984, from 1986 onward the European Community has gone from strength to strength. Many of the supposed omissions or compromises of the SEA are now back on the negotiating table; particularly because in December 1990 at the European Council in Rome, the EC convened two more IGCs with a view to concluding treaties on both EMU and political union by the end of 1991. In the period since the SEA was ratified the EC has made significant progress towards achieving the completion of the internal market by the 1992 deadline. Furthermore the EC was able, in 1988, to agree on a new and more equitable budget package and to make a further effort to reform the CAP – though not enough to satisfy its major critics within the GATT. Perhaps even more importantly the EC has found itself thrust into the limelight at the very centre of European politics as a result of the end of the cold war and of the post war division of Europe.

The new situation in Europe presented an immense external challenge to the European Community only a short time after it had embarked on the not inconsiderable internal challenge of institutional reform and the creation of the single market. On the one hand the end of the cold war can be seen as presenting the EC with a great opportunity to both widen and deepen the integrative experiment, in a Europe no longer divided or dominated by the superpower protagonists. According to this view the cold war placed definite limits on what was achievable within the EC, particularly in the spheres of foreign policy and security; it would see NATO and the need for a US nuclear umbrella as restraints on the development of an EC security identity; and the continuance of the east–west divide was viewed as an inhibition to the enlargement of the EC to include either the neutral states of western Europe or the states of eastern Europe. The end of the cold war could thus be to result in lifting a series of restraints on the west Europeans in their pursuit of European union.

On the other hand there is a view that would regard all the post-war European organizations (western and eastern) as essentially 'cold war institutions' which were unlikely to survive its peaceful conclusion. This view would have led one to correctly predict the collapse of the Warsaw Pact and Comecon but would also have anticipated that NATO and the EC too would have problems maintaining internal cohesion once the discipline of the external threat was removed. According to this view the situation in the new Europe presented challenges to the preservation of the EC's achievements, rather than opportunities for their consolidation and advancement. It was certainly the case that the Warsaw Pact and Comecon have already lost their *raison d'être* and that NATO faces a major restructuring and reconsideration of its role if it is to survive.

However, it is already clear that the EC faces a much more positive role in the new Europe. Both the superpowers have recently demonstrated a desire to distance themselves from the problems and responsibilities of their previous roles in Europe. They would leave the economically successful west Europeans to fend for themselves and collectively to assume responsibility for the economically unsuccessful east Europeans (and possibly the Soviet Union as well). It is certainly the case that the United States and the Soviet Union have significantly reassessed the nature of their relationship with the EC to a point where they both now see the Community as the key to the new Europe, even if their conceptions of that Europe still differ. Uncertainty about the structure of both security and economic development in Europe (which had previously been determined by the east–west divide) combined with this new certainty about the central role of the EC means that the current deliberations within the Community about its future development have implications that go way beyond the EC itself. It is now possible for almost every state in Europe to contemplate not just the desirability or necessity of joining the EC, but the distinct possibility. The present criteria for membership requires a state to be European and democratic; while this may still be used to deny membership to both Turkey and Morocco, all the EFTA states (no longer so concerned about neutrality) and most of the Eastern European states are now contemplating either closer association or membership.

Assuming no great setbacks in the liberalization and democratization of eastern Europe, the Community will increasingly become synonymous with the European continent as a whole. As a result the process that started in 1985, with the 1992 programme and the SEA and which is being continued in the two IGCs, is now seen as being critical to the determination of what has become known as the new European architecture. Commentators are arguing that what is at stake is Europe from the Atlantic to the Urals; and that the decisions taken within and about the EC over the next few years could be as decisive as at the Congress of Vienna in 1814, the Treaty of Versailles in 1914 or the arrangements at Yalta in 1945. The purpose of the concluding chapter of this section is to carry on the account of the development of European union that we began in chapter 2, to discuss how the revitalized Community reacted to, and was affected by, the sudden changes in eastern Europe. It will also consider current developments in the two IGCs in the broader context of the likely evolution of the new Europe in the 1990s.

The impact of change in eastern Europe

We have already noted the fact that before 1989 the EC had reinvigorated itself internally and had taken steps to further develop its foreign policy identity and to add a security dimension to it. As we saw in chapter 7 the EC was still not punching its full weight in the international economy; but it had, with its 1992 programme, attracted the attention of Japan and the United States; it had also forced the EFTA states both to collectively seek a more structured relationship with the Community, and in some cases (Austria and Norway) to make or consider applications for full membership. Following Mrs Thatcher's aggressive statement of her own views on European union in a speech at Bruges in late 1988, a debate on the future of the Community, with herself and Jacques Delors (who was to give his own 'Bruges' speech exactly one year later) as chief protagonists, was already under way. That debate was to be given a new urgency and was itself significantly affected by events in eastern Europe that came to a head in 1989. The EC states had already begun to reconsider their relationship with the Soviet Union in the light of Mr Gorbachev's new thinking, which seemed to involve a desire to have an improved relationship with the west Europeans, but their response had been a very cautious one. Britain was the EC state most concerned that Gorbachev might be seeking to drive a wedge between the Europeans and their American allies, while West Germany was the most receptive to the notion of improved relations with the eastern bloc. The West German stance had already begun to irritate Britain and concern France. The French were worried that West Germany might be contemplating an escape into neutrality in the hope of advancing the cause of German reunification and this led them to seek ways of more effectively binding West Germany into the European Community. One such way of course was to push the Community first of all towards economic and monetary union, and then towards consideration of political union. It became French policy, enthusiastically supported by Jacques Delors on behalf of the European Commission, to seek reassurance from the Federal Republic in the form of support for EC initiatives in this area and it became West German policy to give exactly that sort of reassurance. Jacques Delors, who had developed the three-stage EMU plan, recognized that the Federal Republic's enthusiasm for it could be greatly enhanced if the EC responded to West German anxieties about the need to give assistance to those eastern European governments pursuing reforms.

By April 1989 the EC had adopted a policy of giving aid to eastern European countries like Poland and Hungary who could report progress towards liberalization and democratization, but witholding aid from those who could not, like Romania. Delors pushed for this policy against considerable British reluctance, partly because he wanted West German support for EMU and partly because he wanted to advance Commission competence into a new area. It was by no means clear then that the Commission actually had the capability to operate a policy of conditionality on aid to eastern Europe, given the inadequacy of its information about the economic and political situation in the eastern bloc. Nevertheless, the Commission scored a considerable plus when the G7 (see list of abbreviations), at their Paris summit in June 1989, gave it the task of coordinating not just EC aid but the aid efforts of all the G24 (see list of abbreviations) states towards eastern Europe. As events began to escalate, and in particular as refugees began to stream out of East Germany (the DDR) via a number of routes, West Germany found itself forced to respond rapidly, and sought the assistance of its EC partners. Many of them were fearful about Soviet reactions to any active reponse to events in the DDR in particular, but for West Germany there was simply no choice. Once it became clear that the Brezhnev doctrine was indeed dead and that the Soviets were unlikely to intervene to prop up the DDR, West Germany's EC partners began to worry about the posibility of a German–Soviet deal over reunification that might detach West Germany from both the EC and NATO.

Delors' solution to this came in his Bruges speech in October 1989 when he argued that the twelve member states of the EC should move quickly towards establishing an IGC on EMU. He also proposed that this should be complemented by one on political union, involving the development of a common foreign and defence policy, the introduction of new policy areas and a further reform of the EC's institutions. Delors also sought to link this with developments in eastern Europe by arguing that the single market must be complemented by the Social Charter and an expanded role for the European Parliament, so that the Community would continue to be attractive to those in eastern Europe who sought basic rights, prosperity and democracy. In a direct rebuttal of Mrs Thatcher's minimalist views Delors said 'think of the effect in Prague and Warsaw and elsewhere when the EC declares solemnly, by means of a Social Charter, that it will not subordinate fundamental workers rights to economic efficiency'.

The West Germans, under pressure from the French, hesitated on EMU only as far as its timing was concerned. Chancellor Kohl was anxious that there should be no formal decision on the IGC until after the West German elections, due in December of 1990, because he feared that his voters might view EMU within the EC as a barrier to German unification. It was at this point that the foreign minister Herr Genscher developed his notion of concentric circles of European cooperation in a bid to reconcile the demands of many of his EC partners for West Germany to push ahead on integration, with his own wish not to close the EC off from eastern European states. Mrs Thatcher had begun to argue at this time that EMU and any other aspect of EC deepening should be postponed (preferably for ever!) so that the EC would not become too intimidating an organization for new members to join. It should be added that Mrs Thatcher also believed that the more states that could be admitted into the EC the less likely it was to develop into her personal nightmare of a centralized European union. Genscher however argued that an inner core of EC states willing and able to create a European union should do so and that other European states could associate themselves with such a union depending on their ability to make integrative commitments. Thus the next closest ring would consist of the present EFTA states (and possibly Britain too if it continued to show reluctance about EMU or political union) and they would be more loosely linked to an outer ring of newly democratized east European states. Finally all three circles might be linked with the United States and the Soviet Union in the Conference on Security and Cooperation in Europe (CSCE) process thereby giving some expression to Gorbachev's notion of a common European home (the Bush equivalent of a Europe 'whole and free'). Genscher argued that membership of these circles would not be fixed but that there would be the possibility of states moving from one circle to another as they became capable of sustaining more binding commitments. Thus any European state able to meet the basic conditions of a market economy and a democratic system could begin with a loose form of association but still aspire to eventual full membership. Nearer the centre of course the implicit threat was that some states might chose to advance towards European union without Britain.

As events developed apace in eastern Europe there was much talk of the need for the EC to participate in or even organize a sort of Marshall Plan for eastern Europe. But the problem, then as now, was that, whilst all states were prepared to help in a limited way, only the Federal Republic was prepared to consider the injection of massive funds and then only with the participation of other EC states. Many member states were in any case concerned about the diversion of limited EC funds either from themselves (in the case of the poorer Mediterranean states) or from other policies they supported. In particular fears were expressed, even before the question of reunification arose, that West Germany, the major net contributor to the EC budget, would prefer to redirect its largess from within to outside the Community. In the period between the fall of the Berlin Wall and the confirmation that reunification was both feasible and imminent the West Germans were confronted with the difficult task of both reassuring their EC partners and not antagonizing the Soviet Union. Although they constantly encouraged the EC (and NATO) to coordinate their reactions, events tended to move too fast for their relatively cumbersome procedures, even though EC Foreign Ministers were engaged in an almost constant round of bilateral and multi-lateral meetings. The EC states therefore tended to react at first unilaterally, then engage in bilateral diplomacy and finally attempt to coordinate their responses as a Community. The major actors were inevitably Britain, France and West Germany, though in the first half of 1990 when the issue of reunification and the entry of the DDR into the Community was being discussed, the Irish presidency played a key role. The negotiations would have been very much more difficult if any one of the 'big three' had been in the chair.

For Britain, Mrs Thatcher's stock response was Canute-like in its determination to preserve the status quo and there was precious little sympathy for the German dilemma. Even though the French shared much of Mrs Thatcher's angst about German reunification there was little prospect of Anglo-French cooperation, as the British Prime Minister was also strongly opposed to any acceleration of EC integration, which was the preferred French way of dealing with the German problem. Within the EC the dominant relationship was therefore once again the Franco-German one, and it was by building on its past strength and long history that both countries were able to reconcile their gut nationalistic reactions to events in eastern Europe and preserve a united approach to the development of the EC. French aspirations for EC progress began to centre on the European Council meeting due to be held in Strasbourg in December of 1989; here the French hoped to fix a date for the IGC on EMU to begin, to get agreement on the Social Charter and to extend the Community's programme of aid to eastern Europe, in particular by giving the go-ahead to plans for a European Bank for Reconstruction and Development (EBRD).

However once the Berlin Wall had fallen the United States and the Soviet Union decided to hold a summit in Malta. Fearful that there might be some substance in the slogan 'from Yalta to Malta' and that the superpowers might once again be planning a European settlement without consulting the Europeans in general and the French in particular, Mitterrand called an extraordinary EC summit in order to develop a Community line on events in eastern Europe before the superpowers met. The French enthusiasm for the November Paris meeting was partly related to a desire to prevent eastern Europe dominating the European Council. Nevertheless the real fear, after what had nearly happened at Reykjavik, was that the superpowers might cobble together a European settlement with Gorbachev agreeing to German reunification in exchange for the US accepting that the new Germany would not be a member of NATO. By now most EC states assumed that self-determination in the DDR would lead to reunification, though Mrs Thatcher continued to protest against the speed of developments.

At the Paris emergency summit the EC achieved an impressive degree of unity on the question of aid to eastern Europe and the political and economic conditions that would be applied to it. When it came to the latter the EC Commission sensibly recognized its lack of expertise and agreed to rely on IMF assessments of developments in east European economies. The Financial Times ran a leader on the Monday (20 November 1990) after the summit headed 'Europe's new stature' in which it talked of the EC as a growing actor on the world stage and of the Community, for the first time, 'grasping its political responsibilities'. Building on this enthusiasm France and Germany immediately delivered a joint address to the European Parliament in which they insisted that EC political integration and democracy in the East must go together and that the best response to change in the East was to stengthen EC bonds in order to maintain the Community's 'magnetic' powers of attraction. At the Strasbourg European Council in December 1990 the French by and large got their way at the expense of both isolating and irritating Mrs Thatcher. When the British Prime Minister left Strasbourg after the Community had decided to convene the EMU IGC in December 1990 she acidly noted that Kohl had, with French assistance, fixed a date which 'suits his election but not mine'. That December, the EC was at the centre of a frantic round of multi-lateral discussions; the EFTA countries expressed fears that their potential role was as an EC kindergarten for east European states; the Soviet Union signed the first ever EC-Soviet trade agreement and NATO held its first dialogue with the Community. By the end of 1989 the EC had emerged quite well from the upheavals; it had succeeded in producing a short term response to the need for aid in the East and had gained much prestige from its management of the overall western effort within the G24. It had held its own against the superpowers and had begun to face up to the likelihood of the rapid integration of the DDR into the EC and it had also managed to maintain, even speed up, the momentum of its own internal evolution with the decisions taken in Strasbourg on EMU, the Social Charter and the EBRD.

The positive nature of the impact of change in eastern Europe on the EC has been maintained up to the present day even though the scale of economic assistance required in eastern Europe and the Soviet Union and now in the eastern part of Germany goes way beyond the sort of sums that the EC can muster at present. In 1990 the EC record on the question of German reunification was an impressive one though the major negotiations inevitably involved West Germany, the United States and the Soviet Union. Though Britain and France were given formal roles within the two-plus-four formula they exerted little real direct influence although France continued to attract German support for continued EC integration. This was because, as in the past, France was prepared to trade its own sovereignty (for instance with regard to the establishment of a common currency or a European central bank) in return for the anchoring of a reunified and therefore stronger Germany within the Community. France was thus able to seek positive common ground with Germany by linking reunification and EC integration in a way that the British could never do. Mrs Thatcher came to accept German unity with ill-disguised bad grace and at the same time sought to frustrate moves to further develop the EC. In Germany her cautious and negative statements on reunification were treated with contempt and she found little support in either Moscow, Washington or amongst the other members of the EC. The result was that Britain was marginalized both from the reunification process and from the deliberations that continued about the future of the EC.

The major constraints on the West Germans as they negotiated the internal and external conditions for unity with the DDR came from domestic public opinion and from the need to carry the support of the United States and the Soviet Union. In the case of the Soviet Union this was mainly achieved by the promise of Deutschmarks and in the case of the US, Washington was willing to allow the Germans a free hand provided they could show that they had the support of the Community and this was duly achieved at a European Council meeting in Dublin. Significantly it was also at this meeting that the EC decided to contemplate, at the suggestion of France and Germany, a separate IGC on political union to take place at the same time as the EMU one. Though the initial impetus for the continued development of the EC derived from the success of the 1992 programme and the SEA, it was certainly the case that events in eastern Europe and in particular German unification served to speed up this process; particularly as the Commission and France sought to protect the EC from any German attempt to make links with eastern Europe easier by toning down its EC committment. The timetable for EMU was therefore accelerated, despite some German hesitation based on the practical experience of concluding monetary union with the DDR, and political union was added as an objective.

The changes in eastern Europe and the end of the cold war had also put the question of EC enlargement more urgently on the agenda. From the very start of their revolutions Hungary, Poland and Czechoslovakia in particular and Romania and Bulgaria to a lesser extent, have all sought a close relationship with the EC and have come to regard eventual membership as inextricably intertwined with the successful promotion and preservation of democracy and a free market economy. This interest from eastern Europe, along with the development of the EC internal market, has served to intensify interest in membership amongst the EFTA countries. The end of the cold war has also removed the 'neutrality barrier' that had previously made Austria, Sweden or even Switzerland hestitate about membership of an EC committed to the development of a common foreign (and perhaps defence) policy. The Community has, of course, already effectively taken on a new member with the integration of the DDR into West Germany, and thus the EC, in 1990. Though concern has been expressed about the impact on the EC budget and the long transitional time that will be required for the eastern part of Germany to raise itself to EC standards, the actual process of absorption caused astonishingly few problems within the EC. All the states and the Community institutions seemed anxious to ensure that no barriers were placed in the way of reunification; this meant that they were not inclined to niggle about the transitional details, in stark contrast to the negotiations that surrounded the entry of Greece, Spain and Portugal. The Commission took the lead on DDR entry, as it had done on the coordination of aid, and its considerably enhanced status was underlined by the attention that Delors received from the American press at the Houston G7 summit in June 1990. Throughout this momentous year Delors never missed an opportunity to keep the Commission profile raised high whether by requesting a separate seat at the CSCE, liaising directly with NATO or accepting an invitation to attend all German cabinet meetings that concerned reunification.

One result of this greater role for the EC in general and the Commission in particular has been a constant call from the US for a more structured and formal process of consultation between the US and the EC. Secretary of State Baker referred to this several times in 1990 and indeed an agreement was drawn up that would have involved regular meetings between the US administration and the Community institutions. However in the frictions that arose at the end of 1990 over the breakdown of the GATT talks – itself a good example of the need for a better organized dialogue between the EC and the US – the agreements were not formally concluded, though it seemed certain that they would be in the near future. For the EC this was quite an advance on a few years ago when the US exhibited little interest in dealing with either the EC or EPC but preferred to rely on bilateral dealings with individual EC member states.

The highlight of this period of change came in November 1990 when the thirty-four member states of the CSCE met in Paris to effectively put the final seal on the cold war if not to lay the foundations of the new European architecture. Foundations included: a major conventional arms control agreement; the establishment of a CSCE secretariat; and the promise of regular meetings within the CSCE framework (the outer circle of Genscher's concentric scheme for Europe). However, doubts about internal developments in the Soviet Union and Mr Gorbachev's shifting position remained and meant that the CSCE meeting did little to substantiate the concept, promoted by the Soviets and some east European states, that the CSCE should become an instrument of collective security, eventually replacing NATO and the Warsaw Pact. Indeed, the hopes for the CSCE playing this kind of role in the immediate future were dashed early in 1991 by the actions of the Soviet government which was the only state to veto a suggestion that the CSCE might usefully provide the forum within which the crisis over the Baltic states might be discussed and perhaps resolved. Since the Paris meeting, the cold war has not returned but the search for a new European security order has been confused both by events in the Gulf and by the continued deterioration inside the Soviet Union. As we shall see in the next section, the security debate within the EC, which was a key part of the political union IGC, now revolves less around notions of pan-European security and more around arguments about whether a revitalized NATO, or the EC with a defence competence, or some compromise between the two, will best serve the interests of the EC member states in the new Europe of the 1990s.

Towards European union

The Italian presidency culminated in a European Council meeting in Rome at which it formally convened two new IGCs on EMU and political union. The most striking feature of the meeting was the absence of conflict – in public at any rate – between Britain and her European partners. The replacement of Mrs Thatcher may have changed the tone rather more than the substance of the British position – which remained cautious on the content of both IGCs. But that alone was enough to ensure that Britain's partners were prepared to agree an agenda for the political union IGC which played down the fact that on issues such as the major extension of EC authority into social, transport infrastructure, environmental and research policy most EC states take a different line from Britain (as indeed they do on an increase in majority voting and the powers of the Parliament). The details of the negotiations about EMU have already been dealt with in chapter 8 but it is still worth noting that EMU itself raises a number of contentious political issues. In particular arguments about sovereignty have been raised both by the proposals for a common currency and a European central bank and by the realization of what economic union might mean for the exercise of economic decision-making at the national level. The contrast between the British view of the relationship between national sovereignty and the EC and the predominant view on the mainland of Europe is quite considerable. For the British, both before and one suspects after Mrs Thatcher, the relationship between the nation state (or national government) and the Community has always been seen in zero-sum terms. In other words, given a finite amount of authority or sovereignty, any increase in Community competence or authority has had to be matched by a dimunition of similar power at the national level. In this them and us view of the Community Mrs Thatcher came to believe that if Jacques Delors became more authoritative she would become less so. When Delors chose to address the British TUC and argue that by the year 2000 some 80 per cent of all economic decisions would be taken in Brussels this served only to confirm Mrs Thatcher's concerns about the transfer of authority involved in EMU.

However elsewhere in the Community a different view of national sovereignty and the EC holds sway. For the Germans and, in the context of EMU, for the French as well, increasing Community competence is about creating a shared authority over areas which are no longer amenable to the exercise of individual sovereignty. Most European states do not see the development of the Community as threatening the existence of individual states; they tend to see the Community as a means of collectively achieving objectives which are beyond the grasp of its members operating independently. As such the Community can be seen as a means of preserving not challenging the authority of national governments. Perhaps the major difference between the two positions lies in the fact that, for the British, transfer of competence and authority to Brussels raises the spectre of a 'bureaucratic' Commission and of the talking shop that is the European Parliament. In practice of course not only are the member states responsible for the present state of Community institutions but in practice the transfer of competence to Brussels usually means a transfer to the Council of Ministers. Here major 'framework' decisions continue to be taken on the principle of unanimity, even though more and more of the detailed infilling of these decisions is subject to majority vote. To date, national governments have not relinquished control of decision-making, they have instead chosen to exercise it collectively and in a different place. It is in the Council of Ministers that power is most effectively exercised and the democratic problem that arises is not the unanswerability of the Commission – as Mrs Thatcher would have argued – but the difficulty of holding the Council accountable.

However the argument between Mrs Thatcher and Jacques Delors went beyond a 'theological' dispute about the nature of sovereignty and integration and into the much more interesting realm of political ideology. The true basis of their disagreement, which is of real consequence for the development of the Community, is political. Their visions of Europe differ because one is a free market conservative and the other is a socialist who favours a degree of corrective intervention into the market. This sort of dispute about the future of the Community and the sort of policies that should be pursued seems to be entirely healthy for a grouping of democratic states, indeed perhaps one of the problems in the past was that the debate on Europe was essentially politically neutral. Furthermore the political substance of the Thatcher–Delors debate about the future of Europe is not restricted to the two personalities involved, one of whom has now departed from the scene. In the IGC on EMU it has raised its head again with Germany pushing for the inclusion in the treaty of a clause enshrining a commitment to both the free market and privatization; but coming up against considerable resistance from Belgium which would like to see clauses relating to the need for an interventionist industrial policy; and France which is reluctant to subscribe to a Europeanization of the principle of privatization.

There are of course many ways in which the EMU and political union IGCs are linked, but Germany has sought to put pressure on its EC partners – particularly those who are are less than enthusiastic about some aspects of political union – by insisting that it will only sign the EMU treaty if the equivalent political union treaty is ready to be signed at the same time.

In so doing Kohl would appear to be trying to establish that German sacrifices on monetary union will be compensated for by pushing German policy objectives on political union (Germany is in the maximalist camp on most political union issues). Before the German intervention, progress in the political union IGC had begun to slow down, partly because of the distraction of the Gulf War and partly because many states have come to accept that 1992 or even 1993 may not be the ideal time for reaching decisions about either the institutional structure or the common policies to be pursued in the EC towards the end of the decade and into the next century. Increasingly 1995 or 1996 is being seen as a potential turning point when not only will the single market have been completed but many of the current questions about EC enlargement should have been resolved. Furthermore, it is argued that the shape of the new Europe, and in particular the nature of the required security structures should have become clearer. This would make it easier for the Community to sort out its own role in the new Europe. This sort of thinking is attractive to those who would like to see the political union IGC come up with reformist rather than revolutionary proposals, but it is disappointing for those who would like the EC to exercise leadership and play a full part in actually determining, rather than just reacting to, the shape and nature of new European arrangements. At this point in time (spring 1991) it seems most likely that the political union package will not break very much new ground but will instead cover a number of relatively minor reforms, leaving a number of items to be resolved at a later date. However, even if this does prove to be the case, it is worth recalling the ratchet-like nature of Community progress. Many of the items that will be agreed in the political union IGC are those that were rejected at the time of the SEA and similarly many of those items rejected this time will probably be accepted at a later date.

The political union agenda covers further reform of Community institutions – in particular the question of extending majority voting and the problem of the democratic deficit, the question of subsidiarity, the extension of Community competence into new areas and the further development of EPC with an emphasis on both improving the links between EPC and the EC and extending the present understanding of a security competence into the 'hard' area of defence policy. All these agenda items demonstrate a high degree of continuity with the past and can be traced back through the deliberations about the SEA in the mid 1980s to the European Parliament's draft treaty (see chapters 1 and 2); and indeed further back through the many discussions about European union that took place in the late 1960s and the 1970s (indeed many observers today would trace France's fondness for enhancing the powers of the European Council all the way back to the Fouchet proposals of the 1960's).

It seems certain that the political union treaty will provide for some extension of majority voting in the Council of Ministers but there will be considerable wrangling between the states as to the areas to be covered. Working on the ratchet principle it is probable that those areas like environmental and social policy, perhaps even research and technological policy, that were added to the EC Treaty in the SEA, but which were subject to unanimity, might now have majority voting applied to them. It seems less likely that such a system would apply to either foreign or defence policy were they bought under the ambit of the treaty. The French have proposed that considerable powers over defence policy within the Western European Union be made subject to the rulings of the heads-of-state and government sitting in the European Council and that they too might consider using majority voting on a regular basis. The extension of majority voting will be resisted both by countries like Britain, which fear a general loss of control *vis-à-vis* Community institutions, as well as the smaller states who fear that, in foreign policy, their interests will be subsumed within those of the major states under any majority voting system

Any extension of majority voting combined with the addition of new areas of Community competence in both the political union or EMU treaties will of course raise the question of the EC's democratic deficit. As we have seen, some states (Germany is the most obvious example) support the European Parliament's desire to be given a much greater say in the initiation and approval of Community legislation. It does not seem very likely that the IGC will go the whole way in granting the Parliament colegislative powers but the cooperation procedure may well be extended to more, possibly all areas of EC legislation. The next round of direct elections to the European Parliament will take place in 1994 and it does not look very likely that the Community will by then have agreed on a universal electoral system. Indeed, at present it seems unlikely that the member states will be even able to agree on one site for the European Parliament. At present this uses up a great deal of its credibility in a constant round of travelling between its headquarters in Luxembourg, to Strasbourg where it holds its plenary sessions, and Brussels where the rest of the Community is to be found and thus where the Parliament's committees meet. If the British have their way, very few extra legislative powers will be handed over to the European Parliament and instead the Parliament will be given the more lowly task of keeping an eye on the legality of Community expenditure. Mr Hurd seems keen that a sort of equivalent to the British Public Accounts Committee be created, which would work with the Court of Auditors, to try and prevent fraud and wasteful expenditure. The British would also prefer to deal with the democratic deficit by enhancing the scrutiny powers of national parliaments; they are supported in this by France – not a country usually noted for the strength of its parliamentary tradition – and strongly opposed by Germany and Italy. If there is to be more majority voting, as seems likely, and if the EC is also likely to rely more on the principle of mutual recognition of national standards, it is hard to see how the democratic deficit can be reduced by concentrating on national systems of scrutiny. For they can only hold national ministers accountable and on many issues legislation which will affect one state will either have been developed in another or opposed by its ministers in the Council. Many would argue that if the Council of Ministers is to retain its key legislative role then it will have to stop meeting in secret – at least when it is considering legislation – and that it will probably also have to start publishing a formal record of its voting practices. However the argument about scrutiny is resolved, it would certainly be desirable if national parliaments and the European Parliament could work more effectively together. In particular, if national scrutiny methods are to be effective then ways need to be found to enable members of the European Parliament who usually have expert knowledge of EC legislation to participate in them.

The Parliament is also anxious to both exert more effective control over the Commission and to also increase the independence of the Commission from the interference of member states. The IGC is considering a number of proposals that would give the Parliament the chance to either endorse or give its consent to the appointment of the Commission president – perhaps even of individual Commissioners – on the lines of the 'advise and consent' powers of the US Senate. If the Commission was linked to the Parliament in this way it would make it harder for the member states to attempt to manipulate either the appointment or the work of Commissioners. In this context Mrs Thatcher's refusal to reappoint Lord Cockfield as a British commissioner because of his over-zealous advocacy of the single market programme is often cited. It does seem likely that the states will be able to agree on one thing with regard to the Commission and that is to the idea of limiting each state to just one Commissioner, albeit backed up in some cases by Assistant Commissioners. It is quite evident that at present there are not seventeen portfolios of equal importance to keep the present Commission busy, and with the possibility of enlargement a Commission that exceeded twenty would become unmanageable. The Commission itself would like to see the comitology practices altered so as to make greater use of advisory committees and less use of regulatory committees but the Council, in the absence of evidence that these extra constraints actually inhibit implementation, is unlikely to budge on this.

The British government would like to see the Community taking the implementation of EC legislation much more seriously than it does at present and to that end Britain has suggested that the Court be given the power to heavily fine those states who have failed to implement policies that they have agreed to in the Council. The British government is particularly proud of its good record on implementation, especially of single market measures, and it is deeply suspicious of the practices of some of its partners. Within the British administration there is a view which sees the French as inclined to agree to measures in the Council that they have no intention of implementing, and the Italians of agreeing to measures that they are not capable of implementing. It is certainly reasonable to argue that Britain, when negotiating in the EC tends to argue the finer points precisely because there is a clear intention to implement any decisions taken while other states, on occasion, find it easier to be reasonable in the Council because they either do not appreciate the problems of implementation or because they do indeed intend to avoid them. The British case for stricter control of implementation is not unreasonable and from the British point of view has the added virtue of distracting attention away from political union issues they they would prefer not to discuss.

In chapter 2 we argued that although the principle of subsidiarity is one dear to the heart of the British government it should be cautioned by the fact that it is also a principle that the Commission or the more federally inclined Germans can adhere to. There is a strong movement to have a reference to the principle of subsidiarity written into the political union treaty either in the preamble or as an actual enforceable treaty article. The question that to date remains unanswered is who would be responsible for determining the application of the principle? Who would decide whether a particular objective could either not be achieved at the national level or could be more efficiently determined at the Community level? The most obvious institution to rule on subsidiarity issues would be the Court of Justice but some states would fear its communautaire reputation. It is certainly the case that the American experience would lead some to caution against handing such a power to the Court of Justice. In the US Constitution there is a clause which was designed – like subsidiarity – by the states to limit federal power to those instances where it could be shown that there would be an impact on commerce between states. This is known as the inter-state commerce clause. However, the Supreme Court has consistently found the clause a good reason to extend federal powers because almost everything affects trade. In the European context the principle that power should be exercised at the lowest efficient level of government is one which is entirely political; there is no objective test of what is efficient and the Court of Justice if it is not allowed to act alone is most likely to side with a majority of the Council in a case where the minority wish to argue that the Community does not have competence.

This is not the only problem that is likely to arise over subsidiarity as a governing principle of European union. For the British, federalism means more centralized power to Brussels, but for most Europeans it means more power to the provinces. While Britain clings to subsidiarity as a means of retaining power at the national level, other states – Germany is the classic example – will be arguing that subsidiarity requires the transfer of some powers down below the level of national governments. The British government will not wish to find the Welsh or the Scots or even representatives of South Yorkshire arguing that the subsidiarity clause in the political union treaty places limits on the amount of power that can be concentrated in London.

A great deal of attention has been given during the first few months of 1991 to the place of foreign and defence policy in the political union IGC. There is a strong argument that would like the work of the SEA taken to its logical conclusion. The Commission, on occasion supported by Franco-German statements, would like to see EPC be written into the Rome Treaty and ideally become subject to majority voting. Delors has gone even further and advocated the extension of Community competence into the area of defence policy – again subject to majority voting. The more minimalist position adopted by the British – and likely to carry the day – would settle for the further development of EPC (perhaps by increasing the size and function of the Secretariat) and would fudge the question of defence by seeking to build up the broader notion of security within EPC. The minimalist position would totally reject the notion of either making EPC part of the Rome Treaty or subjecting it to majority voting. The Gulf War gave rise to two competing arguments about the desirability and practicality of the EC moving towards a common foreign and defence policy. Many opponents of the Community in Britain argued that what they saw as the disarray of the Community during the Gulf War – with some states participating in the fighting and others showing great reluctance – suggested that a common foreign policy was just not achievable given the differences that existed between the member states. The British government was careful not to fully endorse these views with Mr Hurd arguing that in fact the record of the EC on the Gulf was not that bad in that, before the fighting broke out, the EC states moved swiftly to pass a number of resolutions not only condemning Iraq but putting economic sanctions into place. AAlthough the Community states were divided over participation in the US-led military action, Hurd argued that it was unreasonable to hold the EC accountable for an area in which it had no competence. Nevertheless the British still tended to use the Gulf War example as a reason for caution in moving towards a common foreign policy. Most other European states drew the opposite conclusion from the Community's experience of the Gulf War and argued that it illustrated the need to create institutions and procedures that would prevent the Community ever again appearing to be either divided or ineffectual.

The arguments about security are related to a much wider debate about security arrangements in post-cold war Europe. There has been a consistent argument that a key role can be played by WEU in all this. The British and the Dutch are prepared to see WEU used as a bridge between the EC and NATO and they are prepared to consider the possibility of WEU taking instructions from the European Council in one or two limited areas. These would be restricted to issues like arms control, counter terrorism and possibly UN backed peace-keeping activities outside the NATO area; but would not be extended to defence policy as such, which both countries would prefer to be handled in the context of NATO. Delors on the other hand would like to see WEU eventually totally subsumed into the Community, with NATO playing less of a military role and serving more to maintain a political connection with the United States. The most likely outcome at present is that the political union IGC will avoid tackling the issue of defence head on and will instead fudge around the looser notion of security. If the Soviet Union had continued to change along the lines anticipated in 1989 and early 1990 then the EC would now be facing the need for a much more radical rethink of its member states' security arrangements than is in fact the case. A growing uncertainty about the likely evolution of the Soviet Union, combined with the impact of the Gulf War, will probably ensure that the cautious wait-and-see view will prevail over the next year or so at least. Eventually however it is reasonable to assume that US defence links with Europe will become much looser, that arrangements will have to be made to replace the security order that NATO and the Warsaw Pact used to guarantee and that the EC will come to play a more significant role in defence matters than it does now or is likely to after the completion of the political union IGC.

Finally, we cannot conclude this anticipation of the role of the EC in the new Europe without a word about the possibility of enlargement. Even before the changes in eastern Europe the Community had decided that it would postpone further enlargement decisions until after the completion of the single market in 1992. The case of the DDR was of course exceptional and made easier by the fact that it was to be admitted after it had become reunited with West Germany. Now, however, the EC faces applications and potential applications from all quarters. Though the states of EFTA continued to gallantly negotiate the notion of the European Economic Area with the EC, most of them increasingly see this as a route to full membership, now that some of the inhibitions about neutrality have been removed. Thus Norway and Sweden seem certain to join Austria in applying for full membership very soon and they all look like quite attractive additions to the Community. Many of the poorer states would prefer to have these rich cousins inside the EC where they can be relied upon to be net contributors to the budget rather than merely associated with the EC and thus gaining all the advantages of the large market without having to pay any of the dues. Of the remaining EFTA countries Finland looks like a longer term bet, Iceland seems unlikely and Switzerland is a state that has not as yet found itself able to join the United Nations. Of the eastern European states only Poland, Hungary and Czechoslovakia are likely to be in a position to sustain EC membership in the 1990s although they could be joined in the near future by one or two states that might emerge from the collapsing Yugoslavian federation. Both Cyprus and Malta have applied to join although both have special problems and Turkey's cooperative stance in the Gulf war has probably significantly raised the price that the Community will have to pay to ward off a serious Turkish application. The most likely development is that, because of the situation in eastern Europe, the Community will in fact enlarge itself quite considerably towards the end of the 1990s. In the cases of Poland, Hungary and Czechoslovakia their claims will be very hard to resist given that the EC states have spent the last forty years urging them to come over to the free market camp. Furthermore the Germans are only too aware that, as with the DDR, unless these countries are encouraged by a positive response, there is a danger of a mass migration westwards by east Europeans determined to get themselves inside the prosperous Community. If the east European claims become irresistible then the present Community may well be grateful to have the prosperous states of Austria, Sweden and Norway assisting in the difficult process of applying the principle of cohesion to the whole of Europe.

The chance of the European Community transforming itself into a European state has not really existed since 1965 when there were just six member states. From then on the Community was always going to evolve along loose federal or confederal lines, but successive enlargements have not had the effect of halting the dynamic of integration and there is no reason to suppose that future enlargements will do so. The European Community has already succeeded in providing a framework within which a number of west European states have transformed and civilized their relations with one another. There is no reason why those states should not now have the confidence to both widen and deepen that framework and thus create a complete European union.

Part IV

Conclusion

Chapter 11

A forward view

David Allen, David Llewellyn and Dennis Swann

Introduction

The SEA, although not a particularly inspiring document, is nevertheless proving to be extraordinarily fruitful, both directly and indirectly. Its dimensions and implications are considerable. Quite apart from the element of achieving the SEM by 1992, we have noted the proposals for EMU and have examined its implications for regional policy, including economic and social cohesion, social policy, environmental protection and R&TD. Quite clearly, sooner or later, the SEA was likely to have a significant impact in the field of political union; that impact has several strands since it relates to the internal governing of the European Communities, to EPC (foreign policy) and potentially to defence matters. The SEA also has key implications for the rest of the world – but notably EFTA and eastern Europe. While all these ingredients are important, it seems to us that the really important ones are the SEM, EMU and political union. It is to these that we now turn.

The SEM

The first point to note is that the Community was extremely adept in the strategy it adopted towards deepening the Community. Had it in 1984 and 1985 decided to start off by proposing to move directly to EMU and political union it would quite likely have failed; it would, to use a phrase, have bitten off more than it could chew. Instead it adopted a phased approach – the SEM first with an expectation that this would pave the way for EMU and political union. That looks like being a successful strategy although the pace at which EMU and political union are approached may have to be a more leisurely one than originally anticipated and not all states may wish to progress at the same pace.

It was possible to be sceptical about the 1992 SEM commitment. In other words to doubt whether the Community would rise to the occasion and finally complete the internal market – a goal which, for the original six, ought to have been achieved by the end of 1969. Scepticism could also be founded on particular cases. Thus whilst it is true that the need for a merger controlling regulation did not feature in the Cockfield Report, such a measure was nevertheless an essential feature of the single market. But the Regulation of 1989 has to be set against a background of inaction which stretches back to the mid-1960s. Or if we take the case of the cross-frontier corporation tax directives agreed in 1990, we recollect that they were first proposed way back in 1969. Stagnation was indeed very much in evidence prior to the Cockfield Report and the SEA. It is therefore pleasant to be able to record that the Community has made extremely encouraging progress with signs of individual states actually competing to outdo each other in legislative terms (at Brussels) during their presidencies of the Council of Ministers. However the SEM will not be wholly complete by 31 December 1992. There are areas where progress is likely to be limited. One is fiscal policy where the absence of majority voting is likely to prove a serious weakness. We have also noted a lack of progress in the maritime sector of the CTP. And there are others. It is also evident from a reading of the accounts presented in earlier chapters that some member states have been allowed periods within which to adjust which stretch well beyond 1992.

It continues to be possible to be sceptical about the size of the likely benefits of 1992. As we indicated at the outset of this book, the Community acted first and calculated afterwards. This sounds like an inversion of the normal order of things but could be defended on the grounds that there already existed a prior commitment – notably the original Rome Treaty's call for the creation of a common market. The size of the gains identified in the Cecchini Report[1] does however seem to be on the high side. Most of the studies of the gains from west European trade liberalization have tended to be low – of the order of 1 per cent of GDP. Admittedly they have been static in character. On the other hand the Cecchini Report focusing on the benefits derived from removing residual barriers (the major barriers in the form of tariffs and quotas having already been removed), but allowing for dynamic effects, comes up with figures several times as large. Some writers, notably Merton Peck, whose study we referred to in chapter 1, have argued that the Cecchini Report overestimates the gains by a factor of two or three. David Llewellyn, in chapter 5, has expressed doubts about the size of the gains to be derived from the creation of a common market for financial services: gains there undoubtedly will be but the Cecchini Report seems to be somewhat too optimistic.

There is of course a riposte to all this and we have in some degree already identified it. Even if the gains from completing the SEM are much less than the Cecchini Report anticipates, the SEM has still proved to be enormously significant. For the plain fact is that the SEM was the centrepiece of the SEA; and the SEA is proving to be equally significant in the broadest sense. It is after all the SEA which helped to revitalize the Community: it has provided the springboard for the drive onwards to EMU and political union; it has helped to establish the Community as a major international economic actor (see the earlier discussion by Christopher Milner and David Allen); and it has exercised a magnetic effect on blocs such as EFTA and eastern Europe and key investors such as Japan.

The benefits will of course depend on what happens after Brussels has put its imprimatur on (mainly) directives and also regulations. The rules of the competitive game will have been adhered to; member states will have to implement those directives. But implementation will not be enough – member states will have to fully act in the spirit of them: in other words there is an enforcement problem. The goal is a difficult one to achieve – for example buy-national attitudes in public procurement are deeply ingrained. The Commission, as we noted earlier, will have to enforce the rules of competition remorselessly and Court of Justice rulings will have to be obeyed. The anomaly whereby erring firms can be fined but governments can get off scot-free seems unfortunate to say the least. There is of course always the problem that in areas such as financial services (see David Llewellyn's contribution), a local firm inevitably enjoys certain advantages which insulates it from competition from without. It is difficult, not to say impossible, to legislate these out of existence.

The full benefits of the SEM will also depend on a complementarity of action in related fields. For example, as Kenneth Button has pointed out in an earlier chapter, deregulation of inter-state air passenger transport will not of itself guarantee substantial gains for the travelling public. Parallel action will be needed to maintain competition; in other words inter-airline agreements and mergers will have to be controlled. Devices which can blunt the edge of competition will have to be addressed – the possible abuses which can arise in connection with CRSs and frequent flyer programmes come to mind. Competitive entry will also depend on the Commission finding a satisfactory solution to the problem of parking slots. Also if the benefits of deregulation are to fully emerge there must be a parallel expansion and integration of the infrastructure such as air traffic control and airports.

The evident success of the Community in making the SEM a reality in legislative terms must in some degree be ascribed to the ability of the Commission to rethink its approach to the problems posed by particular trade-preventing and trade-distorting barriers. The Commission has shown considerable imagination – the decision to go for approximation rather than absolute harmonization in respect of indirect tax rates, to emphasize mutual recognition in the case of standards, to reject recipe laws in the case of food standards and to adopt a new approach to the regulatory problems posed by the freedom to supply services and right of establishment in financial services (see David Llewellyn's comments) are a few instances. However any attempt to apportion credit would be severely deficient if it did not acknowledge the vital role played by the Court of Justice. It is easy to slip into the error of seeing the Court as a kind of passive referee body: on occasions it has acted quite decisively, and at least three particular instances have been highlighted in this book. The first is the *Cassis de Dijon* case which, together with other judgments, helped to simplify the approach to standards. The second was the *Nouvelles Frontières* case which quite literally helped the Commission to pull the carpet from under the feet of the hesitant Council of Transport Ministers. The result was that they sought to regain the initiative by agreeing to deregulate, which is precisely what the Commission wanted. Much the same could be said about the *Philip Morris* judgment which revealed that Article 85 of the Rome Treaty could be applied to mergers. The Commission indicated that it would not hesitate to use its new found power. Again there was the prospect of a loss of initiative on the part of the Council of Ministers. The result was that they agreed to concede a specific power to control mergers – admittedly very much on their terms. But still it did the trick – the Commission had achieved its main objective.

EMU

Because of its implications for national sovereignty and the overall conduct of monetary, fiscal and exchange rate policy, one of the most far-reaching and controversial aspects of the post-1992 EC arrangements centres on plans for EMU. At the time of writing it is the subject of one of the two IGCs. As Brian Tew noted in his chapter, this is not the first time the ambitions for EMU have surfaced, though considerably more progress and momentum is now evident than at any time in the past. It is ironic to recall that the Werner Report and plans for EMU which were agreed in 1969 envisaged full monetary union by 1980.

There are several reasons why the issue has surfaced at this time. The major motive focuses upon the logic of the 1992 internal market arrangements, which have been the subject of other chapters in this volume. The argument is that the certainty of irrevocably fixed exchange rates and the elimination of the transactions costs involved in switching between currencies are necessary in order to gain the full advantage of the completion of the internal market in goods and services. Second, the abolition of remaining exchange controls is judged to create potential instability without a commitment to irrevocably fixed exchange rates. A third reason why monetary union is now being considered more seriously, is the desire by some member states to remove the current hegemony of Germany implicit in the way the ERM operates, coupled with the fact that this power has increased with the unification of West and East Germany. This school of thought wishes to replace the dominant role of the Deutsche Bundesbank by a genuinely European

Central Bank (ECB) which will focus on the monetary policy interests of the Community as a whole rather than that of Germany alone. Fourth, there is a growing appreciation that, as EC countries become more economically and financially integrated, in practice the national conduct of monetary and exchange rate policy does not confer significant real policy independence or sovereignty. We return to this central issue later.

At the political level France in particular viewed monetary union in part as a means of bolstering the Franco-German alliance – which has given France a political influence disproportionate to its economic status. France had become conscious that this alliance could be weakened by German unification, by the closer relationship that had emerged between Germany and the US, and by the declining threat of the Soviet Union which, it was feared, might make Germany more inclined to look east rather than west. Some sources of political opinion in France viewed these trends as undermining the status of France via the Franco-German alliance and sought to harness the power of Germany and share in it.

A major report by the Commission in 1990[2] offers a very extensive outline of the alleged benefits of monetary union which would derive directly from union itself such as lower transaction costs; from a more efficient conduct of economic policy – particularly seen as deriving from a more credible anti-inflation monetary policy through the removal of the devaluation option; and because monetary union would change the behaviour of economic agents – for example, wage bargainers would change their strategies in the light of the non-availability of the exchange-rate escape route. In this last respect EMU is viewed as creating a credible anchor to inflation expectations. The Commission outlines substantial (though highly exaggerated) benefits from monetary union: increased economic efficiency and higher economic growth; higher rates of investment; lower rates of inflation; the elimination of internal balance of payments adjustment problems; a more efficient allocation of capital; a more efficient conduct of monetary and fiscal policy with less conflict between members; removal of speculative capital movements between member countries; and lower real and nominal interest rates. It also sees benefits to be derived from the enhanced strength of the Community in international monetary arrangements and negotiations and from the potential role of the ecu as a major international currency.

On the other hand, the obvious potential costs derive from the loss of the exchange rate as a policy instrument and the loss of autonomy in the conduct of national monetary policy.

We can identify a series of central issues which will determine the nature of the path towards monetary union, the likely eventual outcome, and the speed with which the final position is approached. As they are central to this controversial aspect of post-1992 EC arrangements it is worth considering them in a little detail. They are as follows:

(a) The issue of whether the conditions for a viable monetary union are yet evident and if not, whether they are likely to emerge over the next few years.

(b) The issue of whether monetary union should be seen as the pinnacle of a process of monetary integration, or whether causation should be reversed and the adoption of union be regarded as a means of accelerating the integration process. At the time of the Werner Report this was described as a distinction between the economist and monetarist approaches to EMU.

(c) The role, power and independence of the ECB, and how monetary policy is to be conducted within the union.

(d) The viability of stage two of the Delors plan.

(e) The role of fiscal policy in a monetary union and the extent to which fiscal policy is to be centralized or still left under the jurisdiction of national governments. (Discussed in Tony Westaway's chapter in some detail.) Allied to this is the question of the size of any automatic fiscal transfers in the monetary union (in practice likely to be small given the smallness of the Community budget), and the extent of regional policy mechanisms to compensate for the loss of national exchange rate instruments.

(f) The way the principle of 'subsidiarity' is to be applied.

Below we discuss these issues in the same order. The ultimate issue is whether the conditions for a viable and acceptable monetary union have been achieved. This ultimately reduces to three questions: first, the extent to which the EC approaches the conditions of an optimum currency area; second, the power of the exchange rate instrument; and third, the extent to which independent monetary policy confers the power to influence real magnitudes in the economy and the choice over any trade-off between unemployment and the rate of inflation. The theoretical literature identifies several relevant factors: the degree of price and wage flexibility (the greater this is the more viable is a monetary union); the mobility of labour; the degree of convergence of the constituent regions; the extent and power of regional transfer mechanisms and regional policy; the degree of openness of economies; and the extent to which shocks are common to all regions. These are relevant because they determine either the need for exchange rate adjustments or the power of such adjustments which must be compared with the general benefits of a common currency and any other benefits that might emerge from a monetary union. In other words, a cost-benefit analysis needs to be undertaken comparing the alleged benefits of EMU against the costs of surrendering the independent use of national policy instruments. Clearly, the less that exchange rate changes are needed, and the less power that such changes have, the more viable a monetary union becomes simply because little real sovereignty is surrendered by losing the ability to use this instrument.

Overall, we can observe that prices and wages are not downwardly flexible; the mobility of labour in the EC is low; convergence has increased (most especially with respect to inflation); regional transfer and policy mechanisms are weak; openness (or the volume of intra EC trade) has certainly increased; and that members are still subject to shocks particular to individual countries – the most recent example being German reunification.

On the face of it, therefore, it would appear that the conditions removing the need for exchange rate adjustments are not fully met even though, within the EMS, there have been few changes in central rates in recent years. However, there is considerable doubt as to whether nominal exchange rate adjustments do in practice (in anything other than the short term) have permanent affects on real exchange rates, the balance of payments, or the level of unemployment and output. Because of the growing openness of EC economies, and the erosion of money illusion, there is little evidence that the exchange rate is in fact a powerful instrument to affect long run competitiveness, as any short-term change in real wages tends to be offset by changes in money wage levels. In this case little is surrendered by eschewing exchange rate adjustments.

Equally problematic is the power conferred by having an independent monetary policy. This ultimately comes down to an assessment about the nature of the Phillips curve. The traditional argument against forming a transnational monetary union is that, as it would involve a union-wide monetary policy, it denies national governments the ability to choose their own preferred combination of inflation and unemployment which may vary between countries, either because they face different Phillips curve trade-offs, or because their preferences vary.

In the final analysis, however, this argument presupposes that there is in fact a trade-off between inflation and the level of unemployment: only then can choices be made. In practice, the evidence is against this. Clearly, if in the long-run the Phillips curve is vertical, then the menu of choice disappears and all that an independent monetary policy allows is the ability to choose the actual rate of inflation and not a choice between unemployment and inflation. In this event, as there is no power to determine real magnitudes in the economy, governments might as well simply choose to agree on a common low level of inflation. Nothing of substance is surrendered by collectivizing monetary policy in this case. The evidence certainly casts doubt on the traditional Phillips-curve analysis in the long run. As clear a view as any on this issue was given by Mr Leigh-Pemberton, Governor of the Bank of England, in May 1991 when he asserted: 'I do not believe that monetary policy can, or should, attempt to deliver a target path for real output even in the short run. The objective should be to provide stable prices and the basis for a steady growth of nominal income'.[3] This statement is significant both as a representation of the role of monetary policy and as an assertion of independence. However, the short-term benefits (to the extent that governments believe them to exist) may still be valued. In which case we can argue that, on this criterion, the case for monetary union increases, and the case against becomes weaker, the more that governments believe that there is no long-term trade off, and the less they value any choice offered in the short term.

The ultimate resistance to monetary union is the loss of sovereignty, and this can be both symbolic and real. However, no effective sovereignty is surrendered by giving up instruments that have no power; in practice, this is as much about perceptions as reality. On the assumption that governments will not surrender real power, the issue is about governments' perceptions about their power and perhaps about the fiction that they must believe they have effective power. In practice governments tend to over-state the real power they have and therefore the case against monetary union is partly symbolic.

The overall conclusion is that general economic conditions have been moving in favour of the viability of monetary union (though they are clearly not as favourable as those operating within existing monetary unions or countries), and that the power of exchange rate adjustments, and the ability of monetary policy to influence long term real magnitudes, have been declining. This limits the loss of effective sovereignty implied by monetary union. However, the exchange rate retains some power for some countries and their governments might be reluctant to irrevocably surrender that residual power.

There has always been a major dispute between those who believe the viability of monetary union requires a prior high degree of economic convergence, and those who view monetary union as a grand design step to accelerate the pace of convergence and integration. This has again surfaced with France and Italy in particular adopting the latter approach, while Germany (most notably the central bank) argues that only after the economies have achieved a high degree of convergence can the formal arrangements for monetary union, like an ECB and a common currency, be established. Germany takes the view that an ECB should be established only when it has a real job to do which presupposes that EMU is viable. Above all, it will not allow its own position to be jeopardized until an effective alternative is in place. This debate, and the different positions taken by different member governments, will be central in the coming years and may lead to a two-speed evolution towards monetary union with a faster pace being adopted by those countries demonstrating a high degree of convergence.

A major issue, which is central to the whole debate about monetary union, is the question of the role, power, conduct and independence of an ECB. Any central bank has a pivotal position in the conduct of monetary policy in that its operations determine the money supply, it issues the national currency, and its interventions in the foreign exchange markets have a powerful impact on exchange rates, and it acts as a lender-of-last-resort to the banking system.

The most controversial issue centres upon the independence of the central bank. In some countries (notably the UK) the central bank has little independence in the conduct of monetary and exchange rate policy; the important decisions are taken by Ministries of Finance and hence ultimately by elected politicians. In other countries (the most notable being Germany) the central bank conducts its own monetary policy and is independent of political influence. In these cases the central bank is charged with the overriding requirement of maintaining the value of the currency and a low rate of inflation. It may be argued that price stability is more likely to be achieved in an environment where political influences seeking short-run adjustments to monetary conditions are limited by an independent central bank. Although the issue of political accountability arises, the school of thought which advocates independence of the central bank argues also that governments should not have the power to undermine the value of their currency.

A draft statute for an ECB has been put before the IGC on EMU by governors of existing EC central banks. It is based on the principle of a high degree of independence. In addition, the Bundesbank has submitted its own draft statute and will in practice only agree to the establishment of an ECB if within the union the ECB has at least the same degree of independence as the Bundesbank currently has within Germany. The flavour of the proposal by the central bank governors is given by its first objective outlined in the draft statute: 'the primary objective of the system shall be to maintain price stability'. On independence it is equally emphatic: 'In exercising the power and performing the tasks and duties conferred upon them by the Treaty and this statute, neither the ECB nor a national central bank may seek or take any instructions from Community institutions, governments of Member States or any other body. The Community and each Member State undertake to respect this principle and not to seek to influence the ECB, the national central banks and the members of their decision-making bodies in the performance of their tasks.'

This seems to cast no doubt on the notion that the ECB will be independent in the conduct of EC monetary and exchange rate policy. However, it is not as straight-forward as it seems. The draft statute has been proposed by the central banks themselves and it is not surprising that their bias would be in favour of independence. But politicians might take a different view and the British government has resisted conferring greater independence on the Bank of England. However, the British government may have to modify its stance in the light of the proposed arrangements for the ECB. The development of the ECB may force the government to allow more independence for the Bank of England irrespective of the stance the UK finally takes on EMU. It is notable that during 1990 and 1991 the Bank of England began to assert its position in a series of public statements: it clearly believed it should have more independence.

A flavour of the dispute over central bank independence can be seen in the national attitudes to the operation of the EMS. The system has worked well and its success has been one of the factors inducing further moves towards monetary union. However, it has worked well because it is ultimately a DM bloc, which means in practice that the monetary policy of the system is determined by the Bundesbank. A fixed exchange rate regime requires consistency in monetary policy between countries. Some EC members, such as Belgium, Luxembourg and The Netherlands, have accepted the hegemonic role of Germany simply because of the independence and credibility of the Bundesbank; in effect, these countries share in the credibility of the independent Bundesbank in the conduct of monetary policy. Italy and France, on the other hand, recognize the power of the Bundesbank and that it has effectively operated as the central bank of the EMS as a whole, but their ambition for an ECB is precisely to reduce the hegemony of the Bundesbank and to create an institution in which they have an influence. Neither country is likely to wish to influence an ECB in a more decisive way in the direction of price stability than has the Bundesbank! Their approach is likely to be seen as diluting the commitment to price stability and hence to be unacceptable to Germany. In a nutshell, there is certainly no unanimity on the role of the ECB and the differences could prove to be substantial.

A major issue, therefore, is whether a new ECB might be less able to secure reasonable price stability in a full monetary union than the Bundesbank currently can within the EMS. This will undoubtedly become a major issue in the debate about monetary union and it is not likely that progress will be made without the full agreement of Germany (which effectively has a veto) and this will not be forthcoming without guarantees with respect to the independence and objectives of any ECB. These issues raise powerful political and constitutional issues for member states.

Brian Tew in his chapter describes the three stages of the Delors strategy culminating in full monetary union. There is, however, a major issue as to whether stage two is viable or whether the worst of all worlds will emerge. The problem arises because by that time all exchange controls will have been abolished (including those of the more inflation prone countries), all currencies will be full members of the EMS, and governments will no longer be able to rely on direct credit control instruments. However, within stage two (which is to last for an unspecified time) it will still be possible to change exchange rate central values within the EMS. This brings two potential problems: first, the volume of capital (including speculative) movements will increase which could destabilize the operation of the EMS; second, as exchange rates will not have been irrevocably fixed, governments will not have gained the credibility of an anti-inflation monetary policy which relies upon the commitment to fixed exchange rates. It may be, therefore, that stage two could disintegrate or be appropriate only for a group of countries that are not prepared to move decisively to stage three.

Within most national monetary unions a substantial central budget acts as an automatic stabilizer to cushion changes in relative incomes of different regions. Thus regions which are not competitive (which would have a balance of payments deficit if they were independent but within a larger monetary union experience relatively high levels of regional unemployment) receive automatic fiscal transfers from the centre and pay less to the centre in tax. Combined with regional policy measures these fiscal transfers partly compensate for the absence of a regional exchange rate instrument.

Some countries clearly fear that within an EC monetary union they could experience regional problems which cannot be offset by exchange rate adjustments or a regional monetary policy. They are likely to seek fiscal compensation. In practice, however, the automatic transfers will be small (because of the smallness of the Community budget) and regional policy mechanisms are also not substantial within the EC. This could prove to be a reason for some members not giving up their use of the exchange rate instrument even though, in practice, it may not be very powerful.

One of the key dimensions of monetary union is the extent to which policy is centralized. The Delors Report emphasized the concept of subsidiarity which implies that centralization will only occur in those areas where it is necessary. As stated in the Delors Report: 'the attribution of competences to the Community would have to be confined to those areas in which collective decision-making was necessary. All policy functions which could be carried out at national levels without adverse repercussions on the cohesion and functioning of the economic and monetary union would remain within the competence of the member countries'.

Given the centralist tendencies of the Commission, the applicability of this principle will be subject to substantial dispute as the principle itself is ambiguous. The context is that in principle, monetary union together with the SEM (implying fiscal harmonization) would involve collectivizing a wider range of macro-policy instruments than ever before, and in some fundamental areas.[4] The room for dispute over the interpretation of the concept of subsidiarity is enormous: four alternative tests might be applied when judging whether particular policy mechanisms should be centralized. In the necessity test only those instruments which can no longer be applied nationally will be transferred: this is the minimalist argument. A common-interest test argues that only where members have a common interest will measures be centralized. An attained-better test would centralize only those policy mechanisms which could be more effectively conducted at the EC rather than national level. A fourth interpretation, the materially-affected test, is that measures are only centralized if their national operation would have a significant impact on other members.

This will clearly feature substantially in future negotiations and the scope for major disputes over such a key issue is very substantial. Even the principle itself is totally ambiguous.

Overall, the areas of dispute are substantial and different countries seek different benefits and have different approaches. At the time of writing, Germany's requirement is that there should be a high degree of prior convergence before monetary union will be viable. At the same time, no ECB should be created until it is in a position to execute genuine central bank powers. Substantial differences exist regarding the operation of the ECB, with some countries wanting to erode the hegemonic power of the Bundesbank while others are demanding as high a degree of autonomy for the ECB as for the Bundesbank. Spain, Portugal, Greece and the UK would probably be giving up real power by surrendering their exchange rate. However, the first three also see monetary union as a mechanism for bargaining substantial regional policy grants from the other members. The Commission itself, with its centralist proclivities, views monetary union as a means for centralizing key issues of economic management. The motive of France is twofold: first, it wishes to strengthen the Franco-German alliance which has historically been a central feature of its EC strategy; and second, it wishes to reduce the hegemonic role of the Bundesbank. The motive of Germany is not altogether clear and Germany may in practice prove to be a brake on EMU ambitions; Germany and the UK seem to be converging in this view about EMU. It is not clear why Germany should wish to surrender its existing powerful role. In the past Germany has often been sceptical about EMU. On the other hand, historically Germany has given a high priority to European union and EMU is seen as a contribution to this. As for the UK, it has been probably the most sceptical. Mrs Thatcher was adamantly hostile to the whole concept of EMU both because of the sovereignty issue and because of her deep suspicion of the centralist tendencies of the Commission. As an alternative, and so as not to appear obsessively nihilist, the UK proposed an alternative strategy of using the hard-ecu. This is unlikely to lead anywhere and, at the time of writing, it appears that the proposal will be dropped. At the Luxembourg summit (May 1991) Mr Delors proposed that the UK could sign an agreement to create EMU but reserve the right not to be a full member at the time it would be created. Such a strategy would at least mean that the UK would be part of the bargaining process.

It is unlikely that all countries will be able to adopt a monetary union strategy at the same time. Interests and economic circumstances are too diverse. What is more likely is that a two-speed approach will be adopted where those countries like Belgium, Germany, France, Luxembourg and The Netherlands, which already have a high degree of convergence, and whose independence in monetary and exchange rate policy is recognized to be low, will move towards formal monetary union at an earlier stage than the others. The others will adopt a longer stage two mechanism before contemplating full union. Indeed, this strategy seems to be implicit in the decisions of the Luxembourg summit in May 1991. However, the UK initially resisted this approach; it was clearly sceptical about monetary union both for itself and its partners. The UK may have been adopting a particularly negative approach: not joining EMU itself but also attempting to stop others doing so. The concept of a two-speed Europe met with little favour in UK Government circles. There was a curious anomaly in the UK position. If the UK economy was really divergent from the rest of the EC there may have been a need for a series of changes in the exchange rate and this could have disrupted the operations of the ERM. On the other hand, the loss of credibility it would have suffered through small changes would have been counter-productive and for little gain. If large changes would have been disruptive and small changes not worthwhile, the issue arises as to whether it would have been more appropriate to join a monetary union if one were on offer. It was not entirely clear what standing aloof really achieved. However later indications suggest that the UK became more sympathetic to the notion that a two-speed approach was both more realistic and was also consistent with its long term view that EMU was only viable if accompanied by convergence.

As with many issues in EC debates, a distinction must always be made between rhetoric and reality. There is certainly no common approach agreed by all members. The key is the attitude of Germany which effectively has a veto and no significant move towards EMU would be feasible or viable in the absence of the support of this pivotal economy. Given its two major conditions – sufficient convergence and agreement on a central bank with at least the independence currently enjoyed by the Bundesbank – the German position may have the effect of delaying the creation of a true EMU.

There are two potential dangers. The first is that a two-speed Europe, which is in practice more likely than full monetary union of all members by the end of the century, could undermine much of the current structure of the EC. Second, if, and notwithstanding the conditions required by Germany, an ECB was established with less independence than the Bundesbank, there is a danger that the new system would be less credible than the current EMS.

Either way, it is ironic that what is designed to integrate the EC yet further could in the end divide and fragment it.

Political union

At the European Council meeting in Maastricht in December 1991 the EC member states were due to conclude their negotiations on both EMU and political union. It is already apparent that, whatever their content, the Maastricht treaties – or treaty amendments – will be effectively transitional and that key decisions in both areas will be taken around 1995–6. A treaty on political union is seen by a number of EC states, with the significant exception of the UK, as only the first step towards a more federal European union. The work of the two IGCs is seen as transitional partly because all twelves member states are not yet ready to fully commit themselves in either area and partly because it is now clear that, once the internal market is completed at the end of 1992, the EC will become involved in yet another round of enlargement negotiations.

Even though the attempt to create a European Economic Area with the EFTA countries has now been successful (but see chapter 7 for a qualification) applications for full membership from Norway, Sweden and Switzerland seem certain to join that of Austria which is already on the table. None of these countries present any special problems for the EC and their accession is likely to be even less traumatic, although perhaps not as rapid, as that of the former DDR. More problematic, though even harder to resist, will be the growing expectations of the countries of eastern Europe. The Community has already made significant concessions to Poland, Hungary and Czechoslovakia in the negotiation of the 'European Agreements' but these are unlikely to be enough to ward off their joint determination to enter the EC as soon as possible. As if this was not enough, Turkey, Malta and Cyprus are likely to continue to remind the EC that there are aspirant members on its Mediterranean flank; and a possible future break-up of the USSR could make also the Baltic states and the Ukraine potential applicants. In other words beyond 1992 the EC is likely to become a much larger and even more diverse organization and that is why decisions taken in the current round of IGCs may not prove to be definitive.

Nevertheless a number of interim decisions on political union will be taken in December 1991. On the question of Community competence a number of member states would like to see its extension to new fields such as health, education and culture and its reinforcement in a number of existing areas such as social policy, the environment and R&TD. Not surprisingly the British government is totally opposed to any extension of Community competence but may well be forced to make one or two concessions – perhaps in the social policy sphere. One way of limiting the extension of Community competence is to write a tight definition of subsidiarity into any new treaty. On the question of qualified majority voting (QMV) there will be many states which will cite the success of this experiment in the context of the 1992 programme and thus argue for its extension. Again this will be resisted by the UK with the question of applying QMV to decision-making on foreign policy and defence matters being an absolute sticking point. There has been some pressure to build into any new treaty the concept of European citizenship but this seems likely to be one of those issues that will either be fudged or postponed to a later date. Finally, under the general competence heading, we should note that the southern states would like to expand further the role of the various structural funds. Spain, in particular, is anxious to push the notion of cohesion, which involves providing for massive transfers of funds from the rich north to the poor south of the Community. To the extent that this would involve both enlarging and reforming the Community budget, the northern member states seem determined to postpone this issue until 1992 when negotiations on the future financing of the EC are due to begin.

The UK is keen to pursue the issues of efficiency and financial accountability. It has the second best record in the Community for implementing the measures needed (over 90 per cent) to establish the single market, while Italy has barely managed to turn half the single market measures into Italian law. Similarly while the UK was referred to the Court of Justice 20 times between 1982 and 1989, France was referred 80 times and Italy no less than 160 times. It seems certain that any political union treaty will include measures to improve the effectiveness of Community laws by improving the monitoring of implementation by the Commission and the European Parliament. Even if the implementation problem is dealt with, the question of enforcement will remain; here the powers of the Court of Justice will probably be strengthened giving it the ability to impose significant fines on member states who fail to carry out their obligations. Given the high prevalence of fraud in the Community the treaty is likely to provide for tighter financial accountability. Finally there has been considerable support for the proposal that there should be an EC ombudsman.

As far as the much-debated democratic deficit is concerned the member states are split between those, like the UK, and perhaps France, who do not wish to see the European Parliament be given greater powers and those, like Germany, who say that they are prepared to withhold their final consent to full EMU until there has been a devolution of power to the EC regions and a transfer of legislative authority to the European Parliament. Those opposed to a further extension of the European Parliament's powers argue that democracy in the Community can be better preserved by securing the greater involvement of national parliaments and national scrutiny procedures. It seems likely that the IGC will expand the scope of the cooperation procedure whilst falling short of meeting the Parliament's demands for powers of colegislation shared equally with the Council of Ministers. Much will depend in the future on the ability of the European Parliament itself to get its act together in the face of a natural resistance from the executives of the member states. Until the Parliament conducts all its business in one place (Brussels) and until it finds a way of acting as a coherent whole, it is going to find it hard to enlist the support of European citizens for a greater role in Community life.

Finally we turn to the more fundamental questions raised by the notion of a common foreign and security policy and its relationship to the concept of European union. At one level there is an argument between the maximalists, who would like to see all aspects of foreign and defence policy brought under the legal umbrella of the Rome Treaty with decisions in both areas being taken by qualified majority voting, and the minimalists, who would prefer to keep cooperation in these two areas on an intergovernmental basis outside the Rome Treaty framework. We shall say a little more about this debate below but before turning to the details a more general point needs to be made. We have already questioned the wisdom of attempting to finally determine the policies and procedures of the Community at a time when the likelihood of considerable enlargement in the near future is high. This argument also applies to proposals in the foreign and defence spheres but here another factor also needs to be considered. The debate about the nature of the new post-cold war European security architecture has really only just begun. Although the Warsaw Pact has disappeared and although NATO has made some limited progress in redefining its missions and force structures, much remains in a state of flux and is likely to do so for at least the next three or four years whilst the Soviet Union completes the withdrawal of its forces to within its own borders. It is argued here that the Europeans need more than anything else to engage in a debate about the likely future basis of and challenges to security in Europe. The time to start arguing about the appropriateness of various institutional arrangements is after rather than before a degree of clarity has been reached on the nature of the European security problem. Until then it seems sensible to keep all institutional options open and to make it as easy as possible for any number of different combinations of European states (as well as the US and the USSR) to debate, and where possible reach agreement, on the fundamentals of European security. In brief, 1991 was not a good year for the twelve to try and create definitive and exclusive structures in the foreign policy and security spheres.

Nevertheless the political union IGC has placed the issue firmly on the agenda and some interim conclusions may be reached. Almost certainly there will be some sort of fudge on the broader question of security and the narrower question of defence. While the British and the Dutch would like to see WEU developed as a bridge between the European Council and NATO, the French are in the forefront of those who would like to see WEU developed as an alternative to NATO – an idea which produces an extremely hostile reaction in Washington. Almost certainly, the question of extending the competence of the EC to cover the defence field will be postponed this time around although it may well be that the twelve agree to work even more closely together on security issues like arms control, nuclear proliferation and peace-keeping activities outside the NATO area. The Luxembourg presidency produced a draft treaty in early 1991 which sought to advance foreign and security cooperation, but not to bring it all within the operation of the Rome Treaty. What seems to be emerging is a notion of European union which covers all activity carried out together by the twelve EC member states, whether inside or outside the Rome Treaty. This flexible concept of European union is to be built on three pillars, all of which fall under the direct control of the European Council – the regular summit of EC leaders which stands at the apex of the Union structure. The first pillar consists of all activity that falls under the Rome Treaty while the other two pillars are made up of areas of cooperation between the twelve outside the Rome Treaty framework – namely cooperation in the foreign and security policy area (EPC); and intergovernmental cooperation on various aspects of internal security such as the control of terrorism, major crime and drug trafficking. This notion of European union is naturally attractive to Britain and also probably to France (as long as EMU is firmly incorporated into the Rome Treaty pillar) but is resisted by the Community institutions and by a number of member states led by Germany and Italy. As we suggested above, it is a fundamental argument about the eventual nature of the post-1992 Community which is unlikely to be resolved by the current round of IGCs. It will probably not be until 1996 at the earliest, and possibly not until close to the end of the century before we have a clear idea of how the states of Europe intend to organize their cooperation and manage their interdependence as they enter the next millennium.

Chapter 12

The Treaty on European Union

Dennis Swann

The main body of this book was completed whilst the two IGCs were still in progress. Fortunately it was possible to delay completion so as to include an account of the resulting agreements.

The Maastricht Summit

The reader will recollect from chapter 1 that in December 1990 the Community convened two IGCs – one on EMU and one on political union. In short the Single European Act of 1986 had proved to be not an ultimate destination but only a staging post on the road to greater unification in Europe. The two IGCs culminated in a summit meeting in Maastricht on 9 and 10 December 1991 when the heads of state and government finally reached agreement on a range of issues which formed the basis of a Treaty on European Union. That treaty gives rise to a revised Rome (EEC) Treaty. The new treaty is built on three main pillars. The first pillar consists of provisions relating to the existing EC treaties and primarily those relating to the Rome (EEC) Treaty – the latter is expanded and amended to include among other things articles on EMU. The second pillar is devoted to a common foreign and security policy together with provisions relating to defence. The third pillar covers cooperation among the member states on matters ranging from immigration and asylum policy to the combating of organized crime and drug trafficking. It includes Europol – the embryonic police-intelligence corps. In addition a long list of protocols and declarations are annexed to the treaty. It was anticipated that the treaty would be signed early in 1992 and would hopefully, following ratification by national parliaments, come into force at the beginning of 1993. No later than 1996 the heads of state and government would review the workings of the new treaty.

In the lead-up to the Maastricht Summit considerable differences existed between the member states, with the UK in many areas taking a minimalist view and countries such as Germany taking a maximalist stand. Whilst the UK was able to exert a considerable dampening influence, there is no doubt that the new treaty represented a major step forward on the road to European union. The reader will find the competing ideas in the pre-summit debate on political union laid out in chapter 10 above whilst the rival attitudes to, and problems of, EMU are discussed in chapter 8 and both topics are further considered in chapter 11.

General provisions

The treaty begins by declaring that 'By this Treaty, the High Contracting Parties establish among themselves a European Union'. The idea that the union should have a federal goal, which was in the Dutch draft, was dropped in the face of hostility on the part of the UK. Instead the following wording was adopted – 'This treaty marks a new stage in the process of creating an ever closer Union among the peoples of Europe, where decisions are taken as closely as possible to the citizens'. The closeness to citizens point no doubt reflected UK suspicions about Brussels centralizing tendencies. The treaty also provides for 'citizenship of the Union'. Such citizenship also carries with it rights such as the right to live anywhere in the Community and to vote at local and European elections. Citizens can petition the European Parliament and, if they feel badly treated by EC institutions, they will be able to complain to a newly created EC ombudsman. Outside the Community union citizens could get consular help from any EC government. The principle of subsidiarity was written into the treaty.

EMU

The treaty incorporated an agreement to enter into further phases of a process leading to EMU. The Community had already at the Madrid Summit in 1989 agreed to enter into stage one of the Delors Plan. This involved all the states joining the Exchange Rate Mechanism (ERM) of the EMS. However, further progress was not possible without modifications to the Rome (EEC) Treaty – hence the IGC. The new treaty contains a commitment to engage in an irreversible process and no member state can prevent other states from proceeding to the final stage of EMU if those other states meet the necessary criteria. However, the UK was resistant to the idea of giving a prior commitment and wished to reverse the position of the UK parliament until nearer the final event. A protocol was therefore added enabling the UK to opt out. However, if in due course it meets the criteria for membership of EMU it would not be debarred from participating. It may be that the UK will ultimately wish to join and that the approach of the UK to EMU, federalism and much else was at least in part a reflection of a need to appease anti-European elements within the Conservative party. Because the Danish constitution might require a referendum prior to entry into full EMU, it was also provided that it could be exempted. These arrangements clearly indicate that EMU may prove to be a two-speed affair. The reader will recollect that this possibility was identified by Brian Tew in chapter 8 and is further discussed in chapter 11. The likelihood of this happening will become more apparent below when we come to note that even those who wish to join may not meet the necessary criteria.

The treaty provides that on 1 January 1994 stage two will enter into operation. A European Monetary Institute (EMI) would be established – this will be the forerunner of the European System of Central Banks (ESCB) and the European Central Bank (ECB). Its prime task is to facilitate convergence of economic performance as between member states within a framework of price stability. To this end it will be able to address recommendations to member states concerning their monetary and exchange rates policies. Convergence is of course absolutely essential if member states are to remain competitive in the final single currency stage since the devaluation escape route is then no longer available. The Institute will also monitor the functioning of the EMS. It will take over the tasks of the European Monetary Cooperation Fund. The EMI will be able to hold and manage foreign exchange reserves – the degree to which member states are willing to hand these over will no doubt be a good indication of their commitment to the EMU scheme. The EMI will also be responsible for putting in place the administrative and regulatory arrangements which will be required when the ESCB and ECB finally come into existence. During the second stage member states will also take steps to make their central banks independent.

In 1996 preparations for the third stage will begin. The Council of Ministers will decide by qualified majority vote which member states meet the convergence criteria which qualify them for participation in the final single currency stage of EMU. Five criteria are prescribed. A successful candidate would have to have:

(a) in the year prior to examination an inflation rate no more than 1.5 percentage points above the average of the three EC states with the lowest price rises;
(b) in the year previous to examination a long-term rate of interest within two percentage points of the average of the three members with the lowest rates of inflation;
(c) a national budget deficit which was less than 3 per cent of GDP;
(d) a public debt ratio which did not exceeded 60 per cent of GDP;
(e) a currency which for two years had been in the narrow band of the ERM (of the EMS) and had not been devalued.

In 1991 no more than a quarter of the member states satisfied all these tests. A summit meeting of the heads of state and government would, again by majority, decide whether at least a majority of states was ready for EMU and whether and when to start. If no date is set, another summit will meet before July 1998 and again by qualified majority will decide which states qualify. Those states will automatically adopt a single currency in January 1999 – stage three will have begun. Even as few as two states could therefore form an EMU since the need for a majority of qualifiers will not arise on this latter occasion.

Two observations are appropriate at this point. First, the Community has obviously chosen the Schiller approach (see the discussion of the economist–monetarist debate by Brian Tew in chapter 8 above) in that it has emphasized that convergence must come first. Second, the convergence criteria could give rise to difficulties. Thus the price experience of the best three countries could include one with low inflation and two with relatively high rates. In which case the average will be relatively high and poor performers could therefore be let in.

In stage three those involved in EMU will adopt a single currency in replacement of their national currencies. This single currency, to be called the ecu, should not be confused with the ecu of the ems. Incidentally the UK proposal for a hard ecu (discussed by Brian Tew above) has totally disappeared from the scene. The supply of these new ecus would be determined by the ESCB. The latter would consist of the national central banks together with the ECB. The ECSB would define and implement the monetary policy of the EMU, conduct day to day operations in the foreign exchange market (e.g. the ecu against the US Dollar), hold and manage the foreign exchange reserves of the member states and promote the smooth operation of the payments system. The ESCB will be independent – neither the national central banks nor the ECB will take instructions from Community institutions, national governments, etc. Its primary duty will be to maintain price stability – without prejudice to this it will seek to support the general economic policies of the Community. Whilst it would be independent, it is provided that the Council of Ministers would be able to make decisions concerning the exchange rate policy relating to the ecu. The latter point could give rise to awkward inconsistencies. Monetary union will have implications for national budgetary policy. Member state budget deficits and national debt levels would be subject to limits and failure to take effective action in respect of an excessive deficit could lead to sanctions. These could include financial penalties or the requirement to make non-interest bearing deposits with the Community. Alternatively the European Investment Bank could be invited to reconsider its lending policy towards the guilty state.

Foreign policy, security and defence

The provisions on foreign policy and security can best be viewed as a further development of European Political Cooperation. The treaty quite boldly states that 'The Union and its Member States will define and implement a common foreign and security policy'. It is important to note that this area of activity is not subject to the normal Community processes in that the European Court of Justice will have no powers to oversee common foreign and security policy and the Commission will have little direct role other than ensuring consistency between the Community's external economic policy and the common foreign and security policy and reporting any conflicts to the Council of Ministers. As for the European Parliament, it will have to be content with the fact that it will be informed and consulted. The UK sought to maintain the inter-governmental character of political cooperation (a point made earlier by David Allen) and seems to have succeeded.

The common policy implies that the Council of Ministers will be able to define *common positions*. Member states will be required to ensure that their actions conform to it. The Council may also decide that an area or matter should be subject to *joint action*. This will be on the basis of unanimity although the Council may also decide unanimously to take some detailed decisions on implementing policy by a majority vote.

In the run-up to the summit there was some support for giving the Community a defence role. However, this was opposed by the UK–Italian initiative which seems to have carried the day in that Western European Union (WEU – to which nine of the twelve belong) will be developed as the defence component of European Union. Decisions within WEU will not affect obligations within NATO. The UK was concerned about the possibility that NATO might be undermined and that this might have an adverse effect on the US and its commitment to defending Europe. At the summit in Maastricht the WEU invited the three European Union members who were not then members of the organization (i.e. Ireland, Denmark and Greece) to join or take up observer status. By the end of 1998 the Treaty of Brussels, which set up WEU, will be reviewed. The idea that European Union *might* in time lead to a common defence policy did find its way into the treaty.

The institutions and Community competence

Much play was made by the maximalists of the need to give the European Parliament a much bigger role – this was partly designed to deal with the democratic deficit problem. In the event the Parliament made modest gains – which is very much as David Allen predicted. No advance was made in respect of Parliament's aspiration to initiate legislation. However, it did make progress on several other fronts. In respect of colegislation with the Council of Ministers it has been given a power of veto. Parliament will be able to subject Commission proposals to three readings where it can propose amendments. If the Council of Ministers rejects amendments after the third reading, Parliament, by an absolute majority, can veto the proposal. This veto power applies in relation to laws on consumer protection, health, education, trans-European networks, culture, environment strategy, research and the single market. Parliament has been given extra powers to scrutinize Community finances. The President of the Commission will be appointed by the member states by common accord but after consulting Parliament. On appointment the entire Commission (which will be reduced from seventeen to twelve) will also be subject to a vote of confidence by the Parliament. Parliament will also appoint the ombudsman referred to earlier. It will also have the power to set up committees of inquiry to investigate alleged contraventions of, or maladministration in, the implementation of Community law. The Court of Justice will be able to fine countries which do not implement its rulings.

A new Community institution has been created. This is the Committee on the Regions. It will comprise representatives of regional and local authorities. Members will be appointed by their respective member state governments and will have an advisory role.

Community competence has been extended in a significant number of policy areas (e.g. consumer protection). Proposals in most of these areas will be decided by majority voting. However, on one issue – social policy – the new treaty failed to make progress. In chapter 9 above we noted that the Social Charter was adopted by eleven of the twelve states – the odd man out being the UK. It was opposed to the idea of the Community legislating, notably by majority voting, in this area. It continued to oppose the so-called social chapter in the Dutch draft treaty even when as a concession majority voting had been dropped from most issues. In the end a separate protocol was added outlining an unusual process. The existing social provisions of the Rome Treaty would stand but the eleven would take action in areas outlined in the Dutch draft and on the basis of procedures laid out therein. This meant that some issues would be decided by majority and some unanimously. The Community institutions would play their usual role in this area of policy making but the UK would not attend the Council of Ministers and clearly would not be bound by the resulting laws. This is an untidy arrangement and one which the Community could live to regret. There is indeed every sign that the Commission will fight back. Immediately after the Maastricht Summit it was apparent that it would press ahead with its desire for a maximum 48 hour working week (see chapter 9 above) – arguing that this is a health and safety measure and as such is subject to majority voting. The UK would therefore not be able to block it.

Cohesion

Provisions relating to the demand by the poorer southern countries, led by Spain, that EMU should be accompanied by a transfer of resources from the richer north were not incorporated in the main body of the treaty. Instead a protocol was added. It promised a review of the effectiveness of the structural funds in 1992 (the Community budget was in any case due for reconsideration in 1992). The protocol contains a commitment to set up a Cohesion Fund before the end of 1993 to provide Community financial contributions to projects in the fields of the environment and Trans-European Networks in member states whose GNPs are less than 90 per cent of the Community average. The protocol also indicates the Community's willingness to allow poorer states to contribute a smaller percentage of the cost of Community aided projects. It also recognizes the need to modify the own resources system of financing the Community budget so as to give greater weight to member states' differential abilities to pay. The poorer countries could feel well pleased with all this, coming as it does on top of the 1988 agreement to boost structural spending and steer it towards the poorer members of the Community.

Conclusion

Whilst it cannot be said that the Maastricht Summit was a triumph for the maximalists, there is little doubt that the Treaty on European Union marks a sizeable and decisive step on the road to European unity and we can be confident that the maximalists will be back for more well before this decade draws to a close.

Notes

PART I SETTING THE SCENE

1 The single market and beyond – an overview

1 There are three Communities henceforth collectively the three will be referred to as the European Community or simply the Community.
2 Applications from Malta and Cyprus are now on the table.
3 For a survey of the origins and early history of the Community see D. Swann, *The Economics of the Common Market*, London, Penguin, 1992, pp. 1–18.
4 *Rewe-Zentrale A. G.* v. *Bundesmonopolverwaltung fur Branntwein*, 1979, 3 CMLR 494.
5 For a review of state monopoly policy see D. Swann, *Competition and Industrial Policy in the European Community*, London, Methuen, 1983, pp. 71–60.
6 Strictly this should be periods since new members were given special periods of time in which to conform to the rules relating to tariff and quota disarmament.
7 European Communities Commission, COM (88) 238 final, 2 May 1988.
8 For a review of ECSC intervention powers in action see Swann, 1983, op. cit., pp. 162–76. It has been suggested that the deregulatory philosophy of the SEA could ultimately lead to the watering-down of these policies.
9 For a description of Community decision-making institutions see Swann, 1992, op. cit., pp. 44–64.
10 See Swann, 1983, op. cit., pp. 138–61.
11 See Swann, 1983, op. cit., pp. 149–54 and Swann, 1992, op. cit., pp. 284–7.
12 The history and functions of EPC are laid out in Swann, 1992, op. cit., pp. 59–64.
13 For an account of the main features of the EMS see Swann, 1992, op. cit., pp. 189–204.
14 European Communities Commission, COM (81) 313 final, 17 June 1981.
15 European Communities Commission, *Bulletin of the European Communities*, no. 6, Luxembourg, Office for Official Publications of the European Communities (OOPEC), 1984, p. 12.
16 European Communities Commission, *Bulletin of the European Communities*, no. 11, 1981, op. cit., pp. 92–100.
17 European Communities Commission, *Bulletin of the European Communities*, no. 11, 1981, op. cit., pp. 87–91.
18 European Communities Commission, *Bulletin of the European Communities*, no. 6, 1983, op. cit., pp. 24–9.

19 European Communities Commission, *Bulletin of the European Communities*, no. 3, 1985, op.cit., pp. 102–17.
20 European Communities Commission, COM (85), 310 final, 14 June 1985.
21 The SEA is reproduced in European Communities Commission, *Bulletin of the European Communities*, Supplement no. 2, 1986, op.cit.
22 European Communities Commission, *Nineteenth General Report of the Activities of the Communities*, Luxembourg, OOPEC, 1986, p. 139.
23 European Communities Commission, 1985, op. cit., p. 9.
24 M. Thatcher, *Britain and Europe*, London, Conservative Political Centre, 1988, p. 7.
25 European Communities Commission, *First Survey on State Aids in the European Community*, Luxembourg, OOPEC, 1989.
26 *Reyners* v. *Belgian State*, 1974, 2 CMLR 305.
27 *J. H. M. Van Binsbergen* v. *Bestuur van de Bedrifjsvereniging voor de Metaalnijverheid*, 1975, 1 CMLR 298.
28 For a survey of the regulatory obstacles to free competition in Community air passenger transport see K. J. Button and D. Swann, 'European Community Airlines – Deregulation and its Problems', *Journal of Common Market Studies*, 1989, 27(4): 259–82.
29 Commission of the European Communities, *Research on the 'Cost of Non-Europe', Basic Findings*, vols 1–16, Luxembourg, OOPEC, 1988.
30 M. Emerson *et al.*, *The Economics of 1992*, Oxford, Oxford University Press, 1988 and P. Cecchini *et al.*, *The European Challenge 1992*, Aldershot, Gower, 1988.
31 M. J. Peck, 'Industrial Organization and the Gains from Europe 1992', *Brookings Papers on Economic Activity*, 1989, vol. 2: 277–99.
32 'The European Community An Expanding Universe: A Survey', *The Economist*, 7 July 1990, p. 39.
33 Committee for the Study of Economic and Monetary Union, *Report on economic and monetary union in the European Community*, Luxembourg, OOPEC, 1989.
34 M. Thatcher, 1988, op. cit., p. 4.
35 M. Thatcher, 1988, op. cit., p. 4.

2 European union, the Single European Act and the 1992 programme

1 For an overview see M. Butler, *Europe: More than a Continent*, London, Heinemann, 1986, pp. 85–111.
2 European Communities Commission, *The Intergovernmental Conference: Background and Issues*, London, 1985, p. 1.
3 European Communities Commission, 'Single European Act', *Bulletin of the European Communities*, Supplement 2/86, Luxembourg, Office for Official Publications of the European Communities, 1986, pp. 5–26.
4 T. Worre, 'Denmark at the Crossroads: The Danish Referendum 28 February 1986 on the EC Reform Package', *Journal of Common Market Studies*, 1986, 26(4): 361–88.
5 P. Fontaine, 'Europe – A Fresh Start', *European Documentation, 3/1990*, Luxembourg, Office for Official Publications of the European Communities, 1990, p. 27.
6 For a much more detailed account of EC institutions and decision-making see E. Noel, *Working Together – The institutions of the European Community*, Luxembourg, Office for Official Publications of the European Communities, 1988 or N. Nugent, *The Government and Politics of the European Community*,

London, Macmillan, 1989.

7   For a more detailed account see Nugent, op. cit., pp. 102–3.

8   See Swann's discussion of the merger proposal, chapter 3, above, p. 66.

9   For a detailed account of the early years of European political cooperation see D. Allen, R. Rummel and W. Wessels (eds), *European Political Cooperation*, London, Butterworths, 1982.

10 For a full account of the development of European political cooperation in the 1980s see A. Pijpers *et al.*, *European Political Cooperation in the 1980's: A Common Foreign Policy for Western Europe?*, Dordrecht, Nijhoff, 1988.

11 See Nugent, op. cit., pp. 258–78.

12 See for instance D. Coombes, *Politics and Bureaucracy in the European Community*, London, Allen & Unwin, 1970.

13 See J. Lodge, 'European Political Cooperation; towards the 1990s', in J. Lodge (ed.), *The European Community and the Challenge of the Future*, London, Pinter, 1989, p. 231.

14 Communique of the Paris Summit meeting of Heads of Government, 21 October 1972, *Bulletin of the European Communities*, No. 12, Luxembourg, Office for Official Publications of the European Communities, 1974, pp. 7–12.

15 For a discussion of the Tindemans Review see J. Mitchell 'The Tindemans Report: Retrospect and Prospect', *Common Market Law Review*, no. 13, 1976, pp. 455–84.

16 See D. Allen and M. Smith, 'Western Europe's Presence in the Contemporary International Arena', *Review of International Studies*, vol. 16: 19–37.

17 See D. Allen and M. Smith, 'Western Europe in Reagan's World: Responding to a New American Challenge', in R. Rummel (ed) *The Evolution of an International Actor: Western Europe's New Assertiveness*, Boulder, Westview Press, 1990, p. 229.

18 See J. Lodge, 'European Union and the First Elected Parliament: the Spinelli Initiative', *Journal of Common Market Studies*, vol. 22, 1984, pp. 352–77.

19 See for instance J. Lodge, 'The Single European Act: Towards a New Euro-Dynamism?', *Journal of Common Market Studies*, vol. 24, 1986, pp. 203–23.

20 See A. Adonis and A. Tyre, *Subsidiarity-as history and policy*, London, Institute of Economic Affairs, 1990.

21 J. Rogaly, 'Europe in Thrall to a Slogan not a Principle', *Financial Times*, 7 December 1990.

22 Letter to the *Financial Times*, 17 December 1990.

23 Letter to the *Financial Times*, 13 December 1990.

24 Ibid.

25 See W. Sandholtz and J. Zysman, '1992: Recasting the European Bargain', *World Politics*, vol. 2, no. 1, 1989, pp. 95–128.

26 M. Butler, op. cit. p. 164.

27 P. Taylor, 'The New Dynamics of EC integration in the 1980's', in J. Lodge, *The European Community and the Challenge of the Future*, London, Pinter, 1989, p. 3.

28 Ibid.

29 Ibid., p. 8.

30 See reference 3.

31 Under the present system of qualified majority voting Germany, France, Italy and the UK have 10 votes each; Spain 8; Belgium, Greece, Holland and Portugal 5 each; Denmark and Ireland 3 each and Luxembourg 2. For a measure to be adopted 54 votes out of a total of 76 are required. Abstention does not count towards making a qualified majority nor does it prevent

unanimity where that is required. It is thus possible for two large states to be outvoted under these rules.

32 For a full analysis of the cooperation procedure see J. Fitzmaurice, 'An Analysis of the European Community Cooperation Procedure', *Journal of Common Market Studies*, vol. 26, 1988, pp. 389–400.

33 See Commission of the European Communities, *Twenty-Fourth General Report on the Activities of the European Communities, 1990*, Luxembourg, Office for Official Publications of the European Communities, 1991, p. 360.

34 Ibid.

35 G. Edwards, 'Europe and the Falklands Crisis 1982', *Journal of Common Market Studies*, vol. 22, 1984.

PART II COMPLETING THE 1992 SINGLE MARKET

3 Standards, procurement, mergers and state aids

1 Greece was still in process of dismantling its protection and Spain and Portugal had not then joined.

2 Moreover Article 235 always provided the possibility of taking additional powers if that should prove necessary in order to achieve the objectives of the treaty.

3 European Communities Commission, *Research on the 'Cost of Non-Europe'*, Basic Findings, vol. 6, Luxembourg, Office for Official Publications of the European Communities, 1988, pp. 5–6.

4 See, for example, O. Brouwer, 'Free Movement of Foodstuffs and Quality Requirements: Has the Commission Got It Wrong?', *Common Market Law Review*, 1988, vol. 25, pp. 237–62.

5 *Re Purity Requirements for Beer: E.C. Commission* v. *Germany*, 1988, 1 CMLR 780.

6 European Communities Commission, 1988, op. cit., p. 18.

7 European Communities Commission, COM (85) 603 final, 8 November 1985.

8 The Commission attempted to deal with this by adopting a more rapid process for dealing with adaptations to technical pregress.

9 J. Pelkmans, 'The New Approach to Technical Harmonization and Standardization', *Journal of Common Market Studies*, 1987, 25(3): 251.

10 E. Lawlor, *Individual Choice and Higher Growth. The Aim of Consumer Policy in the Single Market*, Luxembourg, OOPEC, 1989, p. 16.

11 *Rewe-Zentrale A. G.* v. *Bundesmonopolverwaltung fur Branntwein*, 1979, 3 CMLR 494.

12 European Communities Commission, COM (85) 603 final, 8 November 1985, p. 5.

13 For details of technical harmonization procedures see *Official Journal of the European Communities*, C136, 4 June 1985.

14 For a discussion of the European standards bodies see M. Langton, 'Standards and the Single European Market', *European Access*, 1990, no. 1, pp. 16–19.

15 This interpretation is based on Pelkmans op. cit., p. 255.

16 *Official Journal of the European Communities*, L200, 8 August 1987.

17 *Official Journal of the European Communities*, L187, 16 July 1988.

18 European Communities Commission, COM (85) 603 final, pp. 8–9.

19 *Official Journal of the European Communities*, L186, 30 June 1989.

20 *Official Journal of the European Communities*, L186, 30 June 1989.

21 *Official Journal of the European Communities*, L186, 30 June 1989.

22   *Official Journal of the European Communities*, L186, 30 June 1989.
23   European Communities Commission, *Twentyfirst General Report on the Activities of the European Communities*, Luxembourg, OOPEC, 1988, p. 106.
24   *Official Journal of the European Communities*, L205, 13 August 1989.
25   For a detailed treatment see L. Hancher, 'The European Pharmaceutical Market: Problems of Partial Harmonization', *European Law Review*, 1990, vol. 15, pp. 9–33. For a useful introduction see V. Kendall, 'Pharmaceuticals: Missing the 1992 Deadline', *EIU European Trends*, 1989, no. 1, pp. 42–7.
26   *Official Journal of the European Communities*, L40, 11 February 1989.
27   European Communities Commission, *Research on the 'Cost of Non-Europe'*, Basic Findings, vol. 5, part B, Luxembourg, OOPEC, 1988, p. 9.
28   *Official Journal of the European Communities*, L13, 19 January 1970.
29   *Official Journal of the European Communities*, L185, 16 August 1971.
30   *Official Journal of the European Communities*, L185, 16 August 1971.
31   *Official Journal of the European Communities*, L185, 16 August 1971.
32   G. Charpentier and R. Clark, *Public Purchasing in The Common Market*, Brussels, EC Commission, 1974, p. 18.
33   *Official Journal of the European Communities*, L13, 15 January 1977.
34   *Official Journal of the European Communities*, L13, 15 January 1977.
35   See J. H. J. Bourgeois, 'The Tokyo Round Agreements on Technical Barriers and on Government Procurement in International and EEC Perspective', *Common Market Law Review*, 1982, vol. 19, pp. 5–33.
36   *Official Journal of the European Communities*, L215, 18 August 1980.
37   *Official Journal of the European Communities*, L195, 29 July 1980.
38   *Official Journal of the European Communities*, C252, 2 October 1981; C256, 8 October 1981.
39   European Communities Commission, COM (84) 717 final, 14 December 1984, p. 12.
40   D. L. McLachlan, 'Discriminatory Public Procurement, Economic Integration and the Role of the Bureaucracy', *Journal of Common Market Studies*, 1985, 23(4): 366.
41   European Communities Commission, COM (83) 80 final, 24 February 1983, p. 22.
42   *Official Journal of the European Communities*, L127, 20 May 1988.
43   *Official Journal of the European Communities*, L210, 21 July 1989.
44   *Official Journal of the European Communities*, L395, 30 December 1989.
45   European Communities Commission, *Research on the 'Cost of Non-Europe'*, Basic Findings, vol. 5, part B, p. 129.
46   European Communities Commission, *Research on the 'Cost of Non-Europe'*, Basic Findings, op. cit., p. 119.
47   The Cockfield Report did however call for the application of the existing cartel rules to air transport – see chapter 6.
48   *ICI and others* v. *EC Commission*, 1972, CMLR 260.
49   *Europemballage Corp and Continental Can Co. Inc.* v. *EC Commission*, 1973, CMLR 199.
50   It also applies the non-discrimination and state-aid rules to these enterprises, subject to this caveat.
51   *Official Journal of the European Communities*, L204, 21 February 1962. Special arrangements were made for surface transport and agriculture and, as seen in chapter 6, implementation powers were not granted in respect of air transport until 1987.
52   Light metal containers for canned meat and fish.

53 EC Commission, *Das Problem der Unternehmenskonzentration im Gemeinsamen Markt*, Brussels, 1965.
54 For an account of national positions see D. Allen, 'Policing or Policy-Making? Competition Policy in the European Communities', in H. Wallace, W. Wallace and C. Webb (eds), *Policy-Making in the European Communities*, London, Wiley, 1977, pp. 101–8.
55 *BAT and R. J. Reynolds* v. *EC Commission*, 1987, 2 CMLR 551.
56 *Official Journal of the European Communities*, L395, 30 December 1989.
57 Apparently there was a divergence of views on the criteria for assessment. The UK and Germany wanted competition to be the criterion whereas France and others wished to take a broader view. This explains the element of ambiguity which seems to exist in the body of the regulation – see J. S. Venti, 'The "Merger" Control Regulation: Europe Comes of Age . . . or Caliban's Dinner', *Common Market Law Review*, 1990, vol. 27, pp. 8–9.
58 European Communities Commission, *Sixteenth Report on Competition Policy*, Luxembourg, OOPEC, 1987, pp. 13–18.
59 *Official Journal of the European Communities*, L230, 18 August 1986.
60 *Official Journal of the European Communities*, L74, 17 March 1989.
61 European Communities Commission, *Twentysecond General Report on the Activities of the European Communities*, Luxembourg, OOPEC, 1988, p. 198.
62 V. Korah and P. Lasok, 'Philip Morris and Its Aftermath – Merger Control?', *Common Market Law Review*, 1988, vol. 25, p. 352.
63 'Wanted: A New Referee for European Fair Play', *The Economist*, 5 November 1988, pp. 103–4.
64 Agence Europe, *Europe*, 5 January 1990, p. 7.
65 European Communities Commission, *First Survey on State Aids in the European Community*, Luxembourg, OOPEC, 1989.
66 Enforcement does not always follow from Commission discovery. On occasions an industry in one member state may complain about aids to its competitors in another member state – see *Compagnie Française De l'Azote S A* v. *EC Commission*, 1986, 3 CMLR, 385.
67 *Re Aids to the Textile Industry: France* v. *Commission of the EC*, 1970, CMLR 351.
68 *Philip Morris Holland BV* v. *EC Commission*, 1981, 2 CMLR 321.
69 European Communities Commission, *Eighth General Report on the Activities of the European Communities*, Luxembourg, OOPEC, 1975, p. 86.
70 *Official Journal of the European Communities*, L195, 29 July 1980. See also M. Brothwood, 'The Commission Directive on Transparency of Financial Relations Between Member States and Public Undertakings', *Common Market Law Review*, 1981, vol. 18, pp. 209–17.
71 *Re Public Undertakings: France, Italy and the United Kingdom* v. *EC Commission*, 1982, 3 CMLR 144. See also M. Brothwood, 'The Court of Justice on Article 90 of the EEC Treaty', *Common Market Law Review*, 1983, vol. 20, pp. 335–46.
72 *Intermills SA* v. *EC Commission*, 1986, 1 CMLR 614.
73 *Official Journal of the European Communities*, L220, 11 August 1988.
74 European Communities Commission, *Nineteenth Report on Competition Policy*, Luxembourg, OOPEC, 1990, pp. 165–6.
75 *Official Journal of the European Communities*, C83, 11 April 1986.
76 *Official Journal of the European Communities*, C123, 18 May 1989.
77 *Official Journal of the European Communities*, C212, 12 August 1988.

4 The fiscal dimension of 1992

1 See J. Kay and M. King, *The British Tax System*, 5th edition, Oxford, Oxford University Press, 1990 for a discussion of these issues.

2 Ibid., pp. 202–7.

3 C. Lee, M. Pearson and S. Smith, *Fiscal Harmonization: an Analysis of the European Commission's Proposals*, London, Institute for Fiscal Studies, Report Series no. 28, 1988.

4 M. Bos and H. Nelson, 'Indirect Taxation and the Completion of the Internal Market of the EC', *Journal of Common Market Studies*, vol. 27, no. 1, pp. 27–44; P. Guieu and C. Bonnet, 'Completion of the Internal Market and Indirect Taxation' *Journal of Common Market Studies*, 25(3): 209–22.

5 'Report of the Fiscal and Financial Committee' in *Tax Harmonization in the Common Market*, Chicago, Commercial Clearing House, 1963.

6 The UK was operating a system of purchase tax at this time. This was a single stage tax normally charged at the wholesale stage. This enabled manufacturers to trade without making turnover tax payments.

7 The continued existence of twelve separate currencies also imposes additional frontier costs.

8 See C. Jenkins, 'Taxation and the Single Market', *EIU European Trends*, no. 2, pp. 79–86 who claims that surveys show that business regard frontier barriers as being of roughly equal importance with the whole range of technical barriers as an obstacle to trade.

9 A Dutch importer of components produced in Spain for 5500 Pesetas will buy them for 6160 Pesetas (5500 + 12 per cent) or 112 Guilders. The importer turns the components into a fully manufactured product which adds an extra 200 Guilders in value to the product. To this is added a further 40 Guilders in Dutch VAT (or 20 per cent on the value added by the Dutch importer). Thus the Spanish government receives 660 Pesetas and the Dutch government 40 Guilders in VAT payments.

10 European Communities Commission, *Completing the Internal Market*, COM (85) 310 final, 14 June 1985, p. 43.

11 This solution was presented to the European League for Economic Cooperation at a symposium in Brussels on April 21 1990.

12 Agence Europe, *Europe*, 9 May 1990.

13 European Communities Commission, COM (87) 320 final, 21 August 1987.

14 See S. Smith, 'Excise Duties and the Internal Market', *Journal of Common Market Studies*, 27(2): 147–60 who refers to these as compression costs i.e. the costs of compressing the post-duty stages of the production and selling chain.

15 European Communities Commission, *Amended Proposal for a Council Directive on the approximation of taxes on cigarettes. Amended Proposal for a Council Directive on the approximation of taxes on manufactured tobacco other than cigarettes*, COM (89) 525 final, 19 December 1989; *Amended Proposal for a Council Directive on the approximation of the rates of excise duty on mineral oils*, COM (89) 526 final, 19 December 1989; *Amended Proposal for a Council Directive on the approximation of the rates of excise duty on alcoholic beverages and on the alcohol contained in other products*, COM (89) 527 final, 19 December 1989.

16 As far as other goods are concerned, (e.g. playing cards, light bulbs, bananas, coffee, tea, etc.) member states will be allowed to retain the possibility of keeping or introducing excise duties on those products, notably for environmental purposes. However, the overriding aim is to ensure the free movement of goods

and services and thus member states are expected to abolish all excise duties that do not give rise to border controls (except of course for the three product groups discussed in the text), see European Communities Commission, COM (90) 430 final, 26 September 1990.

17 See, M. Devereux and M. Pearson, *Corporate Tax Harmonization and Economic Efficiency*, Institute for Fiscal Studies, Report Series no. 35, 1989; M. Devereux and M. Pearson, 'Harmonizing Corporate Taxes in Europe' *Fiscal Studies*, vol. 11, no. 1, February 1990, pp. 21–35; A. Giovannini, 'Capital Taxation', *Economic Policy*, October 1989, pp. 346–86.
18 Ibid.
19 P. B. Musgrave, 'Interjurisdictional coordination of taxes on capital income', in S. Cnossen (ed.), *Tax Coordination in the European Community*, London, Kluwer, 1987.
20 See Giovannini op. cit.
21 Differences in rates are explained in Devereux and Pearson (1989), op. cit.
22 European Communities Commission, *Corporation Tax and Individual Income Tax in the European Communities*, Brussels, OOPEC, 1971.
23 European Communities Commission, COM (75), 392 final, 23 July 1975.
24 *Official Journal of the European Communities*, L 225, 20 August 1990. (The 1990 guidelines also require all firms engaged in cross-frontier activities to take account of foreign profits or losses.)
25 Ibid.
26 Ibid.
27 Devereux and M. Pearson, (1989, 1990) op. cit.
28 Giovannini, op. cit.
29 European Communities Commission, *Taxation in the Single Market*, Luxembourg, OOPEC, 1990.

5 Banking and financial services

1 European Communities Commission, *Completing the Internal Market*, COM (85) 310 final, 14 June, 1985.
2 Ibid., p. 27.
3 R. A. Eisenbeis, 'The Impact of Securitization' in E. Gardener, (ed.), *The Future of Financial Systems and Services*', London, Macmillan, 1990, pp. 51–71.
4 A. Clark, 'The Regulatory Implications', *Banking World*, October 1989, pp. 18–26.
5 D. T. Llewellyn, 'Financial Intermediation and Systems: Global Integration', in D. E. Fair and C. de Boissieu, (eds), *International Monetary and Financial Integration: The European Dimension*, Dordrecht, Kluwer, 1989, pp. 229–60.
6 OECD, *Competition in Banking*, Paris, 1989.
7 D. T. Llewellyn, *Regulation and Supervision of Financial Institutions*, London, Chartered Institute of Bankers, 1986.
8 M. J. B. Hall, 'BIS Capital Adequacy Rules: A Critique', *Banca Nazionale del Lavoro Quarterly Review*, June 1989, pp. 207–28.
9 D. T. Llewellyn, 'Structural Change in the British Financial System' in C. Green and D. T. Llewellyn, (eds), *Surveys in Monetary Economics*, vol. II, Oxford, Basil Blackwell, 1991, pp. 210–57.
10 A. Steinherr, *The Impact of Financial Market Integration on the European Banking Industry*, Brussels, Research Report no. 1, Centre for European Policy Studies, Brussels, 1989.
11 Op. cit., see reference 9.

12 European Communities Commission, *Research on the 'Cost of Non-Europe'*, *Basic Findings, The Cost of Non-Europe in Financial Services*, (Price Waterhouse), Luxembourg, vol. 9, 1988.

13 R. Watson, 'Insuring a Solution to the Bank Capital Hassle, *Federal Reserve Bank of Philadelphia Business Review*, July 1974, pp. 1–14.

14 J. Mitchell, 'The Consumer and Financial Services in the EC', in J. Mitchell (ed.), *The Consumer and Financial Services*, Belgium, Louvain-La-Neuve, Centre de Droit de la Consommation, 1990, pp. 28–34.

15 Op. cit., see reference 4.

16 European Communities Commission, *Research on the 'Cost of Non-Europe'*, Price Waterhouse, op. cit., reference 12.

17 R. Leigh-Pemberton, 'Ownership and Control of UK Banks', *Bank of England Quarterly Bulletin*, November 1987, pp. 525–6.

18 D. T. Llewellyn, '1991: Financial Services and Competition', *Banking World*, February 1989, pp. 28–34.

19 D. T. Llewellyn, 'Competition and Structural Change in the British Financial System', in E. Gardener, (ed.), *The Future of Financial Systems and Services*, London, Macmillan, 1990, pp. 15–35.

20 D. P. Fraser and D. P. Rose, 'Bank Entry and Bank Performance', *Journal of Finance*, vol. 27, 1972, pp. 65–78.

21 C. Cho, C. Eun and L. Senbet, 'International Arbitrage Pricing Theory: An Empirical Investigation', *Journal of Finance*, vol. 41, 1986, pp. 313–29.

22 Op. cit., see reference 19.

23 Op. cit., see reference 19.

24 Prior to 1983 building societies tended to set a higher rate of interest on large mortgages even though in general the costs and risks of larger mortgages tend to be lower.
    25 e D. T. Llewellyn, 'Banks and the Mortgage Market', *Building Societies Institute Journal*, November 1983, pp. 168–9 and L. Drake, *The Building Society Industry in Transition*, London, Macmillan, 1989.

26 X. Vives, *Banking Competition and European Integration*, CEPR Discussion Paper no. 373, London.

27 Ibid.

28 Op. cit., see reference 18.

29 European Communities Commission, *Completing the Internal Market*, p. 18.

30 Ibid.

31 Ibid.

32 Op. cit., see reference 26.

33 See 'Proposal for a Council Directive for the Implementation of Article 67 of the EEC Treaty: Liberalization of Capital Movements', COM (87), 550 final, 4 November 1987.

34 A. Lamb, *Banking in the European Community 1992*, Occasional Research Paper no. 1, Chartered Institute of Bankers, London, 1991.

35 'First Council Directive on 12 December 1977 on the Coordination of Laws, Regulations and Administrative Provisions Relating to the Taking-up and Pursuit of the Business of Credit Institutions'. *Official Journal of the European Communities*, L 322, 17 December 1977.

36 'Council Directive of 13 June on the Supervision of Credit Institutions on a Consolidated Basis', *Official Journal of the European Communities*, L 193, 1 July 1983.

37 For detail see: 'Proposal for a Second Council Directive on the Coordination of Laws, Regulations and Administrative Provisions Relating to the Taking-up

and Pursuit of the Business of Credit Institutions and Amending Directive 77/780/EEC', *Official Journal of the European Communities*, C84, 31 March 1988.

38 Op. cit., see reference 34.

39 E. Davis, and C. Smales, 'The Integration of European Financial Services, in J. Kay, (ed.), *1992: Myths and Realities*, London Business School, 1990, pp. 205–41.

40 D. Neven, 'Lessons from Industrial Organization for Retail Banking in Europe', in J. Dermine, (ed.), *European Banking After 1992*, Oxford, Basil Blackwell, 1989.

41 Op. cit., see reference 34.

42 'Second Council Directive on the Coordination of Laws, Regulations, and Administrative Provisions Relating to Direct Insurance other than Life Assurance', *Official Journal on the European Communities*, L 172, 12 August 1988.

43 'Second Council Directive on the Coordination of Laws, Regulations and Administrative Provisions Relating to Direct Insurance other than Life Insurance and Laying Down Provisions to Facilitate the Effective Exercise of Freedom to Supply Services', *Official Journal of the European Communities*, L 172, 4 July, 1988.

44 *Official Journal of the European Communities*, L 56, 4 April, 1964.

45 'Second Council Directive of 24 July 1973 on the Coordination of Laws, Regulations and Administrative Provisions Relating to the Taking-up and Pursuit of the Business of Direct Insurance other than Life Assurance', *Official Journal of the European Communities*, L 228, 16 August 1973.

46 'First Council Directive on the Coordination of Laws, Regulations and Administrative Provisions Relating to the Taking up and Pursuit of the Business of Direct Life Insurance', *Official Journal of the European Communities*, L 63, 13 March 1979.

47 M. Emerson, *et al.*, 'The Economics of 1992', *European Economy*, no. 35, 1988, p. 91.

48 'Council Directive Coordinating the Conditions for the Admission of Securities to Official Stock Exchange Listing', *Official Journal of the European Communities*, L 66, 16 March 1979.

49 'Council Directive Coordinating Requirements for Drawing Up, Scrutiny and Distribution of Listing Particulars to be Published for the Admission of Securities to Official Stock Exchange Listing', *Official Journal of the European Communities*, L 100, 17 April 1980.

50 'Council Directive on Information to be Published on a Regular Basis by Companies the Shares of which have been Admitted to Official Stock Exchange Listing', *Official Journal of the European Communities*, L 48, 20 February 1982.

51 'Council Directive on the Coordination of Laws, Regulations and Administrative Provisions Relating to Undertakings for Collective Investment in Transferable Securities (UCITS)', *Official Journal of the European Communities*, L 375, 31 December 1985.

52 European Communities Commission, *Bulletin of the European Communities*, vol. 11, Luxembourg, OOPEC, 1985.

53 'Council Directive Amending Directive 80/390/EEC Coordinating the requirements for the Drawing-up of, Scrutiny and Distribution of the Listing Particulars to be published for the Admission of Securities to Official Stock Exchange Listing', *Official Journal of the European Communities*, L185, 4 July 1987.

54 'Council Directive Coordinating the Requirements for the Drawing Up, Scrutiny and Distribution of Prospectuses to be Published when Transferable Securities

are Offered to the Public', *Official Journal of the European Communities*, L500, 31 December 1989.

55 Op. cit., see reference 16.

56 E. Baltensperger and J. Dermine, 'Banking Deregulation in Europe', *Economic Policy*, April 1987, pp. 64–109.

57 H. Krugman, 'Increasing Returns and Monopolistic Competition and International Trade', *Journal of International Economics*, August 1979.

58 R. Harris, 'Applied General Equilibrium Analysis of Small Open Economies with Scale Economies and Imperfect Competition', *American Economic Review*, June 1984, pp. 1016–32.

59 A. Smith and A. Venables, 'Trade and Industrial Policy Under Imperfect Competition', *Economic Policy*, May 1988, pp. 314–19.

60 J. Revell, *The Future of Savings Banks: A Study of Spain and the Rest of Europe*, Institute of European Finance, Research Monograph, no. 8.

61 Op. cit., see reference 40.

62 D. T. Llewellyn and M. Holmes, 'In Defence of Mutuality', *Annals of Public and Cooperative Economics*, no. 2, 1991, forthcoming.

63 Op. cit., see reference 16.

64 M. Lewis, 'The Theory of the Banking Firm', in C. Green and D. T. Llewellyn, (eds), *Surveys in Monetary Economics*, vol. II, Oxford, Basil Blackwell, 1991, pp. 78–113.

65 W. H. Branson, 'Financial Market Integration: Macro-economic Policy and the EMS', Discussion Paper 385, London, Centre for Economic Policy Research, 1989.

66 Bank of England, *Single European Market: Survey of UK Financial Services Industry*, London, May 1989.

67 M. Boleat, *National Housing Finance System*, London, Croom Helm, 1985.

68 Op. cit., see reference 40.

69 Op. cit., see reference 26.

70 V. Grilli, 'Europe 1992: Issues and Prospects for the Financial Markets', *Economic Policy*, October 1989, pp. 388–411.

71 Op. cit., see reference 39.

72 P. Molyneux, '1992 and Its Impact on Local and Regional Banking Markets', *Regional Studies*, vol. 3, no. 6, pp. 523–34.

73 Op. cit., see reference 70.

6 The liberalization of transport services

1 United Nations Economic Commission for Europe, 'Consumption patterns in the ECE region: long-term trends and policy issues', *Economic Bulletin for Europe*, 1987, vol. 39, pp. 425–82.

2 K. M. Gwilliam, 'Transport policy' in A. M. El-Agraa (ed.), *The Economics of the European Community*, Oxford, Philip Allan, 1980.

3 J. E. Meade, H. H. Leisner, and S. J. Wells, *Case Studies in European Economic Union – The Mechanism of Integration*, Oxford, OUP, 1962.

4 These efforts were not entirely successful and while issues of direct rate discrimination were dealt with satisfactorily, problems of viability of 'tapers' for long distance transport and fixed charges at border crossings were less completely tackled.

5 See, for example, K. J. Button, 'Recent developments in EEC transport policy', *Three Banks Review*, 1979 (123): 52–73; C. Abbati, *Transport and European Integration*, Brussels, Commission of the European Communities, Economic

Perspectives Series, 1987; and K. M. Gwilliam, 'Realism and common transport policy of the EEC', in J. B. Palak, and J. B. Van der Kemp (eds), *Changes in the Field of Transport Studies*, The Hague, Martinus Nijhoff, 1980.

6 K. J. Button, *Road Haulage Licensing and EC Transport Policy*, Aldershot, Gower, 1984.

7 These still go largely unresolved. While Austria, with ambitions to join the EC, has been fairly flexible regarding transit traffic, serious problems still remain regarding the other two states despite, in the case of Yugoslavia, direct EC investment in the country's infrastructure.

8 See P. Cottinet, 'The Allais Report', *Journal of Transport Economics and Policy*, 1967, vol. 1, pp. 90–103.

9 For a critical review of these policies see D. L. Munby, 'Fallacies of the Community's transport policy', *Journal of Common Market Studies*, 1962, vol. 1, pp. 67–98.

10 For example, 'The neglect of Community action in the realm of transport, as well as the failure to fulfil the obligations imposed by the Treaty on the Community institutions, also impairs the development of the general policy of the Community' (European Communities Commission, *Communication from the Commission to the Council Concerning the Community Organization of the Market for Transport*, SEC (71) 3190 final 1971.

11 The European Parliament, concerned about the pace of progress in the late 1970s, for example, commissioned a study by Horst Seefeld, subsequently the chairman of the Parliament's Committee on Transport, which concluded that 'the Council has never had a policy of any kind, but has simply shilly-shallied from one file to another' and went on to add that 'the Commission . . . should not have released the Council from its responsibilities'. (For further comments see *European Parliament Working Document*, S12/78, 1979.)

12 European Communities Commission, 'Progress towards a common transport policy – maritime transport', *Bulletin of the European Communities*, Supplement no. 5, Luxembourg, OOPEC, 1985.

13 M. Feige, 'Transport in the European Community', *EIU European Trends*, 1990, vol. 2, pp. 62–7.

14 European Communities Commission, *Bulletin of the European Communities*, Supplement no. 2, Luxembourg, OOPEC, 1986.

15 European Communities Commission, *Completing the Internal Market*, COM (85) 310 final, 14 June 1985.

16 There seems to be no real justification for this type of division, or at least on the lines drawn. Indeed, the EC in its subsequent work on infrastructure provision sees this as a key element of the transport component of a single market (see Feige, op. cit.).

17 European Communities Commission, *Bulletin of the European Communities*, no. 11, Luxembourg, OOPEC, 1985.

18 Normally quota increases have been agreed in tranches for a number of years (usually three) but Germany and Italy objected to a quota agreement for 1991 and 1992 until transit problems through non-member countries had been resolved since these rendered part of their quota useless.

19 J. Erdmenger, and D. Stasinopoulos, 'The shipping policy of the European Community', *Journal of Transport Economics and Policy*, 1988, vol. 22, pp. 355–60.

20 See, M. R. Brooks, 'A common maritime transport policy: Europe in 1992' in M. R. Brooks (ed.), *Issues in Maritime Transport*, Halifax, Centre for International Business Studies, Dalhousie University, 1989.

21 European Communities Commission, *Medium-term Transport Infrastructure Programme*, COM (86) 340 final, 1986. The priorities were for: improvements in major Community trade routes, especially where there is a heavy burden for transit countries; integration of peripheral areas into the Community network and the construction of high-speed inter-city rail links.

22 European Communities Commission, *Air Traffic System Capacity Problems*, COM (88) 577 final, 1989.

23 See P. J. Kuijper, 'Airline fare-fixing and competition: an English Lord, commission proposals and US parallels', *Common Market Law Review*, 1983, vol. 20, pp. 203–22.

24 See, for example, European Communities Commission, 'Contribution of the European Communities to the development of air transport services', *Bulletin of the European Communities*, Supplement no. 5, Luxembourg, OOPEC, 1979.

25 European Communities Commission, *Civil Aviation Memorandum No. 2 – Towards the Development of a Community Air Transport Policy*, COM (84) 72 final, 15 March 1984.

26 For example, see D. Pickrell, 'The regulation and deregulation of US airlines' in K. J. Button (ed.), *Airline Deregulation: The International Experience*, London, David Fulton, 1991.

27 D. M. Kasper, *Deregulation and Globalization: Liberating International Trade in Air Services*, Cambridge, Mass., American Enterprise Institute/Ballinger, 1988.

28 *Ministere Public* v. *Lucas Asjes and Others*, 1986, 3 CMLR 173.

29 N. Argyris, 'The EEC rules of competition and the air transport sector', *Common Market Law Review*, 1989, vol. 26, pp. 5–32.

30 *Official Journal of the European Communities*, L374, 31 December 1987.

31 K. J. Button, and D. Swann, 'European Community airlines – deregulation and its problems', *Journal of Common Market Studies*, 1989, vol. 27, pp. 259–82.

32 Although in November 1990 there were discussions between a major US CRS operator, and one of the two European systems to merge in the light of the latter's poor financial performance.

33 *Official Journal of the European Communities*, L374, 31 December 1987.

34 Ibid.

35 F. Sorenson, 'The changing aviation scene in Europe', in D. Banister and K. J. Button (eds), *Transport in a Free Market Economy*, London, Macmillan, 1991.

36 Air France subsequently acquired UTA and, via joint ownership by UTA and Air France, Air Inter the main domestic French carrier.

37 These are sometimes confused with cabotage rights but they do not give carriers the right to operate purely domestic services within another member state. Fifth freedom rights allow a carrier to take passengers between countries where the airline is not actually registered but not to operate *within* either of the countries.

38 See also, J. Balfour, 'Air transport and the EEC', *European Access* 1990/2, 1990, pp. 13–15.

39 *Ahmed Saeed Flugreisen and Silver Line Reiseburo GmbH* v. *Zentrale Zur Bekamfung Unlauteren Wettbewerbs eV*, 1990, 4 CMLR, 102.

40 For a variety of technical as well as political reasons it seems unlikely that Europe will ever move to a situation identical to the USA – see K. J. Button, 'Transport deregulation: what are the universal truths?', *Journal of the Transportation Research Forum*, 1990, vol. 31, pp. 87–100. Such a change, however, would, it has been estimated, generate an annual gain of between $1.5 billion and $2 billion annually mainly in terms of benefits to air travellers (see F. McGowan,

and P. Seabright, 'Deregulating European airlines', *Economic Policy*, 1990, vol. 9, pp. 284–344).
41 US carriers are clearly trying to expand into international markets – see Kasper op. cit.

7 The external implications of 1992

1 R. Baldwin, 'The growth effects of 1992', *Economic Policy*, vol. 4, 1989, pp. 248–70.
2 European Communities Commission, 'The economics of 1992', *European Economy*, no. 35, Brussels, 1988.
3 Estimates of cost savings from the abolition of technical barriers, which ranged from 0.5 per cent to 3.2 per cent of current costs, were based on sectoral studies. See M. Davenport and R. Cawley, 'Partial equilibrium calculations of the impact of the internal market barriers in the European Community' in the Documents to the Cost of non-Europe Project, vol. 2, *The Completion of the Internal Market*, Luxembourg, Office for Official Publications of the European Communities, 1989.
4 Cost savings across all EC production due to lower barriers, cheaper intermediate input and immediate scale effects are estimated to range from 0.5 per cent to 6.9 per cent of costs in primary and secondary sectors of activity.
5 This data in fact covers seven of the twelve EC member states; Belgium France, Germany, Italy, Luxembourg, The Netherlands and the UK.
6 Ibid.
7 Some of the dynamic welfare gains of market integration may come in the form of redistributions away from producers currently earning economic rents without significantly affecting production and trade levels and patterns.
8 P. Cecchini, *The European Challenge 1992*, London, Wildwood House, 1988. See also European Communities Commission, op. cit.
9 Baldwin, op. cit.
10 For estimates of these effects see A. Smith, 'The market for cars in the enlarged European Community' in C. Bliss and J. B. de Macedo (eds), *Unity with Diversity in the European Market*, London, Centre for Economic Policy Research, 1990.
11 See *Financial Times*, April 17 1991.
12 *Financial Times*, April 5 1991. See also A. Smith and A. J. Venables, 'Completing the internal market in the European Community; some policy simulations', *European Economic Review*, 32, 1988, pp. 1501–25.
13 See footnote 11.
14 For further development of this idea see, D. Allen and M. Smith, 'Western Europe's presence in the contemporary international arena', *Review of International Studies*, 16, 1990, pp. 19–37.
15 See D. Henderson, *1992: The External Dimension*, New York and London, 1989, for a discussion of the trade policy implications.
16 See M. Calingaert, *The 1992 Challenge From Europe: Development of the European Community's Internal Market*, Washington, National Planning Association, 1988, p. 90.
17 Ibid, p. 92.
18 See D. Allen and M. Smith, op. cit., p. 35.
19 Calingaert, op. cit., p. 83.
20 See *Financial Times*, April 9 1990 and *Financial Times* editorial 'A new deal on dumping', May 21 1990. See also a letter from the EC's Director General for External Relations (Horst Krenzler) rebutting charges of unfairness against the

EC's anti-dumping policies, *Financial Times*, January 19 1989.

21 On the notion of 'aggressive unilateralism' see J. Bhagwati, 'Departures from Multi-lateralism: Regional and Aggressive Unilateralism', *Economic Journal*, vol. 100, pp. 1304–17.

22 Super 301 relates to a provision in the US Omnibus Trade Act of 1988 which declares that if a trading partner of the US is acting unfairly then the US can request it to desist. Failure to do so leads to the possibility of retaliatory action.

23 For a detailed exposition of this idea plus a review of the links between 1992 and the GATT Round see, N. Colchester, 'For fortress read trade laboratory', *The Economist*, July 8 1989, pp. 33–43.

24 See P. Montagnon and W. Dullforce, 'An EC Pitchfork in the Works', *Financial Times*, December 8–9 1990.

25 See chapter 10.

26 See also D. Greenaway, *Implications of the EC 1992 Programme for Outside Countries*, Nottingham, Centre for Research in Economic Development, University of Nottingham, 1990.

27 This applies to shipping as well as air transport. The Jones Act forbids foreign carriers from shipping freight between US ports. Shipping between EC ports will become cabotage after 1992 and will thus provide a base for reciprocity pressure on the US.

28 See G. de Jonquieres, 'The new kid on the block', *Financial Times*, June 28 1989 and 'Waking up to the challenge', *Financial Times*, October 4 1988.

29 M. Walker, 'Fortress vision of a market future', *Guardian*, November 14 1988.

30 Some estimates of the trade and welfare effects of the EC scheme are to be found in R. J. Langhammer and A. Sapir, *Economic Impact of Generalized Tariff Preferences*, London, Trade Policy Research Centre, 1987. The overall merit of GSP schemes is questioned by a number of commentators, see, for instance, J. Whalley, *Special and Differential Treatment for Developing Countries in the Uruguay Round*, Nottingham, Centre for Research in Economic Development and International Trade, 1990. See also C. R. Milner, 'Graduation and reciprocity', in A. O'Brien, R. Thornton and D. Greenaway (eds), *Global Protectionism*, London, Harvester-Wheatsheaf, 1991.

31 M. Huband, 'Africa ill-prepared for challenge from Europe', *Financial Times*, November 16 1989.

32 M. Davenport and S. Page, *Europe: 1992 and the developing world*, London, Overseas Development Institute, 1991.

33 D. Horovitz, 'EC-Central/East European Relations; new principles for a new era', *Common Market Law Review*, vol. 27, 1990, pp. 259–84.

34 S. S. Nello, 'Some recent developments in EC-East European Economic Relations', *Journal of World Trade*, vol. 24, 1990, pp. 5–24.

35 C. R. Milner, J. Presley and A. J. Westaway, 'The impact of the completing of the European internal market on Middle East exports', unpublished paper presented to the BRISMES Conference, University of Durham, 1989.

36 D. G. Mayes, 'The external implications of closer European integration', unpublished paper presented to a Midland Bank Conference, London, 1990.

37 J. Pelkmans, 'Asean and EC-1992', unpublished paper presented to the conference on The External Implications of the Single Market, National Institute of Economic and Social Research, London, 1990.

38 See, for example, R. Vernon, 'European Community 1992; can the US negotiate for trade equality?', *Proceedings of the Academy of Political Science*, vol. 37, 1990. Also S. Woolcock, 'US views on 1992', unpublished paper presented to

the conference on The External Implications of the Single European Market, National Institute of Economic and Social Research, London, 1990.

39 Revision of the GATT code on public procurement is not formally part of the Uruguay Round but is inevitably linked with the outcome of the Round.

40 J. Whalley and C. Hamilton, *The GATT System in the 1990's*, Nottingham, Centre for Research in Economic Development and International Trade, 1990. These authors suggest that this passive role by Japan may disappear during the next decade, given the increased importance of Japan in the world economy and if there is fragmentation of the system.

41 Japan was named, for instance, in May 1989 under the US Super 301 provisions of the 1988 Omnibus Trade Act for unfair trade practices.

42 The Association of South East Asian Nations is the regional trade arrangement covering Brunei, Indonesia, Malaysia, Philippines, Singapore and Thailand.

43 See V. D. Norman, 'EFTA and the internal European market', *Economic Policy*, vol. 4, 1989, pp. 423–49. See also N. Schmitt, 'New international trade theories and Europe 1992; some results relevant for EFTA countries', *Journal of Common Market Studies*, vol. 29, 1990, pp. 53–74.

PART III BEYOND 1992: DEEPENING AND WIDENING

8 Onwards to EMU

1 '. . . a Monetary Committee with consultative status shall hereby be established with the following tasks: to keep under review the monetary and financial situation of member states and of the Community and also the general payments system of member states and to report regularly thereon to the Council and to the Commission; and to formulate opinions, at the request of the Council or of the Commission or on its own initiative, for submission to the said institutions'.

2 P. Coffey and J. R. Presley, *European Monetary Integration*, London, Macmillan, 1971, p. 72.

3 European Communities Commission, *Bulletin of the European Communities Supplement*, Luxembourg, OOPEC, 1970, *Report to the Council and the Commission on the Realization by Stages of Economic and Monetary Union in the Community* (Werner Report).

4 Coffey and Presley, op. cit., p. 39.

5 All the then members of the Community joined the ERM in 1979, but one (the UK) opted out of the ERM until 8 October 1990.

6 When the IMF exchange-rate arrangements collapsed, as they did early in 1973, European currencies ceased to have a par value with the US dollar, and the upper and lower limits for mandatory intervention had henceforth to be expressed by agreeing the par value of each Snake currency in terms of any one of them, thereby determining exchange rate parities in respect of each pair of Snake currencies, the maximum permitted deviation from each of these bilateral parities then being 2.25 per cent.

7 A tighter fiscal stance reduces expenditure on goods and services, including those imported from abroad, and thereby serves to support the FF. But a tighter fiscal stance also requires less government borrowing, which probably means smaller issues of government bonds; hence French bond yields decline; hence investors prefer to buy bonds denominated in foreign currencies (say dollars or DM) and this tends to depress the FF in the foreign exchange market. So it is uncertain whether on balance the FF will be supported or depressed by a change in fiscal stance.

8 The effect on the aggregate balance sheet of French commercial banks of an official sale to nonbanks of FF100 of dollars and an official purchase from banks of FF100 of FF-denominated securities, will be as follows:

Liabilities		Assets		
Bank deposit of the purchaser		Balance at Bank of France	−100	+100
of the dollars	−100	Securities		−100

9 The UK, though not until October 1990 a participant in the ERM, nonetheless participated in the other provisions of the EMS, and hence held ECUs as a reserve asset.

10 Committee for the Study of Economic and Monetary Union, *Report on economic and monetary union in the European Community*, Luxembourg, OOPEC, 1989 – prepared, in response to the mandate of the European Council, 'to study and propose concrete stages leading towards economic and monetary union'.

11 '. . . economic coordination must progress from being the simple academic exercise it tends to be at present. It is for this reason that a new Convergence Decision setting up a framework for a multi-lateral surveillance process within the Community has been put in place for stage one. Until now it has been mainly the pressure exerted at EMS realignments that has acted as catalyst for effective coordination', J. Delors, 'EMU at the Start of Stage One', *Amex Bank Review*, 1990, 17(6): 6.

12 This section draws heavily on a memorandum of evidence of May 1989 submitted by HM Treasury to the House of Commons Committee on the Treasury and Civil Service – see Committee's *Fourth Report*, Session 1988–89, 19 June 1989.

13 'When the exchange rate moves for some reason people decide that it is going to go on moving and pile in and for a short time can make those expectations self-justifying, but it may well be the reason that the expectations can be carried away from fundamentals for a while is because the terms in which most of the relevant people are thinking are what other people are thinking rather than about the fundamentals' – see Bank of England oral evidence to the House of Commons Treasury and Civil Service Committee, Session 1981–82, 21 June 1982.

14 *Financial Times*, 27 July 1990.

15 'Nominal demand growth must be brought under control. The Spanish authorities should tighten fiscal policy, through tax increases and better tax collection, to cut disposable incomes. This would relieve the pressure on monetary policy as the sole tool for managing domestic demand'; in *Financial Times*, 25 September 1990.

16 HM Treasury, *Economic and Monetary Union – beyond Stage One: Possible Treaty and Statute for a European Monetary Fund*, London, January 1991.

17 It is suggested in the UK's proposal for a hard-ecu that in due course the EMF might be authorized to influence the level of hard-ecu interest rates by another route, namely by undertaking open market transactions in securities (for example in ecu-denominated bills, similar to those already on issue by the UK Treasury). However, if the EMF bought securities in the market, this would increase the total quantity of hard-ecu-denominated money without decreasing the total quantity of money denominated in national currencies, thereby conflicting with the UK's professed intention that hard-ecus would be issued only in replacement of other currencies.

18 National Westminster Bank, *International Review*, 18 January 1991.

19 A previous summit had decided the starting date (1 January 1994) for the beginning of stage two.

20 The original Rome Treaty made no reference to monetary union, but the SEA identified EMU as a long-standing objective, though without going into details.

The constitution of the ERM is not contained in the Rome Treaty: instead it is simply an agreement between the central banks of the member states.

21 This line of argument in favour of a two-speed Europe derives from the tradition of the 'economist' school, whose exponent in the 1970s was Karl Schiller, who wanted coordination and harmonization before any rigidity in exchange rates was established.

22 *Greenwell Gilt Weekly*, 17 December 1990.

23 European Communities Commission, 'One market, one money', *European Economy* 1990, no. 44, pp. 63–178.

24 As Roger Bootle puts it in the long quotation, op. cit., see reference 23.

9 The Social Charter and other issues

1 European Communities Commission, *European Regional Development Fund Fourteenth Annual Report*, Luxembourg, OOPEC, 1990, p. 79.

2 European Communities Commission, *Bulletin of the European Communities*, Supplement no. 2, Luxembourg, OOPEC, 1974.

3 M. Thatcher, *Britain and Europe*, London, Conservative Political Centre, 1988, p. 4.

4 See for example, B. C. Roberts, *Delors versus 1992*, London, Bruges Group, 1989.

5 European Communities Commission, *Community Charter of the Fundamental Social Rights of Workers*, Luxembourg, OOPEC, 1990.

6 V. Papandreou, 'Moving On', *Social Europe*, 1990, no. 1, pp. 8–9.

7 European Communities Commission, COM (89) 568 final, 29 November 1989.

8 *Official Journal of the European Communities*, C68, 12 June 1974.

9 European Communities Commission, COM (86) 485 final, 9 October 1986.

10 *Re Disposable Beer Cans: E.C. Commission (with UNITED KINGDOM intervening)* v. *Denmark*, 1989, 1 CMLR 619.

11 European Communities Commission, *Bulletin of the European Communities*, Supplement no. 13, Luxembourg, OOPEC, 1973.

12 European Communities Commission, COM (85) 530 final, 30 September, 1985.

PART IV CONCLUSION

11 A forward view

1 European Communities Commission, *Research on the 'Cost of Non-Europe', Basic Findings*, vols 1–16, Luxembourg, OOPEC, 1988; M. Emerson, *et al.*, *The Economics of 1992*, Oxford, Oxford University Press, 1988; P. Cecchini, *et al.*, *The European Challenge 1992*, Aldershot, Gower, 1988.

2 European Communities Commission, 'One market, one money', *European Economy*, 1990, no. 44, pp. 63–178.

3 See Bank of England, *Quarterly Bulletin*, August, 1991.

4 From the point of view of macro-economic sovereignty national finance ministers will have their wings severely clipped. As we have seen the Delors EMU proposal explicitly envisages an independent central bank. But matters do not end there. EMU is not just about a common currency, but also its rate of interest and its exchange rate against the dollar, yen, etc. The Delors Plan also seeks, as Brian Tew observes earlier, to establish Community control over the size of national budget deficits and their financing. Not only that, but the SEM will yet further

cramp the style of national finance ministers. We can expect approximation of VAT and excise rates. Possibly, as Tony Westaway points out earlier, we may have harmonized corporation tax rates. Only income tax rates are to be left to national discretion. How long will that survive if European citizens, who are destined to be fully mobile (thanks to the SEM), decide to desert high income tax countries? The resources commanded by national exchequers (by taxing and borrowing) will thus be pre-determined. They will however be free to decide how to spend them. Or will they? Community rules also obtrude on the spending side – such as state aids!

Index